Down on Their Luck

Down
on Their Luck

*A Study of Homeless
Street People*

David A. Snow
and Leon Anderson

UNIVERSITY OF CALIFORNIA PRESS
Berkeley · Los Angeles · Oxford

Portions of Chapter 1 have been adapted from David A. Snow and Leon Anderson, "Researching the Homeless: The Characteristic Features and Virtues of the Case Study," in *A Case for the Case Study,* ed. Joe R. Feagin, Anthony M. Orum, and Gideon Sjoberg (Chapel Hill: University of North Carolina Press, 1991). The second part of Chapter 7 has been adapted from David A. Snow and Leon Anderson, "Identity Work Among the Homeless: The Verbal Construction and Avowal of Personal Identities," *American Journal of Sociology* 92, no. 6 (1987): 1336–71; © by the University of Chicago, all rights reserved. The photographs opening Parts I and III are by Larry Kolvoord, © *Austin American-Statesman,* January 7, 1990; the Part II photograph is © Mary Lee Edwards, from the *Austin Chronicle,* March 11, 1988.

University of California Press
Berkeley and Los Angeles, California

University of California Press, Ltd.
Oxford, England

© 1993 by
The Regents of the University of California

Printed in the United States of America

9 8 7 6 5 4 3 2

The paper used in this publication meets the minimum requirements of American National Standard for Information Sciences—Permanence of Paper for Printed Library Materials, ANSI Z39.48-1984. ⊖

To both our immediate and extended families, who have taught us a hundred times over the distinction between a house and a home, and to the homeless we came to know, many of whom have never experienced either in a permanent sense

Contents

Preface

"It was the best of times, it was the worst of times, it was the age of wisdom, it was the age of foolishness . . . it was the season of Light, it was the season of Darkness, it was the spring of hope, it was the winter of despair." So begins Dickens's *A Tale of Two Cities*. A tale of perpetual relevance, it is also of particular relevance to specific historical moments. Clearly one such moment in American life was the decade of the 1980s. Not only was it the best of times for some Americans, especially those at the top of the social hierarchy who prospered further during the Reagan presidency, but it was the worst of times for others, particularly the hundreds of thousands of homeless living on the streets of urban America. During the 1980s few domestic issues generated as much public concern and debate as this scourge of homelessness. As we move into the 1990s the problem remains unabated and the debate continues.

This book reports on a cross-section of Americans who found themselves homeless and, thus, in the winter of despair. It is a sociological case study of a subculture of street life among the unattached adults, mainly males, who lived in or passed through Austin, Texas, between the fall of 1984 and the summer of 1986. Our primary concern is neither with their demographics or disabilities, the foci of so much that has been written about them, nor with the structural causes of their plight, another topic of frequent discussion. We address these issues, to be sure, but we focus our attention primarily on life on the streets as it is experienced by the homeless, that is, on their strategies and struggles to subsist from one moment to the next, materially, socially, and psychologically.

The book was written with several audiences in mind. Clearly we hope it is of value to social scientists interested in the study of homelessness, poverty, and stratification, and in social problems more generally, as well as to those interested in qualitative approaches to studying life on the margins. We also hope the book is of interest to those policymakers who are in a position to make decisions regarding the problem of homelessness. But most importantly, we hope the book finds its way into the hands of the interested layperson and college and university students who, for the most part, live in a world far removed from the subculture of street life and who often harbor glaring misconceptions of the homeless. Having this latter audience foremost in our minds accounts in part for the detail with which some matters are discussed and the care taken at times to elaborate what our professional peers might assume or even take for granted. As we wrote with this broader audience in mind, we have hoped that the book will counter stigmatizing and stereotypic conceptions of the homeless and provide a more thoroughgoing understanding, and perhaps even appreciation, for a particular style of sociological inquiry and practice.

In looking back over the genesis of the book, we have been struck by how it originated largely out of situational circumstances and our particular life experiences rather than as the result of studied, conscious formulation. It is rooted in part in a series of seven trips one of the authors made from Texas to California between 1975 and 1984. The major highway connects with Interstate 20 west of Dallas and Fort Worth, then stretches through Abilene, Big Spring, and Odessa. About midway between Pecos and Van Horn, it is joined by Interstate 10. Together they work their way through El Paso on into New Mexico and thence westward to California. The larger portion of the route wends through some of the most desolate and inhospitable country in North America.

Around Christmas of 1981, the scenery changed noticeably. Hitchhikers, mostly men, dotted the Interstate. Truck stops and rest stops teemed with people carrying packs and sleeping rolls. As the driver approached Tucson the number of hitchhikers increased, triggering memories of the vagabonds of the late 1960s heading for San Francisco along Interstate 5 and the Coast Highway in California. But up close the people encountered on the Interstate between Texas and California in late 1981 bore little resemblance to the transients of the late sixties. They had no flowers in their hair, no blissful expressions. Their weathered, distraught faces were clearly not those of people on their way to a promised land. No, these were the faces of individuals who composed the first wave of what was to become a great flood of homeless by the middle of the decade. Encountering them as he did led the driver to ask himself a number of questions about where they had come from and why they were showing up now, questions that were to become more pressing and focused a few years down the road.

In the case of the other, the seeds of curiosity had been planted much earlier and had been nurtured throughout his life. He was raised a block away from the railroad tracks and frequently encountered hoboes fresh from fruit-picking in the orchards of eastern Washington. By his late teens he had learned to hop the freights and occasionally rode the rails between Seattle and Chicago, sleeping in missions and jails and hanging out in the hobo jungles of Wenatchee, Spokane, and St. Paul. While sharing a pot of coffee with a longtime tramp in Spokane's Hill Yard in the summer of 1971, he received some sage advice that changed his life: "This life's too hard. You're young. Do something easier." Soon after, he abandoned the freights for a more mainstream path. Still, he had not fully understood what the tramp had told him, as he retained his romantic image of the tramps' world of the rails.

A decade later he was working in Alaska as a seasonal employment counselor and a part-time journalist. But he was still drawn toward the margins of society. In these capacities, he worked with a variety of transients, from college students fresh from the Lower Forty-Eight, who slept at the youth hostel and worked day labor in Anchorage while waiting to get summer jobs in remote canneries, to "spitrats," who camped on the Homer spit as they schemed to land berths on "highlining" fishing boats in the Gulf of Alaska. Their bravado and dreams reinforced his lingering vision of the romance at society's margins.

Several years later he enrolled in graduate school at the University of Texas at Austin. At first he was drawn to the day-labor operation of the Texas Employment Commission as a possible research site, since it was a world with which he had some familiarity. But few of the laborers were like those he had encountered before. As he listened to their talk about their troubles and their lives, it became increasingly clear to him that their world was strikingly different from the romanticized transient communities of his past. This disjunction became the source of a gnawing curiosity that suggested an alternative research project.

An opportunity to explore one aspect of this newfound curiosity surfaced in the spring of 1984 when our mutual interests intersected with concerns the City of Austin was beginning to voice about the increase in the number of homeless in its downtown area. The first salvo in what was to become a barrage of complaints was fired by the president of a local jogging club; he was angered by the presence of the disheveled men who had begun to hang around the Town Lake park, drinking by the hike-and-bike trails and sleeping in the bushes by the lake. Spurred by such citizen complaints and genuinely perplexed by this phenomenon of abject poverty in the midst of economic boom, the city sought assistance from Louis Zurcher Jr. and David Austin, both of the Department of Social Work at the University of Texas. By the time Zurcher and Austin broached the matter with us, we had already become interested in the issue. Moreover, recognizing the mental health issues involved in the problem of homelessness, the university-based Hogg Foundation for Mental Health expressed interest in funding our field research.

As the preceding account makes clear, the research project on which this book is based evolved in a contingent fashion out of our own experiences and interests and those of various members of the community in which it was conducted and in which we lived. Research proposals may make a case for why homelessness should be studied in one city or another, but in fact almost all academic researchers have chosen to study the homeless in cities where they have academic or research affiliations. Our case is no different. Additionally, not only was there a dramatic increase in the numbers of homeless in Austin, but their presence was perceived as a serious social problem. Other rationales for the study could be provided—for example, most prior research on homelessness had been conducted in large, northern cities, so conducting a study in Austin offered an opportunity to learn about the problem of homelessness in a moderate-sized, sunbelt city—but they would be pure embellishment. The problem was at our doorsteps, it was regarded as a serious one, and our interest in the daily routines and survival strategies of the homeless could be explored as well in Austin as anywhere else: all reason enough for our study.

During the eight years since the research was initiated, we have accumulated a considerable debt to a wide range of individuals and agencies, and we wish to acknowledge their invaluable assistance. First and foremost, we are indebted to the many homeless individuals who not only shared with us their biographies and their experiences on the streets but also taught us a good bit about surviving on the streets. They number close to 170, but we are particularly indebted to twenty of them who served as our key informants. They are introduced in Chapter 2, but we want to acknowledge here eight of them who were teachers par excellence and with whom we developed especially close ties. They are known in the book as Marilyn, Hoyt, Gypsy Bill, Tony, Tanner, Willie, Tom, and Nona.

Second, we wish to thank members of a host of city, state, and non-profit agencies, institutions, and ad hoc committees, listed here by name rather than by agency affiliation: Major Bagley, Major Belvin, Clint Butler, Lori Cervenak-Renteria, Carol Frank, Vijay Ganju, Ricardo Guimbarda, Jim Grammetbauer, Tony Hearn, Dennis Hogan, Ron Kingsbury, Kent Miller, James Pinedo, Tom Schaefer, Tina Tamez, and Anne Wynne. In many respects, each was as critical to the project as the homeless themselves. We do not suppose that our account precisely matches the ones they would give, but that in no way lessens our deep gratitude for their patience and assistance.

We also received much support in the form of constructive suggestions and comments offered by our academic colleagues, particularly David Austin, Don Baumann, Rob Benford, Bill Bunis, Michael Brown, Dan Cress, Sheldon Ekland-Olson, Joe Feagin, Debra Friedman, Michael Hechter, Joseph Heirling, Randy Hodson, Les Kurtz, Cynthia Phillips, Steve Worden, Richard Workman, and Woody Powell and his Social Organization Seminar at the University of Arizona. In addition to these individuals, we want to single out eight other colleagues to whom we are particularly indebted. Susan Gonzalez Baker and Michael Martin constituted part of the initial data-gathering team and played a central role in collecting the institutional tracking data. They were also reliable sources of suggestion and co-authors of a number of papers resulting from the research. Gideon Sjoberg was a source of considerable support too, providing not only a late-night sounding board for whatever we wanted to discuss but also, on one occasion, the bail money that got one of us out of jail in the wee hours of a Saturday morning. The late Louis Zurcher Jr. was also particularly supportive of the project, especially during its early stages. Finally, we are grateful for the constructive comments and encouragement of Peter Adler, Lyn Lofland, Doug McAdam, and Cal Morrill, all of whom read the manuscript in its entirety.

The Hogg Foundation for Mental Health made the project more feasible by granting two years of generous financial support. We are thus indebted to the foundation, and particularly to Chuck Bonjean for his continuing interest and support both as a colleague and in the capacity of the foundation's vice president.

Ohio University provided support for release time during a critical stage of writing in the winter of 1990, and Barb McIntosh, the manuscript typist in the sociology department at the University of Arizona, labored long and hard and without complaint over draft after draft. Many thanks go to Barb for both her competence and her patience, as well as to Peter Brantley for his computer expertise and assistance. We also thank Sherry Enderle and the rest of the staff in the department at Arizona for their patience and support.

We would be remiss not to acknowledge Naomi Schneider, our editor at the University of California Press. Naomi first learned of the project that culminated in this book when, on one of her editorial treks, she stopped in Austin in the mid-1980s. From that moment on she has been a source of unwavering support and encouragement. The editorial assistance of Amy Klatzkin and Jane-Ellen Long is much appreciated too.

Finally, and most important of all, we want to acknowledge the enduring support and encouragement of our families, particularly our immediate families: Judy, Heather, Maggie, and Pete for one of us, and Mara for the other. In ways that only the immediate family of an author can understand, this clearly is as much their book as ours.

D. A. S. and L. A.
September, 1991

PART ONE

Introduction

CHAPTER ONE

Studying the Homeless

It is a mid-January afternoon. A chilling "Blue Norther" has blown down from Canada into central Texas. A raw wind blows in the alleys and near-freezing rain pelts the streets. Not a day to spend outside. No matter, a twenty-five-year-old man in cowboy boots, a grimy denim shirt, and an oil-stained vest is sprawled on a rain-soaked piece of cardboard beneath his rusted-out black '65 Cadillac parked down the street from the Salvation Army. Aside from two short breaks to get warm, he has been lying under the car since breakfast, trying to install a second-hand starter. If he had had the right tools, he might have gotten the starter in by 10:00 A.M. Now time is getting short for making it to the plasma center before it closes. "If I don't get this car running in the next half hour," he mutters, "I'm going to have to walk the whole three miles to the plasma center in this rain."

Up the block from where the young cowboy is struggling with his car, nearly two hundred people have taken refuge from the cold, driving rain in the Salvation Army's drafty, run-down transient lodge. The Sally, as people on the streets call it, is an anomaly in the renovated downtown area, a diminutive tattered structure dwarfed by glittering high-rises. Inside the Sally's Big Room, some of Austin's most destitute citizens are waiting out the storm. With 200 people, mostly male, the so-called Big Room is bursting at its seams. At the front it is standing-room only.

By the door, several young men with rumpled clothes and unkempt hair pass a cigarette around and peer through the steamed-up windows.

They discuss the dismal employment scene. "People keep saying this is the workingest city in the country, but you couldn't prove it by me," one of them laments. "I haven't been able to get a day's work since I been here."

"And you can write this week off," replies one of his companions, a middle-aged man with a wandering eye and a week's stubble on his face. "You ain't getting nothing in this weather."

Their conversation is interrupted by shouts from the audience of a game show that is playing on a small black-and-white television perched on a card table. Two Sally workers and several of their friends sit by the TV on the few chairs in the room. Behind them stretches a sea of disheveled bodies, discarded newspapers, cigarette butts, and wet paper bags filled with mildewed clothes. Many lie asleep. An acrid blanket of cigarette smoke hangs about four feet off the floor.

A few pockets of animated conversation punctuate the somber mass. Four men in the middle of the room are playing a lively game of hearts. Periodically their banter is halted when their eldest member, a sweet-tempered black man who reeks of stale urine, has such a violent coughing fit that they fear he will pass out.

Nearby, a couple of long-haired young men with two sets of earphones connected to one Walkman pretend to play guitars as they sing along loudly to a rock song no one else can hear. Behind them stands a heavily bearded young man with wild hair and a crude tattoo of a two-headed snake stretching the full length of his right arm. He is throwing karate punches and arguing with an unseen foe. All the while a blond boy who looks to be about twelve years old darts around the room, stumbling over sleepers and leaving a muffled chorus of curses in his wake.

In a back corner of the room, half a dozen men and two women surreptitiously pass around a couple of joints. As the twelve-year-old sails into the back of the room, he sees what they are doing and begins to chant, "People back here are smoking joints! People back here are smoking joints!" Suddenly he is pulled to the floor and punched in the side. "Shut up, you little shit!" yells the man who pulled him down. "You're gonna end up dead if you don't shut up now. What the hell're you doing here anyway? Don't you have a mother or something?"

Squirming and whimpering, the kid slips out of the man's grip and shoots off through the crowd. The man shakes his head disgustedly, then gets up and worms his way through the crowd to the restroom. There he finds a long line of men waiting to use the single toilet. "What's the problem?" he asks, after five minutes during which the line hasn't moved.

"Some guy in there's puking his guts up," a man at the front of the line informs him.

"He better finish pretty soon," the man behind the first says, pounding on the door. "Hurry up in there or I'm gonna go in my pants!" After another minute he steps out of line and heads for the door. "To hell with it," he grumbles. "I'll go outside." He winces as his bare feet hit the wet, cold pavement, and he vows when he goes back in that he'll "find the bastard" who stole his shoes.

As the barefoot man shuffles off to the side of the building, the young cowboy-mechanic sloshes into the Big Room. His clothes are soaked, he's shivering, and his right hand is wrapped in a bloody rag. In his left hand he holds the ratchet set, pliers, and screwdriver he's been using all day. Slowly he weaves his way to the back wall, where several older, crippled men are lying on cots.

"You look like a drowned rat," a little man with a dirty cast on his left ankle tells him. "What happened to your hand?"

The young cowboy drops the tools on the little man's cot. "I sliced it up when the ratchet slipped," he answers wearily. "Still haven't got the starter in. Can I bum a smoke?"

The little man reaches under his blanket, pulls out a package of Bugler tobacco, and rolls them each a cigarette. The man on the next cot watches them enviously. Finally he gets up the nerve to ask, "Can I have a couple of drags?"

"Here, have the rest of it," the little man says, passing him what's left of his cigarette.

The young cowboy slumps down by the cot. His mind is still focused on heading up to the plasma center to sell some blood, but his body is too weary to follow through on it. He's starting to warm up now, but his cut hand throbs and his throat feels scratchy. "Please don't let me catch a cold," he mumbles to himself. "It's for doggone sure I don't need that." He closes his eyes and imagines working a roofing job on a spring day: the smell of hot tar and the sun beating down on his back. Just as he is about to fall into a peaceful dream, the rambunctious blond boy stumbles and falls into his lap. Before the cowboy quite knows what hit him, the kid is up and running through the crowd again.

"No use going to sleep anyway," he muses. "Any time now they'll want us to get in line for dinner." He slouches against the cot, staring blankly at a large, gray-haired woman in a tattered dress. He's been watching her for several minutes before he realizes with disgust that she is tearing scabs off large sores on her arms. The sight disturbs him so much that he gets up and wanders off to the front of the room. He's about halfway to the front when a commotion erupts by the bathroom. "Call an ambulance!" someone shouts. "I think the guy in the bathroom's had a heart attack!"

One of the Sally workers heads over to the bathroom; another goes to call 911. In a few minutes the Emergency Medical Service workers arrive and put the man on a stretcher. One EMS worker keeps asking whether anyone knows the unconscious man's name, but nobody does. They clear a path to the door and rush him out to the ambulance, which speeds away with its siren blaring in the rain.

The cowboy bites his lip as the ambulance disappears. The room hums with nervous excitement, and the blond kid runs around the room shouting, "That man's gonna die! That man's gonna die!"

One of the Sally workers tries to calm things down by collaring the boy and putting a hand over his mouth. Another worker yells out, "Okay, let's get in line for dinner!"

Slowly the crowd reorganizes itself into a long line snaking back and forth across the room. A few determined sleepers lie scattered on the floor. The cowboy feels a fever and a headache coming on. "But at least I'm near the head of the line," he tells himself. "At this rate I'll be able to get a mat by the television after dinner." That provides some consolation for his day of disappointment. After all, he knows, it's going to be a long night.

.   .   .   .

The preceding scene, based on participant observation in Austin in 1985, could have occurred in any of America's urban centers during the 1980s, when they were besieged by increasing numbers of homeless people. The question of just how many Americans were homeless during the 1980s has been hotly debated, with numbers ranging from around 250,000 to over 3,000,000.[1] But a host of other questions spring to mind as well. Who are these people? Where do they come from? What are their lives like? How do they manage to survive physically, socially, and psychologically in this netherworld of the streets that is so alien to most Americans? How do they manage to make sense of lives that strike most of us as waking nightmares?

These questions are relevant not only to the homeless who took refuge in Austin's Sally on that blustery winter day in 1985 but to hundreds of thousands of homeless across the United States. They are also the questions that anchor this book. Our goal is to provide a detailed description and analysis of street life as it was lived by the homeless in Austin, Texas, in the first half of the 1980s. But before turning our attention to Austin, we provide a broader analytic and historical perspective on homelessness. First, we clarify three analytically useful dimensions of homelessness and categorize several distinct varieties. Then we take a brief historical look at street homelessness, the kind of homelessness that we are concerned with in this book.

VARIETIES AND DIMENSIONS OF HOMELESSNESS

Homelessness in one form or another has existed throughout much of human history.[2] Yet even a cursory examination reveals striking differences among homeless individuals and their circumstances. Some people are rendered homeless by mass disasters such as earthquakes, floods, or hurricanes. Others are homeless because the labor they perform forces them into perpetual migration. Some face homelessness when they flee their countries for political or economic reasons. And still others confront homelessness when deep-seated economic and institutional changes push them onto the streets. Each of these groups experience some degree of homelessness, but the nature of that experience often varies considerably among them. These differences can be clarified by considering three separate dimensions of homelessness: a residential dimension; a familial-support dimension; and a role-based dignity and moral-worth dimension.

Homelessness is typically thought of in terms of the first dimension, that is, as a life-style characterized first and foremost by the absence of conventional permanent housing. This residential dimension has been the primary basis for most recent conceptualizations of homelessness.[3] The term "literal homelessness," meaning "those who sleep in shelters provided for homeless persons or in places, private or public, not intended as dwellings," captures this dimension well.[4] Although this dimension is a necessary starting point for conceptualizing homelessness, it is inadequate for distinguishing among the varieties of individuals who share the obdurate reality of residential dislocation, whether for a few nights or weeks on end.

The second dimension is the presence or absence of familial support. We include this dimension for three reasons. First, the concept of family, with its emphasis on social bonds, networks, and the linkage be-

tween individuals and the larger society, is a basic component of sociological theorizing more generally. Second, the inclusion of some notion
of family bondedness is partly consistent with work on earlier generations of homelessness, which focused on the "absence or attenuation of
affiliative bonds that link settled persons to a network of interconnected
social structures."[5] And, third, the family dimension resonates with traditional folk images of the home. The term has traditionally symbolized
far more than simply shelter or a roof over one's head. As John Howard
Payne wrote in 1823 in "Home Sweet Home":

> How sweet 'tis to sit 'neath a fond father's smile,
> And the caress of a mother to soothe and beguile!
> Let others delight mid new pleasures to roam,
> But give me, oh, give me, the pleasures of home![6]

The notion of home in American poetry also includes a feeling of
shared history with significant others, as in Edgar Guest's memorable
"It takes a heap o' livin' in a house t' make it a home,"[7] and the sense
of unconditional support that was captured in Robert Frost's famous
line, "Home is the place where, when you have to go there / They have
to take you in."[8] This image of the home approximates sociological
conceptualizations of the family as a web of mutually affective and supportive relationships. Although recent research indicates that the familial home is often a far cry from the poetic "haven in a heartless
world,"[9] it undoubtedly still performs this function for many, especially in times of crisis. For many homeless, however, this web of relationships has been weakened or shredded.

The degree to which the homeless lack familial support varies, of
course. For some categories of homeless people, such as mass-disaster
victims, familial connections generally remain intact.[10] For most other
categories, including migrant workers, refugees, and street families, familial bonds are often weakened but not totally shattered. The unattached street homeless, though, tend to face their daily lives almost devoid of reliable familial support. Indeed, as we will see in Chapter 8,
many of the homeless never had a reliable familial network to begin
with, and for others it is only a distant memory, seldom functioning
as a source of pleasant reminiscence, much less as a resource that can
be tapped in times of crisis. We thus find it useful to incorporate the
familial-support dimension as a variable that helps distinguish among
different forms of homelessness.

The third distinguishing feature of homelessness is the degree of dignity and moral worth associated with the various categories of homelessness. From a sociological standpoint, to be homeless is, among other things, to be the incumbent of a basic role or master status. These terms refer to statuses that are central to the way we are viewed and the way we view ourselves.[11] Basic roles or master statuses are usually highly visible, are relevant to interaction in most situations, and are generally repositories of moral worth and dignity. Dignity and moral worth, then, are not primarily individual characteristics but instead flow from the roles we play.

Incumbents of different social roles can thus vary considerably in terms of perceived moral worth. Some social roles, such as the occupational roles of physicians or attorneys, tend to imbue their incumbents with considerable prestige. Stigmatized roles or statuses, by contrast, confer disrepute on their incumbents. Implicit in most such roles is an imputation of character defect. This imputation varies in degree among the categories of homeless people, based largely on public perception of the extent to which they are responsible for their plight and the threat they are seen as posing to the safety and welfare of other citizens. Mass-disaster victims, for instance, are seldom seen as having caused their homeless condition or as threatening the larger community, and therefore they are not stigmatized. The situation is more ambivalent in the case of migrant workers and refugees. In contrast, homeless street people are more likely to be perceived as homeless by virtue of their own imperfections or moral failings.[12] Yet even among street people distinctions tend to be drawn. Homeless families and children tend to be treated more sympathetically than homeless street adults. And it is our sense that adult street women are seen as less responsible for their plight than street men, who often tend to be depicted as improvident and lazy individuals who are threats to the property and physical safety of the domiciled.[13] This general perception is reflected in the views of most agencies and individuals who interact with the homeless in a caretaker fashion and who tend to treat homeless men as less worthy or deserving than others.[14] The point, then, is that a community's "span of sympathy" is not as likely to be extended to unattached homeless men as to homeless families, children, and women.[15]

As the preceding discussion demonstrates, homelessness can be viewed as a generic category, with homeless street people constituting a sub-category. Our focus in this book is not on homelessness in general but only on unattached, homeless street adults, mostly male, in the United States in the 1980s.[16] These homeless lived largely in the public domain, and their lives were characterized not only by the absence of conventional, permanent housing but also by an absence or attenuation of familial support and of consensually defined roles of social utility and moral worth. The combination of these three deficits is reflected in the lives and experiences of the street homeless in Austin in the mid-1980s. But these defining characteristics are hardly peculiar to the street homeless of this era. We therefore turn to an historical overview of street homelessness in order to place the street homeless of today in perspective.

AN HISTORICAL OVERVIEW OF STREET HOMELESSNESS

Street homelessness has had a long and varied history throughout much of the world. The preindustrial city was characterized in part by "the omnipresence of beggars."[17] The beggars were just the tip of the iceberg, however, as the preindustrial city contained large numbers of impoverished and organizationally unattached persons who were referred to collectively as "floating populations."[18] It is uncertain just how these people managed to survive. Begging was one common means of livelihood and was sometimes combined with thievery and prostitution, but "much of their time appeared to have been spent hanging about waiting to involve themselves in whatever was happening."[19]

Although the unattached homeless were a common feature of the preindustrial cities of Europe, two overlapping philosophies mitigated their stigmatization. First, folk traditions emphasized the importance of offering hospitality to needy itinerants.[20] Second, during the Middle Ages there was a tendency to idealize poverty. This tendency can be seen in the creed of Saint Francis, who taught "that beggars were holy, and that the holy should live as beggars."[21] It was an age of considerable charity toward the destitute.

This spirit was challenged in the fourteenth century. The change in attitude resulted from multiple social forces in medieval society. Religious values that denigrated poverty emerged, in part due to the discrediting of the Franciscan ideal because of the great wealth that the order amassed, and partly because Renaissance humanists valorized worldly activity and success.[22] But powerful material forces also underlay this ideological shift. The decimation of the population by the Black Death, which struck England about 1348, prompted the passage of the country's first full-fledged vagrancy statute in 1349.[23] Since at that time

England's feudal economy was highly dependent on a ready supply of cheap labor, the first vagrancy statutes were designed expressly to force the dwindling pool of laborers to accept low-wage employment and to keep them from migrating in search of better opportunities. "Every able-bodied person without other means of support was required," according to one observer, "to work for wages fixed at the level preceding the Black Death; it was unlawful to accept more, or to refuse an offer to work, or to flee from one country to another to avoid offers of work or to seek higher wages, or to give alms to able-bodied beggars who refused to work."[24] In essence the statutes acted as a substitute for serfdom, curtailing "mobility of workers in such a way that labor would not become a commodity for which the landowners would have to compete."[25]

A change in the perception of vagrancy and poverty accompanied the passage of these statutes. The sin of sloth, originally conceived as a spiritual vice, was redefined to include physical idleness. Criticism of the homeless in the fourteenth century was minor, however, in comparison to the flood of vigorous attacks unleashed in the Tudor period, beginning about 1485. These signaled a shift from concern with idleness toward a concern with what was perceived as dangerous criminality.[26] A few perceptive contemporaries, such as Sir Thomas More, recognized the poverty and exploitation that were forcing so many people into homeless destitution, but most writers of the period railed against a subculture of rogues and vagabonds that they feared would destroy civilized society. Vagrants were portrayed as cut-throat thieves and sorcerers and often as being in league with the devil.

The same sentiments prevailed on the Continent, as is evidenced by Martin Luther's editing in 1528 of *Liber Vagatorum,* a purported confessional by "Expertus in Truffis" (Expert in Roguery), who revealed the criminal secrets of the vagrant underworld. Luther promoted the publication of the work "in order that men may see and understand how mightily the devil rules in this world."[27]

At the same time that this ideological shift in the public perception of the homeless took place, the number of homeless in England was growing dramatically. The Enclosure Laws and early industrialization are widely recognized as primary reasons for this growth in homelessness, but other factors operated as well. Between the mid-1500s and the mid-1600s the population of England nearly doubled, and the proportion of adolescents, the demographic group most at risk of homelessness, rose as well.[28] In addition to increased competition for resources, members of the lower classes experienced constant increases in rents and food prices during this hundred-year span, increases that were exacerbated by a drop in real wages.[29]

The official response to the growth in vagrancy during the Tudor years was frequently brutal. Although attempts were made to succor the local poor, itinerant vagrants were punished harshly. Military manhunts were organized periodically to round up the homeless, and once arrested they were often summarily subjected to the stocks, flogging, and sometimes even hanging. Branding was common, as was ear boring, which was introduced in a 1572 statute that required all vagabonds to be "grievously whipped and burned through the gristle of the right ear with a hot iron an inch in diameter."[30] Imprisonment of vagrants was common, and they were often confined in the bridewell, an early British version of the workhouse. Conscription into the military was a frequent alternative to harsher options, with vagrants comprising a major part of the period's armies.[31] The Slavery Act of 1547 placed convicted vagrants in slavery for two years, and the Vagrancy Act of 1597 permitted a sentence of transportation to the colonies.

During the seventeenth and eighteenth centuries, many of Britain's homeless, then, were sent to the American colonies as laborers and servants. Still others with few skills or possessions emigrated in the hope of establishing a better life. Life in the colonies, however, was frequently brutal and exhausting, in part because a constant shortage of workers led employers to overwork those they did employ.[32]

In colonial America, two separate systems—both of which had their origins in the Elizabethan Poor Laws in England—existed for dealing with the problem of the poor. The first system was directed toward legally recognized members of the community. Although it was by no means extravagant, some "outdoor relief" was provided to community members who were unable to support themselves. Maximum efforts were made to keep families together, and the workhouse, so common in England, was seldom a preferred method for dealing with the communities' poor during the colonial period.[33] The principle of requiring a pauper to show legal residency in order to receive support, however, had been imported from England, and this created great difficulties for new immigrants and itinerant workers. Colonial America's agrarian economy in many ways encouraged mobile labor, but its system of support was biased against such laborers.

The poor were allowed to petition communities for settlement rights, but they were often denied admittance as bad risks. "There thus arose a kind of transient poor, shunted from community to community because in place after place they were denied settlement rights."[34] The major seaboard cities of the colonial era experienced a particularly heavy influx of nonlocal poor, especially immigrants and sailors. These cities were among the first communities to develop workhouses, shelters, and soup kitchens.[35]

During the pre–Civil War years the American economy suffered several minor economic depressions that swelled the ranks of the homeless, but it was after the Civil War that homelessness rose most dramatically.[36] The war itself displaced tremendous numbers of people. The country also experienced heavy waves of immigration during the later decades of the nineteenth century. And the industrial and agricultural state of the nation demanded large numbers of mobile workers. As one account of this era noted: "The drive of American industry westward opened new kinds of jobs—at the railroad construction sites, in the mines, in the timberlands, on the sheep and cattle ranches, in the orchards. The call was for a special kind of labor, a labor remote from family and community life."[37] The development of the railroad system across the country provided jobs as well as the cheap transportation necessary for those willing to answer this call for a large, itinerant work force. The confluence of these factors gave birth in the late 1800s and early 1900s to the homeless life-style of the American hobo.

During this period hoboes both played a central role in American labor and became a prominent feature of the urban landscape. For all their work in rural areas, the hoboes were, as one observer phrased it, "urbancentric."[38] The reasons were twofold. First, from the 1870s to the 1920s, many major cities contained a district known as the Main Stem (or Hobohemia), to which these men returned when their jobs were finished in the hinterlands or to wait out the winter months. With its lodging houses, pawnshops, saloons, dance halls, and inexpensive restaurants offering "coffee an's" (coffee and donuts or biscuits) for a nickel, the Main Stem provided for all the needs of these migrant workers at reasonable prices. Second, and perhaps more important, the Main Stem contained numerous employment agencies where the men might find new work. Here they could sign on for jobs at remote railroad construction and logging sites and have their transportation paid for. Through these agencies "battalions of workers marched to the pulse of on-again, off-again employment."[39]

In major cities, especially those on primary rail routes, the Main Stem contained a substantial portion of the city's population and businesses.

In San Francisco, the city directory listed one-third of the city's restaurants as located in the Main Stem area.[40] And according to Nels Anderson's classic sociological study, *The Hobo,* Chicago's Main Stem in the early 1920s was populated by "30,000 people in good times and 75,000 in hard times," with roughly half a million transient workers passing through in the course of a normal year.[41]

The Main Stem was politically and intellectually active. Several unions, most notably the International Workers of the World (the I.W.W., popularly known as the Wobblies), worked constantly to recruit hoboes. Chicago's Bughouse Square was a gathering spot for hobo intellectuals, vagabond poets, and revolutionaries. The bookstores of the area sold a wide array of radical literature, including some thirteen publications of the I.W.W.[42]

The hoboes' economic fortunes were better than those of future homeless generations, but their lives, too, had a dark side. The work was unsteady, and they were often subjected to exploitation at the hands of employment agencies and employers. Furthermore, riding the rails was a dangerous business, as over 2,500 men were killed and another 2,600 were injured on the railroads in 1919 alone.[43]

The hoboes occupied an ambivalent place in American culture. On the one hand, they were romanticized as "frustrated Western pioneers with too few lands to conquer."[44] On the other, they were vilified as scoundrels. They were so despised in some quarters that in 1877 the *Chicago Tribune* advised its readers, admittedly tongue-in-cheek, that "the simplest plan, probably, where one is not a member of the humane society, is to put a little strychnine or arsenic in the meat and other supplies furnished the tramp. This produces death within a comparatively short period of time, is a warning to other tramps to keep out of the neighborhood, keeps the coroner in good humor, and saves one's chickens and other portable property from constant destruction."[45]

In the mid-1920s the hobo era died, from a combination of causes. Mechanization of agriculture had depleted the job market for seasonal farm workers. The western frontier had largely been settled. The American economy became strong enough to support large numbers of Americans in more stable jobs. Finally, the railroad, the matrix of the hobo life, had gradually been replaced by automobiles as the major mode of transportation, and those remaining switched from steam to diesel locomotion, a change that made it more difficult to ride the rails.[46]

With the coming of the Great Depression, however, the numbers of homeless people again rose quickly.[47] Testifying before the U.S. Senate in 1934, Nels Anderson estimated that the country contained at least 1.5 million homeless persons.[48] The situation of the homeless had changed dramatically, however, as the Main Stem, home of self-supporting hoboes, was transformed into skid row, where men primarily dependent on charity lived.[49] And unlike the more solidaristic hoboes, transients during the Depression years engaged in little collective organizing. The transition in the skid-row population and its situation is captured in one observer's lament that it was "pathetic to see beggars where rebels once shouted, sang, and whored."[50]

The Depression also witnessed a rise in the number of homeless families and single children on the road. John Steinbeck's *The Grapes of Wrath* realistically portrays the dislocation of the Great Plains refugees who lost their farms and wandered west in search of a new life. Roadside Hoovervilles, named after President Hoover, who had been notoriously unsympathetic to the plight of the poor, sprang up around the country. Police in many communities used their jails as overnight shelters. And in 1932 the U.S. Children's Bureau conducted a study that documented over 200,000 homeless children.[51]

Although in 1933 the federal government began efforts to alleviate the plight of the homeless, the programs were usually modest and often contradictory. The Federal Transient Bureau agreed to pay cities for the shelter and meal costs of nonlocals at established tent camps along the road. But in 1935 the Works Progress Administration took over these functions, resulting in "a significant curtailing of the federal effort on behalf of transient workers" because it strongly supported stiff residency requirements.[52] Furthermore, the transient homeless were kept on the move by local officials who did not want to assume responsibility for their support. In New York state, for example, the money spent on transporting transients out of communities sometimes equaled the amount that was spent on supportive services for the local homeless.[53]

By 1936 many of the Depression's homeless people had been reabsorbed into the work force, but it was only with the onset of the war effort in the late 1930s that the nation's skid-row population diminished appreciably, as the homeless were recruited into the armed services and into war industry. During World War II the skid-row population almost disappeared, reaching a low in 1944, when the city shelters in New York reported an average of only 550 lodgers per day, compared with 19,000 in 1935.[54]

After World War II the federal government provided benefits for veterans in an effort to assist them in the transition back to civilian life and employment. This was the first time in American history that the end of a war did not substantially increase the homeless population.[55]

Skid-row populations grew only modestly in the postwar years, and the demographic composition of skid row changed. The district no longer drew a young and mobile labor force, as it had in the heyday of the Main Stem or even in the Depression. Rather, the cheap food, hotels, pawnshops, soup kitchens, and missions of the Row attracted an older, often disabled population of down-and-outers, averaging over fifty years of age.[56] Some had small railroad pensions, military disability checks, or Social Security income, but the majority scraped by on a meager income from intermittent unskilled labor, frequently supplemented by the sale of blood to commercial blood banks. In 1958, for instance, the median income of the skid-row men in Minneapolis was eighty dollars per month.[57] Most skid-row residents had regular or at least semiregular private accommodations in cheap, single-residence occupancy (SRO) hotels, but at any given time about 10 percent of the population of the Row was either sleeping outside or in free missions and shelters.[58] The skid-row men of this period also exhibited a high degree of residential stability, in striking contrast to the hoboes of the Main Stem and the Great Depression's job-seekers.[59]

The postwar skid row was indeed a smaller, older, and less economically productive version of the once dynamic Main Stem. However, the differences between the Main Stem and skid row were highly exaggerated in the minds of the general public and of the academic community, both of which took a far more pejorative stance toward skid row and its habitués. Skid row was perceived primarily as the part of town that catered to down-and-out drunks. Newspaper cartoons of the period frequently portrayed the men of the Row as social misfits and alcoholic degenerates.[60] Academic researchers supported this perception by focusing the bulk of skid-row research on alcohol problems, despite the fact that only a minority of the population there was actually alcoholic.[61]

In addition to providing inexpensive services for unattached older men at the bottom of the social order, skid row during this period served a broader social function that was consistent with the negative public and academic stereotype of skid-row men. As a geographically distinct district, skid row spatially segregated the stigmatized down-and-outers from the rest of the community. Police tended to keep a watchful eye on the district to prevent spillover into middle-class areas.

By the early 1960s, the populations of America's skid rows had, for several reasons, declined even more dramatically.[62] First, the number of transient workers cycling through the skid rows had continued to decline as the Row no longer functioned as a major labor exchange.[63] Second, the availability of more generous welfare benefits and other entitlements enabled many who would otherwise have been dependent on skid row's cheap housing and services instead to live in other city neighborhoods. Many welfare agencies encouraged their clients to locate elsewhere in the belief that they would thus be saved from the negative influence of the skid-row subculture. Additionally, skid rows around the country fell prey to gentrification and urban renewal. The decline of skid-row populations, therefore, also reflected the demolition of many of the cheap hotels and other services on which the residents had relied.[64]

This decline in the skid-row population around the country led some observers to forecast the eventual disappearance of the skid-row homeless in the United States. Others suggested a more cautious interpretation, arguing that "this decline [was] not due to a decrease in the absolute size of the [homeless] population" but, rather, to its dispersal in American cities.[65] But even those who cautioned against the assertion that the number of homeless was declining did not anticipate the surge in homelessness that was to occur in the early 1980s.[66]

Perhaps as startling as the sudden increase in the number of homeless in the 1980s was the growing recognition that the characteristics of the population were shifting as well. One change was in the age composition of the homeless. In stark contrast to the skid-row men's average age of over fifty, the homeless of the 1980s tended more often to be in the earlier years of adulthood, with a mean age somewhere in the mid-thirties.[67] They were also more ethnically diverse. Although researchers found considerable variation from one community and region to another, most found among the homeless a greater proportion of ethnic minorities than had existed on skid row.[68] The proportion of women had also increased, as had that of families.[69]

The differences between the homelessness of the skid-row era and that of the 1980s extended beyond demographics. Most significantly, it included a shift in the public perception of the problem of homelessness. Urban renewal and the gentrification of skid rows around the country had destroyed the urban niche in which many of the homeless of the previous period had existed. As a result, the homeless of the 1980s were more visible and faced more frequent contact with domiciled citizens than had their earlier counterparts. Because of this increased visibility and contact, coupled with the dramatic growth during the 1980s in the sheer numbers of homeless, homelessness generated more public interest and debate during the decade than did almost any other domestic issue. One result was a plethora of research reports on the topic.

Indeed, it is probably not too farfetched to assert that academics or researchers in the social-service sector have generated reports of one kind or another on the homeless in almost every community throughout the country. In a monograph reviewing many of these studies, for example, the author noted that his "working bibliography on the homeless exceeds sixty single-spaced pages of entries, of which three-quarters are from 1980 or later."[70] The vast majority of the more recent studies that contain primary data share two fundamental characteristics. Most are based on questionnaire surveys of the homeless or of shelter providers, and most are concerned primarily with the demographics and disabilities of the homeless.

Evidence of the first tendency can be readily gleaned from the research literature, but it is also clearly indicated by a General Accounting Office report (1985) summarizing research on the homeless. This overview identified one hundred and thirty studies or reports, seventy-five of which contained primary data. Thirty of the seventy-five were based on street and shelter surveys of the homeless; the remaining forty-five reported data retrieved from shelter providers. There was nothing resembling a case study or ethnography among these studies. Clearly, there has been a proliferation of research on the homeless since 1985, but with the exception of a few studies such as Jonathan Kozol's *Rachel and Her Children* and Irene Glasser's *More Than Bread,* most of this recent research has been of the survey variety.[71]

The tendency to focus on the demographics and disabilities of today's homeless is also evident in both popular and social science literature. Indeed, it is difficult to find current publications on the homeless that go much beyond enumeration of their demographic characteristics and presumed disabilities, such as mental illness, alcoholism, and poor health.[72] These focal concerns are congruent both with the interests and agendas of funding agencies (such as the National Institute of Mental Health, the National Institutes of Health, and the Robert Wood Johnson Foundation) and with the kinds of data best procured by questionnaire surveys. The resultant findings certainly advance understanding of the demographics and some of the disabilities of the homeless, and they are of some utility to service agencies interested in doing something about or for the homeless, but they tell us little about actual life on the streets. Thus, it seems reasonable to assert that such survey studies of today's homeless have tended to deflect attention from questions and issues pertinent to an understanding of the nature and texture of street life, and particularly from the perspective of the homeless themselves. They have generated, in other words, what Clifford Geertz has called "experience distant" rather than "experience near" constructions and understandings.[73]

Since it was the latter type of understanding we were most interested in securing, and since we were particularly interested in learning about the survival routines of the homeless and how these routines vary among them, we thought an ethnographic field study would be the appropriate research strategy. It was with this in mind that we began our field research of homeless street people in Austin, Texas, in September of 1984.

LOCAL CONTEXT AND PROCEDURES

Nestled on the eastern edge of Texas's verdant hill country, Austin has long been perceived by both natives and visitors as the state's garden spot. As the state capital, the home of the main campus of the University of Texas, and the seat of progressive country music, Austin has been regarded as a cultural oasis as well. In the decade between 1975 and 1985, it was also one of the sunbelt's shining boomtowns, nearly doubling its population, from around 250,000 to close to 450,000. But its booming economy and growing population did not shelter it from the scourge of homelessness. On the contrary, its very prosperity and growth seemed to give rise to a number of local homeless and to attract even larger numbers from other states and cities. The fact that it is located on the interstate between Dallas and San Antonio and is connected by several highways to Houston, two and a half hours to the east, placed Austin at the intersection of the flow of homeless between three of the country's ten largest cities. For these and other reasons that will be discussed later, the ranks of Austin's homeless population swelled during the first half of the 1980s.

Estimates of the size of Austin's daily homeless population during the mid-1980s ranged from a low of around 650 to a high of 4,000, with perhaps the most reasonable estimate being 1,000 to 1,300.[74] Although this and other estimates of the size of Austin's homeless population are open to debate, there is no mistaking the dramatic growth in that population during the first half of the 1980s. This growth is clearly demonstrated by the increase in services provided to the homeless by the Salvation Army, by Caritas (a local charity agency), and by the Texas Employment Commission (TEC). The Salvation Army, for example, served 4,928 people in 1979 and 11,271 in 1984—an increase of 128 percent. That the vast majority of these individuals were indeed destitute and undomiciled is suggested further by the quantum jump in lodgings and meals provided by the Salvation Army during the same time period, from 16,863 to 156,451, an increase of 828 percent. Caritas experienced an even more phenomenal increase of 1,602 percent in the services it provided during this period, and TEC witnessed a 72 percent increase in day-labor applicants between 1982 and 1984. Even though there is some duplication in services, both within and across agencies, the rate of increase in the number of homeless served by each agency is so robust that the conclusion is unmistakable: whatever the exact number of homeless living in or passing through Austin in the mid-1980s, the city had experienced a remarkable leap in the size of that population since the late 1970s.

This pool of homeless street people was the focus of the case study we conducted between 1984 and 1986. Our primary research interest was not with their demographics and disabilities but with three other considerations: the repertoire of material, interpersonal, and psychological strategies and routines the homeless fashion or appropriate to facilitate their survival; the variation in the use of these strategies among the homeless; and the array of factors that shape these survival strategies and routines. In short, we were most interested in the subculture of street life as it manifested itself in the lives of the homeless.

To respond to these interests we had to direct our research to meet four basic criteria. First, it had to be appreciative of the institutional contexts in which the routines and experiences of the homeless are embedded. Second, the research had to attend to the perspectives and voices, not just of the homeless, but also of other groups whose actions affect the daily lives of the homeless. Third, it had to use a variety of procedures in order to tap a range of data sources. And, fourth, the research had to be longitudinal, capturing events and happenings as they unfolded over time. In addition, we wanted the research to permit the discovery of unanticipated findings and unexpected data sources.

CONTEXTUALIZATION

Concern with contextualization is predicated on the contention that social actions and events can be adequately understood only in relation to the social contexts in which they are embedded. In practice, a contextual orientation manifests itself in a persistent commitment to understanding how actions or processes are produced and reproduced or changed by their interaction with other elements within a particular sociohistorical context.

In our research we were interested not only in the repertoire of survival strategies fashioned or appropriated by the homeless and in their corresponding daily routines but also in the factors that shaped these strategies and routines. Repertoires of survival strategies do not emerge willy-nilly. They are the product of the interplay between the resourcefulness and ingenuity of the homeless and local organizational, political, and ecological constraints. An understanding of the experience of homelessness and how it is managed thus requires consideration of the local matrix of social service and control agencies and commercial establishments that deal directly with the homeless. Accordingly, in addition to spending over four hundred hours in the field with homeless individuals, we spent another two hundred hours with agency personnel, police officers, local political officials, and neighborhood activists. This aspect of the field research was facilitated by ongoing examination of relevant agency reports, news releases, and articles and editorials in the *Austin American-Statesman,* the city's daily newspaper. These considerations take us to the second feature of the research.

MULTIPERSPECTIVAL ANALYSIS

To contextualize social activities, issues, and processes involves more than providing a descriptive overview of the encompassing context. It also requires consideration of the voices and experiences of the range of actors of focal concern, of the perspectives and actions of other relevant groups of actors, and of the interaction among all of them.

We attempted, therefore, to identify and map the social settings and organizations and the types of homeless that together constituted the subculture of street life in Austin. Relevant social settings and organizations included the major institutions or agencies (e.g., Salvation Army, the city hospital, the city police department), commercial establishments (e.g., plasma centers, labor pools, bars), and spatial or territorial niches (e.g., campsites, bridges, parks, street corners) that were central to the daily rounds, life-style, and prospects of the homeless. Social types, in contrast, connote characteristic ways of thinking and acting among individuals within a given context.[75]

Since we were interested in documenting the diversity of relevant settings and types of homeless, we employed a type of nonprobability, judgmental sampling technique called maximum variation sampling.[76] The mode of procedure is almost Darwinesque: it is to sample as widely as possible within the specified sociocultural (ecological) context until exhaustion or redundancy is reached with respect to types of adaptation or response. We thus spent time with as many homeless as possible in the settings most relevant to their daily lives in Austin. In total, over six hundred waking hours were spent with 168 homeless men and women and with other individuals dealing with them in one capacity or another in the twenty-five street settings and organizations shown in Table 1.1.

Here it is important to emphasize that our interest in street life as it was experienced, whether from the differing standpoints of the homeless or of the agencies that dealt with them, meant that we were primarily interested in "perspectives in action" in contrast to "perspectives of action."[77] Perspectives in action are accounts or patterns of talk formulated for a particular end in a naturally occurring situation that is part of some ongoing system of action, such as when a homeless street person panhandles a passerby. Perspectives of action, by contrast, are constructed in response to the queries of researchers or other outsiders, as when a street person tells a researcher about panhandling. Perspectives of action are thus produced "not to act meaningfully in the system being described, but rather to make the system meaningful to an outsider."[78] Both perspectives yield useful information, but they are of different orders. Perspectives of action are ex post facto accounts that place the action in question within a larger normative framework; perspectives in action contain the cognitions and feelings that are inseparable from the sequences of action themselves. The more interested researchers are in lived experience and the management of everyday routines, the more critical to their project is the elicitation of perspectives in action.

We attempted to elicit such perspectives primarily by two means: interviewing by comment, and listening unobtrusively to conversations among the homeless that arose naturally rather than in response to the researcher's intervention.[79] This listening took two basic forms: eavesdropping, which involved listening to others in a bounded interactional encounter without being part of that encounter, as could be done when waiting in meal lines or in day-labor offices; and a kind of nondirective, conversational listening that occurred when we were engaged in encounters with one or more homeless individuals. The elicitation of perspectives in action through these means enabled us, we believe, to gain

TABLE 1.1   FOCAL SETTINGS

1 +	*ABC Plasma Center*
2 +	*Angels House* (Austin's only soup kitchen)
3	*Austin Police Department*
4	*Brackenridge Hospital* (city hospital)
5	*Bunkhaus* (a men's dormitory)
6 +	*Caritas* (private, nonprofit welfare agency)
7	*Central Assembly of God Church*
8	City Planning and Zoning Commission meetings
9 +	"The Drag" (street constituting western border of University of Texas campus)
10 +	Labor Corner
11 +	*Labor Pool*
12	*Legal Aid Society*
13 +	The Lounge (demolished in spring of 1985)
14	*Mental Health and Mental Retardation* (MHMR; state and local agencies)
15	*Oak Springs De-Tox Center*
16	*Salvation Army Alcohol Center*
17 +	*Salvation Army Shelter* (Sally)
18	*Stratford House* (private alcoholism center)
19	Task Force on the Homeless (City of Austin)
20	Texaco Truck Stop
21 +	*Texas Employment Commission*
22 +	Town Lake Parks and Bridges
23 +	Whataburger (on the Drag)
24	Winter Shelter
25	*Wright Road Farm* (for recovering alcoholics)

+ Plus signs indicate major stopping and/or hanging-out points that comprise the daily round of the homeless in Austin. Italics indicate agencies whose personnel were interviewed regarding the homeless and agency services.

a reasonable approximation of a multiperspectival understanding of street life as it was actually lived by the homeless.

TRIANGULATED RESEARCH

The third feature of our research is that it was heavily triangulated. Triangulation has traditionally been associated with the use of multiple methods in the study of the same phenomenon,[80] but it can also occur with respect to data, investigators, and theories.[81] Broadly conceived, triangulation entails the use of multiple data sources, methods, investigators, and theoretical perspectives in the study of some empirical phenomenon.

The logic underlying triangulation is rooted in the complexity of social reality and the limitations of every research methodology. The basic argument is that social reality is too multifaceted to be grasped adequately by any single method. Consequently, rather than debate the merits of one more or less flawed method vis-à-vis another, it is better to combine multiple strategies so that they make up for one another's weaknesses.[82]

With that philosophy, we pursued two basic research strategies. One entailed extensive ethnographic research among the homeless and the settings in which they found themselves; the other was to track a sample of homeless through a set of core institutions.

Ethnographic Strategy   We have discussed our interviewing and conversational procedures, but we have said little about how we positioned ourselves in relation to the homeless. The position or role the field researcher claims or is assigned, it has been argued, "is perhaps the single most important determinant of what he [*sic*] will be able to learn," for it "largely determines where he can go, what he can do, whom he can interact with, what he can inquire about, what he can see, and what he can be told."[83]

With that in mind, we positioned ourselves in relation to the homeless in the role of a "buddy-researcher." Although not discussed explicitly by other researchers, it is a role that has been used in a number of studies of street-corner men, hoboes, and tramps.[84] In this role, one of us hung out with the homeless on a regular basis, making the daily institutional rounds with them as individuals and in small groups. As a friend, the buddy-researcher provided his companions with minor necessities on occasion, such as small loans that were not expected to be repaid, clothes, rides in an old Toyota, and a sympathetic ear for their hopes, troubles, and fears. The buddy role entailed receiving as well as giving. The homeless shared some of their resources with the researcher, who as a friend was expected to accept such offers.[85]

In keeping with the buddy role, the researcher tried to avoid distinctive dress by wearing old clothes similar to those worn by most homeless, although his were generally cleaner. He also avoided the use of academic English.[86] It should be emphasized, however, that the researcher did not attempt to pass as a homeless individual. He frequently brought up his researcher status by mentioning his research and university affiliation and by asking questions homeless people were less likely to ask (e.g., personal questions about an individual's past). The research role gave a credible reason for inquiring into such personal matters, while the buddy role generated enough trust and goodwill that the homeless responded.[87]

The researcher, by virtue of his status as a friend of homeless individuals, could participate in most activities with them. However, although many of his experiences on the streets could approximate those of the homeless, they could never be quite the same, since the option to leave the streets was always available. On the day following a murder at the Salvation Army shelter, for example, the buddy-researcher could participate in the discussion of the event with a group of homeless men while waiting in the dinner line, but he had not had to experience the trauma of the event. Later that evening, when one small group of these men huddled nervously together for protection in the Sally shelter while others, who were afraid to stay at the shelter after the murder, went out on the streets in search of less dangerous sleeping places, the researcher returned to his home for the night. And when the buddy-researcher was arrested with two homeless men one evening, he experienced the arrest and jailing but was bailed out later the same night, whereas the two homeless men did not have that option.[88] In sum, although the researcher's role granted him access to a variety of street situations and experiences, the fact that he did not fully disengage himself from his other roles allowed for the ever-present prospect of escape from the streets, thus diluting the direct experience of homelessness.

Rather than using his personal experiences on the streets as the primary data base, then, the buddy-researcher collected data from the homeless themselves. Their behavior and conversations were recorded in a stepwise fashion, beginning with mental and jotted notes in the field and culminating in a detailed field narrative based on elaboration of these notes. These narrative elaborations constitute the ethnographic data log on which much of the book is based.

The data derived from our field observations and encounters were supplemented by taped, in-depth, life-history interviews with six homeless individuals who had been on the streets for lengths of time ranging from two months to fourteen years. Each of these individuals was a key informant, with whom we had numerous contacts.

Although it might be argued that much of the behavior and talk secured during field encounters represented a reaction to the researcher's
presence rather than a naturally occurring phenomenon among the
homeless, our field experiences suggest that this was not the case. Most
of the homeless were apprised of our researcher status, but they typically lost sight of it as we continued to spend time on the streets with
them. This forgetfulness was forcefully illustrated one night when one
of us gave an ill, homeless woman a ride to a health clinic. On the way
back from the clinic to the abandoned warehouse where she was going
to spend the night, she asked, "Are you sleeping in your car these days
or down at the Sally?" The researcher had explained his situation to
this woman many times during the previous two and a half months, but
she had forgotten or had not fully believed what he had told her. This
should not be surprising, however, in light of the dramaturgical thesis
that individuals tend to respond to and identify others more in terms of
their proximate roles or actions than in terms of their claims to the
contrary.

Tracking Strategy   In addition to studying the homeless ethnographically, we tracked a random sample of 767 homeless through a network
of core institutions with which they had varying degrees of contact.
This data source provided a detailed portrait of the demographics and
disabilities of the homeless in Austin, and it also enabled us to learn
more about the institutional contacts and experiences of the homeless
and to cross-validate information on each case by comparing independent institutional records.[89] Implementation of this tracking strategy
was contingent on the resolution of four problems: constructing a reasonable sampling frame; securing identifying information on each case;
selecting the core institutions; and negotiating access to their institutional records.

The first problem was resolved by using as our sampling frame all
homeless adults who had one or more contacts with the local Salvation
Army between January 1, 1984, and March 1, 1985. This yielded an
unduplicated count of 13,881 homeless persons. The decision to use
this population as our sampling frame was based on the assumption
that the total number of homeless who had contact with the Salvation
Army at any given time during this fourteen-month period comprised a
reasonable approximation of the number of homeless who had been in
Austin for one or more days during that same time period. Several con-

siderations justified this assumption. Foremost was the fact that the Salvation Army operated Austin's only public shelter for the homeless and was the only facility in Austin that provided free showers, breakfast, and dinner.[90] Consequently, we assumed that nearly all homeless men and women in Austin would have had occasion to utilize the Salvation Army at least once.

Our ethnographic research revealed that this assumption was essentially correct. Only two subgroups of homeless were underrepresented: women, and a scant number of street men whose daily routines did not encompass the Salvation Army. Women were underrepresented for two reasons. First, the majority who used the Salvation Army had children and utilized its family services. As a consequence, their records were kept in a separate family file. We chose not to sample from this file because the difficulty of disentangling individual from family data seemed excessive for what comprised less than 9 percent of the individuals who had contact with the Salvation Army in 1984. The other reason for the low proportion of women in the sample is that the majority of childless women had developed means of survival independent of the Salvation Army. The younger ones in particular attached themselves to men with some income or resources that allowed them to stay away from the Salvation Army, a point we will return to later. The other subgroup underrepresented in the sampling frame was the relatively small number of homeless men whose daily routines seldom brought them into contact with the Salvation Army. Since these subgroups, taken together, comprised a comparatively small proportion of the homeless in Austin, and since they were represented in our field sample, we felt justified in using as the sampling frame the 13,881 homeless who had registered at the Salvation Army during the period of our sample.

The problem of securing identifying information to track cases through the other selected institutions was resolved by the Salvation Army's practice of requiring all first-time users to fill out a registration card that asks for name and Social Security number, if any, as well as some demographic and background information. Upon receiving permission from Salvation Army officials to use this identifying information for tracking purposes, we randomly drew 800 cards and then negotiated access to the records of six other local and state agencies. These included Austin's major city hospital, Caritas, the city police department, the Texas Employment Commission, the state department of mental health and mental retardation (MHMR), and the local community mental

TABLE 1.2   NUMBER OF HOMELESS IN
TRACKING SAMPLE, BY AGENCY

Agency	Number of Cases	Percentage of Sample
Salvation Army	767[a]	100.0
Texas Employment Commission	348	45.4
Caritas	294	38.3
City police department	248	32.3
City hospital	181	23.6
Texas MHMR[b]	84	11.0
Austin/Travis County MHMR[b]	78	10.2

[a]Number of usable cases from a sample of 800 drawn randomly from a population of 13,881 individuals who registered at least once at the Salvation Army between January 1, 1984, and March 1, 1985.
[b]MHMR = Mental Health and Mental Retardation.

health center. These agencies were selected because of their centrality in the lives of the homeless living in or passing through Austin and because each had amassed data relevant to much that has been hypothesized about today's homeless. We searched each agency's files for some record of contact with our sample cases. When a match was made, all data on that case were coded onto a surveylike instrument that had been constructed on the basis of prior inspection of the record forms of the agencies. Once these data were computerized and cleaned, we were left with a usable tracking sample of 767 cases. Table 1.2 shows the percentage of the total sample matched at each agency.

In sum, our data were derived from three sources: (1) ethnographic encounters with 168 homeless individuals on the streets of Austin over a two-year period; (2) records of seven local and state agencies through which we tracked 767 homeless; and (3) the community itself—that is, the agencies, governmental units, commercial establishments, and ecological niches associated with the lives of the homeless. These data sources were tapped by a mixture of procedures: participant observation and informal interviews in the case of the homeless; participant and nonparticipant observation, coupled with formal and informal interviewing, in street agencies and settings; and a systematic survey of institutional records. In order to tap the various data sources by these means, the traditional "lone ranger" approach characteristic of most urban ethnography, was inappropriate.[91] Instead, a team of researchers was developed, consisting of four individuals with different but complementary and overlapping tasks. Two members of the team were responsible for the tracking data, another assumed the role of primary ethnographer among the homeless, and the fourth functioned in a number of capacities—coordinating the research, negotiating access to agency records and interviewing agency personnel, and functioning occasionally as a street ethnographer as well as a detached observer or sideline coach in relation to the primary street ethnographer.

Regarding the relationship between the roles of the buddy-researcher and the detached observer, it is important to note that rarely was a day, an evening, or a series of days in the field not followed by a debriefing session that involved discussion of field experiences with their methodological and theoretical implications, and development of plans for subsequent outings. Conscious and reflective enactment of these two roles enabled us simultaneously to maintain involvement and detachment, thereby facilitating management of the insider/outsider dialectic characteristic of much ethnographic research.[92]

CAPTURING SOCIAL PROCESSES AND CHANGE

A fourth major research concern was to capture processes of psychological adjustment, interpersonal relations, and material adaptation as they unfolded over time. To capture such changes requires that the researcher have extended access to the same settings and that the principal actors, both individuals and organizations, be observed at different points in time.

We were able to pursue this objective. Since ethnographic fieldwork involves prolonged and persistent observation within a bounded sociohistorical context, it is ideally suited for sustained contact with the same individuals across time and for grasping changes in behavior and orientation among those individuals. We had repeated contacts with many homeless individuals in a range of settings, in some cases extending for nearly two years. All totaled, we had 492 ethnographic encounters with our field sample of 168 homeless adults, averaging three encounters per person, with a high of twenty-five.

The tracking strategy, which was longitudinal in design, also enabled us to trace the institutional contacts and careers of the homeless across time, in many cases over several years. All totaled, the 767 individuals in the tracking sample had 30,400 contacts with the seven core institutions, over a span of time ranging from one day to twelve years.

The longitudinal character of both the ethnographic and tracking strategies enabled us to observe, not only different patterns of adaptation with variation in length of time on the streets, but also the transition from one pattern to another and what events and experiences were affecting these changes.

OPEN-ENDED RESEARCH

The final concern underlying our research was that it not foreclose discovery of unanticipated findings and data sources.[93] Indeed, several of our eventual focal concerns were not fully anticipated initially. Upon entering the field, we coded our observations broadly, into twenty-five focal settings and thirty cultural domains.[94] In time, however, variation in the number of data entries contained in each respective category showed that some of the settings and domains were more central than others to the daily lives of the homeless.[95] Those files that bulged with data became the foci of our analysis. Thus, our discussions of work, social relationships, and meaning and identity do not rest so much on a priori concerns as on what we actually observed and heard as the research progressed.

In addition to the emergence of a number of focal concerns, the possibility of tracking the homeless institutionally surfaced only after we had been in the field for several months. Initially, we thought we would conduct only an ethnographic study. In time, however, the study broadened methodologically, as we became aware of the possibility of tracking the homeless and then took the steps necessary to compile the tracking sample.

THE ISSUE OF GENERALIZABILITY

In the preceding pages we have provided a rationale for the case study we conducted, we have placed that study in historical context, and we have described our underlying research concerns and how we dealt with them methodologically. Whatever the strengths of the resultant research, it is confronted by a vexing issue that haunts every case study. We refer to the issue of generalizability or typicality. To what extent is our portrayal of street life in Austin and the adaptive strategies and routines of the city's homeless representative of homelessness elsewhere, and to what extent is it peculiar to homelessness in Austin? If we cannot answer this question, then of what utility is the case study we conducted?

Satisfactory answers to questions of the first kind, which are prompted by the positivistic contention that the production of generalizable findings is social science's most basic activity, depend on the degree of comparability among the cases in question. The more similar the relevant community contexts and the more alike the populations being studied, the greater the generalizability from one case to another. Since nearly all of the research on the homeless across the country is based on cross-sectional surveys, with relatively little attention paid to the community contexts, it is difficult to assess the extent to which these contexts differ from one case to another. Austin certainly differed from other cities in having only one shelter for the street homeless and in enjoying a booming economy during a portion of the period during which the research was conducted. But, as we see in subsequent chapters, striking similarities also appear.

The issue of demographic comparability is easier to assess, since there is a wealth of demographic data on the homeless across cities. Table 1.3 compares the homeless in the tracking sample with the homeless in other samples compiled during the mid-1980s in a number of southern and western cities. In each case, the majority of the homeless are male, under forty years of age, and single or unattached. Considerable similarity also emerges in terms of education and military experience. However, ethnic composition seems to vary with city size and minority base: the larger the city and its minority base, the greater the proportion of minorities in its homeless population. All in all, though, the table shows that the homeless in the tracking sample are quite similar to the homeless elsewhere, or at least to the homeless in the South and the far West.

This apparent demographic comparability between the homeless in Austin and a number of other cities suggests that some of what we report may hold for the homeless more generally. But we do not want to overstate the case for generalization, especially statistical generalization.[96] After all, the virtue of ethnographically based case studies of the kind we have attempted to conduct resides in their dense contextualization, their concern with process and the fluidity of social life, and their attention to the voices and experiences of individuals in their daily lives. Adherence to these values can result in in-depth examination and possible debunking or refinement of existing folk and theoretic presumptions about the life-style, subculture, or people in question. While the findings of such case studies may not be fully generalizable in the

Selected Demographic Variables	Tracking Sample[a] (N: 767)	San Antonio[b] (N: 139)	El Paso[c] (N: 197)	Phoenix[d] (N: 195)	Los Angeles[e] (N: 269)	Portland[f] (N: 131)	Nashville[g] (N: 117)	Birmingham[h] (N: 150)
Gender:								
Male	90%	90%	97%	86%	78%	85%	85%	78%
Age:								
Mean	35	34	33[i]	37	37	38	35[i]	40
Under 40	73%	—	71%	61%	63%	60%	—	54%
Over 60	1%	—	3%	3%	6%	7%	7%	6%
Ethnicity/race:								
Anglo	75%	60%	—	64%	49%	77%	79%	69%
Black	12%	15%	—	9%	32%	6%	21%	31%
Hispanic	12%	25%	—	17%	10%	4%	—	—
Native American	1%	—	—	9%	6%	10%	—	—
Other	—	—	—	1%	3%	3%	—	—
Marital status:								
Married	8%	14%	3%	13%	6%	12%	14%	7%
Unattached (single, divorced)	92%	86%	97%	87%	94%	88%	86%	93%

Education:								
Completed high school	58%	—	49%	60%	64%	47%	30%	57%
Some postsecondary	18%	—	18%	34%	38%	24%	21%	—
Military veteran:								
Yes	49%	—	—	46%	36%	46%	42%	—
Current residential status:								
Local resident	9%	—	39%	7%	14%	23%	36%	51%
From within state	39%	26%	—	7%	5%	—	—	15%
From out-of-state	52%	74%	61%	86%	81%	77%	64%	35%

[a] Percentage male is based on the total population of men, women, and children registered at least once at the Salvation Army in 1984. The remaining figures are based on the tracking sample. These figures correspond closely with those of Baumann et al. (1985), based on their August, 1984, street survey of homeless in Austin. They also found a small proportion of women on the streets (only 7 percent), a mean age near 35, 74 percent Anglo, and 91 percent unattached.

[b] Based on a survey conducted in an emergency shelter over a three-week period in February and March, 1984. Residential data based on place of birth (San Antonio Urban Council, 1984).

[c] Based on a survey conducted in an emergency shelter during March and April, 1983 (El Paso Task Force on the Homeless, 1984).

[d] Based on a survey conducted in food lines, shelters, and urban camps in March, 1983. Residential data based on response to question concerning place of origin (Brown et al., 1983).

[e] Based on a survey conducted in shelters, in soup lines, on skid row, and in other areas from December, 1983, to May, 1984 (Robertson et al., 1985; Ropers, 1988).

[f] Based on a survey conducted in 1983 (Caulk, 1983).

[g] Based on survey and enumeration data gathered in 1986 and 1987 (Lee, 1989).

[h] Based on survey and enumeration data collected in February, 1987 (LaGory et al., 1989). The 31 percent under ethnicity/race was in the original called simply "nonwhite."

[i] Median.

conventional sense, they can identify presumptions and generalizations that do not fit the case and can thereby alter existing understandings.[97]

This leads to a second, and perhaps more important, function of the ethnographic case study: its up-close, naturalistic focus can put its readers in touch with the lives of others and thereby reduce the distance between "us" and "them."[98] The generation of such an understanding is much too valuable for social scientists to ignore, especially when considering marginal populations and subcultures, such as the homeless, that are frequent objects of stigmatization and dehumanization. We thus leave the issue of the generalizability of our findings to the reader to ponder, but we do hope that the subsequent chapters reduce the distance between the homeless, as we came to know them, and those who take hearth and home for granted. If an ethnographic case study can enlarge the span of sympathy and universe of discourse of its readers while simultaneously prompting reconsideration or extension of existing theoretic presumptions, then it must be judged a worthwhile endeavor. It is our hope that this one does a bit of both.

A NOTE ON TENSE, VOICE, AND LANGUAGE

Although it is customary for academic texts to be written in the past tense, this convention has not been followed strictly by ethnographers. Instead, much ethnographic writing is couched in the present tense, and for good reason. The present tense creates a greater sense of immediacy and realism, it captures more accurately the character of events as they were observed and experienced by the researcher, and it more accurately preserves the voices of the informants. Because of these considerations, it seemed to us that the present tense would often serve our interests better than the academic past tense. Accordingly, we have written much of the text in the present tense. However, we have not ignored recent criticisms of the tendency of the ethnographic present to freeze its subjects and their activities in time and space.[99] Our attention to this issue should become clear in a number of subsequent chapters, particularly the final one, and in the epilogue.

A related critique of traditional ethnography, as well as of more traditional research procedures, argues that researchers should try to examine their objects of research from as many perspectives as possible.[100] Others have made a similar call recently, suggesting that ethnographic research and writing should be "dialogic" and "polyphonic" and that the voices of the array of actors pertinent to a particular social world should be privileged over that of the researcher.[101]

What is being called for at least in part, it seems, is the kind of multiperspectival strategy that we pursued by triangulating our research in terms of informants, situations, and researchers. We have thus endeavored to be polyphonic in the sense of including the voices of a number of different sets of actors relevant to street life in Austin. But we have also explicitly and consistently sought to put into the foreground the voices of the homeless themselves, since it is their adaptive behaviors and experiences that are the central concerns of this book. Of course, not all of their voices are equally privileged. Some are featured more than others for reasons that will be elaborated in the next chapter, but those privileged voices are, we believe, representative of the cross-section of homeless we came to know.

We do not presume, however, that we have privileged their voices in an uncontaminated fashion. It is our book, not our homeless informants'. We are the choreographers or narrators, so to speak. We recognize that our discussion provides second-order interpretations of the homeless people's own interpretations of their experiences.[102] But we do believe that our descriptions and interpretations are reasonable approximations of what we were privy to, in that they are restrained both empirically and methodologically. We did not create the settings, the characters, the behaviors, or the life histories and experiences that constitute the empirical basis for the book; we tried to let the voices of the homeless speak loudly and clearly throughout; we refrained from editing their talk or excising their often colorful and profane language; we characterized them as individuals we and others knew, that is, some as sweet and gentle, others as cussed and rough; and we attempted to keep in the forefront of our consciousness the often dehumanizing consequences of the social scientist's antiseptic gaze. These empirical and procedural restraints notwithstanding, most of what we observed and heard was filtered through the sociological eyeglasses we brought to the field. This is neither new nor particularly damning, for it could hardly be any other way. Ethnography is and always has been an interpretive enterprise involving the mediation of frames of meaning between the world of those studied and that of some imagined audience.[103] We can only hope, then, that the subsequent chapters prove to be effective mediations in the sense that they are not overladen with distortions and that they form a meaningful bridge between the world of the homeless and that of our readers.

CHAPTER TWO

A Grounded Typology
of Homeless Street People

In the preceding chapter we delineated several varieties of homelessness and indicated that in this book we are concerned primarily with the lives and routines of "homeless street people," the most destitute and degraded of all of the homeless. Situated at the bottom of America's class structure, they are in many respects the contemporary equivalent of the floating population of Europe's preindustrial cities and the lumpenproletariat of its nineteenth-century industrializing cities. But to describe homeless street people in such broad terms deflects attention from their daily lives and obscures significant variation among them. If there is one point of agreement about the homeless, it is that they do not constitute a homogeneous population. But the question remains unanswered, exactly how, other than demographically, do they differ, and to what extent? Our aim in this chapter is to address that question by constructing a typology of homeless street people that is grounded in their own world and that captures the similarities and differences among them as they go about the business of trying to survive physically, socially, and psychologically. We begin with an overview of the process of typologizing and the considerations influencing how we proceeded.

AN EXCURSION ON TYPOLOGIZING

The process by which members of some empirical domain are categorized and ordered in terms of their similarities and differences is called typologizing. The resulting classificatory scheme directs the observer's attention to certain aspects of the phenomenon under study. A typology thus functions as a conceptual tool.[1]

In ethnographic fieldwork, typological construction begins with a taxonomic analysis and then proceeds to what is called componential analysis. Taxonomic analysis identifies the members of a category of meaningful phenomena within a particular sociocultural context. It begins with a category of meaning or cultural domain, such as social relationships, and then enumerates the members of that category according to a particular question of interest, such as "What kinds of social relationships are there?" Thus, a preliminary taxonomy of social relationships might include stranger relationships, acquaintanceships, friendships, blood relationships, and conjugal relationships.

Taxonomic analysis increases understanding of the empirical world by grouping elements in terms of one or more similarities. However, a more fine-tuned understanding can be achieved by considering how those grouped elements differ among themselves. Componential analysis, as this search for differences among members of a particular taxonomic category is called, constitutes the second major step in typological construction.[2] In a taxonomy of social relationships, for example, a componential analysis would consider how each relationship varies in terms of dimensions such as initiation, duration, intensity, and termination.

Although typologizing in this manner is one of the basic analytic steps in social scientific investigation, it is by no means peculiar to social science. As a basic cognitive process that makes the world more manageable by reducing and ordering its complexity, it is often the first step taken by people in general to deal with some problematic feature of their environment. The kinds of typologies produced by social scientists will invariably differ in certain respects, however, from those of the individuals whose behaviors are the object of inquiry, since the purpose of the two sets of actors are somewhat different. Folk or lay typologies are constructed by participants within a particular social system in order to render action within that system more intelligible and orderly. Social-science typologies, by contrast, are typically constructed, not for action within the system under study, but to facilitate an understanding of those systems, or aspects of them, in accordance with certain basic social-science concepts and principles. These "constructed" or "second-order" typologies are not all of one stripe, however. Some constitute reasonable approximations of folk typologies; others are more distant and abstract. The difference is nicely captured by William James's distinction between two kinds of knowledge embodied in the word "understanding."[3] One is represented by the phrase "acquaintance with," the other by "knowledge about." To be acquainted with a set of actors, the behaviors they engage in, and the context in which both are embedded presumes a direct, intimate familiarity with each; to have knowledge about them denotes a more abstract, distant, and secondhand kind of understanding that may exhibit little awareness of direct experience. Constructed typologies that fall toward the "acquaintance with" end of the continuum can be thought of as "folk-elicited," those at the other end as "abstracted," and those in between as "mixed."

The typology we elaborate is of the mixed variety. This is largely because we were unable to elicit a set of typological distinctions that functioned for the homeless as a lingua franca. Our encounters with them elicited a range of typifications—"tramps" and "bums," "transients," "the crazies," those "who take what they can get," those "who fuck with you," those "who don't give a shit," and those "running from a bad marriage"—but we never acquired a sense that a shared folk typology had emerged among the homeless on the streets of Austin. This is not surprising, considering that these homeless comprised at first glance a highly heterogeneous aggregation. Perhaps that is why the only characterization that seemed generically appealing portrayed the homeless in Austin as people who were, beyond all else, "down on their luck." Most of the other characterizations seemed to cluster according to the various types we will identify later in the chapter and seemed to function primarily as statements of identity clarification and assertion. Thus, although the homeless we encountered did not provide us with a widely shared folk typology, they did alert us to several possible dimensions of contrast and to a number of subtypes. We will return to these considerations shortly.

A CONTEXTUALLY GROUNDED TYPOLOGY
OF HOMELESS STREET PEOPLE

Two core principles undergird our mixed typology. The first asserts that behavior cannot be properly understood apart from the social context in which it occurs. This suggests that the behaviors of the homeless should be viewed first and foremost as adaptations to environmental exigencies. The second principle is that behavioral patterns can best be understood diachronically or processually, that is, as they evolve over time. At the aggregate level, this indicates that the relationship between time on the streets and behavioral patterns should be assessed. At the individual level, it calls for consideration of street careers. We attend to these two principles by conceptualizing in subcultural terms the context in which the homeless find themselves.

Broadly defined, a subculture connotes a fairly distinctive mélange of behaviors, artifacts, and cognitive elements that together characterize the way of life of a set of individuals and distinguish them from other groups or aggregations within the larger society. Subcultures tend to congeal among a set of individuals who share one or more common traits or dilemmas, have corresponding interests, and are likely to be associated with one another.[4]

Since the seeds from which subcultures germinate are structurally embedded, the behavioral (what people do), artifactual (what they make or use to do it with), and cognitive (the meanings people give to things) elements that coalesce to give a subculture its distinctiveness can be construed in part as adaptations to structural exigencies and opportunities. Thus, subcultures are not sui generis phenomena but originate in processes of accommodation and resistance to social forces and changes in the lives of collectivities of individuals.[5] The nature of the relationship between the subculture and the larger society can be quite variable, however. In some cases individuals who share ethnic, national, or religious values may resist structural incorporation because they feel those values to be threatened by cultural assimilation. In such cases, salient values and the rituals that celebrate them give a subculture its distinctive character.

But shared values do not constitute the cornerstone of every subculture. If values are construed as life-style preferences thought to be worthy of protection and promotion, then clearly there are subcultures that do not rest on this ideational bedrock, at least not initially. All too often, individuals find themselves thrown together in a common fate or dilemma not of their own choosing. Under such circumstances a way of life may develop that is indeed distinctive, but that does not inspire celebration and promotion. To the contrary, many of those who are forced to endure it may abhor the life they are leading. What these similarly situated individuals have in common is not a strong and recognizable set of values, but a shared fate and the determination to make do as well as they can. This common predicament and associated survival problems may give rise to an identifiably unique set of behaviors, daily routines, and cognitive orientations and may thus be construed as a subculture, albeit a limited or incomplete one.[6]

Our observations indicate that the social world of the homeless constitutes such a limited subculture. It is a social world that is not of the making or choosing of the vast majority of the homeless, at least not initially, but into which most have been pushed by circumstances beyond their control. Nor is it a social world that is based either on a set of shared values or on a set of activities that typically inspire joint celebration and promotion. It is, however, a social world in which its inhabitants share a unique fate: that of having to survive in the streets and alleys of America's cities and along the highways and railways that connect them.

Like people everywhere, the homeless must eat, sleep, eliminate, make ends meet, and carve out a sense of meaning and self-respect. The homeless, however, must attend to these survival requisites without the resources and social-support structures that most of us take for granted. Because they are at the bottom of the status system, the homeless also lack the role-based sources of dignity and self-respect that typically accrue to those higher up in the social hierarchy. Additionally, life on the streets is often permeated with an omnipresent sense of uncertainty. There are no guarantees that what facilitated survival today will work tomorrow. Consequently, the homeless must frequently scramble anew each day in order to stay afloat. It is these stark and obdurate realities that give the world of homeless street people its distinctive character and that make their world so alien to most Americans. The manner in which the homeless attend to the shared fate of life on the streets is not uniform, however. Just as there is variation in the patterns of adaptation associated with most subcultures, so there is variation among the homeless, and these differences constitute the basis for the following typological distinctions.

Table 2.1 lists eight life-style, cognitive, and temporal variables that are key to understanding adaptation to life on the streets and that can serve as dimensions of contrast. Each of the first seven dimensions constitutes either a life-style or a cognitive component of subculture. The life-style component represents the behavioral repertoire of the street subculture of the homeless. The first four dimensions in Table 2.1 are of that order.

The *work/livelihood* dimension encompasses all activities engaged in by the homeless to get money and other items that can be exchanged for goods and services that facilitate physiological and psychological survival on the streets. Most of the homeless regularly pursue a limited range of such strategies rather than the entire gamut. In effect, they

TABLE 2.1   SUBCULTURAL DIMENSIONS
OF CONTRAST

I. Life-style dimensions
  1. Work/livelihood
    1.1 Wage/day labor
    1.2 Selling goods and services
    1.3 Selling plasma
    1.4 Begging and panhandling
    1.5 Scavenging
    1.6 Theft
    1.7 Income supplements (e.g., transfer payments)
  2. Range/mobility
    2.1 Interstate
    2.2 Intrastate/intercity
    2.3 Intracity
  3. Sleeping arrangements
    3.1 Shelter
      3.1.1 Paid shelter (e.g., flop house)
      3.1.2 Free shelter (e.g., Salvation Army)
    3.2 Nonshelter
      3.2.1 Sleeping rough (e.g., sidewalk)
      3.2.2 Personal/private (e.g., old car)
  4. Substance use
    4.1 Alcohol use
    4.2 Drug use

II. Cognitive dimensions
  5. Identity talk
    5.1 Distancing
      5.1.1 Categoric distancing
      5.1.2 Specific (within category) distancing
      5.1.3 Institutional distancing
    5.2 Embracement
      5.2.1 Categoric embracement
      5.2.2 Specific (within category) embracement
    5.3 Fictive storytelling
      5.3.1 Embellishment
      5.3.2 Fantasizing
  6. Daily routines taken for granted
  7. Talk/plans about getting off the street

III. Temporal dimension
  8. Time on the streets
    8.1 Less than 6 months
    8.2 6 months to 1 year
    8.3 1 year to 2 years
    8.4 2 years to 4 years
    8.5 More than 4 years

become specialists in a few survival activities. Of course, if one cannot engage in his or her preferred specialty on a given day, other possible options may be pursued, but frequently in a hierarchical fashion. We can, then, speak of survival repertoires. These survival specialties and repertoires are understandably the focus of considerable attention during the waking day and together function as a useful criterion for distinguishing among the homeless.

The second life-style dimension of contrast is the *range* or *mobility* of the homeless. Do they travel from one state or city to another in search of work or a more congenial climate? Or are they locals who tend to stay put? At least since the time of Nels Anderson's research on the homeless of the 1920s and 1930s, extent of mobility has been found to be a useful wedge for distinguishing among homeless men.[7]

The next life-style dimension that reflects differences in the adaptive patterns of the homeless is their customary *sleeping arrangements*. In most urban areas, sleeping options range from various kinds of shelters, to "sleeping rough" on sidewalks and park benches or in alcoves and weed patches, to more private arrangements, such as abandoned cars and buildings and personal campsites under bridges. Whether a person's customary sleeping arrangement is the preferred one depends on the options available. But we found that, given a range of options, preferences will be exercised that further distinguish among the homeless.

The fourth life-style dimension is *substance use,* which encompasses both alcohol and drugs. Alcohol has long been regarded as one of the central defining features of the subculture of homeless men, and particularly of those congregating in the skid rows of American and British cities.[8] Indeed, the prevailing public conception of the homeless man, at least since the itinerant train-riding workers of the late 1800s and early 1900s disappeared from the American scene, has been of a disheveled man nursing a bottle of cheap wine. This image still has considerable currency. Yet, just as studies of the skid-row homeless of the 1950s and 1960s found variability in alcohol use, so research on the homeless of the 1980s has found similar variation.[9] We, too, discerned differences in the drinking behavior of the homeless we studied. Some individuals were chronic drinkers; others rarely, if ever, drank. Similar variability was found concerning the use of drugs.

The next three dimensions are aspects of the cognitive component of subculture, that is, they pertain to matters of orientation and meaning. Since most sets of activities can be pursued without internal commitment to them, caution must be exercised to keep from inferring subjective attachment from behavioral involvement.[10] Action and cognition may be aligned, of course, but one does not necessarily imply the other. The behavior of some individuals can be anchored in the life-style of street subculture, but with their cognitive orientation regarding self and future rooted elsewhere. Conversely, some identify with and express internal commitment to life on the streets. The three cognitive dimensions in Table 2.1 not only cover these possibilities but do indeed reflect cognitive variability among the homeless.

The *identity talk* dimension covers the meanings attributed to self by the actor during the course of interaction with others. Identity talk is indicated by self-designations and self-attributions that speak to the actor's actual or desired conception of self in relation to others and the situational context. Such talk tells us something about the social worlds and individuals with whom the actor identifies.

The *taken-for-grantedness* dimension focuses on the extent to which life on the streets is regarded as problematic rather than routine and customary. Presumably, the more life on the streets is taken for granted, the more habituated the person is to its routines and vicissitudes and the less likely he or she is to seek sanctuary and to think about disengagement.

The last cognitive dimension is *talk or plans about getting off the street*. The use of this dimension as a criterion for differentiating among the homeless is grounded not only in the existence of such talk but also in the variability of its occurrence. Some of the homeless talked almost incessantly about getting off the streets; others mentioned it only occasionally; and some, seemingly resigned to life on the streets, never mentioned it at all.

The eighth and final dimension of contrast is *time on the streets*. Its inclusion is consistent with the previously mentioned processual principle, which holds that, all else being equal, behavioral patterns and cognitive orientation ought to vary with the length of exposure to any particular set of objects or circumstances. Accordingly, we would expect the adaptive patterns and orientations of the homeless to differ enough with the amount of time they have been on the streets that it should be possible so to identify discrete types of homeless street people.

Using these eight dimensions of contrast as the basis for categorizing the 168 homeless street people whom we encountered, we discerned the types listed across the top of Table 2.2. We conceive of three of them—the recently dislocated, straddlers, and outsiders—as generic types, with

TABLE 2.2   MEAN SCORES FOR LIFE-STYLE AND
TEMPORAL DIMENSIONS, BY TYPE OF HOMELESS*

	Recently Dislocated	Straddlers	
		Regular	Adapted
	(N: 31)	(N: 56)	(N: 5)
Work/livelihood:			
Wage/day labor	1.52	1.02	2.00
Selling goods and services	.26	.71	.20
Selling plasma	.19	.68	.20
Begging and panhandling	.16	.18	0
Scavenging	.06	.11	0
Income supplements	.23	.27	.20
Range/mobility:			
Interstate	.67	.79	.40
Intercity	.71	1.02	.40
Intracity	.58	.96	.40
Sleeping arrangements:			
Paid shelter	.19	.23	1.00
Free shelter	1.10	1.07	1.00
Sleeping rough	.23	.32	0
Personal/private	.39	.61	0
Substance use:			
Alcohol use	.23	.59	.40
Drug use	.19	.48	.20
Time on the streets:			
Mean time	4.3 mos.	1.2 yr.	2.4 yr.

* Portions of this table will be elaborated in subsequent chapters.

	Outsiders				
Tramps		*Bums*			
Traditional (N: 9)	Hippie (N: 15)	Traditional (N: 30)	Redneck (N: 5)	*Mentally Ill* (N: 17)	
.89	.13	.27	.20	.29
.22	1.10	.43	.80	.29
.11	.87	.13	1.00	0
.77	.93	.73	.60	.41
.22	.20	.83	.20	.65
.33	.13	.40	.20	.71
1.67	1.07	.20	.20	.29
1.78	.97	.17	.20	.35
1.11	.53	.20	1.20	.53
.20	0	.03	0	.06
.67	.13	.67	0	.71
1.11	1.47	.70	0	.65
.22	.33	.83	2.00	.41
.89	1.33	1.67	2.00	.29
.11	1.67	.30	1.20	.29
6.1 yr.	3.2 yr.	4.4 yr.	2 yr.	1.3 yr.

the latter two encompassing seven subtypes. Table 2.2 profiles and compares these types in terms of the life-style and temporal dimensions by indicating the mean score for each dimensional attribute for each type. Mean scores were derived by summing numerical values assigned to each attribute for each type and dividing by the total number for each type. Each of the 168 individuals in the field sample was assigned a numerical value of 0 to 2 depending on the relative frequency with which it was determined that he or she engaged in each of the dimensional activities. The determination of relative frequency was made on the basis of observed behaviors and conversational encounters. If we acquired, on the basis of these two data sources, a sense that an individual was an extensive user of day labor, for example, then he or she was assigned a value of 2. If day-labor use was a less frequent but still salient feature of an individual's street life-style, then a value of 1 was assigned. And if the individual rarely used day labor, as far as we could determine, then a value of 0 was assigned. A mean score of 1.67, for example, suggests rather extensive engagement in the activity in question, whereas a score of .20 indicates relatively little engagement. Inspection of the table indicates that although there are similarities among some of the types for specific dimensional attributes, there is also considerable variation. Additionally, each type is different in terms of its overall dimensional profile. The eighth type, which comprises the mentally ill as a variant of the outsider genre, also differs in terms of certain cognitive and behavioral characteristics that are peculiar to the mentally ill, thus making them a strikingly distinct category.

With these classificatory criteria and analytic considerations in place, and with Table 2.2 as a point of reference, we are in a position to elaborate the types and to introduce twenty homeless individuals who were among our key informants and who will serve as exemplars of each type.[11]

THE RECENTLY DISLOCATED

Whatever the causes of homelessness, the adaptive behaviors and cognitive orientation of those individuals who find themselves on the streets for the first time show marked similarities that distinguish them from the homeless who, with the exception of some of the mentally ill, have typically been on the streets longer. When individuals first hit the streets they are understandably frightened by the stark and strange new world they have entered. They are afraid of the unkempt company in which they find themselves. They do not know who, if anyone, to trust. And they do not know how, if at all, they will survive. In many respects, they find themselves in an anomic state wherein conventional road markers have disintegrated. Consequently, the recently dislocated tend to gravitate toward local caretaker agencies, particularly those, such as the Salvation Army, that provide food and shelter.

The uncertain and alien world that initially confronts the recently dislocated tends to induce them to think about their past experiences and identities, sometimes with favorable embellishments. The juxtaposition of these two tendencies often gives rise to a strong desire to return to the world from whence they came. Not only is the talk of the recently dislocated peppered with plans for getting off the streets, but their behaviors are directed fairly consistently toward doing so; for example, they are among the most frequent seekers of both conventional employment and day labor. Additionally, they disavow the social identity of a street person and are quick to stress to others that they are not like most of the homeless in whose company they are found. The recently dislocated thus find themselves in the perplexing and stressful situation of being cognitively oriented to the larger sociocultural context but physically mired in life on the streets.

Roughly 19 percent of our field sample fell into this category. As is indicated in Table 2.3, which compares the types in terms of gender, age, ethnicity, length of time on the streets, and the mean number of contacts we had with each type, the recently dislocated are demographically similar to the remainder of the field sample, except that they tend to be somewhat younger and have been on the streets for a much shorter period of time. Tom Fisk, Tony Jones, and Sonny McCallister are examples of this type.

Tom Fisk   Tom is a twenty-five-year-old white man who was born in Vancouver, Washington.[12] His parents separated when he was eight years old, and he and his five sisters and brothers were raised in a series of foster homes. Tom dropped out of high school in the eleventh grade to join the army. He was discharged from Fort Hood, Texas, and moved into nearby Killeen to stay with friends he had made during his time in the service. For the next eighteen months he remained in Killeen, working sporadically for roofing contractors. During that time he was arrested and convicted of stealing a motorcycle.

In the summer of 1984 Tom came to Austin to take a roofing job he had been offered by a contractor, but the job fell through just a

TABLE 2.3 COMPARISON OF TYPES OF HOMELESS IN TERMS OF SELECTED VARIABLES

| | Totals | Recently Dislocated | Straddlers | |
			Regular	Adapted
Distribution of sample:				
Number of each type	168	31	56	5
Percent of total		19%	33%	3%
Gender:				
Male	86%	81%	91%	100%
Ethnicity:				
Anglo	83%	94%	80%	100%
Age:				
Mean age	36	26	33	35
Under 26	20%	58%	20%	0%
26 to 35	45%	29%	48%	60%
36 to 45	15%	10%	20%	20%
46 to 55	9%	3%	9%	20%
56 to 65	11%	0%	4%	0%
Time on the streets:				
Less than 6 months	24%	77%	18%	20%
6 months to 1 year	14%	23%	21%	20%
1 year to 2 years	17%	0%	36%	0%
2 years to 4 years	28%	0%	25%	40%
More than 4 years	17%	0%	0%	20%
Number of contacts:				
Mean number	3.0	1.8	3.3	5.4

Outsiders				
Tramps		Bums		
Traditional	Hippie	Traditional	Redneck	Mentally Ill
9	15	30	5	17
5%	9	18%	3%	10%
100%	87%	83%	100%	71%
78%	93%	73%	100%	71%
52	31	47	31	32
0%	7%	0%	0%	18%
11%	93%	20%	100%	59%
22%	0%	23%	0%	12%
11%	0%	20%	0%	6%
56%	0%	37%	0%	6%
0%	0%	0%	0%	35%
0%	0%	0%	0%	18%
0%	20%	7%	40%	6%
22%	73%	33%	60%	29%
78%	7%	60%	0%	12%
2.8	2.5	3.5	2.4	2.9

few weeks after he started it. For the next several months he worked part-time for a fly-by-night contractor who seldom paid him for his work. Most nights, he slept on the roofs of apartment complexes they were repairing or in the old car his boss had given him as partial payment for his work.

It was during this period that we first met Tom. He was helping reroof the apartment complex in which one of us lived. Late one afternoon he came by chance to the researcher's apartment to ask for a drink of water. He spent the next hour drinking iced tea in the air-conditioned apartment, talking about how his fondness for the roofing trade was being dampened by his current employer's failure to pay him. As a consequence of not being paid, Tom was forced to go to the Salvation Army for meals. Later, when his car was impounded and he had to sell it or lose it, he began sleeping at the Salvation Army as well. Tom found all of this terribly frustrating, because he had developed considerable affection for a woman in Killeen and he deeply wanted to impress her. At the time of our initial encounter, Tom had been on the streets only about a month. A year later he sent us a letter from Ocala, Florida, where he was still living on the streets.

Tony Jones   Tony is a black man approximately thirty years old. He was born and raised in Chicago, where he continued to live with his wife and infant son until he lost his job as a security guard at a steel mill. At the time he was also having trouble getting along with his wife. He therefore decided to leave Chicago and go to Baton Rouge to stay with his sister and look for work. After he had been there only a few days, however, they got into an argument and he moved into the Baton Rouge Salvation Army. After two unsuccessful weeks of looking for a job, Tony decided to go to Houston, but the labor market there proved no better, so he moved to Austin. Almost immediately after reaching town he managed to land a job as an appliance repairman. Tony stayed at the local Salvation Army, though, since he did not at first have the money necessary to rent an apartment.

It was at the shelter that we first encountered Tony, waiting in a long line for the shower. Not only was Tony easily distinguished from most Salvation Army users by the neatness of his clothes and appearance, but he himself was quick to point out his differences from those around him. He boasted about his self-sufficiency, indicating that, unlike others on the streets, he knew "how to handle money" and was "saving to get an apartment in about a week." He made it clear that he wanted no part of life on the streets. Tony had been on the streets for only two to three weeks when we first met him. Having landed a steady job, he soon located a rooming house in which he rented a room. Two weeks later he was back at the Salvation Army, however, having moved out of the rooming house because of its disorderly and unsanitary condition. But within another week and a half he had moved off the street again, at which point we lost contact with him.

Sonny McCallister   Sonny is a nineteen-year-old white male who was born in Arkansas but grew up in the Carthage, Missouri, area, where he lived until he "decided to split" in the autumn of 1984. Things were chaotic there, and neither of his parents wanted him to stay with them. He said the trouble began several years ago when his mother, whom he described as "a real religious type" for whom "everything is a sin," decided to place him and his brother in a religious school his parents could not really afford. His father worked regularly in a lumber mill but did not make enough money to send Sonny and his brother to a private school. This conflict strained his parents' already unstable marriage, and they divorced when Sonny was sixteen.

For the next two and a half years Sonny bounced back and forth between his parents, not getting along with either and failing to make any progress in school. Sonny wanted out, but he had nowhere to go. His difficulties with his father reached crisis level when his father had him committed to a mental hospital for a month. When Sonny was arrested for shoplifting shortly after his release from the hospital and his father threatened to have him committed once again, Sonny decided it was time to leave. He hitchhiked to Tulsa, and after four days there he got a ride with a trucker all the way to Austin.

We first met Sonny about a week after his arrival. He was doing day labor as a roofer's helper, hot-tarring an apartment complex. His boss constantly derided him for his lack of strength, but he grimly worked on in the afternoon heat, despite his frail physique. Like Tom, who had befriended him, Sonny did not get paid. For the next six weeks Sonny and Tom hung out together on the streets, selling plasma regularly and sleeping in the back of Tom's car. As tension between them mounted, Sonny began to seek other situations. Ultimately, he developed a relationship with an older non-street male who took him into his home. When we last spoke to Sonny he had been living for about a week with his new friend, with whom we suspect he was sexually involved.

STRADDLERS

If a recently dislocated person's efforts to get off the streets continually meet with failure, he or she frequently changes in self-orientation and behavior. A person's fear of the homeless environment tends to diminish as it becomes familiar. The homeless person makes new acquaintances and becomes more adept at finding food, shelter, and companionship. At the same time, memories of the past begin to fade, being replaced in part with new experiences that are often strikingly incongruous with the past. Just as past and present become disconnected, so does the relationship of present to future lose continuity and clarity. There is a desire, on the one hand, to tie the future to the past by escaping from street life. On the other hand, planned ways of getting off the street tend to become increasingly unclear, and there is a tendency to slip into lassitude, letting the days flow by without taking any action. Frequently, at this stage talk and action are inconsistent. Plans of action are highly changeable, especially plans to seek work. Even the self-identity of the homeless person undergoes change. No longer does he or she so strongly distinguish self from others on the streets. Although the homeless person at this point does not positively identify with others on the streets, there is a recognition of a shared plight.

We have termed this type of homeless individual the "straddler," drawing on the anthropologist Victor Turner's notion of liminality.[13] According to Turner, "[T]he attributes of liminality or of liminal *personae* ('threshold people') are necessarily ambiguous, since this condition and these persons elude or slip through the network of classifications that normally locate states and positions in cultural space. Liminal entities are neither here nor there; they are betwixt and between the positions assigned and arrayed by law, custom, convention, and ceremonial."[14] The straddlers in our typology are those individuals who are in such a state of liminality or status ambiguity. They are at a critical turning point in their lives, with one foot in the domiciled world of their past, with which they still identify and feel some continuity, and one foot planted in street life. We identify two types of straddlers, the "regular straddlers" and those we term the "institutionally adapted."

REGULAR STRADDLERS

Regular straddlers are those homeless individuals who are in the situation of status ambiguity and passage just described. In time they will either find a way off the streets or drift into the outsider status wherein both life-style and cognitive orientation are anchored in the streets. As indicated in Table 2.3, 33 percent of the field sample fell into this category, with a mean age seven years older than the recently dislocated and a ten-month-longer period on the streets. Three of the homeless who fell into this category are Willie Hastings, Ron Whitaker, and Pat Manchester, each of whom we came to know quite well.

Willie Hastings   Willie is a thirty-six-year-old white man from Dallas. When he was six years old his parents divorced and he went to live with his father. His father married a woman who allegedly abused Willie. The abuse apparently had his father's endorsement. For example, when Willie was nine years old his father beat him so severely he was "unconscious for a month." After that he was sent to live in a Methodist group home for five years. "Those years," he told us, "were the best years of my life." At the age of fourteen he was sent to live with his mother, but he found the situation with her so unpleasant that he ran away and returned to his father. His father, he says, then introduced him to child prostitution. After he had engaged in sex for money with adult men for a while, he began to think of himself as gay. It was not until several years later, when he was in the navy, that he experienced heterosexual sex—with a young prostitute whom he soon married. He hit the streets after his wife died, and he had been on the streets for about two years in Dallas and Houston before he came to Austin.

Shortly after he arrived in Austin, we met him on a street near the university. He was walking to the north side of the city, where he hoped to get a half-day job as a taste-tester for a new brand of chewing tobacco. He offered us his services as a guide and informant, claiming to have a B.A. in sociology and to have operated a homeless shelter himself in the past. Willie was a very sociable and likable fellow, as well as an accomplished storyteller. He seemed to know as many people on the streets as anyone we met. He worked sporadically at various jobs in Austin for several months, then disappeared mysteriously, leaving behind many worried acquaintances and his few personal belongings.

Ron Whitaker   Ron is a twenty-two-year-old white man who was born in California. His parents died in a car accident when he was a senior in high school. When Ron graduated from high school he joined the army for two years. He returned to California after he was discharged, living in cheap hotels until his $600 in savings was depleted.

He had since been on the streets in cities throughout the western United States. In the fall of 1983 he was staying in a cheap hotel in Denver and working as a short-order cook for a fast-food restaurant, but when he lost his job he decided to head south. He had no particular destination in mind, but when he caught a ride with a man headed to Austin he decided it would be a good place to stay for a while and look for a job.

We first encountered Ron at the Salvation Army the day after he arrived. He initially talked incessantly about the local job opportunities, his desire to find permanent employment, and his fear that his tattered appearance and lack of a telephone would hurt his chances of landing a job. He did work sporadically, however, and sold plasma regularly. Occasionally he would maniacally work two jobs at a time in the hope of making enough money to get an apartment, but the stress would wear him out within a couple of weeks, and he would quit both jobs and hang out disconsolately at the Salvation Army and the plasma centers. Ron stayed in Austin for nearly four months and then, during one of his disconsolate periods, reportedly headed for either Orlando or San Diego.

Pat Manchester   Pat is a thirty-three-year-old white male from New Jersey who migrated to central Texas in 1981 in search of employment. He worked fairly consistently until August of 1984, when he lost his job as a construction laborer in a nearby community. He then moved to Austin and found himself on the streets, unable to secure a permanent job that paid enough for an apartment. As time dragged on, Pat's life increasingly came to be characterized by occasional day labor, selling plasma, and a growing dependency on the Salvation Army. During the five-and-a-half-month period between his initial contact with the Sally and when he left Austin in late January, 1985, Pat had eaten 222 meals at the Sally and had slept there 105 times.

We first met Pat in the Salvation Army dinner line one afternoon after he had been on the streets for about two months. He had sold plasma that morning and used the eight dollars he received for it to buy some beer and a paperback. Half-drunk by the time he arrived at the Sally, throughout the afternoon he sat on a laundry bag full of his possessions and read his western novel. He told us that he liked to get an early place in the dinner line so that he could get supper and still manage to get in the bed line in time to get a place for the night that was close to the television. Pat was coming to take life on the streets for granted, although periodically he found himself thinking about getting off the streets. Perhaps it was the resurfacing of such thoughts that prompted him to leave Austin in search of greener pastures, or perhaps it was the discordant image of himself he received from a local newspaper story on homelessness in which he was one of the featured street people. Whichever was the case, Pat disappeared a few days after the story appeared. That was nearly six months after he had first found himself on the streets of Austin.

INSTITUTIONALLY ADAPTED STRADDLERS

A second type of straddler involves the suspension of passage from one status to another. It is a transitional state, but one in which the status of those so situated is frozen temporarily between two social worlds and their corresponding life-styles. The most conspicuous examples come from such holding institutions as prisons and asylums, where individuals find themselves assigned to institutionally structured liminal statuses. We encountered a few such people on the streets. All were marginal workers for agencies serving the homeless. These individuals have found off-street niches, but ones that are structurally part of the subculture and social ecology of street life. The incumbents of such niches thus still have one foot on the streets. With jobs that fall somewhere between day labor and steady work, and with the guarantee of shelter and meals as part of their pay, their survival repertoires differ considerably from those of the rest of the homeless. But these straddlers do come directly from the streets, and they tend to evince the orientation of the regular straddlers, although on average they are a few years older and have been on the streets twice as long. Our exemplars of this type, which constituted only a small percentage of the field sample, are Hoyt Page and Tanner Sutton.

Hoyt Page   Hoyt is a thirty-seven-year-old white male from Dallas who has been on the road for most of his life. Orphaned as a child, he was moved from one living arrangement to another, residing first with his grandparents, then with aunts and uncles, and then in an orphanage. At the age of thirteen, while still in the orphanage, he claims to have strangled to death a boy who had been mercilessly taunting him about his bed-wetting habit. For this, Hoyt was moved again, this time to a correctional institution for juvenile delinquents. Later he joined the army, and after he was discharged he got married. Things went well for a while, but then he and his wife parted, and his life was shattered. It was then that he first hit the streets.

For the next ten years he led a substance-oriented life-style, using "speed" frequently, drinking heavily, and working only sporadically. He eventually realized that the life he was living would destroy him. Hoyt left Dallas and headed south to Austin, where he immediately sought work with the Salvation Army. Since Hoyt is a bear of a man who stands 6'6" and weighs over 300 pounds, the Salvation Army was quick to offer him employment as a monitor for the dinner line. His easygoing, friendly disposition fitted the job well.

We first met Hoyt in the dinner line, as he walked along talking to the men and sharing his cigarettes with anyone who asked. For the next nine months, Hoyt worked as both a line monitor and a truck driver, in exchange for room and board and $134 a week. He took pride in his work and seemed especially pleased that he was working regularly. It was a step forward, but he knew it was only a stopgap measure. In time he would either have to slip back onto the streets or find permanent employment that paid him a living wage and took him away from the influences of the street which had become a part of him.

Nearly nine months after our initial encounter with him, Hoyt's prophecy came true. He left Austin, leaving no indication of where he was going. Several months later we learned that he was back in Dallas—not on the streets, though, but in a veteran's hospital, where he was being treated for his drinking problem. Apparently Hoyt had come to the realization that if he was to ever make it off the streets permanently, he would first have to attend to his chronic drinking habit.

Tanner Sutton   Tanner is a twenty-nine-year-old white man who is badly disfigured by burn scars from a childhood accident. Like Hoyt, Tanner was orphaned as a child and shuffled from one boys' home to another. At the age of twenty-two he married and landed a job as a janitor in a college in Beaumont, Texas. A few years later he lost his job because he was unable to perform the more strenuous duties demanded of him. Soon after he lost his job, his marriage fell apart. He then took to the streets and has been homeless in Texas for a little over two years.

We first encountered Tanner during a dinner at the Salvation Army at which he broke into a tirade about evolution and reincarnation, claiming that humans had "devolved from a higher being." With his burn-scarred, dust-covered body and his wild long hair, Tanner looked like an ascetic just returned from the wilderness. At first hearing he sounded like a rambling fool. He apparently struck others at the dinner table as mentally ill; they rolled their eyes and chuckled to each other as he ranted on. We learned over time, however, that Tanner is literate and a constant reader, spending a good deal of time in libraries and secondhand bookstores. He is knowledgeable about the occult, spiritualism, and higher forms of consciousness and is particularly fond of the writings of Carlos Castaneda, the mystic-anthropologist who has written extensively on his apprenticeship to a Yaqui Indian shaman.

Shortly after our initial encounter, Tanner was hired by the Salvation Army as a night monitor in its transient lodge. Like Hoyt, he received board and room, but Tanner was paid only $5.00 per week for his less demanding job. Tanner saw himself as having taken a step up, as less of a street person than before. But with an income of $5.00 per week it was highly improbable that he would ever accumulate the funds needed to move into an independent living situation. Tanner's new status thus represented a reprieve at best. At the Sally, Tanner often talked enthusiastically about traveling to Washington, D.C., to pursue his "occult studies" at the Smithsonian Institute. Perhaps that is where he headed when he quit his job and left Austin four months after we met him.

OUTSIDERS

We have noted that the recently dislocated homeless may drift into the transient state of liminality as they become attuned to life on the streets. Our observations also indicate that individuals in this liminal status may, in turn, drift further into street life, with both their cognitive orientation and their daily routine riveted on surviving on the streets rather than on making it off. Such homeless individuals have become *outsiders,* the third generic category in our typology.

The concept of outsider is widely used, with several different emphases.[15] The variant that captures most clearly what we mean by the term is provided by Victor Turner. Turner notes that just as there is "the betwixt-and-between state of liminality, there is the state of outsiderhood, referring to the condition of being either permanently and by ascription set outside the structural arrangements of a given social system, or being situationally or temporarily set apart, or voluntarily setting oneself apart from the behavior of status-occupying, role-playing members of that system."[16] We would only add that outsiders, as we have observed them, exist apart from the larger system not only structurally but also cognitively. They are individuals for whom street life has become taken-for-granted. They often see themselves in terms of various street identities and not merely as individuals who are down on their luck. As a consequence, they rarely talk about getting off the street. They are people for whom the past and the future have collapsed into the present.

These similarities notwithstanding, outsiders reveal some striking differences. They can be divided into three subtypes: tramps, bums, and the mentally ill.

TRAMPS

The terms *tramp* and *bum* have long been part of the typological lexicon of the streets. During the first half of this century, the most widely diffused typology for distinguishing among the homeless was the folk schema that differentiated among hoboes, tramps, and bums. The distinction rested on two dimensions of contrast: mobility and work. The hobo was a migratory worker, the tramp a migratory nonworker, and the bum a nonmigratory nonworker.[17] Some slippage undoubtedly occurred among the types, but the vernacular of the road during the first third of the century made much use of these distinctions. The hoboes, particularly, regarded themselves as the "kings of the road" and scorned the tramps and bums. As one celebrated " 'bo," who managed to secure an audience with Teddy Roosevelt, exclaimed, "You may call them hoboes if you will, but do not confound hoboes with tramps and bums."[18]

By the 1950s this threefold distinction had apparently lost its conceptual utility. The concept of the hobo seemed to have died. Whether its decline in usage on the streets resulted from the disappearance of the hobo and his subculture or from a blurring of the previous distinction between hoboes and the tramps and bums is unclear. What does seem certain, though, is that by the latter third of the century, homeless street people were seldom imputing or avowing the hobo identity. The tramp and bum constructs were still part of the lexicon, however. Thus, an ethnographic study of homeless men in Seattle in the late 1960s found that both were used, but *tramp* was preferred.[19] Subsequent research has not found the term to have such generic appeal among homeless men, however. A more recent biographic travelogue about a tramp named Carl revealed, for example, that tramps are quite clear about the distinctions between themselves and those called bums.[20] As Carl put it, "We're not the same at all. They just don't want to do nuthin'. They just sit there and bum—you can't get one of them to work if you tried."[21]

We found that these stereotypic characterizations were still in use among some of the homeless on the streets of Austin. We therefore retained the terms as descriptors of several types of the homeless we encountered.

Three dimensions distinguish the tramps in our typology. They are highly migratory, with a much larger range than the other homeless. Their travels are typically patterned rather than random. And they possess a strong sense of independence and self-control that prompts them to look down both on street novices who have not yet learned the ropes and on those who subsist largely on handouts from organized charity and who accept substantial support from social services. Alcohol is fairly central in the lives of tramps, but not as much so as it is in the bums' lives. Tramps, like the other outsiders, seem to have resigned themselves to life on the streets and tend not to look ahead to a life beyond the streets. Their embrace of street life is frequently reflected in a tendency to discard their given names in favor of street names.

Approximately 15 percent of our field sample were classified as tramps. They fell into two subtypes, traditional tramps and hippie tramps.

TRADITIONAL TRAMPS

Traditional tramps are the heirs of the hobo life-style, which is based on a cycle of working, drinking, and migrating. Their preferred livelihood tends to be wage labor, and their travels are largely determined by seasonal and regional variations in labor markets. Most are unlikely to stay put for long, however, since they also claim a strong impulse to travel. Traditional tramps frequently see themselves as "brethren of the road." Like all the outsiders except the mentally ill, traditional tramps drink heavily, but their drunks tend to be more scheduled than those of other outsiders.

Nine of the twenty-five tramps were classified as traditional tramps. As is indicated in Table 2.3, they are the oldest homeless in our sample, with a mean age of fifty-two. They also have the longest tenure on the streets, averaging nearly six years. Shotgun and Banjo are the two traditional tramps we came to know best.

Shotgun   Shotgun is a forty-nine-year-old white man who was born in Juneau, Alaska. He is a self-proclaimed tramp and artist who claims to have received a B.F.A. from a college in Boston in the early 1960s. After college, he told us, he taught for a short time in a ghetto high school, but he quickly grew dissatisfied with his life and took to the road, leaving behind his wife and two daughters. He has been on the road for fourteen years, leading a migratory life. In recent years he has worked on ranches in Montana during the summers and has wintered in Austin.

We first met Shotgun as he wandered the streets on a cold winter day, drunk and ostensibly looking for a detox facility to which a policeman had referred him. Once engaged in conversation and sobered with a couple of cups of coffee, he changed his mind about admitting himself to detox, saying, "It's too humiliating to go into detox sober." Nearly a month after this initial encounter, Shotgun disappeared, yielding to the itch to move on or deciding it was time to begin the annual trek back to Montana.

Banjo   Banjo is a forty-five-year-old white man. At the age of sixteen he ran away from home in Arkansas to take a job with a carnival. He has lived a transient life ever since, occasionally settling in one or another Christian commune. He is a devout Christian and carries a banjo with "Wealth Means Nothing Without God" painted on the case.

Banjo was first encountered sitting beside his banjo case in the Salvation Army dinner line on the afternoon after a murder had taken place at the Sally. Most of the men had been frightened by the murder, but Banjo appeared calm. He told us that he had nothing to fear, because he was a Christian and the Bible promised that God would be with him even in "the valley of the shadow of death." Like Shotgun, Banjo had been coming south to Austin each winter for several years. His itch to move on did not appear quite as strong as Shotgun's, however, as Banjo had been in Austin for nearly five months by the time we lost contact with him.

HIPPIE TRAMPS

Hippie tramps are the heirs of the 1960s counterculture. Apparent throwbacks to an earlier era, they identify with counterculture values and the rock heroes of that period, practice arts and crafts, use and sell drugs, and hang out together on the streets in an almost communal fashion. They frequently travel to the "Rainbow" reunion of old hippies that is held annually at various locations throughout the country. They live squarely in the present, but with an eye toward the past rather than the future. As one hippie tramp who had been around for some time commented wistfully, "The most memorable experience in my life was when I smoked dope on Jimi Hendrix's grave."

Hippie tramps travel a good bit, having the second largest range among the various types of homeless. Both alcohol and drugs are central to their life-style, but they use drugs more than any other of our types, and they make their living partly by selling drugs to college students.

In Austin the hippie tramps hung out in a student housing and shopping area along the main street that borders one end of the University of Texas. This section of the street has long been known as the Drag, prompting students to refer derisively to the hippie tramps and other homeless who frequent it on occasion as "Drag worms." This did not deter the hippie tramps from staking out this area as their home base or from peddling, panhandling, and occasionally performing to get money from students and other passersby.

Fifteen of the tramps fell into this category. With a mean age of thirty-one, the hippie tramps average twenty-one years younger than their traditional counterparts.[22] They have also been on the streets for a shorter period of time, an average of around three years. We came to know Rhyming Mike and Gimpy Dan well.

Rhyming Mike   Rhyming Mike is a thirty-three-year-old white man from Oxnard, California. He says he left home several years ago to travel around the country, and he hangs out on the streets with other hippielike tramps when he finds them. He spends a good deal of his time writing poems, and he frequently offers to compose poems for people on the streets if they will give him a little spare change. Such poem titles as "Dogs and Tramps," "Blood Bank Blues," and "Cross-Road Refugee" reflect his experience on the streets and his tramp orientation.

Rhyming Mike was first encountered at the Renaissance Market on the Drag. He was involved in a heated argument with a merchant who said Mike was scaring off customers. When Mike refused to leave the bench he was sitting on, the merchant got a hose and started washing down the area, getting closer and closer to the bench. A fight between the shop owner and Rhyming Mike seemed imminent when Mike suddenly changed his mind, offering to leave the area as long as it was understood that he was doing it of his own free will and could come back whenever he wanted. We walked up the street about a block and sat on a curb with Mike while he smoked several joints, recited his poetry, and philosophized about life as a tramp.

Gimpy Dan   Gimpy Dan is a thirty-three-year-old white male, also from California, who claims to have been on and off the streets for around eighteen years. He says he quit school and left home in his early teens and that his "only education since has been reading *Freak Brothers Comics*."

We first saw Gimpy Dan sitting on a parking lot curb near the university as he talked with street acquaintances who hung out in the area. Occasionally he would break off the conversation to walk down a nearby alley and sell joints and hits of acid to college students. He walked with a cane, having an obvious back problem for which he had been dubbed Gimpy Dan or Bad Back Danny. In this and subsequent encounters, he talked repeatedly about his travels around the country, saying that he plants marijuana wherever he goes and then returns the next year to see if it has grown and is ready to be harvested. He told us on one occasion that the past year had been a particularly busy one in that regard, adding that "I'll be a rich man next year if all my fields work out."

BUMS

In the vernacular of the street, as we noted above, the term *bum* has traditionally meant a nonmigratory nonworker whose range is usually within the confines of a local skid-row area and who is a chronic alcoholic. Although this image is stereotypic, it contains elements that typify a number of the homeless we encountered. Moreover, we heard some homeless describe certain fellow travelers as bums, and a few others defined themselves as such. We thus incorporate the term into our typology, but without any intention of impugning the character of those so categorized.

Individuals in our field sample classified as bums consistently had two characteristics in common that clearly distinguished them from others: their limited range of travel, and their heavy use of alcohol. Not all the individuals who exhibited these two characteristics were similar in other respects, however. We thus distinguish between traditional bums and redneck bums.

TRADITIONAL BUMS

The traditional bum comes closest to the popular image of the skid-row alcoholic. Not only are the traditional bums relatively immobile and heavily dependent on alcohol, but they also rather infrequently engage in wage labor. This is not so much because they are lazy as because they have become indifferent or because they are physically debilitated from years of hard living and drinking. Instead, they survive by a mixture of begging, peddling, scavenging, charity hand-outs and social-service support. They seem resigned to this style of life, and they live from day to day, rarely thinking beyond the moment, largely because they know that tomorrow holds little in store for them that is different from today.

Eighteen percent of our sample were classified as traditional bums. Their mean age was forty-seven, making them the second oldest type, and they averaged nearly four and a half years on the streets. Representative of the street people who fell into this category are Gypsy Bill, Marilyn "Mom" Fisch, Nona George, and JJ and Indio.

Gypsy Bill   Gypsy Bill is a thirty-two-year-old white man from New York. He is a small man with a striking appearance: about four feet six inches tall, blind in one eye, and with a severely deformed back on which he has had nine surgical operations. Before the Reagan administration cutback of the Social Security disability rolls, Gypsy, then a married man, received Supplemental Security Income checks and worked a part-time janitorial job. But in the fall of 1982 Gypsy was cut from SSI, and his marriage disintegrated at about the same time. He hit the road and hitchhiked to Austin, where he has remained ever since, living in the parks along the lakes near Austin in the summers and close to the Salvation Army during the winters. At both sites Gypsy stays in an old car he purchased with money he earned at a landscaping job shortly after he came to Austin. He has rarely worked at such jobs since then, because his deformed back makes such work extremely difficult. His chronic drinking has compounded his plight, depleting his fitness and his interest in most kinds of day labor. After he bought the car, Gypsy survived primarily by panhandling, scavenging, and procuring hand-outs from local charities.

We first met Gypsy Bill at one such charity that gives sandwiches to the homeless between 10 A.M. and noon each day. Gypsy told us he had an appointment later that day for a physical exam to see whether he could qualify for reinstatement on SSI. We gave him a ride to the doctor's office and listened to him talk about how he had learned to live on the streets. It was clear that he had come to identify himself as a street person, frequently referring to himself as a "bum" and "an expert dumpster diver." Gypsy was eventually reinstated on SSI, but he continued to live on the streets, in part because of the insufficiency of SSI payments and in part because he had grown accustomed to street life.

Marilyn "Mom" Fisch   Marilyn is a forty-nine-year-old, five-foot-tall white woman, born in Halifax, Nova Scotia. She has been married and has several children. She and her husband were living in West Virginia when he died in 1968. From what we gathered, her life has spiraled downward ever since that time. Marilyn is an outgoing woman many of the younger people on the streets call Mom, but she can be very combative when drunk and on several occasions has been banned from various establishments frequented by the homeless.

We first met Marilyn as she was handing out discarded burritos in an alley near the Salvation Army. She was drunk at the time and talked about how she regularly provided food for her "people" on the streets because she knew what it was like "to be so hungry you're ready to eat dirt." During the next year we had twenty-five contacts with Marilyn, more than with any other homeless person. She functioned as a key informant, introducing us to the ins and outs of life on the streets, as well as to other street people.

Nona George   Nona is a forty-six-year-old emaciated, toothless Native American woman from Oklahoma. She had been on the streets of Austin for nearly ten years when we first encountered her at a Sunday worship service for the homeless held by a church located on the outskirts of the city. Nona and the other homeless in attendance were transported there by a church bus that picks people up near the Sally each Sunday morning. Before and after the service Nona captured the attention of several people as she told tales of her frequent fights with other homeless and the number of agencies she had been barred from for unruly behavior. She talked of hard drinking and of her dozens of arrests for public intoxication, which we verified when we examined her file at the City Police Department. "I give them a different name every time they arrest me, just to give them trouble," she boasted.[23] "And one time I even swiped the judge's coffee when they had me in court." Except for two stays in the hospital for pneumonia, Nona remained on the streets throughout our research.

JJ and Indio   JJ and Indio are two old drinking buddies who struck us as prototypes of the skid row alcoholic. JJ is a sixty-five-year-old black Austinite. Indio, who came from a small town about fifteen miles northeast of Austin, is a fifty-year-old Hispanic. Both had been on the streets of Austin for close to five years when we first met them. That was at dusk one evening as they sat in a parking lot near the Salvation Army sharing a quart of beer and a bottle of wine. JJ dozed off sporadically while Indio sobbed as he talked about his divorce some fifteen years earlier.

In subsequent encounters with them we rarely found them either sober or separated from one another. One exception was on Thanksgiving morning of 1984, when a sizable number of homeless were waiting for a church bus to take them to the church's Thanksgiving dinner. The bus was almost full when it arrived, and there was a mad rush to get on. Old JJ was right in the middle of the crowd rushing the bus, and he fell and knocked others off balance, too. But he got back up, dusted himself off, and sat on the curb until the next bus came. Once again everybody rushed the bus, leaving JJ in the dust. He did manage to make it to the door, however, and asked the bus driver whether there was room for one more. When the driver shook his head no, JJ replied with deferential resignation, "You're a good man, sir." Then, having had enough hassle for one day, he stumbled off down the street.

REDNECK BUMS

Redneck bums constitute a variant of the bum type that is probably peculiar to the Southwest. They are similar to the traditional bum in their relative immobility and heavy use of alcohol, but they are strikingly different in other respects. Their livelihood is based primarily on a mixture of selling plasma, peddling, and panhandling, whereas the traditional bum does little of the former. They also tend to hang out together, in an almost ganglike fashion, and they are noticeably proprietary, claiming as their own turf a former used car lot across the street from the Salvation Army. When they do move locally, which is rarely beyond the plasma center two miles to the north, they typically do so together. Occasionally they travel out to the lakes to "party." With long hair and beards, they look somewhat like the hippie tramps on the Drag, but they prefer country music to rock and alcohol to drugs. They are also a much less convivial bunch than the hippie tramps. They are contentious, often daring other homeless to come onto their turf, and they bear the signs of past frays. Most have facial scars and teeth missing from past fights, as well as frequent black eyes and cuts on their faces or hands and arms. This country, "macho" orientation, coupled with the fact that they are "homeguards" who drink more heavily than the rest of the homeless, led some of the other homeless to dub them "redneck bums."

Only 5 of the 168 homeless with whom we had some contact fell into this category, but more than that hung out together. We came to know one of them, Bill-Bob, quite well.

Bill-Bob   Bill-Bob is a white, bearded thirty-two-year-old native of Texas. He had been on the streets for a little more than a year at the time of our initial encounter. That was on a hot afternoon in a plasma center parking lot where Bill-Bob and the gang were having a beer party. Bill-Bob was glassy-eyed and incoherent. While stumbling around, he grabbed one of the gang leader's beers and refused to give it back. Not given to negotiation, particularly on a hot Texas afternoon, the gang leader kicked Bill-Bob solidly in the groin, whereupon he fell to the ground moaning as his spilled beer foamed into his beard. In subsequent encounters, he was somewhat more coherent, but rarely without companions or without a beer in his hand.

THE MENTALLY ILL

The last type within the outsider genre and the final category within our typology is that of the so-called mentally ill.[24] We include in this category neither what are termed substance abusers nor those who evince evidence of depression, but only those who give some indication of being severely impaired psychiatrically within the context of street life.[25] We include this category not only because there are some people on the streets who are so impaired, but also because their survival repertoire is somewhat distinctive.

Three criteria were used as indicators of mental illness: prior institutionalization; designation as mentally ill by other homeless individuals; and conduct that is so bizarre and situationally inappropriate that it would be likely to be construed as symptomatic of mental illness by most observers. Classification of those within our field sample as mentally ill was contingent on evidence of at least two of the three criteria.[26]

The first criterion is the most straightforward. Prior institutionalization is generally taken as indicative of mental illness at some point in one's past. But since prior institutionalization does not necessarily mean current dysfunctionality, it cannot be used as a sufficient indicator of present mental status. Indeed, we encountered several individuals who had been institutionalized but who were currently functioning quite competently in their present circumstances. But even if prior institutionalization were in principle a satisfactory indicator of current mental functioning, it would not have been sufficient for us, since we were unable to ascertain whether each of the 168 individuals in the field sample had ever been institutionalized.

The use of typifications by the homeless themselves as a second criterion rests on the assumption that however mental illness may be conceptualized, it is, from a sociological standpoint, "bizarre behavior" that makes face-to-face interaction improbable, risky, or exceedingly difficult for peers of the individual.[27] If so, then people who share similar sociocultural niches ought to have some sense of who among them is "crazy" or "mentally ill." Accordingly, we listened for such designations and judgments among the homeless and sought to elicit and confirm them in conversational interviewing when appropriate.

The third field criterion is based on the premise that some behaviors and patterns of talk prompt the designation of "madness" or "mental illness" across subcultural groups and populations. These typically tend to be behaviors and streams of talk that are so grossly incongruent with the context or situation that they would appear to most observers to be strikingly bizarre, aberrant, and inappropriate.[28] The following encounter provides a graphic illustration of such behavior:

> A heavy-set, middle-aged woman who had been walking alone on the sidewalk and singing came over and sat beside us on the curb as we waited to catch a bus to a church service for the homeless. Immediately after telling us her name, she said, "I'm from one of 5,000 planets which have beings superior to humans. People on those planets watch earthlings on TV, but they find them repulsive. You're ugly to me too." She went on, "I have been reincarnated on earth and trained to be a scientist so that I can inform God about scientific developments on earth. But earth science is bullshit! I know because I saw a picture on the front of *Scientific American* that was supposed to be a nebula in space, but I recognized it was a photograph I took a long time ago of a dirt clod under a microscope." Then when asked if she knew who we were waiting for, she replied, "We are waiting for the last pure descendants of the Romans who are going to feed us."

While many behaviors might be construed as peculiar or deviant, there are probably relatively few that are so dramatically beyond the pale of everyday discourse and rationality that they are unambiguously indicative of mental illness. When they do surface, however, designation of the person associated with them as mentally ill "usually pro-

ceeds with relative ease and consensus" for both insiders and outsiders.[29] The stream of talk reported above is illustrative of the sorts of
behaviors that we took as symptomatic of some degree of mental illness, provided that they were recurrent and verified by one of the other
criteria.

Ten percent of the homeless we encountered in the field met at least
two of the above criteria for mental illness.[30] This alone sets them apart
from the other homeless, but they are also distinguishable by their survival repertoire. They are among the most immobile of the various types,
rarely moving voluntarily beyond their daily orbit. Within this circuit,
they survive primarily by taking handouts, scavenging for food from
garbage receptacles, and begging. In some cases, survival is occasionally
facilitated by financial aid from governmental welfare programs. Our
observations indicate that the mentally ill scavenge more than any of
the other types except the traditional bum and that they are the most
frequent recipients of federal income supplements. They are also distinctive in that their daily routine does not include much use of either
alcohol or drugs. Finally, the mentally ill appear to be outcasts even
among the outsiders. They are avoided by the other homeless as much
as possible, and they seem to reciprocate in kind. Of all the homeless
with whom we had contact, the mentally ill were clearly the most reclusive and socially isolated. In many respects they are not only the most
distant of all the homeless from the larger sociocultural world, but they
are also strangers in the street world of the homeless. As Hoyt explained
one evening over a couple of beers:

> I see people coming to the Sally who are mentally ill. They're sick and men-
> tally incapable. They're not drug addicts. They're just people who need to
> be in a hospital. I mean, these people are harmless, most of them. They're
> not violent, but there's something there that they just can't help themselves.
> Now you can take an alcoholic and sober him up, or even a drug addict.
> Maybe you can get him thinking, talk to him and get him thinking positively
> about himself, make him think he's a little better than he thinks he is, you
> know. But these people, no matter what you do for them, they're going to
> be the same. . . .They're crazy. They don't belong on the streets.

The seventeen homeless within our field sample whom we classified as
mentally ill averaged thirty-two years of age and around nine months
to one year on the streets. Jorge Herrera and Lance McCay were the
two we came to know best.

Jorge Herrera   Jorge Herrera is a forty-two-year-old Hispanic man
from Corpus Christi. He has been on and off the streets for twenty

years. In 1966, at the age of twenty-three, Jorge was admitted to Austin State Hospital for psychiatric problems. He ran away from the hospital and was sent back on several occasions, but when we first met him he had been out of the hospital for ten to twelve years. When asked how long he has been on the streets in Austin he simply says, "For a long, long time." Police records show that he has been arrested occasionally over the past fifteen years for aberrant behavior, including screaming that he was being chased by ghosts.

We first saw Jorge on a hot spring afternoon as he sat against a wall along the Drag. He was in bad shape that day: his body shook in periodic spasms, and mucus covered his long mustache and beard. He said that he had been "very sick from eating bad food" lately, but that he did not need to go to the hospital. As he muttered, he kept nodding off, then waking to scratch his ankles, which were covered with sores. Encounters with Jorge over the next year revealed that he was not routinely as comatose and incoherent as he had appeared that day. He was, however, a highly visible figure who seemed to be recognized by most people whose daily routines intersected with his.

Lance McCay   Lance is a thirty-two-year-old white man who had been on and off the streets for ten years at the time of our first encounter. During this period he had also been in and out of Texas state mental hospitals and halfway houses. But most of his past ten years had been spent on the streets of Austin, even though his parents lived in Houston and were well off financially. Lance had a manic personality and a quick, uncontrollable temper, for which he took Lithium. He wrote poetry and autobiographical notes almost daily, and he believed himself to be an up-and-coming writer.

We first met Lance at the Salvation Army. He was carrying a large manila envelope that he refused to put down, even during dinner. He told us it contained a poetry manuscript he had recently completed. He explained that he had recently left a halfway house for the mentally ill so that he could travel to New York City to find a publisher for the manuscript. Although Lance was not as conspicuous as Jorge at first glance, we came to learn that he was more erratic and unpredictable, thus making sustained interaction with him equally difficult.

SUMMARY

In the preceding pages we have distinguished among the homeless street people in our field sample by categorizing them into empirically discrete types according to their adaptive activities or survival repertoires. We have delineated the life-style, cognitive, and temporal attributes used as dimensions of contrast, articulated the rationale for using these dimensions, highlighted some of the ways in which the types differ in terms of these criteria, and introduced representative examples of each type. The end product is an empirical and conceptual scaffolding that can be used to explore in greater detail the nature of life on the streets and to discern different patterns of adaptation among the homeless. Like any scaffolding, ours is only a platform from which to work, a springboard for diving into the social world under investigation. Much remains to be done if the subculture of street life is to be apprehended and the daily routines and survival repertoires of the homeless are to be grasped. The task of the next section, then, is to attend to these concerns by detailing the factors that shape the subculture of street life and by elaborating the similarities and differences in the ways the various types of homeless go about the business of surviving materially, socially, and psychologically.

PART TWO

Life on the Streets:
Daily Routines
and Survival Strategies

CHAPTER THREE

The Subculture
of Street Life

At 4:30 A.M. Austin is a city asleep. Traffic lights blink amber in the empty streets. The only places open are a few all-night restaurants, self-service gas stations, and convenience stores, and even they seem to be napping. It will be another sixty minutes before the clerks at the convenience stores start brewing coffee and setting out donuts for the morning crowd. At the Salvation Army downtown transient lodge the night monitor flashes the lights and then leaves them on. More than seventy men fight off the discomfort of the early awakening. Sitting on the two-by-six-foot sleeping mat on the floor, a man slowly gathers his few belongings: a bag with a spare pair of pants and a girlie magazine, a tattered jacket, and shoes used as a pillow, less for comfort than to keep them from being stolen. For most, having to get up so early is just the grim conclusion to a bad night. It's not easy to drift off to sleep in a noisy, smoke-filled room crammed with strangers. Hoyt Page, who has spent twelve years in and out of such shelters, describes the situation:

> You're tired, you're hungry, you stink, and you're in there with a bunch of people you don't know and they're tired and they stink. I don't care who you are, you could stand your own feet and your own farts, but sometimes guys puke on themselves, or they shit on themselves. And say you're in there trying to make it—you're trying to save your money. . . . It'll get to you and you'll think, "God, I need a drink. I need to get outta here. I need to get high." Try to lay down and you gotta get up the next day and go to work. Can't sleep. Can't rest. You'd rather go out and sleep on the street, but you're scared of what's out there.

But it's a place to stay, at least for most of the night.

The men stack their mats at the back of the room and amble outside to the breakfast line under the red-and-white Salvation Army sign. In summer some of the men are shirtless; in the colder months some are wrapped in blankets or cardboard instead of a coat. Usually at least one or two are barefoot.

It will be dark for another hour, an hour most of the men will spend waiting on the sidewalk. Groggy and withdrawn, they stand quietly in the breakfast line or walk around to the side of the building to relieve themselves.[1]

After half an hour the men at the front of the line get impatient. A few climb up on a ledge to look into the dining room. They speculate on what is going to be served for breakfast and complain about having to wait. But an ex–speed freak who has been on and off the streets for the past fourteen years has learned to stay calm. "If there's one thing you don't want to do in this town," he says, "it's get in a hurry."

By a quarter past five the first group of men are let into the dining room and seated shoulder to shoulder in front of already dished-up plates. The menu varies, but not a lot. It was oatmeal and stale pastries for a while. Now it's powdered eggs that are almost cold by the time the men get to them. A fifty-six-year-old man who was recently released from the Huntsville prison after six years of incarceration comments, "There's a right way and a wrong way to fix powdered eggs. Leave it to the Army to find the wrong way." There's white bread and commodity butter on the table too, but the best part is the styrofoam cup full—more often half-full—of coffee. The Sally does not provide sugar, but some of the men have learned to pick up packets of sugar at fast-food spots for their morning coffee. Sometimes the coffee is hot, but usually it's lukewarm. Still, it helps the men wake up. Some liven up as they eat, chatting about their plans for the day. But most just drain their coffee cups and head back out into the dawn.

At a quarter to six a few weathered old men, barely able to stand at this time of day, stumble off into the darkness to find a business doorway, a vacated building, or some other sheltered spot in which to go back to sleep. The younger men, especially the recently dislocated and the straddlers, head out to look for work. By half past six they have deserted the Sally for the day.

Some men who have a little money in their pockets forego breakfast at the Sally. They cross the river and walk south about ten blocks to a twenty-four-hour fast-food restaurant. There for only $1.33 they can buy a newspaper, a cup of hot coffee with a free refill, and a sausage-and-egg taco. But many of the men do not even have enough for the coffee; they are eager to start looking for a job for the day. These men go directly from the Sally to one of the several spots around town where the homeless congregate in the hope of finding wage labor.

Not all of the city's homeless are up and about by 6:00 A.M., however. For the reasons given by Hoyt, as well as the desire to sleep beyond 4:30 and to exercise a little autonomy, many of the homeless prefer sleeping arrangements other than those provided by the Sally shelter. Some of the homeless who have been working may choose to spend a few dollars on a cheap motel, often sleeping two, three, or more to a room in order to stretch their money. Even though it is only for a night or two every now and then, the warm bed, quiet sleep, and private shower add up to an almost idyllic retreat from the street. Others sleep in cars parked around the Salvation Army. The number of cars with sleepers is always changing, but there are at least a dozen at any one time. Sometimes the cars are missing one or more tires, which have been sold or stolen. But a car does not need tires to shelter three or four homeless, allowing them to sleep until sunrise or later, protected from the elements and from other homeless as well. Those who do not have access to cars or vans or who prefer to bed down alone may "sleep rough" under bridges, in abandoned buildings, in alcoves, in isolated weed patches, or in small "jungles" with other homeless.[2]

On almost any morning more of the homeless can be found having fashioned or appropriated for themselves one of these exterior niches than sleeping in the Sally. Whatever the reason for sleeping rough, it is seldom done without some awareness of the risks: vulnerability to mean-spirited citizens, other homeless, or probing surveyors; inclement weather; and menacing varmints such as Texas fire ants and brown recluse spiders.[3]

One popular jungling area is adjacent to one of the day-labor gathering places. Here men wrap themselves in their jackets and soiled blankets and sleep in the weeds and dirt beside a metal building. Here, too, a few women stay with their male friends. During one five-month stretch, Marilyn Fisch often spent the night here with her twenty-eight-year-old male companion, Smitty, whom she referred to as her common-law husband. They slept on a large piece of plastic they put on the ground under some scrub trees. While this was their "home" they suffered from the dangers of sleeping rough. Marilyn battled two ulcerated sores from brown recluse spider bites for over a month, and they constantly had to ward off the relentless fire ants with insecticide they sprayed around their piece of plastic. Smitty claims to have been attacked by a group of other homeless men, receiving a knife wound in his abdomen that required twenty-eight stitches, and Marilyn was hospitalized with pneumonia during a rainy spell. Still, they preferred living out because it allowed them to sleep together. Neither the church charities nor the Sally accepted their common-law marriage—not surprisingly, since Marilyn had had a series of "old men" during her time on the streets. This time, though, their relationship was reminiscent of traditional marital roles, refracted through the prism of homelessness. Smitty would often rise early and scurry off in search of work while Marilyn stayed in camp, cleaning things up, visiting with other homeless, and nursing a bottle of warm beer or vodka and coke.

By 8:30 to 9:00 A.M., most of the homeless who will find wage labor for the day are out on jobs. The rest—the unlucky job seekers and those who are too discouraged to look for work—have turned their attention to other ways of making do. Some have hiked three miles north to the city's two plasma centers, a few have wandered over to the main branch of the city's public library—more to escape the elements than to read in peace[4]—others have drifted to the park along Town Lake, some are just hanging out on selected street corners killing time, and still others have begun to make their way to a local charity that hands out sandwiches on weekday mornings.

.   .   .   .

So begins a day on the streets. It is not a day that is totally unstructured, however. It may appear that way from the standpoint of the domiciled citizen and, indeed, it may be because of that appearance that street life is occasionally romanticized.[5] But from the standpoint of those who live it, street life has a definitive order and rhythm that are suggestive of a subculture of street life.

It is not a subculture in the conventional sense, though, in that it is neither anchored in nor embodies a distinctive set of shared values. Rather, as we emphasized in the previous chapter, its distinctiveness resides in a patterned set of behaviors, routines, and orientations that are adaptive responses to the predicament of homelessness itself and to the associated conditions of street life. But there is more to this subculture than the homeless and their adaptive behaviors and routines. The political climate with respect to the homeless affects how they spend their days. The matrix of social-service and control agencies and commercial establishments that deal directly with the homeless also shapes their routines and options. In addition, the ecological distribution of these institutional facilities and what we term marginal space within the community helps to define the contours of street life. And, finally, the texture of street life is further influenced by a kind of emergent moral code that provides a tenuous guide to the elaboration of behavioral routines and interpersonal relationships.

Developing an understanding of the subculture of street life thus requires examination of the institutional, political, ecological, and moral constraints that affect the adaptive responses the homeless fashion in order to survive. In the subsequent chapters in this section we explore the adaptive responses themselves, but in the remainder of this chapter we examine the various contextual factors that facilitate and constrain those adaptations.

ORGANIZATIONAL AND POLITICAL CONSTRAINTS

Street life in Austin, just as in every other community throughout the country, is embedded in a loose network of organizations that range from social-service agencies to neighborhood associations and governmental task forces. These organizations not only affect the survival opportunities and resources available to the homeless but also contribute to the texture of street life. In attempting to understand the relative importance of the various organizations that comprise this constraining matrix we are concerned not so much with their manifest or ostensible functions as with how they actually respond to the homeless from day to day and with their underlying operating perspectives.[6] Simply put, we focus on what the various organizations do and on the working ideologies that organize and justify their activities.

We discerned five patterns of functioning or response among the various organizations intervening in the lives and routines of the homeless in Austin. Table 3.1 presents these five patterns, along with their operating perspectives and organizational carriers. We discuss each of these patterns in turn.

ACCOMMODATIVE RESPONSE

In *The Urban Villagers,* Herbert Gans notes that a significant feature of the urban landscape, especially in low-income areas such as the Italian-American one he studied in Boston's West End, is the existence of a

TABLE 3.1   ORGANIZATIONAL RESPONSES
AND PERSPECTIVES

Organizational Response	Operational Perspective	Local Organizational Carriers
Accommodative	Sustenance-oriented caretaker	Salvation Army Caritas Angels House Texas Employment Commission
Restorative	Treatment-oriented caretaker	
	Medical perspective	City hospital Mental Health and Mental Retardation Detox units Substance treatment programs
	Salvationist perspective	Assembly of God church Detox units
Exploitative	Market-oriented	Plasma centers Labor pool Labor corner Bunkhaus
Exclusionist/ Expulsionist	NIMBY* perspective	Neighborhood associations
Containment	Harassment	Police department

* "Not in my back yard"

spate of "caretakers." They encompass the "agencies and individuals who not only give patient care, but other kinds of aid that they think will benefit the client, and who offer aid as an end in itself, rather than as a means to a more important end."[7] Generic examples include medical and psychiatric facilities, case-work and social-welfare agencies, many employment agencies and educational programs, and various facilities for the down-and-out, such as the missions and single-room-occupancy tenements (SROs) that lined the skid rows of the past.[8] The landscape of the urban world the homeless know is dotted with an array of such caretakers. Not all of them are of the same stripe, however. Some function primarily in an accommodative fashion; others are essentially restorative.

The accommodative response attends to the basic subsistence needs of the homeless, particularly the need for food and shelter. As a mode of response that helps the homeless manage street life, it facilitates their survival as homeless persons but does little to help them off the streets. This pattern of functioning characterizes the work of most shelters, missions, and soup kitchens, including, in Austin, the Salvation Army, Caritas, Angels House, and the day-labor operation of the Texas Employment Commission, which we will discuss in the next chapter.

Of the various organizations and agencies that cater to the homeless in Austin, none offers more accommodative services than the Salvation Army's downtown shelter. As we noted previously, the Sally is the only facility that provides free shelter, free breakfast and dinner, and an opportunity to shower, and until mid-1985 it was the only shelter of any kind in town. Its liberal shelter policy also heightened homeless persons' dependence on it as a place to stay. Many shelters restrict lodgers to only two or three nights in a row, but the Sally has an open-door policy: admission is based on a first-come, first-served queue system and the willingness to abide by the Sally's few regulations. Homeless individuals can stay night after night, provided they queue up early enough to get their lodging ticket and provided they are sober at the time the door opens and do not have a history of "making trouble" on previous stays. This is not the ideal policy, of course. The social-service director told us that he tried to initiate "a program where a person is allowed to stay for only one week" and is then required to talk with the director "about his situation and come up with a cut-off date." But he conceded that the increasing number of homeless and "the pressure from the city to keep them off the streets" have made it difficult to institute such a program.

These considerations notwithstanding, the Sally actually shelters only a small proportion of the city's homeless. The reasons are threefold, having to do with space, atmosphere, and availability. The dormitory, built at a time when the need for shelter was not so pressing, has room for only twenty-two beds. These are given to the Sally's homeless employees, parolees from the Texas prison system, and occasionally, if there is room, "first nighters."[9] All others are lodged in the recreation room, which is transformed into a sleeping area at night. The Sally can accommodate only around ninety homeless men and another twenty homeless women and children. This dearth of shelter space becomes particularly problematic when the temperature begins to plummet. Recognizing the need for additional shelter, especially during the winter, in 1983 the city council opened a vacant warehouse for use as a makeshift shelter from December 1 to April 30. This provided shelter for around 350 homeless and was operated by the Sally. But the net gain was only 240 shelter spaces, since for lack of personnel to staff both places, the Sally closed its own shelter during this five-month period.

Except for an occasional cold, blustery day, however, the winter shelter is rarely filled to capacity. One reason for its unpopularity is its dreary, forbidding, almost ominous ambience. It is an old meat-packing warehouse with barren concrete walls, a roof that leaks, and iron rails along which sides of beef used to move still hanging from the ceiling. It makes occupants feel truly "warehoused" and reminds them of how far they have fallen. As one observer noted, "There's something ill-boding about down-and-out live men being housed in a building that in its better days was used to house dead animals."

What makes matters even worse is that many of the homeless sleep on two-by-six-foot mats that are too thin to protect them from the bone-chilling cold of the stained, cracked cement floor. The smell of chemicals used to sanitize the four Port-a-Boy johns pervades the warehouse, and a cloud of cigarette smoke hovers midway between the roof and the cement floor. The constant cacophony of coughs, hacks, and muffled talk, punctuated by an occasional scream, makes it impossible to sleep soundly. In fact, the warehouse is not regarded so much as a place to sleep as a temporary retreat from the elements, especially the rain and the cold. Because of such conditions, which a number of well-traveled homeless regarded as among the worst they had experienced, the winter shelter averaged only around 150 lodgers per night.

In Austin, as elsewhere, then, many of the homeless turn their backs on available shelter space. Most do so not because of insanity or judgmental incompetence, as some officials would have us believe, but because of the deplorable and often dehumanizing conditions in shelters.[10] "Fuck it, man," replied one straddler when asked why he did not use the winter shelter, "the conditions at the dog pound are better than in there. I ain't no animal. Hell, I deserve better." Hidden in such comments is a more subtle but perhaps salient reason why the homeless often eschew shelters in favor of makeshift sleeping arrangements: they are exercising a bit of autonomy in a world in which their choices and options are highly constrained.

There are good reasons, then, why many homeless do not embrace existing shelter arrangements. This is further borne out by the finding that the use of free shelter varies considerably among the different types of homeless identified in the previous chapter. The most frequent users of free shelter, with mean scores of 1.00 or above, are the recently dislocated and the straddlers. The remaining types have scores ranging from .71 for the mentally ill to almost 0 for the redneck bums, suggesting that differences in sleeping preferences are also at work in accounting for differences in sleeping arrangements.

Besides such social psychological considerations and spatial constraints, a third factor limits the number of homeless the Sally shelters: its facilities are simply not open or available to all who seek to use them. Like Lazarus at the gate, some homeless are turned away. This is not really surprising. As do all people-processing and service organizations, the Sally must make choices about whom to assist, both because their resources are limited and because the orderly dispensation of services is contingent on client control. As the major in charge of the Sally commented:

> I'll sleep and feed almost anybody, but such help requires that they be deserving. Some people would say I'm cold-hearted, but I rule with an iron hand. I have to because these guys need to respect authority. . . . The experience of working with these guys has taught us the necessity of rules in order to avoid problems.

Thus, the Sally tends to close its doors to the momentarily inebriated, the chronic drunks, and "the troublemakers," those who are deemed both undeserving and difficult to control. In actuality, only a small proportion of the homeless who knock at Sally's door fall into one or more of these categories. But some do, including a number of our key informants. Marilyn, for one, was occasionally denied access to the Sally because of drunkenness. And her friend Nona George, who is a chronic alcoholic, was banned for extended periods of time for both drunken and unruly behavior. In fact, she would boast on occasion that she had been "86'ed from the Sally for giving them a lot of shit."

For all of these reasons, then, the Sally shelters only a small proportion of the city's homeless—perhaps 10 to 20 percent on any given night. But it is the only inn in town, so to speak, so it is the place the homeless turn to when they are new to Austin, when they have been dislodged from their private sleeping arrangements by the police or construction crews, or when the weather turns bad. Even seasoned street veterans like Banjo and Gypsy Bill are driven in by the weather on occasion. One wet, snowy January day when the temperature hovered in the twenties and the Sally opened its rec room early, we found both Banjo and Gypsy, along with two hundred other homeless, bunched together in search of warmth. Banjo much preferred a weed patch or jungle to the Sally, but "the weather was just too damn nasty," he told us. And Gypsy, who customarily slept in his stranded car, "couldn't sleep all last night because of the cold." "I shivered all night," he said. "I didn't have enough blankets to keep warm."

Like bad weather, hunger drives some reluctant homeless into the Sally. As was noted previously, the Sally is the city's only provider of free breakfasts and dinners. In 1984 it served 122 breakfasts and 182 dinners per day. The meals are seldom eaten without complaint and speculation about their "actual" ingredients. One evening, for example, near-consensus was reached that what was alleged to be meat and mashed potatoes was really "Alpo and potatoes." But the meals are eaten, nonetheless, because they momentarily quiet the rumbling of empty stomachs and they are free.

Before relocation of the Sally became a political issue, the homeless would line up for dinner as early as they wanted. But pressure from neighbors of possible relocation sites prompted the Sally to improve its image by demonstrating that it could control its clients. One strategy was to restrict the times at which the homeless could line up for the evening meal. Before the restriction, often four to six men were sitting against the Sally's wall by 11:00 A.M. on Saturday (when food is not available elsewhere) or by 2:30 P.M. on a weekday. After the Sally's downtown location became an issue, the staff forbade the men to line up before 3:15 P.M. They were instructed to congregate instead in the parking lot across the street and wait until the major came out and gave them a nod. Twenty to forty men would then rush across the street to queue up.

Being at the front of the Sally dinner line means more than just getting an early dinner. It also guarantees a good spot for the night in the shelter. On a particularly busy night it may even make the difference between securing a place to stay in the shelter and not getting one. Those at the front of the dinner line also had a chance of showering at the Sally, until it changed its policy, opening the showers only to staff, families, and women staying overnight.[11]

The Sally offers a few other services, such as free used clothes and shoes, and even some counseling for women and families, but for the most part, at least for unattached males, its services are limited to the provision of food and shelter. This is also true for Caritas and Angels House, two other agencies that figure prominently in the local subculture of street life.

Caritas is a private, nonprofit charity started by a local Catholic priest and funded by city and county grants, United Way, and several local churches. It provides an array of services to the local poor, including housing and financial assistance for families, employment counseling, clothing vouchers for use at a nearby St. Vincent de Paul, bus passes for travel to and from work, and vouchers for rooms at local motels.[12]

Although none of these services is earmarked specifically for the homeless, they utilize a number of them, as nearly 38 percent of the tracking sample has had one or more service contacts. Most of the services, such as the bus passes and clothing and hotel vouchers, have been accommodative in nature. Few of the homeless in our sample received employment or housing assistance, in part because the bulk of the assistance available is reserved for families and in part because many of the homeless are not deemed worthy of such assistance, at least in comparison to other constituents. Like most social-service agencies confronted with an imbalance between increasing demand for assistance and available facilities and resources, Caritas found it necessary to reduce its pool of eligible clients by distinguishing the deserving from the undeserving. Thus, when a homeless person requests services, he or she is referred to a caseworker who will screen for, among other things, the person's "salvageability." As the director of Caritas explained:

> When these people come in, you've got to size them up, see what they're really like. . . . It's important that the caseworker not be too cynical, though. Otherwise they would never offer services to anyone. But it's also important to look for something in the individual that makes you feel they might be salvageable.

The losers in this winnowing process typically are the unattached homeless adults, particularly the males. But their service-seeking is not completely in vain, since Caritas operates a free-sandwich program each weekday morning. Here the homeless can pick up two bologna sandwiches and a vitamin-fortified beverage between 9:00 and 11:00 each morning. Since this is the only free-food program operating between 6:00 A.M., when the Sally stops serving breakfast, and 11:30, when Angels House opens for lunch, it is Caritas's most heavily used service.

In 1984 Caritas handed out sandwiches to 130 homeless per day, and on any given weekday morning a dozen or more homeless could be seen eating their sandwiches and hanging out on the large front porch. Some of them napped, others clustered into small conversational groups, talking about recent and past experiences. Still others kept to themselves, tossing pieces of bread crust to the pigeons, and a few drifted off into their own world, seemingly oblivious to those around them. Occasionally a person with a shopping cart full of belongings or aluminum cans would park his or her cart, mount the steps to the porch and front door, pick up a sandwich or two, and then return to the cart and move on. A few day laborers who managed to get a late job stopped by to pick up sandwiches before going to their job sites. But most of the homeless who came for a sandwich or two lingered for a bit, whiling away a portion of the morning.

There are few places in the downtown area where the homeless are not discouraged from passing time, but the Caritas porch is one of those few. Caritas thus provides not only a late breakfast or mid-morning snack, depending on one's perspective for that day, but also a temporary refuge.

By late morning, though, the porch is nearly deserted. The sandwich service has closed for the day and many homeless have begun to migrate to the city's only soup kitchen, about a mile away. Angels House, a church-supported charity, provides the city's only free lunch. It is operated by a strict evangelical brother of the Benedictine order, who sees his mission as one of "reaching people with effective values." He realizes that this is a rather idyllic objective, especially when people are down-and-out and hungry, so he concedes that "our more immediate concern is with keeping their bodies alive" by providing hot lunches. "The body," he explains, "is the vehicle of our ministry."

Angels House attends to this mission by serving an average of 150 lunches each weekday between 11:30 in the morning and 2:00 in the afternoon. The fulfillment of this mission, however, has not been a particularly easy task. Located on the downtown edge of the East Austin barrio, Angels incurred the wrath of residents and small businessmen in the area, who complained frequently and vociferously about "the riffraff" the kitchen attracts. As the director explained in a letter sent to supporters:

> Some of our neighbors have routed them [the homeless] from the sidewalks. One merchant brought over to me one morning a sack full of trash, dumping it at my feet. "Here!" he said. "Keep the trash from your derelicts to yourself!" I replied: "I'm afraid they're OUR derelicts!" Yes, our neighbors have

borne their burden poorly . . . no neighborhood in Austin wants the needy.
. . . Eggs have broken our window, paint has smeared our walls, neighbors
have criticized our presence to the City Council.

The director responded by trying to limit the time the homeless are
in the area. A sign on the front of the building reads: "Please do not
come to this area before 11:15," and the homeless are expected to eat
their meal and leave immediately. No loitering or post-meal socializing
is tolerated. The director supervises the meal and maintains a high degree of orderliness in the operation. As is illustrated by the following
excerpt from a handout the director gives new kitchen users, Angels has
almost as harsh an image of the people it serves as do many of their
angry neighbors:

> WELCOME TO ANGELS HOUSE! Angels House is a Christian ministry to per-
> sons who need a meal. . . . A person who comes to Angels House for help
> should realize that he or she has a serious life problem including bad habits,
> some of which are willful idleness, lack of self-discipline at the job site, al-
> coholism, drug abuse including nicotine addiction, chronic faultfinding with
> others and general unruliness. ANGELS HOUSE DOES NOT EXIST TO SUPPORT
> PEOPLE WHO WILLFULLY AND CONSISTENTLY INDULGE ANY OF THESE BAD
> HABITS. Evidence of refusal to turn away from these bad habits . . . will be
> grounds for denying help at Angels House. YOU MAY BE ASKED TO LEAVE
> AND NOT RETURN TO ANGELS HOUSE UNTIL YOU WANT TO LEAD A NEW LIFE.

Angels House provides a hot lunch, but it is not particularly hospi-
table otherwise to the homeless. The director is quick to follow through
on his threat to deny meals to those who do not meet his behavioral
standards. Marilyn and many of her acquaintances were banned from
Angels for having shown up drunk, and those who do use the kitchen
quickly return to the west side of town after they eat. Unlike the Caritas
porch, Angels' patio dining area is not a secure retreat in which to pass
time.[13] It is a place to get a hot lunch, though, and it thereby facilitates
the survival of some of the homeless.

The Benedictine brother in charge of Angels would like to do more
than help the homeless subsist. His primary mission, he unabashedly
asserts, is "to save souls" by introducing "people to the values found in
the Scriptures." He sees the homeless as being on a "spiritual pilgrimage" of sorts and thus "open to spiritual regeneration." But neither he
nor others have been very successful in fulfilling this mission, as he ad-
mits readily but in frustration. He ascribes the derailing of the mission
to the overwhelming number of homeless and to agency preoccupation
with "keeping bodies alive," with resultant neglect of "their Christian

values." It is in this regard that he frequently chastises both Caritas and the Sally. "Both are failing their spiritual mission," he says, because "they are not saving souls." [14]

In some respects the heads of Caritas and the Sally would agree with their evangelical critic. "We would like to do more," mused the Sally's major one day in a moment of realistic reflection, "but as it is now we're little more than a turn-key operation. We accommodate them the best we can, but that's about it."

The homeless are also keenly aware of this accommodative function and its insufficiency. As Tony Jones, the recently dislocated man from Chicago, observed as he was standing in the dinner line one evening, "The Sally doesn't really do anything for these people. It just gives 'em something to eat and a place to sleep, but it doesn't really help them get off the streets." Echoing Tony's sentiments, Banjo observed that "everybody's back in the same spot in the morning as they were the night before, because the Sally don't do anything here but give people food and a place to sleep." Banjo had a solution—one that would put a smile on the face of the director of Angels House. An ardent, born-again Christian, Banjo saw salvation as the answer. "People need something to put their faith in, but most street people don't have anything," he preached. "They're like shifting sand. But God is solid rock." The problem, as Banjo saw it, was that the Sally had abandoned its mission. Instead of saving souls and giving the homeless "something to put their faith in," the Sally was merely "feeding and sleeping."

Neither the major nor the Sally's social services director would take exception to Banjo's lament. On the contrary, this disjunction between their idealized mission and what they were actually doing was a constant source of frustration. They could rationalize it by pointing to the growing imbalance between the demand for assistance and available facilities and resources, but the fact remained that they were conducting "little more than a turn-key operation" that left their clients standing in "shifting sand."

This dilemma is clearly not the Sally's alone. As we have seen, Caritas and Angels House also found themselves sustaining physical functioning to the neglect of the more lofty objective of spiritual and economic renewal. To highlight this disparity between the idealized functions of these agencies and the services they actually deliver is not to disparage those services. Indeed, many of the homeless, including most of the recently dislocated, would be hard-pressed to survive were it not for the food and shelter provided by these agencies. But the fact remains that these services are basically accommodative: they help the homeless endure life on the streets rather than escape it.

RESTORATIVE RESPONSE

A second set of organizations that deal with a segment of the homeless approach them primarily from a treatment-oriented rather than a sustenance-oriented perspective. Their general aim is to attend to actual or perceived physiological, psychological, or spiritual problems that are seen as impeding their clients' functioning. The response these caretaker organizations make to the homeless is more rehabilitative than accommodative. Examples of such institutions include mental hospitals, outpatient mental-health facilities, regular hospitals, drug and alcohol rehabilitation clinics, detoxification facilities, various counseling services, and some skid row–like missions that make access contingent on participation in salvationist rituals. In Austin, at least four caretaker organizations or agency complexes fall into this treatment-oriented category. They include the city's major hospital, the state's mental health and mental retardation facilities, several detoxification facilities and substance-treatment programs, and the homeless outreach program of the Central Assembly of God Church.

None of these treatment-oriented caretaker facilities is concerned with the problem of homelessness per se. Rather, their attention is focused on homeless individuals and the problems they are perceived as having, be they physiological, psychological, characterological, or spiritual in origin. Agency personnel recognize that many of the homeless are on the streets because of socioeconomic forces beyond their control. Even the head preacher of the homeless ministry at the Assembly of God church conceded that some of the homeless he knows "are on the streets because of social circumstances." But this group, often referred to as the "new poor" or "the new and temporary homeless," is seldom seen as comprising more than 20 to 30 percent of the homeless. The majority are seen as riddled with physical or mental problems, interactional incompetencies, and characterological flaws. Such a view is not surprising. Not only do these remedial caretaker organizations see some homeless who indeed suffer from such problems, but since the agencies have neither the mandate nor the wherewithal to alter socioeconomic forces, they are unlikely to focus on such issues. What they can do, however, is exactly what they do: treat individual ailments, whether actual or perceived, or arrange for such treatment.

This commonality notwithstanding, these caretaker organizations espouse a variety of treatment-oriented ideologies. At one extreme, as is noted in the middle column of Table 3.1, is the medical model or perspective, and at the other is the salvationist or conversionist orientation. The former see many of the problems of the homeless as symptomatic of illness or at least as treatable within a medical framework. The salvationists, by contrast, identify the issue as one of moral weakness and spiritual degeneration. The city hospital and mental-health facilities approach the homeless from a medical standpoint, whereas the Assembly of God church is almost purely salvationist. The several detoxification facilities slide on this continuum, but tend to be skewed toward the salvationist orientation.

These remedial caretaker organizations also vary in the scope of their aims. Some seek only to repair debilitating physical ailments as quickly and cheaply as possible so that the client can be sent on his or her way, typically back to the social niche from which he or she came. This is the approach taken by the city hospital, where the vast majority of the homeless are seen on an outpatient basis, typically in the emergency room, and then sent back onto the streets. This pattern of contact is clearly reflected in our tracking data. As is indicated in Table 3.2, which shows the distribution of hospital contacts among the homeless in the tracking sample, 94 percent of the 174 homeless with one or more contacts received outpatient treatment in the emergency room; in other words, they were treated and released. In contrast, fewer than 25 percent received inpatient treatment; that is, less than a quarter ever stayed overnight in a hospital bed.

The kinds of contacts these homeless had are at least partially explicable by the sorts of problems that sent them to the hospital: cuts and abrasions (20 percent), followed in descending order by alcohol- and drug-related ailments (13 percent), fractures and sprains (12 percent), and skin infections (11 percent).[15] However, although such ailments are acute rather than chronic, there is little question but that the healing process would be expedited if some homeless with these ailments were hospitalized. Marilyn's experience with a broken ankle provides a case in point. She slipped on ice one wintry January evening while on her way to a motel room she and four other homeless were renting for the night. The next day she went to the city hospital and was diagnosed as having a sprained ankle. The ankle was taped and she was sent on her way with instructions to stay off her feet. Such directions are difficult enough for the domiciled to follow; when a person is homeless and her

TABLE 3.2   NATURE OF CITY HOSPITAL
CONTACTS AMONG THE HOMELESS

Type of Contact	Homeless Persons with Contact in Each Category		Total Contacts in Each Category	
	(N: 174)		(N: 508)	
	No.	%*	No.	%
Inpatient/nonemergency (regular admission)	(15)	8.6	(19)	3.7
Inpatient/emergency (admission through emergency)	(25)	14.4	(31)	6.1
Outpatient/emergency	(163)	93.7	(401)	78.9
Hospital clinic	(23)	13.2	(57)	11.2

*Total for this column is more than 100 percent because many of the homeless had contacts in more than one category.

feet are her primary mode of transportation, they are impossible. Not surprisingly, then, Marilyn returned to the hospital a few days later complaining of persistent pain. Her ankle was examined again and rediagnosed as broken. It was placed in a cast and she was again sent on her way, albeit with crutches this time. Clearly her ankle would have benefited more from several days of bed rest than from beating the pavement to and from the hospital. But hospitalization, even just for a bed, is quite expensive, so the homeless and other indigents are dealt with as outpatients.

Exceptions occur, of course, as when an acquaintance of Marilyn's, nicknamed Giggles, was hospitalized for several days before she died of cirrhosis of the liver. Giggles was obviously in a life-threatening situation, and it is in such situations that the homeless are most likely to be hospitalized. But we suspect that the number who are seriously ill is far greater than the number who are admitted to a hospital bed. For one thing, the homeless tend not to be very attentive to their physical condition until they are incapacitated, as Marilyn was, or gravely ill, as was Giggles. Physical complaints that prompt remedial action by the domiciled, middle-class citizen are likely to be ignored by the homeless.[16] Not only do the needs of daily subsistence seem more pressing, but medical facilities that treat the homeless are not always within easy walking distance. Thus, Tom Fisk had deep, infected cuts on his right hand for several days before he went to the hospital. Gypsy Bill ignored an infection on one hand until it began to move up his arm. He was diagnosed as having a staph infection, given some antibiotics, and sent back onto the streets. And a young female hippie tramp failed for some time to seek medical attention for a severe leg infection. She had initially broken an ankle and had had a cast put on it at the city hospital. When she was sleeping rough shortly afterward, fire ants crawled into the cast and infected her encased foot. The end result was gangrene and several weeks in the hospital.

Such hospitalizations are rare, though, not only for the reasons indicated above but also because the hospital is disinclined to keep the homeless overnight because they are financial liabilities. According to one of the hospital's administrators, the homeless cannot pay their own way, they find it difficult to qualify for medical financial assistance because of residency requirements, and the funds provided by the city to help cover the hospital's "indigent" debt have not kept pace with the city's growing indigent population and its utilization of the hospital. Consequently, the hospital tries to avoid inpatient care for the homeless except in life-threatening situations. Still, 81 percent of the total cost of treatment for the homeless in 1984 was in the inpatient category, even though fewer than 25 percent of the homeless who received medical care from the hospital received such treatment.[17]

In practice, then, the hospital has dealt with the homeless in a Band-Aid, revolving-door fashion, quickly dispensing remedial assistance and sending them back onto the streets. And, in time, many return for further treatment, as is indicated by the fact that 50 percent of the homeless in our sample with hospital contact had at least two contacts and 26 percent had four or more contacts.

A similar short-term, revolving-door pattern is evident in the relationship between the homeless and the state's psychiatric hospital system and local mental-health centers. This pattern is due in no small part to the outpatient orientation of the local catchment center, but it also surfaces upon inspection of the length and frequency of institutionalization of the homeless within the state hospital system. Of the eighty-four homeless in the tracking sample who were institutionalized one or more times, two-thirds were hospitalized for less than thirty days, and none stayed longer than three months.[18] The frequency of these commitments, which were voluntary in nearly 60 percent of the cases, ranged from one to fifteen, with two-thirds having one or two commitments.

The remaining third experienced a revolving-door pattern of brief, re-peated voluntary stays—entering from the streets and exiting back to the streets.

Lance McCay's experience is illustrative. During the four-year period between September, 1980, and October, 1984, Lance was institution-alized on fourteen different occasions. Nine of the commitments were for seven days or less, two were for one to two weeks, and four were for between one and three months. Jorge Herrera's record is less clear, but he, too, was institutionalized within the state hospital system on numerous occasions between 1966 and 1974. What is more, both Lance and Jorge continued to be obviously mentally ill, whatever the diagnos-tic criteria used.

Contact between the homeless and the mental health system is not extensive, at least not in Austin. All told, 16 percent of the tracking sample had one or more contacts with this system: eighty-four with the state institutions, seventy-eight with the local outpatient center, and thirty-eight with both. Clearly, the mental health system does not figure as prominently in the subculture of street life as either the accommodative street agencies or the city hospital. But it still casts a shadow over the lives of around a sixth of the homeless.[19] It tends to be revolving-door contact, though, like that with the city hospital, characterized by a brief encounter, often followed by a series of visits. Moreover, any treatment is of the stop-the-bleeding rather than cure-the-wound variety. Some of the homeless in need are attended to, but they are not so much cured as restored to a level of physical or psychic functioning that allows them to limp back to the streets.

The Central Assembly of God Church is also in the business of res-toration, but from a salvationist rather than a medical operating per-spective. Its central objective with respect to the homeless is to move them toward a more responsible life-style by converting them to the way of the Lord. Underlying this objective is the view that the homeless are partly responsible for their own plight, as is evidenced, according to the preacher, by "their excessive carousing and drinking." From his vantage point, the homeless are rather "like the errant sheep" in the parable of the good shepherd that is "in need of a lesson in order to keep it from straying off." Obviously, the pastor sees himself and his congregation in the role of the good shepherd, trying to salvage the homeless by, in his words, "getting them high and drunk on Jesus." As he reminds his regular church members on occasion, "we have been blessed because God has given us a place in the street ministry."

Because the church is located on the outskirts of the city, it buses the homeless to its premises from several points downtown. The major service for the homeless runs from 9:30 to 1:00 on Sundays, attracting, on average, 125 to 150 homeless. The morning begins with donuts and coffee, while several regular church members circulate among the homeless exchanging pleasantries and attempting to bolster their spirits. Then, after an hour-long gospel service, a hearty meal is served. In the restroom at the back of the building in which these services are conducted are several showers, which are in use throughout most of the morning. The homeless are instructed to limit their showers to before and after the service, but occasionally someone will slip in during the service. At one point during one of the services, for example, a feisty young homeless man came running out of the restroom yelling, "I'll give ten dollars to whoever finds the motherfucker that stole the radio out of my pack while I was showering!" Halting his sermon, the preacher ran to the back with an assistant and quieted the irate man. He then returned to the pulpit, using the interruption as an occasion to remind the homeless of the persistent attempts of the devil to frustrate the work of the Lord.

For most of the homeless who make these Sunday mornings at the church part of their weekly routine, the appeal is not so much the gospel service as it is a solid Sunday meal and an opportunity to shower. The church functions much like the traditional skid-row rescue mission, offering food and other amenities in exchange for attendance at its gospel services.[20] Most of the homeless think it is a fair exchange, though; otherwise they would stay away. As Pat Manchester explained:

> You gotta sit through an hour's ear-banging. But then they feed you like kings. Yeah, it's worth it. I had three plates of spaghetti today, and salad and cake and pie. And last week they had chicken-fried steak.

Not all of the homeless find value only in the meals, however. For some the gospel service provides the attraction. Banjo, for one, comes every week and "looks forward to it all week long," he says, " 'cause it gives me a spiritual lift for the rest of the week." Willie Hastings, too, looked forward to the spiritual fellowship of the services and frequently went to Sunday evening services as well when he could get a ride. For at least a handful of homeless individuals, then, the church functions somewhat in accord with its idealized mission of spiritual restoration.

The final set of restorative caretaker organizations that affect the lives and routines of some of the homeless are the drug and alcohol rehabilitation facilities. Of the four such facilities in the area, two deal almost exclusively with the homeless. One is an in-town facility operated by the Salvation Army; the other, a rural facility operated by a private, nonprofit corporation. Both facilities provide residential treatment for chronic inebriates, especially of the traditional tramp and bum varieties. The majority of the clients of each facility are older than the average street person, and they are long-term alcoholics. Many of them, according to the head of the Salvation Army rehabilitation facility, "come into the program in rough physical shape . . . with ulcers, parasites, and broken bones that haven't healed right and need attention." Even more damaging, she emphasized, is that "they have all sunk into moral turpitude as alcohol has taken control of their lives." Or, as the ex-alcoholic in charge of day operations at the rural facility described his constituency, "They are real down-and-outers." As a consequence, he added, "This is not a place for virgins."

The treatment programs at both facilities are AA-oriented and thus are skewed toward the salvationist perspective. This quickly appears at the Salvation Army's evening meetings, where much of the time is spent discussing the "second step" of the AA doctrine: "Believe that a power greater than ourselves can restore us to sanity." Such a step may not be easy. One of the men we came to know, a fellow in his mid-thirties named Alvin, complained that he was "just unable to take that leap of faith." He was not the only homeless person to express such reservations. Still, these detox and rehab facilities, as they are commonly called on the streets, provide a place to dry out and regain a modicum of health. Thus, when the homeless leave, they typically are better off physically than when they arrived.

Yet these rehab programs are only partially successful at best. They restore their clients' health so that they can function physically, but they seldom provide the resources or training their clients need in order "to get back into society." Consequently, clients often end up back on the streets after being discharged. This was a constant concern for Alvin, as we will see in the next chapter. Moreover, once back on the streets, they quickly return to their old ways and frequently end up in another detox program. The day operator of the rural rehab facility told us that "most of the men who are here have been in and out of treatment program after program." We had sensed this anyway, especially after getting to know Shotgun, Hoyt, Nona, and Willie Hastings, all of whom have experienced that revolving door.[21]

Like the city hospital, mental health facilities, and Assembly of God church, the detox and rehab facilities seem more effective at dispensing palliatives than curatives. In each case, an attempt is made to restore the physical, mental, or spiritual health of the homeless sufficiently to return them to the streets in better shape than they were in when they entered the facility. But these restorative agencies, whether their treatment is medically or spiritually based, seem to do little to help their clients climb back into the domiciled world. They are, then, only restorative in part and thus complement the more accommodative caretaker agencies.

EXPLOITATIVE RESPONSE

A third set of organizational actors that cater to the homeless do so from a market-oriented perspective. This perspective, unlike the caretaker perspectives, shows little authentic concern with the welfare of the homeless. Rather, the homeless are commodified as sources of cheap labor and plasma or are approached as just another set of consumers. In either case, the homeless become objects of economic exploitation.

Several commercial organizations in Austin deal with the homeless in this fashion. The two plasma centers near the university clearly fall into this category, as do the two downtown day-labor operations, one sanctioned by the city and the other run by a Houston-based corporation.

The Houston-based company also operates the Bunkhaus, a hundred-bed barracks-style boarding house in east Austin, about three miles from its downtown day-labor operation, the Labor Pool. Although the Bunkhaus is a late addition to the institutional sector of the city's street subculture, it quickly came to be favored by some of the homeless as a place to stay at night because it has showers available and has fewer restrictions than the Salvation Army. The men can bring beer into the boarding house and drink while watching the color cable television, and they sleep on army-style bunks instead of mats. There is a catch, though. It cost $6.50 per night. This amount, insignificant for most working non-homeless, means a good deal to the homeless, for whom work is unsteady and wages are minimal. Nonetheless, the Bunkhaus is generally full. The lights go out at 10:00 P.M. and on at 5:00 A.M. Free coffee is served from 5:00 to 5:30, and a van is available for a ride downtown to the Labor Pool, where the men can sign on for day-labor jobs.

In return, the corporation siphons off a portion of the wages earned by those lucky enough to secure a job for the day. A van awaits those who want to return to the Bunkhaus for the night. Thus, if a homeless person grosses $15.00 for four to five hours of work, his net after the Labor Pool takes out income tax, Social Security, and other deductions and the $6.50 for the Bunkhaus is a little less than $5.50, barely enough for dinner and a couple of beers or a bottle of "Thunder Chicken" or "Mad Dog 20/20." When the $6.50 extracted for the Bunkhaus is added to the money the Labor Pool received from the employers for the labor exchange services provided, it becomes clear that the company is conducting a profitable business. Indeed, it is already operating in three other Texas cities, and the manager has commented, "We're doing so well that we're planning to expand to other cities!"[22]

As we will see in the next two chapters, the plasma centers also find the homeless to be a source of profit, as do those building contractors and other industries who hire the homeless for day labor. This exploitative response is not without some benefit to the homeless, though. A cheap place to sleep and money, albeit minimal, for giving blood or working by the day facilitate the daily survival of the homeless. But the exchange relationship is uneven and exploitative: money is being made off of the homeless at a rate that is seemingly far greater than the value they receive in return.

EXCLUSIONIST/EXPULSIONIST RESPONSE

In whatever city the homeless find themselves, their daily routines and survival options are likely to be affected by a political climate that slides on a continuum ranging from generosity to hostility. At one end of the scale, the homeless are objects of sympathy who are seen as victims of social forces and bad luck. At the other, they are objects of fear and scorn who are thought to have chosen this way of life and who therefore should be run out of town or at least constrained ecologically so that they do not contaminate respectable citizens. Both orientations can be found in most communities, and which sentiment predominates is likely to vary over time. But at any particular moment within a given community, the political climate with respect to the homeless is likely to be skewed in one direction or the other. If it is in the direction of sympathy, the homeless are likely to feel more welcome and to have greater latitude for pursuing their survival routines. If hostility rules, then they are likely to feel less welcome and to have less elbow room for making do. Either attitude is likely to affect their survival routines.

In Austin, the dominant sentiment and corresponding political climate became increasingly hostile as the city's homeless population began to mount in the early 1980s and the pending relocation of the Salvation Army shelter became a community issue. Outcroppings of something other than sympathetic concern for the homeless first surfaced in 1982, when City Hall began to receive a steady flow of complaints from business proprietors around the Salvation Army shelter and from citizens using the nearby park system along the river. One of the more persistent complainants, a real estate broker whose office was several blocks east of the Sally, related that although he knew "the homeless have their problems," they also "create big problems," especially "when you get hundreds of them together hanging out in the same area. They shit in the bushes. They steal and sleep in our yard and on our porch, and they hassle the customers. You name it," he complained, "we've had it." To strengthen his case, he took us on a tour of his property, pointing out the sleeping "nests" the homeless made in the bamboo and weeds and even the scattered piles of feces where they had relieved themselves.

At the urging of this complainant and other concerned citizens, in the spring of 1983 the city formulated its initial Task Force on the Homeless. Its appointed members included four business proprietors and representatives from the Sally, the police department, Caritas, TEC, and three other social-service agencies. Its chair, who also headed the Greater Austin Track Club, had gotten involved because he "was sick and tired of being hassled by the homeless while running along the river."[23] Six months later the task force issued a list of recommendations, including establishment of a controlled day-labor pick-up site; strict enforcement of city ordinances that prohibit sleeping in public places, begging, and public intoxication; construction of a minimum-security detention center for persons arrested on misdemeanors such as public intoxication; and establishment of a temporary winter shelter.[24] Taken together, the recommendations seemed aimed at controlling and segregating the city's homeless population. The task force was not oblivious to the needs of the homeless, but, according to one of its members, it felt that "there's a real danger of doing too much." As this individual explained, "Word travels fast in the underground of street people. Austin has a problem because of a good climate and the abundance of work anyway. So if we provide good social services the word will get out, and pretty soon . . . trouble."

Trouble over the homeless was already beginning to percolate within the community, but it was hardly due to the provision of services. With only one legitimate street shelter, one soup kitchen, and a mid-morning sandwich spot, Austin's street services for the homeless were meager in comparison to those available in other cities of similar size. Instead, the rumblings of citizen unrest were over the pending relocation of the Salvation Army.

The Sally had to move not only because the building was too small but also because its weathered appearance was out of step with the glittering redevelopment of much of the downtown. Moreover, the land it sat on was coveted by developers, one of whom eventually bought the lot for $1,500,000—$750,000 cash plus title to 3.74 acres several miles south of the downtown but still within the city.

The path to a new site was thorny, engendering rancorous community opposition as it wound its way through one prospective neighborhood after another before ending up back in the downtown area within a block of the city police station. Underlying citizen opposition to the "frightening possibility" of the Sally relocating nearby was the repeatedly voiced fear that "thousands of womanless, homeless men" would inundate their neighborhoods and "rob their homes" and "rape the women." Thus, in one prospective neighborhood, signs were hung on doors asking, "Do you want your women raped and your children mauled?" In another, residents appeared before the city council carrying placards that read "Vagrance [sic] and kids don't mix" and gave testimony highlighting the threat to women and children posed by the homeless. One neighborhood resident emphasized "how the neighborhoods will be unfit for raising children," and another angrily asked the council whether they understood the "impact these womanless men will have on schoolchildren, on women, and on families." The local Catholic university located adjacent to one of the prospective sites joined the resistance, similarly framing its opposition in terms of the danger the homeless posed to its students. As the chairman of the university's board of trustees emphasized on three different occasions at one board meeting: "We have to be able to reassure the thousand coeds on campus, and I don't think we can."

Such beliefs and fears were succinctly rationalized by a prominent local resident in one of her occasional columns written for the city newspaper:

> What the good people of Austin and everywhere have come to fear are the unpredictable ones who have joined the vast army of the indigent and who are being dumped on Sally as the last resort. I speak of the young, strong, but stoned druggies whose next move may be robbery, assault, or murder

... [and] the criminals dumped by the justice system from overcrowded prisons and jails and left to prey on the innocent, just as they did before incarceration. Salvation Army is not to blame because the nature of the clientele has changed from the hobo of the 1930's to the wino of the 1950's to the unpredictable stranger of the 1980's. But neither are the upstanding citizens of Austin to be blamed for looking over their shoulders.

Thus, the dominant local perception of the homeless evolved from one that portrayed them as public nuisances whose routines interfered with those of other citizens to one that framed them as dangerous criminals who threatened the lives and property of others, particularly women and children.[25] The result was a decline in sympathy for the homeless and the emergence of an exclusionist/expulsionist response that said, "Don't put the homeless in my backyard, and if they're already there, get rid of them."[26] For the homeless, this meant a darkening of the cloud that already hung over their heads, a corresponding narrowing of their survival options, and increased official attentiveness to some of their daily routines. Shotgun, the traditional tramp who had traveled widely, was street-smart, and claimed to "have a sense about these things," related one morning at the outset of the Sally furor, "the police here used to be less into hassling street people than in other places I've been. But I've got this funny feeling that something's about to happen, like the police are going to start coming down on people."

CONTAINMENT RESPONSE

Shotgun's premonition was grounded not only in the contentious political climate spawned by local neighborhood associations but also in the increased vigilance of the police. The police were not particularly enthused about getting involved in this political issue, however. For one thing, there was reluctance to deal with "the wider social problems." One of the officers in charge of the uniform patrol division made this clear on several occasions. He emphasized that "it stretches our responsibility and resources to have to deal with problems like homelessness." There was also a sense that whatever the police did, "it won't be enough as long as this Sally thing is an issue." But, most important, the police were keenly aware that neighborhood claims and fears had little empirical substance. Their own preliminary figures on crime among the homeless who had been arrested revealed that only 5 percent were arrested for felonies, around 62 percent for public intoxication, and the remaining 33 percent for other misdemeanors.[27] Thus, at one of the

initial meetings of the city's second Task Force on the Homeless a perceptive police officer explained, "The problem with the homeless . . . is
not necessarily how criminal they are, but how the public perceives
them to be criminal. What is actually true and what the public feels or
is afraid of may be two different things."[28] And indeed they were. But
neighborhood assertions drowned out the actual facts, pressuring the
police into greater vigilance toward the homeless.

Like most police work, the police response toward the homeless was
essentially reactive, in that it was conducted in response to calls for
increased vigilance. But it was conducted, not on behalf of the homeless, but for the benefit of other citizens who were the primary complainants.[29] This distinction was not lost on the homeless. Hoyt, who
worked at the Sally, often complained about the treatment he thought
the homeless received relative to other groups. He told us a number of
times, "We can call the cops down at the Sally, and it takes them forty-
five minutes to get there." To illustrate, he related the following instance:

> Did you see the fight here a couple of weeks ago with the James Gang [the
> redneck tramps]? . . . About forty-five minutes after the police were called,
> they arrived. And there's a fight out there in the middle of Second Avenue,
> stopping traffic for fifteen minutes or so. In other parts of town, the police
> would come faster, you know. Guys on the streets see that and they don't
> think it's fair. They got their own problems, you know. It's no wonder a lot
> of them hate the cops!

Marilyn's sentiments were similar, as the following excerpt from our
field notes shows:

> As we were walking in the vicinity of the Sally early this morning, we spotted
> Marilyn from a distance. She had on a pair of baggy, ragged jeans, and she
> was limping worse than the last time we saw her. When we got closer, we
> could see that her face was swollen. She seemed in pretty bad shape, and we
> thought she might have just come off a long drunk. But she was stone sober.
> She greeted us, then shook her head dispiritedly and stretched out her arms
> for us to look at. There were two open wounds the size of dimes on her left
> arm, and both arms were scraped. We asked her what had happened. She
> said she was "jumped the other night by three men." She "was walking back
> from Brackenridge to find a place to sleep for the night when three men
> hanging out in front of Twin Liquors followed me and drug me into an
> alley." There "they stripped off my clothes, beat and kicked me, and robbed
> me of twenty-five bucks, a necklace, and my watch." They also "put ciga-
> rettes out on my arms." When we asked whether she had reported the inci-

dent to the police, she said she "never even considered it. The law wouldn't
do anything anyway. They'd just say I'm a tramp and let it go. The law won't
help a tramp."

Many of the homeless, then, seemed to see themselves as victims rather
than beneficiaries of police work. This is not surprising, considering the
other characteristic feature of the police response to the homeless. It is
captured by the word *containment*. Applied to the homeless, containment is a mode of response that seeks to minimize the threat they pose
to the sense of public order by curtailing their mobility or ecological
range and by reducing their public visibility. Its aim, as one police officer put it in an offhand way, "is to keep the homeless out of the face of
other citizens."

The police department pursued this objective through four interconnected lines of action. One entailed stricter enforcement of existing ordinances regarding begging, public intoxication, and disorderly conduct, coupled with an appeal to City Hall to pass ordinances prohibiting
both the use of city land between 12:00 midnight and 5:00 A.M. and
"sleeping in any public place, vehicle or building not designated for
overnight sleeping."[30] In order to assure enforcement of these ordinances, the police asked for both additional manpower and a minimum-security detention center to avoid overcrowding the city jail with
persons arrested on misdemeanor charges. This latter request seemed
especially reasonable in the light of police statistics suggesting that most
homeless arrests were for misdemeanors and the fact that violations of
the existing and proposed ordinances are misdemeanors. The most visible outcomes of the requests, though, were an increase in the number
of foot patrolmen and the addition of a mounted patrol in the downtown area, concentrated on the revitalized Sixth Street strip of bars and
honky-tonk clubs that functioned as the hub of the city's night life and
on the Drag, where the hippie tramps hung out. Plainclothesmen were
also dispatched to the Drag.

The result was a more enthusiastic and focused vigilance that smacked
of harassment. Whether the harassment was attributable to officially
formulated policy or to overly zealous and unconstrained street officers
is unclear. That it occurred, though, seems incontestable. Not only was
it felt by the homeless, but we too observed it rather frequently. Late
one afternoon at the south end of the Drag, for example, we saw a
panhandler, to whom we had just given some change, shoved up against
a sign by two preppily dressed young men. Thinking they were a couple

of college students harassing the guy, we ran over to them to intervene. As we approached, they pulled out their police IDs and told us, "Get out of here if you don't want to be a part of it." They then proceeded to empty the man's pockets and frisk him, whereupon one of them said, "What do you think you're doing, asking me if I want to fight? Now pick up your stuff and get off my street." We followed them into a nearby convenience store to press them a bit about what had just transpired. They were obviously uninterested in talking, but they did say they were undercover police officers whose job was "to arrest transients on the Drag." They justified their aggressive action in this case by claiming the guy had "tried to pick a fight" with them—a reversal of what had actually happened.

On another occasion, when we were sitting on the ledge outside the Sally talking with Pat Manchester and some other homeless, we observed a similar instance of questionable police action:

> Several police cars pulled up in response to a call from the Sally about a troublesome drunk. Two officers got out and were greeted by a couple of guys working at the Sally. They pointed out the drunk, who was propped up against the building. The police told the man to get up and put his hands on his head. After he struggled to his feet, the police frisked him. As he was being frisked the drunk stepped on one of the officer's shoes. The officer shook his head and told the guy, who was too inebriated to understand, "Well, now you did it. . . . Now I'm going to have to get you for assault." This statement wasn't lost on the other homeless, one of whom said, "Man, that's tight. Step on a cop's shoe and he gets you for assault." The other officer, apparently wanting to get some action too, came over to the rest of us on the ledge and told us, "Get up, turn around, and put your hands on the ledge." He then proceeded to frisk us.

In this and the previous episode we see police action toward the homeless that is unprovoked and excessive, and that seemingly disregards the issue of culpability. Previous research on police work on skid row has noted that although "it is well known that policemen exercise discretionary freedom in invoking the law," the exercise of such discretion was particularly pronounced on skid row where there was little regard for questions of culpability and heightened ad hoc decision-making.[31] These observations apply equally to police work we observed among the homeless, with the addendum that it often had a flavor of harassment.[32]

All of these police behaviors were experienced one evening when one of us was arrested with two homeless males near Sixth Street, in the downtown area. As we were sitting under a bridge on the bank of the creek with a couple of open cans of beer, two police officers approached. They demanded identification and asked about our places of residence. When the two homeless men were unable to provide IDs and admitted having stayed at the Salvation Army, they were immediately arrested and handcuffed for violation of the city's ordinance prohibiting open containers of alcohol near the Sixth Street area. The researcher, who had provided an ID and a local address, was simply told to leave the area. It was only after he protested the arrest that the researcher was arrested too. The arresting officer informed him, "I was going to let you go because you're cleaner than they are and you have a place to stay." On another occasion, riding with a downtown beat officer for a night, one of us witnessed several university students having alcohol confiscated but not being arrested for the same open-container violation.

These contrasting experiences underscore the discretionary and ad hoc nature of much police work, as well as its harassment of the homeless. Whether these measures had the effect of containing the homeless to a smaller area is difficult to determine.[33] But they most certainly made the homeless more circumspect about where they roamed, hung out, and slept. Hoyt, who had been on the streets in several cities, including Dallas, was particularly sensitive to the furor over relocation of the Sally and to the harassments of the police. He commented one afternoon, "It looks like we're going to have to be looking over our shoulders more now than ever before. It used to be that Austin didn't have a bad reputation on the streets. But it ain't that way anymore. It's getting as bad as Dallas."

ECOLOGICAL CONSTRAINTS

We have seen how various organizational and political responses to the homeless facilitate or impede their survival. In either case, these responses function as constraints on the subsistence activities and daily rounds of the homeless. Another set of constraints that function in a similar fashion are essentially ecological in character and are manifested in two ways. One is through the existence and accessibility of marginal or interstitial space within a community; the other is through the ecological distribution of both this marginal space and the various facilities that cater to the homeless.

MARGINAL SPACE

The recently dislocated homeless and recent arrivals from other cities quickly learn to take into account community spatial distinctions when they map their daily rounds. Indeed, their survival is contingent on doing so, especially in communities where the problem of homelessness has been defined by some actors as a struggle over territory, as occurred in Austin. The relevant criterion for the homeless is not so much property rights as the functional value the space has for the host community. That is, the critical questions are not who owns the property or whether it is public or private land, but whether it is of importance for domiciled citizens.[34]

Such functional considerations suggest that space can slide on a continuum ranging from prime to marginal.[35] Prime space can be defined as space that is either being used routinely by domiciled citizens for residential, commercial, recreational, or navigational purposes or has symbolic significance. In the latter case, the space is not being used directly, but its value resides in what it symbolizes—order rather than disorder, civility rather than incivility. Marginal space, by contrast, is of little value to regular citizens. In most communities, abandoned buildings, isolated weed patches, alleys, the roofs of buildings, the space under bridges, vacant lots, impoverished, run-down residential areas, warehouse districts, and skid rows are all marginal spaces.

Marginal space is ceded both intentionally and unwittingly to the powerless and propertyless. It is ceded intentionally for the purpose of containment and control, as was the case with the traditional skid row.[36] It is ceded unwittingly when domiciled citizens and control agents pay little attention to their property, be it public or private. But the definition of space can change as fast as attention can be refocused. Marginal space can thus quickly be reconstituted as prime.[37] We have already seen that this occurred repeatedly in Austin as citizen groups collectively redefined marginal land in or near their neighborhoods as prime in order to ward off the relocation of the Sally on that land. This process of spatial redefinition and reappropriation has been heightened during the past fifteen years in most American cities as a result of vigorous gentrification and redevelopment programs.[38] Indeed, the relocation of the Sally itself was necessitated in large part by the revitalization of the city's downtown, which included the demolition of a number of seedy bars just north of the Sally on the main street and the transformation of Sixth Street from a strip of cheap and funky bars that catered to skid-row types, among others, to an upscale honky-tonk area frequented primarily by college students and "yuppies."[39]

The consequences of these processes of spatial transformation are twofold for the homeless: they are dislodged from areas traditionally appropriated by the down-and-out, particularly in central cities, and thereby the marginal space available to them is reduced; and they are therefore forced to spend more time in prime space, thus increasing their public visibility and the probability of citizen complaints and eventual arrest.[40]

Many of the homeless in Austin were keenly aware of this double-edged dilemma. Some complained bitterly about the erosion of "safe places to hang out," as Gypsy put it. JJ and Indio, the two old drinking buddies, noted with a rare trace of anger that it was becoming increasingly difficult to find places to drink in seclusion. As Indio put it in one of his more sober moments, "There used to be lots of places down here where no one would bother you. But it ain't that way no more. Too goddamn many fancy buildings going up." Aware of the greater risk of detection associated with drinking in prime space, the more circumspect tried to make sure they drank in the marginal or interstitial spaces that remained in the downtown area. This did not always work, though. With the increased vigilance of the police and the open-container ordinance for the Sixth Street area, even marginal spaces were not always safe retreats in which to drink, as we learned firsthand. Because of these increased risks, many of the homeless hanging out in the downtown area took measures to camouflage their drinking, such as keeping their bottles in paper bags. For example, one evening we stopped at a gas station carry-out to buy a couple of quarts of beer to share with Hoyt. When we returned to the car with the beer, Hoyt sent one of us right back for a couple of paper bags, commenting with a chuckle, "Boy, are you guys green! If you're gonna make it on the streets, you gotta learn to cover your ass!"

DISTRIBUTION OF FACILITIES AND MARGINAL SPACE

The problems posed for the homeless by the erosion of marginal space in the downtown area are magnified by the limited availability of such space in other accessible areas of the city and by the widespread distribution of caretaker organizations and commercial facilities that figure in their survival routines. Many large cities once had fairly well defined skid-row districts where street agencies were concentrated. In Austin, however, such facilities are distributed over an area that stretches from three miles to the north of the Sally, where the main plasma center is located at the northern edge of the Drag, to two miles to the south of the Sally, where the homeless frequent a fast-food restaurant. Its width varies considerably, from two miles of city park land running east and west along the river just south of the Sally, to a one-mile area running from First Street on the south to Fifteenth Street on the north, to a narrow swath no more than several hundred yards across at the northern and southern extremes, except for a six-block by four-block area where the hippie tramps hang out across from the university.

This area constituted the in-town range of the city's homeless. A number would drift out to the lakes that are scattered through the hill country, and some would "jungle-up" with other homeless in a hill country encampment, as Gypsy did on occasion. But nearly all returned to town from time to time, and when they did, their activities were confined to this range. Its extended and contorted dimensions are due to the decentralized distribution of the previously discussed facilities, the absence of much marginal space within the range, and the fact that the only way to get from one facility to another is by trekking through prime space.

The upshot of these ecological constraints for the homeless is that they not only spend a good portion of each day hiking from one subsistence node or hangout to another, but also find themselves spending a considerable amount of time in prime space. The homeless in urban America have always had to spend some time in prime space, of course, as they often had to "venture into high-risk, prime areas" in order to secure the wherewithal to survive.[41] Gentrification and redevelopment in central cities and the simultaneous increase in the numbers of homeless on the streets have greatly exacerbated the problem for the homeless, however, not only in Austin but throughout the country. Simply put, less marginal space is available in many cities to accommodate more homeless. When a decentralized social-service system is added to these factors, we have a formula for what occurred in Austin: the dispersion of the homeless over an extended range that includes much prime space, with a corresponding increase in their visibility and their contact with other members of the community.

Taken together, these observations indicate how the routines and life-styles of the homeless in Austin have been affected by various ecological factors, including changes in the use and definition of space.

They also help to explain why concern with the control and containment of the homeless has become such a heated issue in some communities. As the homeless filter into the spatial preserves of other citizens and their respective routines begin to intersect, traditional territorial understandings are violated and a sense of "urban unease" begins to develop.[42] People who are perceived as out of place have long generated fear and anxiety in those who have a strong sense of place.[43] And that fear and anxiety are taken into account by most homeless as they negotiate their daily routines. They learn not only to "look over their shoulders," as Hoyt told us to do on several occasions, but also "where to walk and hang out, and when," as Pat Manchester claimed he quickly learned when he arrived in Austin.

MORAL CONSTRAINTS

A final constraint on the adaptive behaviors and routines of the homeless is a moral code of sorts. Moral codes function something like a relief map: they delimit the boundaries for exploration without specifying exactly what to do each step of the way. They do not determine the content of social action, but they provide guidelines for the elaboration of behavioral routines and interpersonal relations within a specific sociocultural context. Moral codes are constraining rather than determinative cultural phenomena, and they appear to be almost universal features of the social landscape.[44]

Traces of a moral code were clearly evident on the streets of Austin in both the comments of some of the homeless and in what they did and did not do when they were together. One thing they did not do as often as might be expected is "fuck with each other," as Willie, Hoyt, Tanner Sutton, Banjo, Gypsy, Marilyn, and Nona, among others, related on numerous occasions. To use less colloquial terms, they were surprisingly restrained about victimizing each other either physically or verbally. They clearly have the opportunity to do both with considerable frequency. For instance, highly embellished storytelling is fairly rampant on the streets, but, as we will discuss in a subsequent chapter, we rarely heard the homeless call one another's stories into question.

Nor do the homeless rob or assault one another to the extent that might be supposed. Some students of criminal behavior have suggested that the convergence in time and space of motivated offenders, suitable targets, and the absence of capable guardians against crime increases the prospect of direct-contact predatory offenses such as assault and robbery.[45] Clearly, these three conditions are present on the streets, yet most of the homeless do not victimize each other criminally. To be sure, they victimize each other, as we saw when Marilyn's male friend was allegedly stabbed by several homeless and when Marilyn herself claimed to have been mugged by "three local street people who were out to get me." Moreover, the homeless victimize each other criminally at a higher rate than they do non-homeless persons. Victim/offender figures derived from arrest data on the homeless tracked through the police department show, for example, that over a twenty-seven-month period the homeless victimized another homeless person 32 times out of 1,000 and other citizens only 2.8 times out of 1,000.[46] These rates would be even more discrepant if all predatory offenses perpetrated by the homeless against other homeless were reported and then acted upon by the police. Even then, however, criminal victimization of the homeless by the homeless would still be far from the modal type of association among them.

A central reason why the homeless are disinclined to prey on each other more than they do is because life on the streets is indexed to a moral code that manifests itself most clearly in a widely and frequently articulated phrase: "What goes around, comes around." It is the street version of the karmic principle that one reaps what one sows. In the vernacular of the street, Hoyt told us one evening, it essentially means "if you don't want somebody to fuck with you, you don't fuck with them." Turning more philosophic and expansive, he added:

> It's karma, but it can be stated in Christian terms too—you know how it goes, "Do unto others as you want others to do to you." Yeah, I believe that what goes 'round, comes around. That's why when I get clothes or shoes down at the Sally, I give 'em away instead of selling 'em. I could sell 'em, but it wouldn't be right for me. It's like selling a coat to a guy when it's freezing out. This way my conscience doesn't bother me.

This principle is practiced in two ways. One variant says, "Don't fuck with me and I won't fuck with you!" It is a kind of truce that keeps potential antagonists apart and thus has an atomizing effect. Biographic strangers remain biographic strangers. They tread the same water but do little to help each other stay afloat. This was Tony Jones's attitude during his stay on the streets. "I'll mind my business," as he put it, "and I hope others will do the same." He was preoccupied with getting off the streets and wanted little to do with the other homeless.

The other way this karmic code is practiced is more in keeping with the widely acknowledged "norm of reciprocity."[47] This stance pulls the homeless together, creating at least a tenuous sense of mutuality and solidarity. Since the operation of this code will be elaborated in more detail in a subsequent chapter, it will suffice here to ground its salience as an associational principle in two illustrative encounters. The first occurred during our second week in the field. One of us, talking with Ron Whitaker in the early evening, offered him a cigarette. He took it without a bat of the eye, but immediately responded by offering a drink from his Coke and saying, "See, man, I'm all right! I share, man! I don't just take shit." If you get, then, you are obligated to give, either immediately or at some point down the road. And if you want something now but those around you know you failed to give in the past in a similar situation, you are unlikely to get what you want, as was clearly illustrated one morning at the Labor Pool:

> A distraught man was anxiously trying to bum a smoke. Earlier in the morning he had been trying to trade donuts for a cigarette at the Sally. He didn't succeed, since few homeless have any cigarettes to spare on Monday mornings. Now, at the Labor Pool, he finally hit upon a fellow who agreed to give him one. But this fellow's buddy interfered: "No fucking way, motherfucker. Don't give him any. The motherfucker won't give anybody else one when they ask him." So the proffered smoke was withdrawn, and the man who wanted one, more desperate than ever, took a dime out of his pocket and asked if anybody would sell him one.

He eventually found a taker, and he was out only a dime, but perhaps more important, he had learned firsthand about the meaning of "what goes around, comes around."

Do the homeless generally adhere to this moral code? Some do and some do not, and those who do only do so some of the time. But, then, moral codes never elicit one hundred percent adherence. Masturbation occurs in monasteries, snitches can be found in prisons, tattlers exist in most classrooms, military cadets sometimes cheat, and, as we have seen, the homeless victimize each other criminally at a rate higher than they do the non-homeless. Slippage occurs within any subculture. Moreover, there are often individuals within the subculture who are guided by a different standard. This was made clear to us one afternoon when we were talking about street life with Willie, Ron, and Tanner. They contended that there are two kinds of people on the streets:

> "There are the 'what goes around, comes around' people and the 'take what you can get' kind," Willie said. Ron agreed. "Yeah, the 'take what you can get' kind are rip-offs. They fuck with you, and you can't trust them. But the 'what goes around, comes around' kind are guys like us." "That's right,"

Tanner added. "If you don't fuck with us, we don't fuck with you. And if you do something for us, we remember it."

Which one is ascendant on the streets of Austin? Clearly, it is the karmic code, "What goes around, comes around." If it were not, then the homeless would victimize each other much more than they do, both verbally and physically, and street life would be more of a Hobbesian hell than it is. To be sure, such behavior can be found on the streets, especially among the redneck bums. But there are also traces of civility and morality, as when we first encountered Marilyn passing out scavenged burritos to "my people."[48]

SUMMARY

The essence of the subculture of street life, we have suggested, resides not so much in a distinctive set of cherished values as in a shared fate and the adaptive behaviors and routines the homeless fashion in order to deal with that fate. But those adaptive behaviors and routines are not fashioned willy-nilly. Rather, they are embedded in and structured by a set of organizational, political, ecological, and moral constraints that constitute the cornerstones of the subculture of street life. In this chapter we have identified and examined these constraining cornerstones as they materialized in Austin, and we have provided glimpses of the daily routines and experiences of the homeless as they are filtered through or affected by these constraints.

With these contextual considerations in place, we are now in a position to examine how the homeless fashion and refashion survival routines out of the limited opportunities and resources available to them as they try to make do materially, interpersonally, and cognitively. It is these survival routines that give street life its distinctive flavor. They also underscore, as we will see in the following chapters, the ingenuity, resourcefulness, and resilience of many of the homeless.

CHAPTER FOUR

Wage Labor and Institutionalized Assistance

"A man's work," it has been said, "is one of the more important parts of his social identity, of his self; indeed of his fate in the one life he has to live."[1] Few students of work would disagree. As one has noted, "[T]he human species have no greater entanglement with an artifact of their own creation than they have with work. . . . For a great many individuals in industrial society the entanglement is complete: they both work in order to live and live in order to work."[2] Karl Marx, perhaps the foremost student of work and the labor process, would have understood such observations well; he argued long ago not only that humans reproduce themselves through their labor but that the nature of the lives they lead is determined in large part by the kind of work they do and for whom they work.[3]

An understanding of the way of life of individuals and of the aggregations they comprise, then, requires consideration of their work and the factors that shape it. This is as true for the homeless as it is for the more fortunate, since all social strata are characterized in part by their material survival strategies. Accordingly, in this and the next chapter we examine the repertoire of material survival strategies employed by the homeless. We seek to answer two basic questions: What are the nature and the range of strategies the homeless fashion for the purpose of acquiring money or material goods for personal use or exchange? And what are the factors that shape this repertoire? We also identify variations in subsistence activities and orientations among the different types of homeless.

In this chapter we consider only the more conventional means of material subsistence: wage labor and various forms of institutional assistance. Then, in the following chapter, we examine the compensatory, non–wage labor survival strategies pursued by the homeless in the shadow of more conventional material subsistence.

WAGE LABOR

In the early 1920s Nels Anderson argued that "all the problems of the homeless man go back in one way or another to the conditions of his work. The irregularity of his employment is reflected in the irregularity of all phases of his existence. To deal with him even as an individual, society must deal also with the economic forces which have formed his behavior."[4] The context and character of homelessness have changed since Anderson's day, but work still remains a central dilemma in the lives of the homeless. Indeed, as we will see in Chapter 8, the fact of homelessness itself results in part from problems and trends associated with the world of wage labor. We thus begin our exploration of the work world of the homeless by considering their experiences with wage labor.

REGULAR WORK

Wage labor customarily refers to the exchange of labor for an hourly wage. Since wages can be officially regulated or situationally negotiated, such jobs can vary considerably in terms of actual wages and in how those wages are determined. At one end of the continuum are jobs for which wages, time, and place of work are prearranged. This is regular work, work as traditionally conceived.

It is the unavailability or inaccessibility of regular work that makes work one of the central dilemmas in the lives of the homeless. Conventional wisdom, however, often holds instead that the homeless eschew regular work because they are lazy.[5] Proponents of this belief argue that large numbers of unskilled jobs are available that the homeless are simply unwilling to take, thus suggesting that these people are unemployed and on the streets largely because they are undisciplined and slothful. "They don't want to punch a clock," as a local police officer put it. "Most don't want a steady job. They're content to be the way they are." This view was stated even more sharply in a letter to the editor of the local newspaper disagreeing with a guest editorial that contended that "on any given day more homeless want work than can find it." "Horse-feathers," the writer responded:

> Even for the unskilled or semi-skilled, the daily classified section is filled with job offerings that go unanswered. So long as the community is willing to support the various types of bums who make the rounds of the hand-out agencies, their numbers will continue to increase.[6]

Such sentiments, although stated more diplomatically, have found considerable support in higher places. In the spring of 1981, President Reagan noted that in a recent Sunday *New York Times* "there were 45-1/2 pages of help wanted ads, and in the *Washington Post,* there were 33-1/2 pages. . . .[of] jobs calling for people of every range that you could imagine." In the light of such observations, the president wondered, "How does a person in any of those skills justify calling themselves unemployed when there's a fellow spending money and saying, 'I've got a job, come fill my job'?"[7]

This seemingly popular notion that the homeless are unemployed because they are lazy begs three empirical questions. First, what are the skill levels of the homeless? Second, are there enough decent-paying jobs for which the homeless qualify? Third, do the homeless really fail to pursue these jobs, and if so, why?

Job Experiences and Skills   We address the first question by examining the regular occupational identities and experiences of the homeless. Upon initial registration at both the Sally and the Texas Employment Commission (TEC), the homeless were asked to indicate their occupations. All but fourteen of the tracking sample did so at one of the two sites, thus providing occupational self-identification for 753 homeless individuals.[8]

The distribution of occupations among the 753 homeless is indicated in column 1 of Table 4.1. It shows that only 5 percent claimed white-collar occupations, whereas 81 percent identified themselves as blue-collar workers, the majority of whom were general laborers, mainly in the construction industry.[9] An additional 12 percent claimed occupations in the service sector, mostly lower-level food-service jobs such as short-order cook, dishwasher, or waiter. Insofar as occupational self-identification can be used as an indicator of occupational skill, it is clear that the vast majority of homeless are unskilled or semi-skilled at best.

This generalization is also suggested when we examine the most recent regular work experiences of the homeless. Columns 2 and 3 of Table 4.1 provide information bearing on regular work experience.

Column 2 reveals that the vast majority of regular jobs held by the homeless before their initial contact with TEC were also of the unskilled to semi-skilled variety. Over 50 percent of the 348 who had registered with TEC one or more times had held a semi-skilled or unskilled job in the blue-collar sector at least once, with the modal category again being general laborer. Nearly another third had held service jobs, mostly in the food-service and janitorial sectors.[10]

These same patterns are also evident when we turn to the most recent regular work experiences of our twenty key informants. As indicated in column 3, 80 percent had been employed at least once as blue-collar workers, mostly as general laborers, and 35 percent had worked one or more times at a food-service or janitorial job. To illustrate even more concretely, Tom Fisk and Sonny McCallister, two of our recently dislocated informants, and Willie Hastings and Pat Manchester, two regular straddlers, had all worked most recently as general laborers, and none of them claimed more specific and refined skills. When asked what they could do best, for example, both Tom and Sonny mentioned roofing, which for them involved little more than hauling tar and shingles up and down ladders.

Taken together, these three sets of observations clearly indicate that the homeless living in or passing through Austin have relatively few occupational skills that can be used to secure jobs beyond the lower level of the secondary labor market.[11] Furthermore, to the extent that occupational skills constitute an individual resource, it is clear that the homeless suffer a serious resource deficit.[12]

This deficit becomes even more striking when the occupational profile of the homeless is compared with that for the U.S. and the Texas work forces, as is shown in columns 4 and 5 of Table 4.1. Whereas slightly over 40 percent of the state and national male work forces were employed in white-collar jobs, only 5 to 9 percent of the homeless were ever so employed.[13] Moreover, even this small number was congregated in sales and clerical work, the bottom tiers of white-collar work. The differences are equally striking for blue-collar work: 68 to 80 percent of the homeless were blue-collar workers, in comparison to 44 and 47 percent for the U.S. and Texas male work forces.

These findings, coupled with the previous observations, demonstrate not only that the homeless have few job skills, but that they are much less skilled than most of the American work force.

The Want Ads   According to some observers, this obvious resource deficit should not necessarily function as a deterrent to finding work,

	Avowed Occupations (N: 753)	Most Recent Regular Work Experiences[a] (N: 348)	Recent Job Experiences of Key Informants (N: 20)	U.S. Male Work Force[b] (N: 56,004,690)	Texas Male Work Force[c] (N: 3,705,550)
Professional & technical	1.6	—	5.0	13.9	12.1
Managers & administrative	0.1	0.9	—	12.6	12.2
Sales	1.9	2.0	—	9.1	9.9
Clerical	1.9	6.0	—	6.9	6.1
Total white-collar	5.5	8.9	5.0	42.5	41.3
Craft workers (skilled)	21.6	18.1	25.0	20.7	23.9
Mechanics & repairers	4.1	2.6	15.0	6.6	6.7
Construction craftsmen	17.1	15.5	10.0	7.4	9.6
Operatives (semi-skilled)	13.1	19.8	10.0	16.9	15.9
Factory operatives	6.9	14.9	5.0	9.7	7.9

Transport operatives	6.2	4.9	5.0	7.2	7.9
General laborers (unskilled)	46.3	30.1	45.0	6.2	6.9
Construction laborers	38.5	22.1	40.0	1.1	1.6
Stock & material handlers	4.5	4.9	—	1.9	1.9
Total blue-collar	81.0	68.0	80.0	43.9	46.8
Food service	8.2	14.0	15.0	2.6	2.1
Cleaning & building service	2.0	12.3	15.0	3.2	2.7
Total service workers	12.4	29.2	35.0	9.2	7.6
Farmworkers & related	1.1	3.1	10.0	4.3	4.3

[a] Figures in this column are derived from TEC data. Totals add to more than 100 percent because many of the homeless claimed more than one recent regular work experience.

[b] Figures derived from Tables 89 and 104 of *1980 Census of the Population: General and Social Economic Characteristics*, Vol. 1: *U.S. Summary* (Washington, D.C.: Government Printing Office, 1981).

[c] Figures derived from Tables G1 and G8 of *1980 Census of the Population: Texas*, Vol. 1 (Washington, D.C.: Government Printing Office, 1981), chapter C, part 45.

TABLE 4.2   JOBS IN CLASSIFIED LISTINGS
AVAILABLE TO THE HOMELESS, SUMMER 1985[*]

Occupations/Jobs	Listings		Available to Homeless	
	No.	%	No.	%[a]
Professional & technical	624		—	—
Managers & administrative	61		—	—
Sales & retail	539		18	3.3
Clerical	292		—	—
Total white-collar	1,516	(63.9)	18	1.2
Craftsmen & operatives	423		17	4.0
General laborers	42		26	61.9
Total blue-collar	465	(19.6)	43	9.2
Restaurant/food service	176		39	22.2
Household/child care	144		—	—
Hotel	19		4	21.1
Other	51		8	15.7
Total service	390	(16.5)	51	13.1
General total	2,371		112	4.7

[*] Summation of listings that appeared in the *Austin American-Statesman* on four randomly selected days in the summer of 1985. See note 14 of this chapter for criteria used to determine the availability of jobs for the homeless.
[a] Proportion of jobs available to the homeless for each occupational category.

however. As noted earlier, some believe that perusal of the want ads in almost any local daily indicates that jobs are abundant and thus readily available for anyone who wants to work. This presumes, of course, that there is no glaring discrepancy between the requisite skills for the advertised jobs and the skill level of the pool of potential employees.

In order to assess this issue, we examined the job advertisements in the classified section of the local daily newspaper on four randomly selected days in the summer of 1985. Table 4.2 presents our findings. Nearly two-thirds of the advertisements were for white-collar jobs, with professional and technical jobs as the modal listing. When these figures are compared with those presented in Table 4.1, which show the homeless to be predominantly semi-skilled and unskilled workers, it becomes clear that there is a mismatch between the jobs listed in the want ads and the skill level of the homeless. This mismatch becomes even more striking when we consider that the majority of the remaining jobs for which many of the homeless might qualify under ideal conditions are unavailable to them because they lack such requisite job resources as references, drivers' licenses, tools, clean clothes, a telephone number, and a permanent address. Thus we found that only 4.7 percent of the 2,371 listings could be counted as real job possibilities for the homeless.[14]

In the light of this finding, the presumption that the want ads typically contain an abundance of jobs for which the homeless qualify appears to be empirically unfounded, at least for Austin. We found that no more than a handful of homeless in Austin generally read the want ads. They are not eager to spend their few precious nickels on a local daily. More important, though, most ignore the paper because they have learned from experience that they gain little from pursuing jobs advertised in the newspaper. For reasons we will discuss below, the odds are stacked against them in securing these jobs.

TEC Job Referrals   The odds are stacked against the homeless in securing regular work in general, whatever its source. But many of the homeless are nonetheless persistent in their pursuit of such work. At the time of their initial contact with the Sally, fully 85 percent of the tracking sample's 600-plus individuals from another Texas city or from out of state indicated that they had come to Austin in search of work.[15] All but a small handful said they were unemployed, but the vast majority (82 percent) claimed they had been out of work for less than seven months. The majority of the tracking sample, then, were recently dislocated and arrived in Austin reportedly eager to find work.

The institutional agency they customarily turned to first in this quest was the Texas Employment Commission (TEC), the statewide agency that provides referrals for regular work and occasionally for day labor. TEC's downtown office is located one and a half miles north of the Sally, roughly in the middle of the daily orbit of the city's homeless. The TEC's central location and the avowed interest of the majority of the homeless in finding regular work suggests that a sizable proportion of the homeless would establish contact with TEC. And indeed they do. Nearly 50 percent of the tracking sample used TEC's job-referral services on one or more occasions. This comprised a pattern of contact that exceeded that for every other agency except the Salvation Army.

Additionally, 45 percent of these individuals (21 percent of the entire sample) initiated contact with TEC before they reached the Sally. To put this datum in practical terms, many homeless tried to find regular work in Austin through TEC even before they looked for a free meal or shelter.

These observations suggest a fairly strong work orientation among many of the homeless. Corroboration of this orientation is provided by the responses of the homeless to a number of questions at the time of their initial TEC contact. Their responses, shown in Table 4.3, reveal that almost 100 percent preferred long-term over short-term work and a full-time rather than a part-time job. Nearly all of them also indicated that they would work any shift. Additionally, most were not fussy about their prospective wages. Over a quarter expressed willingness to work for the minimum wage or less, and a clear majority said that around $4.00 per hour would be acceptable. Taken together, these responses indicate that many of the homeless would accept almost any steady work.

So what was the nature of their experience with TEC in search of regular work? In a word, frustrating! Of the 348 individuals with TEC contact who sought regular wage labor, 248 received one or more referrals for such jobs, with an average of 4.4 per person. But, as is shown in Table 4.4, fewer than 30 percent of the referrals led to a job.

What happened? Did the homeless in question fail to follow up on the referral? Not at all. As is also shown in column 1 of Table 4.4, fewer than 10 percent failed to respond to the referral. Instead, most (89.3 percent) were rejected for the job. Thus, TEC did not prove to be a much more reliable source of regular work than the want ads.

Obstacles to Regular Work   The rejection of the homeless as job applicants, as well as most other difficulties they experience in seeking regular work, stems in large part from the fact that they are at an immediate disadvantage vis-à-vis other prospective employees. The sources of disadvantage are of two kinds. One concerns their low skill levels, which we have already discussed; the other concerns the particular circumstances of street life that together comprise a set of obstacles to securing regular work. The first such obstacle results from the disjunction between employer expectations and the realities of street life. Most employers seeking to hire permanent employees, even in low-paying, unskilled jobs, expect new workers to satisfy certain minimal qualifications. At the most basic level, they expect prospective employees to

TABLE 4.3   INDICATORS OF WORK
ORIENTATION AND MOTIVATION AMONG
HOMELESS WITH TEC CONTACT

| | Respondents | |
Indicator	No.	%
Desired length of job	218	100
Long-term	213	97.7
Short-term	5	2.3
Desired work week	216	100
Full-time	215	99.5
Part-time	1	0.5
Preferred shifts	215	100
All shifts	212	98.6
Only one shift	3	1.4
Minimum acceptable salary	201	100
$3.35 or less	56	27.9
$3.36 to $4.00	57	28.4
$4.01 to $5.00	53	26.4
More than $5.00	35	17.4

meet certain standards of dress and appearance. Homeless people, however, seldom have much spare clothing. Aside from the dilemma of securing extra clothes, they are faced with the problem of storage. Some
of the homeless use their own or a friend's car to store their belongings,
but most do not have this option; besides, to store clothing in another
homeless person's vehicle is to risk losing it. Others carry extra clothing
in a bag or rolled up in a sleeping roll, but toting a bag or bedroll is
awkward and can tip off employers that the person is homeless. And
even a person who has been able to secure clean clothes in which to go
job hunting is still faced with the difficulty of finding a place to take a
shower, as we have already seen, as well as money for toiletries and a
haircut.

The search for regular work is further impeded by the lack of local
job references and a stable work history. Employers utilize job applications and references to help weed out potentially unreliable appli-

TABLE 4.4   TEC WAGE-LABOR EXPERIENCE OF
HOMELESS MEN IN AUSTIN

TEC Experience	Regular Work	Day Labor
Number of tracking sample seeking work through TEC	248	277
Percentage of total number (348) with TEC contact	71.3%	79.6%
Job referrals received	1,094	2,159
Average number of referrals per person	4.4	7.8
Percent of referrals resulting in a job	27.4%	97.0%
Reason for not receiving a job:		
Homeless rejected	89.3%	NA
Job filled	2.0%	NA
Homeless failed to respond	8.7%	NA

cants. They infer prospective work performance partly on the basis of the past work record. The homeless job applicant who lacks a relatively stable work history and local references may thus be perceived as a high risk and not be hired if other applicants are available. Some may try to pass as domiciled, but lack of local work experience and an address or phone number may give the street person away. Such problems were illustrated late one afternoon when we encountered Ron Whitaker. He was noticeably distraught, having just been told by a woman at a nearby Arby's, who had already said she was going to hire him, that she had found someone with previous Arby's experience and would not be needing him after all. We asked him how he had filled out his application and he replied, "I gave a fake address on it since I knew I wouldn't get a job if I put the Sally down as my address." He did not put down a phone number, though, telling her he was "new to town and hadn't gotten a phone yet." He continued:

What got to me was that the assistant manager had handwritten the application for me since they needed workers so bad. I thought that was a good sign and it got my hopes up. But after she told me she was going to hire me, she must've had second thoughts. She must've figured out that I'm a transient, otherwise why would the "Help Wanted" sign still be in the window?

You know, it's really depressing when you apply for a minimum-wage job that is only part-time and they won't even hire you for that.

Such experiences underscore the sort of disadvantage the homeless person faces when seeking even low-pay regular work. But the disjunction between the demands of the regular wage-labor market and the life situation of the homeless is perhaps even more clearly illustrated by the problems the homeless person faces when he or she does obtain a steady job. One such problem in Austin was that of finding transportation to and from the work site. The city's public transportation system was not of much help. It was a modest system at best, and it did not serve the city's suburbs, where there were numerous construction sites and openings for unskilled labor.

Such transportation problems are exacerbated by the bureaucratic nature of the facilities serving the homeless. Meal times and sleeping schedules are firmly set. If a homeless person's employment does not mesh with these schedules, he or she is left without food and/or a place to sleep. One evening, for instance, we met Tony Jones at the Salvation Army after he had finished work. His new job as an appliance repairman had kept him past the Sally's dinner time, but more frustrating for Tony was the fact that he would be unable to spend the night at the Sally, because the facility was full by the time he arrived. "I don't care though, man," he told us. "This is my last night down here anyway. I've got a big paycheck coming tomorrow and I've got a place lined up to stay. I can stay up all night tonight if I have to—it won't be the first time."

The homeless person trying to work a regular job, then, is often torn between the demands of work and the bureaucratic strictures of caretaker agencies. The wages from low-paying jobs are seldom sufficient for them to afford motels and eating out, and cheap rooming houses, especially with cooking facilities, are extremely scarce. When Willie Hastings secured a steady job on the graveyard shift at a fast-food restaurant, he was told that he could sleep at the Sally only from the time it opened its sleeping facility at 7:00 P.M. until he had to leave for work at 11:00. When he overslept one evening and arrived at work four hours late, he got into an argument with the assistant manager that resulted in his being fired.

Tom Fisk coordinated his personal and work schedules by sleeping on the roofs of buildings he and his employer were reroofing. When his employer gave him an old '65 Cadillac as partial payment for his work,

Tom quit sleeping on the roof and slept in the car on the job site—until the police ran him off. He told us:

> It was around 11:30 and kinda cold that night and I already had my boots and socks off when they come up to the car and asked me to step out. And they wanted to look through the trunk, and I told 'em, no problem. And I says, "Would you mind if I put my boots and socks on? My feet are freezing." And the officer says, "No, just get out here. It won't be but a few minutes." And my feet were starting to hurt. And it was really starting to bug the shit outta me. And finally they says, "The manager would like you to leave." And I says, "Hey, no problem. If I run outta gas, then I don't make it to work." But I made it all the way down to Denny's on an empty tank and called my boss in the morning.

Low-wage jobs tend to reinforce dependency on the street agencies with whose schedules they conflict. As a result, the homeless person who finds a low-paying, regular job is frequently unable to manage sustained work at such jobs but tends, instead, to work them for short periods of time until he or she is forced back to the street agencies for survival. A revolving-door pattern emerges in which regular work becomes temporary and cyclical. After his disappointing experience with Arby's, for instance, Ron managed to get two dishwashing jobs in town, one in a fraternity and the other at a restaurant seven miles north of the Sally. He worked the two jobs maniacally for a couple of weeks, bragging, "I'm in good shape now, and all on jobs nobody else wants." He claimed it was not difficult to find a place to sleep, but one evening when we were giving him a ride from work back to the Sally he fell asleep in the middle of a conversation. Within two weeks Ron had quit both jobs and was talking of moving to Florida. Within a month, however, he had secured another kitchen-helper position at a downtown restaurant. Again his initial optimism was dampened by his inability to sustain his work routine without a place to stay that matched his employment schedule.

Experiences such as these show that the inflexible structure of the regular wage-labor market is not responsive to the situation of the homeless. This is hardly surprising. Research on consumer practices among the urban poor has shown that "normal marketing arrangements, based on a model of the 'adequate' consumer (the consumer with funds, credit, and shopping sophistication)" are not responsive to the situation of the poor.[16] Similarly, the normal arrangements of the regular labor market, based on a model of the "adequate" job applicant or worker, are not responsive to the situation of the homeless. But whereas some merchants may find it to their advantage to adapt marketing arrangements in order to tap the lower-class market, employers have little incentive to adapt their demands and practices to accommodate the homeless as long as other job applicants are available. Consequently, in adapting to life on the streets, the homeless must locate and engage in more flexible and reliable strategies for material survival.

DAY LABOR

Whether they wake in the Sally shelter, a motel room, a building alcove, a car, a weed patch, or under a bridge, the homeless usually face each new day broke or nearly so. Even though food and shelter can often be procured for free, other basic amenities such as cigarettes, coffee, and beer must be purchased or acquired through some other effort. One of the most pressing daily problems for the homeless is to find a way to get some money almost immediately.

Many of the homeless deal with this dilemma in part by seeking casual, day-labor jobs. As the term *day labor* implies, these jobs are secured on a day-by-day basis. They are, in essence, jobs without a tomorrow. They typically involve some form of manual labor, from yard work for homeowners to construction labor to unloading vans for businesses, and they seldom pay more than minimum wage. Day labor has irregular hours, changing locales, and pay that is usually lower than regular work and frequently is negotiable.

In spite of its irregular character and low pay, day labor has several advantages for the homeless compared to regular work. The laborer is paid in cash on the same day he or she works. This is of no small importance to individuals who seldom have much loose change. Another major advantage is that transportation is provided to and from the work site for most day-labor jobs. In addition, acquisition of a day-labor job seldom requires a neat and clean appearance. And, finally, neither a recent work history nor job references are necessary for securing day labor. In Austin there were three major sites where the homeless would congregate in search of day labor.[17]

Texas Employment Commission   Until the spring of 1986, the major source of day labor was the downtown office of TEC.[18] In 1984 an average of 110 homeless would come to look for work daily. These prospective day laborers were segregated from the regular job seekers in a room filled with wooden chairs nailed to slats so that they could not be moved around. Queuing up to apply for work usually began on the preceding evening, with ten to fifteen men lining up their bedrolls on the driveway beside the day-labor entrance. By 5:45 in the morning another fifteen or so homeless, many of whom had slept in the little alcoves on the outside of the building, had also queued up in the hope of getting first dibs on job referrals. By the time the security guard arrived at 6:00 A.M., there was already a semblance of order in the line, and those still asleep were roused and coaxed to fall into line.

When the office opened at 7:00, the job seekers signed in and waited to be called to go out on jobs. A TEC "Labor Pool Rule" board was posted on the wall. It announced: "Everyone will sit in one chair. Do not lay down on several chairs or you will be asked to leave." Another rule warned against drinking: "If we determine that you are drinking or drunk, you will not be referred and the police will be called." Nonetheless, the security guard spent most of his time watching the men who were hanging around outside the office, and on any morning a few men could be observed surreptitiously nursing a bottle inside. But most of the men just sat and waited, reading a discarded paper, smoking cigarettes, and waiting some more in the hope of hearing their names called for work.

How successful was TEC's day-labor operation? How reliable was it as a source of wage labor? Its day-labor operation was clearly a more reliable source of work for the homeless than its regular work service. As is shown in Table 4.4, 2,159 day-labor referrals were received by the 277 individuals in the tracking sample who utilized TEC day-labor services, and 97 percent of those referrals resulted in a job. Thus, receipt of a referral generally guaranteed a day-labor job. The problem, however, was that application for such a job was no guarantee of a referral. In fact, only 45 percent of 67,600 day-labor applications at TEC over a three-year period resulted in job referrals. Waiting from 6:00 to 9:00 each weekday morning, then, offered less than a fifty-fifty chance of getting a job. Moreover, the jobs seldom lasted for a full eight hours, and the pay was typically not much above minimum wage. These features of day labor, as well as the nature of such work, were driven home one day when one of us secured a day-labor job out of TEC with Ron Whitaker and Pat Manchester:

> When Ron's name was called for a job, he told the day-labor interviewer that I had a car and got me out on the job too. We were to unload garage-door parts from a van. The day-labor interviewer gave us a referral card and told us the employer was guaranteeing four hours of work at $4.00 an hour.

Pat Manchester was sent with us, and we stopped at Caritas to pick up some sandwiches before we went to the job. At the job site the boss put us to work unloading sixteen-foot sections of garage doors. Ron, who had the flu, had trouble doing the work. He asked the boss for several breaks and for some money to go up the street and get a Coke. The truck driver helped Ron with some of the heavier pieces and told us how much he appreciated our help, but he also told us at one point, "Man, you're the saddest bunch of workers I've ever seen. Just what's wrong with you?"

Pat replied, "We're starving, that's what's wrong. You wouldn't be smiling either."

The truck driver responded, "Well, I'm real sorry about that, but what the fuck can I do? That's just the way things are sometimes."

After the van was unloaded, the driver told the boss that we had done a good job and that he ought to hire us full-time. The boss asked us what time we had gotten to the warehouse. Ron told him we had gotten there at 8:00 A.M. The boss shook his head and replied, "Listen, the van didn't even get here until nine o'clock, and you weren't here when he got here. I said I'd guarantee four hours' work and I'll pay you for that, but nothing more." When the boss went to write out the check, Ron shrugged, saying, "It was worth a try."

We were given a check for $48.00 in Pat's name and went to a bank to get it cashed. We divided the money and went our separate ways. Pat said he was going to the plasma center since there was still enough time to make another ten bucks selling plasma. Ron had me drop him back at TEC so he could try his luck again. And I headed home, tired and stiff, knowing full well, like Pat and Ron, that the $16.00 I had earned would not take me very far if that were all I had and I were really on the streets.

In April, 1986, when TEC was forced to trim its services due to statewide budget cuts, day-labor services were the first to be cut. "If we ever open up a day-labor office again," the office manager told us, "we'll have it in a separate building. These people are just too disorderly to have around our regular offices." Nonetheless, for a number of years TEC offered, albeit grudgingly, day-labor services to this "filthy and disorderly lot." At the same time, another agency in town was going out of its way to court homeless workers. The homeless called it the Labor Pool.

The Labor Pool   The Labor Pool is located in a small dilapidated building six blocks from the Salvation Army. It is run by the previously mentioned Houston-based company that operates similar employment agencies in three other Texas cities.

By 6:15 each weekday morning, between fifty and seventy men and a few women are crammed into the Labor Pool shack, drinking twenty-five-cent cups of coffee and waiting for jobs. Behind the counter where the dispatcher works hang a row of orange hard hats, with a stack of work clothes, and a couple of shelves on which the belongings of the homeless who secure jobs can be stored for the day. The Labor Pool contracts with employers to provide them with laborers and typically pays the men not much above the minimum wage. A few of the men get more for especially arduous or skilled work, and occasionally a man with a vehicle who is willing to take other men to the job site with him is paid $4.00 per hour. The men must sign in each day, but if a man does good work and the employer requests him back, he can get a "repeat ticket" that assures him the same job the next day. A sign behind the counter states: "If you have a repeat ticket you *must* show up one hour ahead—NO EXCEPTIONS."

About 6:30 A.M. the first vanload of men is transported out to job sites. The rest of the job seekers wait their turn and more show up through the early morning hours to sign in. According to the woman who runs the Labor Pool, on an average day ninety-five to a hundred workers "get out on jobs." Statewide, the Labor Pool operation places an average of a thousand homeless workers per day. The work is primarily unskilled: cleaning bottles for Pepsi, doing clean-up on construction sites, and hot-tar roofing. Upon returning to the Labor Pool after work, the homeless laborer is given a check for the day, which is cashed on the spot. For four hours of work, a laborer grosses about $15.00 and nets approximately $12.00.

The Labor Corner   The third site for securing day labor is referred to on the streets as the Labor Corner. It has an interesting history. In 1974 TEC closed an employment office it had operated for many years just a few blocks east of the Sally. When the office closed, employers continued to use the corner as a contact point with homeless men staying at the Salvation Army. A couple of years later, businesses in the area began to complain about the labor seekers hanging out all day on the corner. The police responded to this pressure by patrolling the area more vigilantly, and the day laborers responded to the police patrol by moving down a block toward the major Austin freeway on which most prospective employers came into town. The homeless job seekers had not been congregating long at the new location before the owner of a nearby dairy began complaining to the city. In about a year the city decided officially to move the Labor Corner eight blocks west to a corner equipped with a portable toilet and benches.

To the homeless, where they wait for jobs is less important than getting them. Most mornings by 6:30, ten to twenty men are standing on the edge of the sidewalk, watching the vehicles coming down Second Avenue. When one slows down and pulls over, the men rush to the car to find out what kind of work is being offered and what the pay will be. Since the competition is usually stiff, it is not uncommon for one or more of the men to jump into the bed of a contractor's pick-up truck without even asking about the type of work or the wage. Folklore and personal stories on the corner warn of the dangers of such overzealousness, telling of occasions when an unwary worker was paid five dollars for a day's backbreaking landscaping or nothing for eight hours of hot-tar roofing. Nona George told us, for instance, of having "accidentally" gotten a job while talking with friends at the Labor Corner:

> This fella wanted somebody to go mow the lawn and clean the flower beds at his condominium, and nobody there wanted it, so I said I would go. And he had me out there, using the lawn mower and digging in flower beds all day. So when I finished, the son-of-a-bitch didn't even bring me all the way back downtown. We stopped at a Seven-Eleven and he bought me a quart of beer and a pack of smokes. For a day's work. Told me "thanks" and wouldn't even give me a ride the rest of the way downtown. That's some shit, isn't it? Said he was going to pay me five an hour.

Although there is no assurance that the verbal promise of an employer will serve to protect against such exploitation, not even to discuss the matter before accepting the job seems doubly unsafe. But since there are never enough jobs to go around, the desire of a broke and homeless person to earn some money often overrides the fears of exploitation.

Some of the homeless endeavor to get first shot at prospective employers by moving east toward the freeway. During the morning hours the police patrol the area, pushing the men back toward the officially designated Labor Corner. But serious job seekers cannot afford to stay there. As one twenty-eight-year-old black man told us in frustration, "You just can't get a goddamn job if you stay where they want you." Occasionally a particularly persistent seeker after day labor refuses to move back to the Labor Corner and ends up arrested. Usually, however, the homeless comply—until the police leave.

As they wait for employers to drive by, some of the homeless ward off boredom and discouragement by smoking joints or drinking beer if they have the money, and by telling each other stories. At the Labor Corner a person with a good story can almost always find a willing audience. Other homeless sit on the curb reading paperbacks or the newspaper. Some lean up against a wall or chain-link fence and doze off. To the casual observer driving by it may appear that only a few of the homeless are really interested in landing a job, but what the observer does not realize is that by 9:00 A.M. many have already been waiting for two or even three hours. Also, for many of them, this take-it-or-leave-it demeanor seems to be in part a reaction to the intense competition. It takes a particularly aggressive attitude to run out to a truck that has stopped in the street, haggle against eight or ten other people, and convince the prospective employer that you are the one to hire. Faced with such stiff competition, some of the homeless just sit on the curb and "watch the circus," as one disgruntled homeless man described the scene. Furthermore, the Labor Corner is also frequented by many Hispanics who live in east Austin and who are often more aggressive than most of the homeless. Resentment is voiced in ethnic slurs when the Hispanics are out of earshot. Many of the homeless believe that "the Mexicans drive the wages down by accepting anything."

The lore on the Labor Corner has it that the best jobs are offered by private individuals, who are likely to hire the worker for less demanding work at a higher wage and to toss in lunch as well. Not all private jobs live up to expectations, however, as is illustrated by the following field notes describing a morning's work off the corner with Willie Hastings:

I had told Willie I was looking for work this morning. While I was talking to Pat, I saw Willie run out to a new Ford pick-up and jump into the cab to talk with the driver. Willie motioned for me to come over. He opened the door for me and said the man had a job for us. The man said he wanted us to come out to his home to clean up and mow the yard. He wasn't very talkative and seemed a bit nervous about being with us. When we got to his house he had everything already set out to put us to work. He had me go around the front and back yards scraping up dog shit (and there was lots of it) in fairly tall grass before Willie came by and mowed the grass with a lawn mower. After I finished he had me do some trimming around the driveway and then rake while Willie loaded the pick-up bed with junk from the backyard. The fellow didn't work with us, but he did come out to check on us periodically. Willie worked pretty hard at first, but then slacked off when we'd worked for about an hour and a half and the guy hadn't told us we could take a break. Willie told me that most of the time when he's worked for people at their homes they've been really nice to him, feeding him and not making him work too hard. He said this fellow was a slave-driver and that he wasn't going to do any more than he had to. We finished at 11:30 A.M. The fellow gave us $12 each for three and a half hours of work and drove us back into town, saying only that we'd done a good job. He dropped us off back at the corner. As the man drove away, Willie sneered to one of the other guys on the corner, "That rich asshole wouldn't even give us a break."

Problems with Day Labor   The reliance of many of the homeless on day labor has a number of drawbacks which must be understood as essential ingredients in their daily lives. Perhaps most deleterious to efforts by the homeless to pull themselves up by their own bootstraps is the sporadic nature of such employment. As has been pointed out, even on a good day no more than half of the homeless who apply to TEC or the Labor Pool are able to obtain day labor. At the Labor Corner the percentage seeking employment unsuccessfully is even higher. Furthermore, even during good times, when work can be found almost every day, it is seldom possible to work a full forty-hour week, since many of the jobs last only a few hours. Additionally, much of the work, such as landscaping and construction site clean-up, is outside, which makes it particularly vulnerable to shutdown in bad weather. Furthermore, little work is available on Saturdays and virtually none on Sundays. This means that the homeless who secure day labor during the week must try to save a portion of their meager earnings to tide them over through the weekend. As one forty-year-old homeless male commented, "I put quarters and dimes off to the side all week for 'Sunday money,' but I always end up spending it all on Saturday."

There are other ways in which day labor is unstable. Seldom does a worker have the opportunity to work for the same employer over an extended period of time. Employers utilize day laborers primarily for occasional needs, such as unloading vans. Moreover, the homeless person has difficulty keeping in touch with employers since he or she does not have ready access to a phone. Pat Manchester, for instance, acquired semi-steady employment for several weeks doing yard work for a physician who lived on the outskirts of town. The physician did not give Pat his telephone number, but Pat did not think to ask for it, either. During bad weather Pat's only means of keeping in touch was to go to the Labor Corner and wait. "If he doesn't show up," Pat stated dejectedly, "it means I'm not working that day."

Elliot Liebow, in his analysis of the work world of black street-corner men in the 1960s, noted several reasons why these men were less than enthusiastic and aggressive in pursuit of such jobs as were available to them. Objective factors included low pay, closed doors in the

labor market due to unionization, lack of transportation, the arduous-
ness of the work, and lack of basic skills. The bottom line, however,
noted Liebow, was "the plain fact that in such a job he cannot make a
living."[19]

Times have not changed in that regard. Nearly twenty years later,
the homeless in Austin were faced with the same problem. As a forty-
two-year-old homeless man from Pittsburgh who had been working out
of the Labor Pool told us despairingly:

> If you're working the Labor Pool, you're making at most, say, 25 dollars a
> day. Meals cost you $4.50 or so and cigarettes are over a buck. Then a bunk
> at the Bunkhaus is $6.50 a night. If you drink, forget it. You can't make it.
> And if you don't go to work one day, there goes your bankroll.

Day-labor employers seldom provide benefits, such as medical insurance, unemployment insurance, and social security contributions, that
are normally provided by conventional employers. Frequently even such
basic provisions as worker's compensation are not provided.[20] More
immediately frustrating to the homeless worker than not receiving benefits, however, is the possibility of being paid less than the negotiated
wage. The homeless person is seldom in a position to argue over such
exploitation, as can be seen from Nona's experience. In fact, we often
heard about day-labor employers who skipped out without paying the
workers at all, as in an incident recalled by Marilyn:

> We went and worked on this job a week. The boss said he'd pay us at the
> end of the week. We were there the day he got $2,500. And he took us to
> the Tamale House and said he was going to go to the bank and cash the
> check and come back and pay us, but he never came back and nobody got
> their money. See, he was a subcontractor and there was four of us working
> for him. We were out there floating and taping, putting up plaster and paint-
> ing. And we got the job done and we were down there waiting for him to
> come back and pay us. He said he was paying each one of us $5 an hour.
> But none of us got paid and nobody's ever seen him around since. So that's
> what you gotta worry about at the Labor Corner.

An even more serious danger lurking in the world of day labor is the
risk of work injuries. For the homeless person without a supportive
social network to fall back on, an injury on the job can be an even more
catastrophic setback than for most workers. Furthermore, some day-
labor employers seem unscrupulously willing to evade their responsibility to assist injured employees. The evangelical activist who ran Angels
House railed against city support of the Labor Corner on just these

grounds. He frequently recounted the story of a young man who came to the soup kitchen one day with acid burns on his face. The man was hired off the Labor Corner to use acid to remove cement from metal siding. When the worker's face got splashed with the acid, the employer took him to the county hospital's emergency room and told him to run inside while he parked the truck. When the young man went in, however, the employer disappeared. Similar stories were often told at the Labor Corner and the Salvation Army. Our field notes contain numerous examples of work injuries, and in the Salvation Army dinner line we frequently saw workers on crutches or with an arm in a sling.[21]

In understanding the work orientation of the homeless, then, it is important to recognize the demoralizing nature of the work experiences they confront. The jobs available to them are low-paying, short-term, and irregular. Added to this is the threat of employer exploitation and negligence. These frustrations and inequities are not transparent to the recently dislocated, however. Not only do they often look intensively for wage labor, but many of them exude persistence and optimism. Like other Americans supposedly imbued with a strong work ethic, many of the recently dislocated believe that if they only look hard enough, they too will find work that provides a living wage.[22]

A touching illustration of this orientation was provided by Tiny, a thirty-two-year-old man who slept beside one of us one winter night in the downtown warehouse run by the Sally. As he lay stretched out on a skimpy mattress on the cold cement floor, he talked about himself. Tiny came from Mississippi, where he had worked in a variety of jobs since high school, mostly construction, heavy equipment operating, and farming. He said that he used to drink heavily for several years, but that he had been on the streets only twice before. The first time, he got off the streets by going back to live with his parents; the second time, he moved in with friends. His most recent job had been in a factory that made industrial tubing. One day when he was driving home from work Tiny picked up a twenty-one-year-old woman hitchhiker. She was broke and alone with no place to go, so he had her come home with him. They fell in love. He referred to her as "my fiancée" and said that "we're planning to get married as soon as possible." But the tubing plant he was working at had recently closed and there had been no other work in his hometown, so Tiny and his fiancée decided to leave town in his old pick-up and look for work elsewhere. They had gotten as far as Kansas when the engine blew. With what little money they had left Tiny sent his fiancée off to stay with her mother until he could manage to find a job. People he met on the road told him there "was lots of work to be had in Austin," so he "came down here" and had been here ten days. He worked the first few days and had hopes of working steadily. His spirits bolstered, he called his fiancée at her mother's house and told her that it would not be long before he could send for her. She wanted to come right away, but he told her, "Rent down here is high and it'll take a while to get enough money together to get an apartment." He told her that if she came now she would have to stay with him on the streets. That convinced her to stay with her mother a little longer. Now, however, the money he had earned from his first few days of work was gone and he had not yet found another job. He was worried, since the last time he had talked to his fiancée she had told him she was going to have to leave her mom's place very soon and was thinking about hitchhiking to Austin. He pulled out a picture of her he carried in his wallet, commenting, "She's pretty to me, and she don't ask for money. All she needs is tender loving care." Just before we went to sleep, Tiny turned and said, "I know I can find work tomorrow. I'm just going to keep walking from one place to the next until I do."

Such persistence and optimism are not stable attitudinal resources. Instead, they are highly vulnerable to erosion by the frustrations the homeless encounter in their experiences with day labor. Alvin Gouldner argues that the "norm of reciprocity" is a universal component of moral codes and "makes two interrelated, minimal demands: (1) people should help those who have helped them, and (2) people should not injure those who have helped them."[23] When homeless workers, struggling as they do against heavy odds to keep afloat in the world of wage labor, are not paid or are injured and not assisted, their material survival is obviously endangered. But, perhaps even more important, their faith in the moral order of the world of wage labor is undermined. Observation of a number of such experiences, combined with a growing realization of the undependability of such work, is bound to diminish commitment to it as a means of survival.

In time, then, whatever optimism and enthusiasm existed with respect to the world of wage labor begins to sour. As a consequence, pursuit of wage labor through such facilities as TEC, the Labor Pool, and the Labor Corner starts to wane. This alienation process clearly manifested itself in our tracking data. As is revealed in Table 4.5, the longer the contact with Sally, and presumably the longer the time on the streets, the less frequent the contacts with TEC. Individuals whose contact with Sally spanned only one day show a median number of

TABLE 4.5   RELATIONSHIP BETWEEN TIME ON
THE STREETS AND TEC CONTACT

Time on the Streets *	Number of Homeless	Median Number of TEC Contacts
1 day	71	2.8
2 to 14 days	71	0.5
15 days to 2 months	69	0.12
2 to 6 months	59	0.06
6 months or more	67	0.03

* As indicated by length of contact with the Salvation Army.

TABLE 4.6   MEAN SCORES FOR DAY LABOR AND MEAN
TIME ON THE STREETS, BY TYPE OF HOMELESS PERSON*

	Mean Score for Day Labor Use	Mean Time on the Streets
Recently dislocated	1.52	4.3 months
Regular straddler	1.02	1.2 years
Traditional tramp	0.89	6.1 years
Hippie tramp	0.13	3.2 years
Traditional bum	0.27	4.4 years
Redneck bum	0.20	2.0 years
Mentally ill	0.29	1.3 years

* Mean scores close to 0 indicate infrequent use, those in the vicinity of 1 indicate occasional use, and those approaching 2 indicate extensive use.

contacts with TEC nearly ninety-five times that for individuals with a span of contact covering six months or more. This difference is clearly exaggerated, since most individuals whose contacts with the Sally are compressed into one day have been on the streets for a longer period. But it is not so much the absolute figures that are of interest as it is the pattern they reveal. The same pattern of declining day labor use was observed among the homeless in our field sample. Table 4.6 shows both the mean scores for pursuit of day labor among the different types of homeless and their corresponding mean time on the streets. Day labor is utilized most frequently by the recently dislocated and the regular straddlers, the groups that have been on the streets for the shortest periods of time. Thus, the longer individuals are on the streets and the more they drift into the subculture of street life, the less likely they are to rely on day labor as a means of survival. The only apparent exception to this process of alienation is the traditional tramps, but their use of day labor is more cyclical than routine. Moreover, as outsiders, they have in any case already drifted far from the world of regular work and its cultural underpinnings.

Taken together, then, the findings presented in Tables 4.5 and 4.6 point to an inverse relationship between wage labor as a means of survival and time on the streets, and thus they suggest that experience with the world of wage labor leads to diminishing reliance on it as a subsistence strategy. Such a process of alienation is understandable, considering the array of frustrations and difficulties the homeless confront in their dealings with that world.

But where or to whom do the disenchanted homeless turn in order to survive materially? If some of them are shut out of the world of wage labor or eventually eschew it, then how do they make do economically? As we will see in the next chapter, most drift into the world of shadow work. But the survival of some is facilitated by various forms of institutionalized support. We therefore turn now to consideration of such assistance.

INSTITUTIONALIZED ASSISTANCE

The term *institutionalized behavior* refers to lines of social action that are patterned in accordance with normative traditions, political legislation, or the mission and operational requisites of organizations, be they churches, corporate firms, or soup kitchens and shelters. Wage labor is institutionalized, as are several other forms of material support some of the homeless receive. The two basic forms of such institutionalized material assistance are institutional labor and income supplements.

INSTITUTIONAL LABOR

Institutional labor is work within and for agencies that is performed by agency clients or constituents.[24] Two varieties of such work were available to some of the homeless in Austin: jobs with accommodative street agencies that serve the homeless, such as the Salvation Army, and work within caretaker rehabilitative agencies that treat homeless substance abusers.

Working for "the Sally"   The day-to-day operation of the local Salvation Army requires, among other things, a sizable work force. Aside from the administrative staff and a handful of volunteers, virtually all of the Sally's workers are homeless who use the agency's facilities. According to its director of services, "There are two basic employment categories for homeless workers. We begin them on 'grant status,' which means we give them a bed upstairs and five dollars a week for the work they do, like clean-up in the dining room. Then, if they do well, they have a chance to be hired as regular staff. The resident manager, the door manager, and the cook are all staff who started on grant status."

Although upward mobility from grant status to wage labor is possible, many employees stay on grant status for some time. Tanner Sutton, for instance, began working for the Sally in an official grant position as one of several night monitors at the shelter. As a grant status employee receiving five dollars per week, three meals per day, and a bunk in the workers' dormitory, Tanner felt a big improvement in his life situation. "When I used to be on the streets," he told us shortly after getting the job, "I never had any money for books or xeroxing, but now that I'm working I've got a little when I need it—at least for a few days, if I don't spend it all on cigarettes. Now I can go to the used book store and even buy a book. I don't have to stand there to read it."

Tanner kept this job for several months without being offered a chance to move into a higher-paying, minimum-wage position. Openings in the higher-paying positions are not nearly as frequent as in grant positions, and in fairness to the Sally it must be said that there was little Tanner was capable of doing. After working the job through the winter, he left Austin in mid-spring, ostensibly to visit the Smithsonian Institute and pursue his occult studies.

Those among the homeless who have talents and abilities needed by the Sally are occasionally recruited to wage-labor positions directly, without a probationary contract period. When Hoyt Page first arrived in Austin he approached the shelter director. "I told him, 'I ain't gonna lie to you. I have a problem with drinking. But I won't drink on the job, and I won't come in drunk at night. And I need a job to get my life straight.' " Hoyt's immense size and affable disposition made him a natural choice for the recently vacated position of dinner-line monitor. He was hired as a regular staff worker immediately, receiving the minimum hourly wage plus room and board. Of course, the Sally can employ only a handful of homeless in comparison to the vast number it serves.

Working for Rehab Programs   Drug or alcohol rehabilitation programs offer the homeless person a modest income and room and board
in a relatively stable environment, at least in comparison to life on the
streets. The explicit goal of such programs is to salvage substance abusers who are thought to have "ruined their lives," and work is seen as
an integral part of the salvaging process. The head of one Austin rehabilitation program told us, "We use work therapy here for rehabilitating them. You see, one of the biggest problems an alcoholic faces when
he tries to come off drinking is how to deal with his idle time." His
assistant elaborated:

> By the time they get here, these men have sunk about as low as they can go.
> You can't just clean them up physically, you've got to do it behaviorally as
> well. These men have lost the ability to work regularly, and part of our
> program is getting them rehabituated to that and getting them experiencing
> the improved self-esteem that goes with it.[25]

The homeless are less likely to see their problems as stemming from
drinking.[26] Nonetheless, by going along with agency personnel to some
degree, they can get off the streets for a while, and, in most programs,
earn five to twenty dollars per week while working (usually forty hours
or more per week) and attending AA or similar substance-abuse meetings. Thus, some of the homeless, whether or not they are in need of
drug or alcohol rehabilitation, use these programs as a temporary escape from the grueling trials of street life, a fact some agency personnel
willingly admit.[27] As one agency director explained, "Last winter when
it snowed, we had a waiting list a mile long, but mostly it was people
who just wanted a place to stay out of the cold. Street people are wise
enough to know how to get in here when they want to. We take self-
report as evidence of addiction and the word has gotten around. They
know it."

The homeless, especially those who are in need of rehabilitation, face
a dilemma when they reach the end of such programs. The programs
do not generally provide sufficient funds or follow-up services to let
clients stay off the streets once they are discharged. For example, Alvin,
who is thirty-three years old, has spent nearly two years on the streets
of Austin, surviving for the last year mostly by scavenging, panhandling, selling plasma, and, to a lesser extent, homosexual prostitution.
"Then one morning," he told us, "I woke up hung-over and sick in an
abandoned apartment complex. I could hear a bulldozer knocking over
part of the building when I woke up and I thought, 'Fuck it, I'm just

gonna lay here and let them take me with it.' But when the 'dozer started getting closer, I decided to try to get into this program and get off the streets." Alvin had been a resident at the rehabilitation center for a month when we first met him. He was attending compulsory AA meetings regularly and working as the agency's daytime receptionist. He confided, however, that he was uncertain about his future:

> What's worrying me most is that I can't see how I'm going to make it once I get out of here. They start you out at seven bucks a week and raise it two bucks per week until you get to twenty. But that's not enough so that I'll be able to save anything for when I get out. I mean, I'm fine while I'm in here, but they only let you stay seven weeks, and when they kick you out you don't have anyplace else to go or money to get by on. That's why the guys in this program have been in other ones—they end up going from one program to another, living on the streets in between.

A month later Alvin was still at the rehab center, having been allowed to stay beyond the usual seven weeks because he was a good worker who impressed the counselors as sincerely working the program. He was still anxious about his future, however:

> They're letting me stay because they need me, but it's hard. They expect you to reach out, you know, but how? Like they want you to find an AA sponsor, but it's hard because anybody you find here has probably only been in AA a couple of months at most. And you can't save any money. A lot of the guys sneak off to the plasma center just to have enough money to stay in cigarettes and coffee. So it looks like I'm going to leave here broke and end up without a job, back drinking on the streets.

Whereas Alvin perceived the rehab counselors as at least trying to help him, some of the homeless see certain rehabilitation agencies almost completely in terms of exploitation. Willie Hastings told us of a program in San Antonio where he had been a client:

> They're supposed to be helping you, but it's nothing more than a rip-off outfit. They get you up at five in the morning and you have breakfast and an early morning AA meeting, then they take you out and you spend all day working landscaping jobs for this guy. He gives you two bucks a week and a place to stay. He tells you that if you stay for the whole eight-week program, they'll set you up in an apartment, but I've never heard of anybody lasting that long with him. Last time I was there I quit with three other guys and we stole some of his weed-eaters and a lawn mower. It's slave labor, man. Now the guy has to come to Austin to try to get people for his program because people on the streets in San Antonio know what he's doing.[28] See, that's why I'm saying it's a rip-off.

Neither street-agency jobs nor rehab institutional labor provides work for more than a handful of the homeless. Of the 168 homeless we came to know in some capacity, seven were or had been employed by the Salvation Army, one worked for the Bunkhaus, and five did wage labor for a rehabilitation agency. The jobs provided by such agencies are obviously merely a drop in the bucket of what is needed. Moreover, they seldom get anyone off the streets; rather, they place the homeless worker in a liminal status, neither completely on nor removed from the streets. The work provides little, if any, sense of progress except initially, and its location within the subculture of street life means that it gives workers and clients neither a sense of realistically attainable regular work nor a personal identity beyond the streets. Such positions offer few social contacts with people who are not homeless. Furthermore, such positions—especially agency jobs—are plagued with tension and role conflict.[29] Although recently recruited from the streets and still in direct contact with street acquaintances, agency workers are expected to distance themselves from those individuals and to identify with the agency. In dealing with this tension the homeless generally receive little support or understanding from their non-homeless superiors. As the Salvation Army services director explained to us, "We tell them not to associate with the guys on the streets so that we can maintain equality and keep them from showing favoritism to their friends." However reasonable such strictures may seem, they create considerable role conflict and push institutional straddlers into a social void. These institutional positions are therefore often seen by their incumbents as little more than what have been aptly termed "stations of the lost."[30]

INCOME SUPPLEMENTS

Institutionalized income supplements to the homeless take two forms: transfer payments and intrafamilial handouts.

Transfer Payments   Transfer payments are simply monies collected by the state and transferred back to citizens who qualify for their receipt. The United States, like many Western industrial countries, offers two main types of transfer programs: universal ones, such as Social Security, Social Security Disability (SSD), and unemployment compensation; and means-tested programs, such as General Assistance, Aid to Families with Dependent Children (AFDC), food stamps, Special Supplemental Food Program for Women, Infants, and Children (WIC), and Supplemental Security Income (SSI).[31]

Both our tracking and our field data indicate that most of the Austin homeless do not receive much income from either kind of program. At the time of their initial TEC contact, for example, only 13 percent of 348 indicated that they had recently received unemployment compensation, and fewer than 1 percent claimed receipt of some form of welfare compensation. Moreover, such assistance is typically supplemental at best, as only 6 of the 168 field informants counted transfer payments as their major source of income.[32]

The reasons the homeless in Austin do not receive a larger share of these benefits are rooted in a set of circumstances and qualifying criteria that undermine both their eligibility and the accessibility of the dispensing agencies. The universal transfer programs are essentially social insurances in which receipt of benefits is contingent on having first paid into the system. These programs are typically organized through employers who withhold employee deductions and pay employer contributions. Only a small proportion of the work engaged in by the homeless is with regular work employers, and day-labor employers seldom bother with the paperwork or expense of withholding taxes or Social Security, much less provide for workers' compensation or unemployment coverage. Even if their employers did attend to these matters, however, the majority of the homeless would be ineligible for Social Security benefits, since their mean age is thirty-five and Social Security eligibility begins at sixty-two, except for the disabled. Additionally, the limited availability of regular work for the homeless in Austin, as well as the transience of many of them, makes it difficult to qualify for unemployment benefits.

It is not surprising, then, that most of the homeless are unable to collect from universal transfer programs. What is surprising, though, is the degree to which the homeless fail to meet general requirements for means-tested programs. The problems the homeless face in qualifying for such programs are not related to their financial means, for clearly most of them are financially needy, but to their failure to meet other requirements.

One particularly restrictive stipulation for both AFDC and WIC is that the recipients either have children or be pregnant. Thus the majority of the homeless, whether in Austin or elsewhere, find themselves ineligible for these forms of assistance by virtue of being unattached adults.

Another pervasive restrictive requirement is that of residency. Documentation of state or local residency is required by most government-based services, as well as by many locally based private charities. Since homelessness means, most fundamentally, having no residential address, residency requirements bar the homeless from assistance.[33] This problem is exacerbated by the extensive mobility of some of the homeless. Straddlers and tramps, with their high degree of interstate and intercity mobility, often have not been in town long enough to qualify as residents, and neither have the recently dislocated who have come in search of work.

Ironically, some of the facilities that provide shelter for the homeless actually foster mobility. Although the local Salvation Army is fairly liberal, many shelters allow only a limited number of nights of free shelter, after which clients must pay a nightly fee. According to Banjo, this is "one reason why so many street people are transient. If the shelters across the country would let people hang out for free a little longer," he told us, "then maybe more street people could get some coins together for a real place to live. But no, the policies of most Sallies and shelters force us to keep on the go."

A final set of barriers confronting the homeless are associated with the bureaucratic structure of the agencies that dispense transfer payments and benefits. In keeping with the bureaucratic principle of specialization, transfer programs are spread throughout a community's social-service system rather than being housed in a single agency or facility. Such decentralization frequently makes it difficult for the most needy citizens to reach these agencies. This is particularly true for the homeless, who seldom have much discretionary income to spend on public transportation and even more rarely own any form of transportation themselves.[34]

Even if the homeless find their way to the appropriate agency, they may encounter another obstacle: the not infrequent inflexibility of the bureaucratic operatives themselves. Students of bureaucracy have often noted that the bureaucratic principle of standardization often leads to pernicious rigidity with respect to individual client needs and circumstances and that this tendency is most pronounced among those "bureaucrats . . . who have the greatest amount of contact with lower-class clients."[35] As a consequence, those at the bottom frequently find their dealings with transfer-dispensing agencies demeaning and alienating. What often makes such encounters even worse is that many homeless clients seldom have much knowledge about either the array of programs for which they might qualify or the rules of the bureaucratic game.[36] For all these reasons, then, the homeless frequently find it not worth their while to pursue the monies or services for which they might be eligible. When they make the attempt, they often give up because of the frustration and humiliation they experience.[37] A graphic case in point is provided by Hoyt's attempt to gain information about a literacy program for which he thought he might qualify. He had already made several telephone inquiries and told us that he thought he was "being given a run-around." He asked us to give him a hand, and we agreed. We had to make twenty-two phone calls over the course of four days in order to secure the information Hoyt needed. When we agreed to assist him, we had no idea that what seemed like a simple task would prove to be so time-consuming and frustrating. And we had a personal telephone at our disposal, as well as experience with client-centered bureaucracies. What proved to be an onerous task for us must be far more frustrating, as well as expensive, for the homeless. It is understandable, then, that many of the homeless fail to pursue benefits that are rightfully theirs.

These frustrations notwithstanding, some of the homeless, as we have already noted, do receive income from transfer payments. This is more likely to be the case with the older ones, such as JJ, who have officially retired and are drawing Social Security pensions, and the disabled ones, such as Gypsy Bill. Gypsy received SSI for several years before he was abruptly cut from the rolls, and then again three years later, when he was reinstated after his third administrative appeal. Lance McCay, one of our mentally ill informants, was also among those who were initially cut from SSI only to appeal and be reinstated later. Unlike Gypsy, who had managed to stay off the streets until he was cut from SSI, Lance had never been able to stabilize his life, with or without SSI. He had experienced episodes of homelessness before he was dismissed from the rolls, and again after he had been reinstated. As he despairingly told us one evening, "I've got to get myself together! I've just got to get myself off the streets. But every time I get my check I blow it in four or five days. I hate myself for it. It makes me so mad! I got over $2,500 once and I blew it in two weeks. So I'm still on the streets."[38]

Receipt of such large checks is clearly the exception rather than the rule. Moreover, it is our sense that relatively few of the homeless receive transfer payments in an amount that would enable them to get off the streets. In this respect they have definitely fallen through our society's "safety net."

Familial Handouts   A second kind of income supplement available to some homeless individuals comes directly from their families rather than

TABLE 4.7   RECEIPT OF INCOME SUPPLEMENTS
BY THE HOMELESS, BY TYPE

	Mean Score for Income Supplements	Ranking Among Repertoire of Material Survival Strategies
Recently dislocated	0.23	3
Regular straddler	0.27	4
Institutional straddler	0.20	2
Traditional tramp	0.33	3
Hippie tramp	0.13	5
Traditional bum	0.40	4
Redneck bum	0.20	4
Mentally ill	0.71	1

being filtered through the government. Such intrafamilial financial support is a relatively widespread economic phenomenon in the United States, particularly in the middle and upper classes. Among other things, parents often assist their children attending college and during the early years of their marriage—so often, in fact, that we can speak of such patterns of assistance as being almost institutionalized.[39] Although we met some homeless individuals who received familial economic support, such support did not appear to represent a very substantial source of income even for those who received it. Lance McCay received the most substantial familial support of any individual in our field sample. One Christmas Lance visited his parents in Houston for several days and returned to Austin by Greyhound bus on the day after Christmas. When we encountered him in a fast-food restaurant a few hours after his return, he excitedly displayed a wide array of presents: a couple of cartons of cigarettes, clothes, notebooks, toiletries, a transistor radio, a five-ounce gold paper clip, and a big, fancy duffle bag to hold it all. He was particularly fond of the paper clip, saying that it showed his parents' feelings for him. He said they had also given him "quite a bit of money."

As a member of a well-to-do family Lance is an exception among the homeless. More commonly, familial support comes in the form of small amounts of cash and "care packages." Occasionally the recipient sells the items in the packages at cut-rate prices to "get some cash up," as one young man did with the new clothes his mother sent him at Christmas.

Considering the lower-class status of the homeless and their families, this lack of familial support is predictable.[40] Poor families have few economic resources to spread among their members in times of need. As a consequence, the homeless are unlikely to receive much financial support from their families.

It appears, then, that familial handouts provide the homeless with even less reliable financial support than transfer payments. In fact, when these two sources of financial assistance are combined, we find that they are the major source of support in Austin only for the mentally ill. As is shown in Table 4.7, where a mean score of near 0 indicates infrequent receipt of income supplements and a score approaching 1 indicates occasional receipt, we see that it is only for the mentally ill homeless that income supplements inch toward moderate salience as a means of material survival. It is clear, then, that income supplements did not figure prominently in the day-to-day survival repertoire of most unattached homeless adults in Austin.

SUMMARY

Consistent with the premise that an understanding of any aggregation's life-style requires consideration of its repertoire of material survival strategies, in this chapter we have examined the roles of regular work, day labor, and institutionalized assistance in the material survival of the homeless in Austin. We have seen that the vast majority of the homeless express interest in securing work when they first find themselves on the streets in Austin, that they are willing to work full-time, whatever the wage or shift, and that most do indeed look for work, both regular work and day labor, at least for a while. But regular work is largely unavailable to the homeless, and day labor, being short-term, irregular, and low-paying, does not provide them with steady incomes, much less a route off the streets. Additionally, the job-seeking efforts of the homeless, particularly the recently dislocated and the straddlers, are encumbered by a host of obstacles that further undermine the dependability and utility for survival of work as conventionally conceived. And neither public assistance nor familial handouts go very far in filling the void.

To what extent do these findings differ from what has been observed among the homeless in other cities across the country? At first glance, it might be argued that the experiences of the homeless in Austin with wage labor and institutional assistance differ considerably from those of the homeless elsewhere, because the majority of the homeless we studied comprise a self-selected population consisting of individuals with unusually strong work orientations. Yet when we compare the homeless in Austin with those in many other cities it becomes clear that they do not differ in any significant way. As we noted in Chapter 1, they are quite comparable demographically. Moreover, research into the employment activities and income sources of the homeless across the country has shown that the vast majority are either working or looking for work,[41] and that some form of employment is often cited as the most frequent source of income.[42] But, just as in Austin, such work as can be found is typically less than full-time and the wages are usually minimal. The result is that the income the homeless derive from wage labor across the country is irregular and seldom sufficient to support them even on the streets.

The data on institutional assistance across the country indicate that it is of some help to some of the homeless but is clearly not as much help as is often supposed. Most studies, however, have found a higher proportion of homeless receiving institutional assistance, particularly transfer payments, than we found in Austin.[43] We suspect these differences are due to variations in the distribution of gender and age groups, and the proportions of disabled, those actively looking for work (not yet totally discouraged workers), and local and state residents. Several studies have reported, for example, that the receipt of public assistance is greater among female homeless, especially those with children.[44] These differences notwithstanding, it is important to note that the findings coming from cities around the country contradict the idea that most of the homeless are on the dole. Moreover, the public assistance that does find its way into the hands of the homeless is supplemental at best: it is not sufficient to sustain most homeless recipients, much less enable them to get off the streets.

It is clear that even those homeless who are beneficiaries of public assistance must supplement it in order to survive on the streets. Some of them, we know, do so by turning to wage labor. But, for reasons already discussed, that is rarely a full solution. Moreover, the frustration and uncertainties associated with the world of wage labor tend to diminish reliance on it as a salient subsistence strategy. As the homeless give up on wage labor and find themselves unable to receive adequate public assistance, they must develop other strategies for material survival. We turn, then, to these other subsistence strategies in order to round out our understanding of how the homeless manage to survive on the streets of Austin.

Shadow Work

It's 8:30 on Sunday morning. There are only a few cars on the streets, and even fewer pedestrians, except near the Sally, where some homeless have begun to congregate to await the bus that will take them to the Central Assembly of God Church on the outskirts of town. As we walk toward this pick-up point, we hear some rustling in a large garbage dumpster and then see a head pop up. It's Gypsy, already at work scavenging for salvageable items: food, clothing, tin cans, and other throwaways he can use directly or sell on the streets or in pawn shops.

On another day, at noon on the Drag, we notice two long-haired hippie tramps panhandling passersby. "Hey, man, you got any spare change? Just a quarter?" they ask. It's Gimpy Dan and a sidekick trying to make ends meet. A bit further down the Drag, in front of the major campus bookstore, sits another homeless person playing a beat-up guitar and singing songs about Jesus. It's Banjo trying to coax passersby to toss some loose change into his guitar case. And just around the corner, by an open crafts area, we spot Rhyming Mike reciting his street poetry in exchange for a few nickels and dimes.

That evening, when we queue up for dinner at the Sally, we observe two rather infirm and weather-beaten men, both in their fifties or sixties, scouring an empty parking lot across the street for aluminum cans. One spots a Coke can, picks it up, and drops it into a plastic garbage bag held open by his partner. It is Indio and his friend JJ. The bag is bulging—they have had a productive day.

While we are still waiting in the dinner line we see two fellows in their mid-twenties leave the queue and scurry across the street to talk to Bill-Bob and his redneck friends. They make a quick exchange and then sprint back to the dinner line. Grinning, they say they got a good deal: "A couple of joints for two bucks each." Across the street Bill-Bob is smiling too, probably because he has just added a dollar or two to his cash supply.

Later, stretched out in the winter warehouse, we hear the barely audible voice of a homeless entrepreneur. Walking through the cavernous room after lights-out, he whispers, just loud enough to be heard over the coughing and muffled conversations, "Joints! Joints! Joints for sale!"

.   .   .   .

In each of the preceding vignettes, we see one or more homeless persons at work. It is not work as traditionally conceived, to be sure. But it is work, for in each case attention and energy are riveted on the procurement of money or other material goods for personal use or exchange. Unlike wage labor, though, in these activities there is little to no regularized exchange of labor for money. Nor are the activities officially sanctioned or their time and place bureaucratically controlled.[1] Instead, they are compensatory subsistence strategies that are fashioned or pursued in the shadow of more conventional work because of exclusion from existing labor markets, because participation in those markets fails to provide a living wage, because public assistance is insufficient, or because such strategies provide a more reliable means of survival. We call these compensatory, non–wage labor subsistence strategies "shadow work."[2]

Besides being unofficial, unenumerated work existing outside the wage labor economy, shadow work is characterized further by its highly opportunistic and innovative nature. It involves, at the very minimum, the recognition and exploitation of whatever resources and unofficial markets happen to be available whenever a few dollars are needed. As Jacqueline Wiseman observed in her field study of skid-row alcoholics in the 1960s, "When the skid row man thinks of getting money, he . . . must show ingenuity in creating something out of nothing. Thus, he thinks in terms of objects, relationships, or short-term tasks that can be converted into enough cash to take care of current needs—liquor, food, shelter, incidentals."[3] The same is true of many of the homeless we came to know. They trade their personal possessions, sell their plasma, scavenge through the refuse of others in search of salable items, perform in prime space, and panhandle passersby. Seldom does any one homeless person engage in all of these activities consistently, but often, as need and opportunity arise, they combine various of these strategies with day labor and/or public assistance, or they develop individual repertoires of shadow work. The homeless we studied are not only people of needs, but, in the words of one observer of their contemporaries in another city, "grudging players in a rough theater of improvisation."[4]

In this chapter we explore this characterization by examining the nature and range of shadow work pursued by the homeless in Austin. Four categories of such work were identified during the course of our field research: selling and trading, soliciting donations in public places, scavenging, and theft. We consider each variety in turn, noting, as well, the extent to which the different types of homeless engage in the various kinds of shadow work.

SELLING AND TRADING

As in the domiciled world, so among the homeless, too, the sale and exchange of goods and services are central forms of shadow work. We observed three basic variants of sales work among the homeless in Austin: selling and trading junk and personal possessions, selling illegal goods and services, and selling plasma.

SELLING AND TRADING JUNK AND PERSONAL POSSESSIONS

Sale of junk and personal possessions is not uncommon among most social classes.[5] Among the working and middle classes, these exchanges take the form of weekend garage sales, and among the upper classes they manifest themselves as estate sales.[6] Among the homeless, however, sale of junk and personal possessions takes on a distinctive cast. For one thing, the proceeds are much more fundamental to their subsistence than is typically the case for other strata. If and when the homeless peddle personal items, it is not because they have no use for them or want to clean house, so to speak, but because they need cash. Additionally, the homeless usually have few personal possessions. Their sales thus vary according to what they have recently purchased, scavenged, received as a gift, or stolen. Whatever their source, the sales items most often consist of clothing such as jackets, belts, and shoes, watches and rings, calculators and cassette tapes, and cigarettes and beer.

The asking price for such goods is low, undoubtedly because the other homeless, who make up the primary market, have little money to spend. There are exceptions, though. One afternoon we observed a twenty-eight-year-old male trying to hawk a new pair of jeans his mother had sent him. As he sat on the sidewalk, propped up against a building in the middle of the city's downtown night-life section, he would hold up the jeans as men walked by and yell out, "Man, they're brand new jeans and they're not hot!" They *were* new, too, with the labels still attached. He eventually sold them for $11.00 to a fellow who appeared to be a college student, an extraordinarily good price for a street sale. Sometimes an energetic peddler will attempt to sell his wares to the more affluent university market. For example, when Lance McCay was short of cash he would sell students his gifts from home or items he had purchased with his Social Security money, as when he sold his $400 briefcase for a mere $10 to a college student.

The sales price is usually considerably lower than even $10 or $11, though, not only because the homeless peddle primarily among each other, but also because the goods for sale are often cheap, recycled items in poor condition, items most people would regard as junk. One evening, for instance, we observed an elderly man going from group to group at the Salvation Army, trying to sell a rusty alarm clock he insisted would work even though no one could get it to run. On another occasion a young black man walked beside the Sally dinner line, hawking several old and well-worn *Playboy* magazines. "This is fine stuff," he told the men in line as he tantalizingly showed them the centerfold photos. "And only a buck apiece." He generated obvious interest, but it was Sunday evening, when few of the homeless have any loose change. Consequently, the *Playboy* hawker could find no buyers.

Among the few homeless who own vehicles, the selling or trading of auto parts is common. When times are difficult and work is scarce, they sell tires, batteries, or other parts, expecting, of course, to buy replacements in more prosperous times. Unfortunately, there are many more bad days than good, and homeless car owners frequently find themselves selling off one part after another. This creates problems for them, since a car that is not running cannot be used for transportation and is likely to get numerous parking tickets. In the late winter Gypsy Bill got together enough money to buy an old but functional car from another homeless person, but he quickly had to sell several parts, including the battery. He avoided parking tickets by enlisting the help of friends to push the car from one parking spot to another. When he was arrested on an outstanding warrant for failure to pay a traffic ticket, he was unable to move his car for several days and it was impounded. Tom Fisk also had his car impounded from a parking spot when he was in jail. Tom called the towing company and was told that it would cost $20 to get the car out. While in jail, Tom talked to the booking sergeant about his car problems. The sergeant offered to buy the car from him for $200. When we met Tom on his way to the plasma center on the day he got out of jail, he was trying to decide whether or not to sell the car. "Sure, it's worth more than $200," he told us, "but you got to figure the shape it's in and that I don't have the money to get it out. I'm going to sell some blood just to get some money up for smokes and something to eat. Tomorrow I'm going to have to go down to the police department and talk to him." As we found out later through a letter Tom sent us from Florida, he did end up selling the car at a bargain price to the police officer.[7]

Pawn shops also provide a market for personal possessions, especially jewelry and tools. The amount a pawn shop will pay for an item is usually far below its value, but the possibility remains of redeeming the item. Just as with car parts, however, there is the risk of falling behind and not being able to catch up, as is illustrated in a comment by a former carpenter waiting for day labor at TEC one morning:

> I could be getting better work than this if I just had my tools, but they're in the pawn shop downtown. I wouldn't let 'em give me no more than 30 bucks when I pawned 'em so I wouldn't have trouble getting 'em out. But work's been so slow I haven't even been able to get that much together yet.

SELLING ILLEGAL GOODS AND SERVICES

An alternative form of selling pursued by some of the homeless is the sale of illegal goods and services, particularly drugs and sex. Not all the homeless are involved in this form of sales work, though. The recently dislocated, whose energies and hopes are still focused on wage labor, tend to shy away from such illicit activity, as do the mentally ill, who have neither the interactional skills nor the persistence to be much good at it. And the majority of both traditional tramps and traditional bums seem either too old, too rickety, or too inebriated to get involved competitively in either drug trafficking or prostitution. That leaves the regular straddlers, hippie tramps, and redneck bums, all of whom are involved in varying degrees in this illicit form of shadow work, particularly in drug-dealing.

Drug Dealing   Although drug dealing can be readily observed among regular straddlers as well as hippie tramps and redneck bums, it is not as salient to the survival of the straddlers as it is for the other two types. For them, and particularly for the hippie tramps, drug dealing is more commonly a primary subsistence strategy. There are other differences between the groups. Regular straddlers deal drugs predominantly to other homeless individuals, and each deal usually involves only one to three joints of marijuana.[8] Sellers solicit customers in locations where the homeless gather in the downtown area. In the mornings there are usually several people at the Labor Corner and the Labor Pool selling joints at "two bucks apiece, three for five dollars." In the afternoons, individual sellers walk up and down the Sally dinner line soliciting buyers, and in the evenings it is common for sellers to walk along the rows of mats in the Sally's sleeping quarters, calling out in muffled tones, "Joints! Joints!" The number of sales regular straddlers make on a given day is highly dependent on the amount of money being funneled into the street economy from day labor and other forms of shadow work. When the street economy is good, sales are brisk. But when the weather turns bad, curtailing day labor, and on the weekends, when day labor is scarce and the plasma centers are closed, few people have the money for joints.

A few regular straddlers whom we observed selling drugs seemed to engage in this economic activity almost exclusively. One of them, a stocky young man in his mid-twenties who went by the name of Streeter, carried two cigarette cases filled with joints on his daily rounds of the major gathering spots for the homeless. One morning at the Labor Corner we saw him do a particularly good business, making a dozen transactions within half an hour. Except for occasional day labor or, during slow times, the sale of plasma, Streeter did not pursue any other work. A similar repertoire was followed by one of the few Native Americans we met on the streets. Known as "Medicine Man," he worked the same spots as Streeter and a few others, but he was somewhat more proprietary about the Sally dinner line. He could be seen working it vigorously evening after evening, and he did not take kindly to others infringing on "his turf," although there was little he could do about it except make threatening gestures.

Unlike Streeter and Medicine Man, most regular straddlers who sell drugs do so infrequently and as a supplement to other economic activity. During one of his periods of manic employment, Ron Whitaker purchased an ounce of marijuana at a time, rolled it into thin joints, and sold enough to pay for the ounce. He could then smoke what was left for free. Many others on the streets spoke of this as a shrewd and frugal practice and engaged in it when they could. Since the economic fortunes of the homeless are dependent on external circumstances, however, often when times were good enough that one person was able to buy a quarter-ounce, others were able to do so as well. As a result, the market would diminish and price wars would develop as individuals undercut each other in an effort to earn back their investment.

The redneck bums also cater primarily to other homeless, but they tend to work together as a team rather than individually. Additionally, they are rumored to sell better-quality marijuana. And, unlike the straddlers, the redneck bums seem to have a steady supply. Sometimes when the straddlers are unable to score, the rednecks do a particularly brisk business, as can often be seen by the number of homeless darting back and forth between the Sally dinner line and the street corner where the rednecks hang out.

The drug trade of the hippie tramps is strikingly different from that of either the straddlers or the rednecks. Their turf, as we have said, is around the Drag, adjacent to the university campus. Partly as a consequence of having staked out this niche, the hippie tramps sell drugs predominantly to people outside their own group, especially to students from the university. The market around the Drag is considerably more affluent and stable than the homeless market, except during school breaks, when the students disappear. Sales are typically larger, too—in the quarter-ounce to ounce range for marijuana—and the variety of drugs sold is greater. We observed on a number of occasions the selling of psychedelic drugs and various forms of "speed." For example, one mid-afternoon as we were chatting with Gimpy Dan and several other hippie tramps on a side street off the Drag, two punk-looking college-aged women approached the gathering and asked where they "could get some acid." Gimpy told them he "could get them Red Star for $5.00 a hit." He had one of the women walk with him up the street for half a block while the other stayed with us. Apparently he needed to check with an associate on the availability of the acid. After he found the man and talked with him a bit, Gimpy and the woman returned. He told them he would have the acid in a while and instructed them to "get lost and come back and see me in half an hour." As they walked away, he assured them that Red Star acid is the best around. "Ask any of the tramps around here," he yelled to them, "and they'll tell you that Red Star is the best."

We left before the transaction was completed—if indeed it was—but such encounters were fairly common. Whether the hippie tramps dealt more expensive drugs, such as cocaine, is unclear. We never observed them doing so, but there was considerable talk among them about such drugs as well as claims of having used them. Such talk notwithstanding, we suspect that more expensive drugs were seldom distributed by the hippie tramps.

Prostitution   The second form of illicit sales work observed among the homeless is prostitution, both homosexual and heterosexual. That some of the homeless would engage in prostitution should be expected, considering their dire economic situation and the fact that prostitution has long been recognized as an activity often pursued by individuals with limited economic prospects.[9]

Our observations indicate that homosexual prostitution is the more prominent, in large part simply because there are more homeless men than women. It is pursued more often by the younger homeless men. How widespread it is among the homeless is unclear, however. Three of our key informants openly admitted to engaging in prostitution, but many more homeless talked about having been approached by men who offered to pay them for sex. Furthermore, when dinner-line conversation among the homeless turned to "rolling queers," it seemed that everyone within earshot chipped in with one or more experiences of having robbed a gay man during a prostitution encounter. One Sunday evening, for instance, a lanky weather-beaten man in his mid-thirties rambled on to an interested gathering about once having gone home with a gay man he had "drugged with three Quaaludes." "Then," he boasted, "I split with his Caddy, a stereo, and a new TV and sold them on the streets for twenty-five hundred bucks." Having the crowd's attention, he continued by recounting an episode with "this other dude who's an accountant here in town who used to give me fifty bucks to tie him up and fuck him. But once I got him tied up I'd just take the rest of his money and split." Another man, who appeared to be about five years younger despite having lost several front teeth, responded, "Let's go find that guy and offer to do a double on him." The younger man then proceeded with a story of his own:

> I went into this bar one time—it was a peter bar, but, hell, I didn't know it—and this guy offered me fifty bucks to go home with him. So we get there and he tells me he wants me to fuck him in the ass, and I told him "Man, I gotta be drunk to do that." So I kept mixing him doubles and me singles

until he passed out. Then I swiped his car and took off down the freeway, only I was drunk on my ass and I kept bashing into the other cars, so I pulled off and went to sleep. Next morning I woke up, man, that car was beat to shit.

We suspect that such talk about preying on gay men is not only highly embellished but offers the homeless a relatively safe way to discuss an activity that is fairly common, while still allowing them distance from the stigma of homosexuality. In these stories they can admit contact with homosexuals and even, obliquely, some sexual activity. But by focusing on predation as the central theme of such encounters, they can avoid identification with gays.[10]

The homeless do not always need to seek opportunities for prostitution. Sometimes they are approached by gay men in the course of other activities, as is exemplified by an experience one of us had while in the field:

> As I walked back toward the Sally on the bridge, a little before noon, I was approached by a small, nicely dressed man who offered me a cigarette and walked beside me, asking me questions. "Have you been getting much work lately?" he asked. When I replied no, he asked if I was married and had any children. When I told him I wasn't married, he stopped and said, "I'll pay you ten dollars to fuck me." He said we could go do it under the bridge or in an abandoned building down the street. When I told him I wasn't interested, he stopped walking with me across the bridge.

However, the three key informants who openly discussed prostitution with us admitted having solicited customers. Sonny McCallister told us that when he had needed money in Missouri, "I'd go up to the park and hang around the restrooms and make some money from the queers." Willie Hastings, who claimed to have been introduced to prostitution by his father, pointed out to us several homeless young men who, he said, engaged in extensive prostitution. "Man, I know they're doing it," he told us. "I've been there and I know what they look like and what they do. They go up to a street they call the meat rack and wait for guys to drive by and pick them up. Or they go up to the dirty bookstores by the university and hang around outside or stand in the back with their pants unzipped and hard-ons sticking out, just waiting."

We also observed a few instances of heterosexual prostitution among the homeless. They were all situations in which a single woman was managed by a man to whom she exhibited some degree of attachment. In one case a man in his early twenties did a brisk business for a couple of weeks arranging sex for $20 and up between his young girlfriend and men who were staying at the Salvation Army. A case of cheaper prostitution was witnessed one afternoon at the plasma center: a man was soliciting men to have sex with his wife in the back of their pick-up truck for $8 to $10—the amount received for a plasma donation.

Heterosexual prostitution appeared to be relatively rare, however, as a result of the paucity of women on the streets, the unwillingness of those who are there to engage in such activity, and the lack of much disposable cash among most homeless males. More common for homeless women was a sort of serial monogamous or polygamous prostitution in which a woman attached herself to one or more men in exchange for support. As one homeless male told us, "You wonder why there's not very many women living on the streets? It's because those women are living with men who aren't on the streets, you know. They've worked out some kind of arrangement, whether it's sex or whatever, where they can be living with some guy." Marilyn Fisch, who was present during this discussion, agreed with the man's assessment and elaborated:

> A lot of girls are going into doing what they have to do to get a place where they can sleep at night. That's why a lot of these girls are hanging out in bars, just to do what they can to get a place to shower and sleep. . . . Like Debby. You've seen Debby. She got run out of the Sally and she's doing whatever she can. She's sleeping with guys in their cars or underneath bridges, running dirty. They do it even though they don't want to just 'cause they got to get off the streets. They stay at a bar in the daytime while the guy goes to work, and then they get a motel room. That's what Debby's doing. And there's Carol. And there's JoAnne, who's living back there in the alley with five or six guys. It don't look right for her to be living with them, but that's the only way she can survive.[11]

SELLING PLASMA

In a world of limited and irregular opportunities to make a few dollars, an outcropping of economic regularity stands out like a beacon on a dark night. The blood banks or plasma centers are unique in offering the homeless a sure opportunity to pick up a few dollars. Perhaps this certainty helps explain the upbeat ambience of the blood bank compared to the anxious gloom that pervades the day-labor spots. As with most things the homeless do, there is a trade-off to selling plasma—in this case, sitting for an hour and a half with a needle in the arm—but it is a trade-off that many find worthwhile, especially when their pockets are empty.

Austin has two plasma centers, both located nearly three miles north

of the Sally, near the university campus. Some of the homeless check
out the day-labor spots in the morning and then, if they do not land a
job, go to Caritas for a sandwich and then to the main plasma center to
"sell some blood." Others try to avoid the long wait to sell their plasma
by foregoing the search for a job and getting to the doorstep by 8:00
A.M., when the center opens. Paid plasma donors are allowed to sell
plasma twice a week. They are paid eight dollars for the first donation
and ten dollars for the second. On Monday mornings, which is usually
the busiest morning since the homeless have so few opportunities to
make money on the weekends, at least thirty broke and homeless individuals will be sitting in front of the plasma center when the doors
open. The "Plasmapheresis Informed Consent Form," which donors at
the Austin Plasma Center must sign, explains the plasmapheresis procedure:

> The clue to this procedure is the word "plasma." In plasmapheresis you
> donate only your plasma, the straw-colored liquid portion of your blood
> which the body replaces much more rapidly than red blood cells. Your red
> blood cells, which, if donated, would take your body several weeks to re-
> place, are returned to you. By giving only your plasma, you can safely donate
> as often as twice a week.
>
> The plasmapheresis requires removing 500–600 ml of whole blood, sep-
> arating the red blood cells from the plasma, and returning the red cells to
> you. The procedure is repeated a second time through the same needle punc-
> ture. 600 ml is withdrawn from donors weighing 175 pounds or more; 500
> ml from donors weighing less.

Posters at the plasma center focus on society's need for plasma and
the beneficence of the donors, on the one hand, and on financial incentives for continued selling of plasma, on the other. One poster shows a
man sitting in a plasma center while his blood is being extracted for
plasmapheresis. The caption underneath the picture reads: "This man
is a paid blood donor. He represents one-third of all the blood donors
in America. We owe him a debt of gratitude." Another poster shows a
smiling adolescent hemophiliac sitting on a bicycle, with the caption:
"Hey Plasma Donor! Thanks!" These posters are slick, colorful, and
professionally made. The signs promoting financial incentives, hand-
made by the plasma center staff, are less professional and more direct.
One proclaims: "$ BONUSES! $25.00 Drawings at the end of the month.
2 Winners every month!" Another states: "$20 Bonus for the 7th do-
nation in the month."

The income from regular plasma donation is an important means of subsistence for some of the homeless. At \$18 per week plus the \$20 bonus for the seventh donation of the month, a homeless individual can earn about \$95 per month selling plasma. If calculated in terms of hourly wage, taking into account the long walk to the plasma center, the long wait there, and the hour and a half to two hours the process takes, the homeless individual earns little more than \$2.50 per hour. Nonetheless, it is a guaranteed \$2.50, as opposed to the uncertain money to be made from day labor. Some of the homeless plan their otherwise unpredictable weeks around their guaranteed plasma sales, as is illustrated in the following excerpt from a conversation overheard between two homeless males in their mid-twenties as they waited in the plasma center to be called for their Monday morning donations:

> "Hey, tomorrow I'm going to the Labor Pool and get some work."
> "You got a car?"
> "No, you 'spose I'll just end up sitting around then?"
> "Yeah, I always do."
> "Well, I'm gonna try it. I need a forty-dollar day bad. I can get my ten bucks here on Wednesday if I don't get out tomorrow."

In *The Gift Relationship: From Human Blood to Social Policy*, Richard Titmuss pointed out the serious ethical implications of developing a system of paid plasma donors drawn to a large degree from the homeless population. "With the great expansion in plasmapheresis programs in recent years," he wrote in the 1970s, "the problem of the effects on the donor's health of frequent and repeated donations has emerged as an important public health issue."[12] He went on to quote a physician who argued that one of the most serious ethical problems of plasmapheresis as it is operated in the United States paid-donor system is "the exploiting for its proteins a population which is least able to donate them—the poorly nourished Skid Row population."[13]

This exploitative process has been even more evident in the 1980s and 1990s, as the ranks of the homeless have expanded to include far more than skid-row alcoholics.[14] One of the more pernicious effects of frequently selling plasma relates to the difficulty many of the homeless have in maintaining their body weight. The plasma centers have weight requirements, but many of the homeless try to circumvent them. Marilyn, who when we met her was no longer healthy enough to sell plasma, told us how she used to deal with the weigh-in at the plasma center: "I'd put rocks in my shoes and my pockets and then I'd go in and get on the scales. It worked for a while, but then one day some rocks fell

out of my pocket, and after that they 86'ed me from the plasma center."
Tom Fisk, who was 6'1" and weighed only 130 pounds but still donated
plasma, told us of similar problems he faced when living in his car in
Killeen, Texas:

> I'd been selling blood all along and it wasn't no problem. Then, one day, I
> go in—and I'm really needing money bad—and they weigh me and say,
> "You're too underweight to donate." So I left and drank a lot of water and
> came back, and they weighed me again and said the same thing. By that time
> I was getting pretty pissed off, so I left and put some rocks in my pockets
> and came back. They said, "We're not letting you donate today." Well, I got
> kinda belligerent about it 'cause there weren't no reason not to let me and I
> was desperate for money. And they called the police on me.

For some of the homeless, the moral taint of donating blood is more
salient than the health risks. As a thirty-four-year-old man said in an
interview at an Austin alcohol rehabilitation center: "I've done all kinds
of things for money, including selling my body to men for sex, but
nothing has ever made me more ashamed or made me feel dirtier than
selling my very blood." Many of the homeless, however, grimly engage
in this activity, recognizing it as an unfortunate economic necessity on
which they have become dependent. Rhyming Mike captured this sentiment well in a poem he aptly titled "Blood Bank Blues."

I was heading down the highway, heading toward the end,
I didn't have no money and I couldn't find my friends.
That's the way, that's the way, you know it had to be.
Sometimes I wonder if I'm crazy or is it just poverty.

I made it to New Orleans where my wallet drew a blank.
So I made this withdrawal at the local blood bank.
That's the way, that's the way, it seems it had to be.
I had them vampires in their white suits sucking all the blood from me.

They gave me nine dollars, told me, "Thanks a lot,
Please come again another day." Seems I got what they want.
That's the way, that's the way, you know it had to be.
Guess you have to give them what they want, 'cause money doesn't grow on
    trees.

Now I'm back out on that highway, still heading toward the end.
I still don't have my money and I still can't find my friends.
That's the way, that's the way, it seems it had to be.
You know the blood bank blues have sure 'nough put the drain on me.

TABLE 5.1   SALES OF GOODS, SERVICES, AND PLASMA, BY
TYPE OF HOMELESS PERSON*

	Mean Score for Selling Goods and Services	Mean Score for Selling Plasma
Recently dislocated	.26	.19
Regular straddler	.71	.68
Institutional straddler	.20	.20
Traditional tramp	.22	.11
Hippie tramp	1.10	.87
Traditional bum	.43	.13
Redneck bum	.80	1.00
Mentally ill	.29	0

*Mean scores near 0 indicate infrequent use, those in the vicinity of 1 indicate occasional use, and those approaching 2 indicate extensive use.

Just as we observed variation in the frequency with which the various types of homeless pursue day labor and the other forms of sales work, so are there differences with respect to selling plasma. Table 5.1 presents the mean scores for each type of homeless for sales of both plasma and other goods and services, irrespective of legal status. Here we see that selling plasma figures significantly in the survival repertoire only of the regular straddlers, hippie tramps, and redneck bums. With the exception of the mentally ill, each of the other types sold plasma, but not very often. It is still somewhat foreign to the recently dislocated, many of whom initially find repugnant the prospect of selling their blood in order to survive.

The story is somewhat different for the traditional bums. Most do not find it revolting to sell plasma. To the contrary, many, like Marilyn, have sold their plasma in the past. Now, however, the vast majority are too alcoholic or too anemic to qualify as donors. Additionally, their physical condition makes it difficult for many of them to hike the three miles from the downtown area to the plasma centers. Like the skid-row alcoholics, many of the traditional bums we came to know have a fairly narrow daily orbit beyond which they rarely stray. JJ, Indio, and Nona George are cases in point.

The traditional tramps are considerably more mobile than the bums, but most of them are also older and alcoholic. Also important, though, is the prideful resolve of some of them to make it through their street smarts and cunning and through day labor. Thus, they also eschew plasma sales as a form of shadow work, but for a rather different set of reasons than either the recently dislocated or the traditional bums.

When we compare the mean scores of selling plasma with those for the previously discussed forms of selling combined, we see that it is only for the regular straddlers, hippie tramps, and rednecks that both types of selling appear to figure fairly prominently as compensatory subsistence strategies. Although the scores for selling goods and services are higher than for selling plasma, except for the rednecks and the institutional straddlers, it is clear that among the homeless in general there is a similar pattern of reliance on selling as a means of survival.

SOLICITING DONATIONS IN PUBLIC PLACES

A somewhat different pattern emerges for the public solicitation of handouts through begging and panhandling.[15] Both strategies are used most frequently by outsiders, and particularly by traditional and hippie tramps and traditional bums, the groups with the longest spans of time on the streets. The mean scores for both the recently dislocated and regular straddlers are below .20, for example, indicating infrequent engagement in this variety of shadow work. In contrast, the mean scores for the traditional and hippie tramps and the traditional bum are .77, .93, and .73 respectively, all within the range of moderate engagement.

The reason for this disparity resides, we suspect, in the nature of begging and panhandling. Both involve fleeting attempts to persuade others to part with a sum of money, usually quite small, without providing anything tangible in return. As such, they are antithetical to the work ethic, which decrees that honorable subsistence involves the exchange of labor for pay or, at the very least, making do without handouts from others. As a consequence, begging and panhandling can engender considerable shame and embarrassment in individuals still imbued with the work ethic as conventionally understood, as are most recently dislocated and many regular straddlers. Tony Jones, who had been on the streets for only two to three weeks when we first met, told us, for example, "I got too much pride to beg. As long as I got my hands and feet, I'll be damned if I'll get on my knees and beg." And Ron Whitaker, who has been homeless somewhat longer, said that when he first hit the streets he "found panhandling downright embarrassing." He learned to swallow his pride, however, when his pockets were empty and he had exhausted his other options. As he put it, "You can't let pride get in your way. I used to and still do sometimes, but there are times you have to ask people for a couple of quarters because you ain't got a dime." [16]

Apparently the sense of shame that some homeless attach to begging and panhandling is minimal or nonexistent for the outsiders. Most have been on the streets too long or have drifted too far from the world of regular work and its underlying values to permit them to circumscribe survival activities. Moreover, as Ron Whitaker began to realize, the exigencies of street life have a way of withering prior constraints and understandings.

But even outsiders differ among themselves in how they elicit money from passing strangers: some beg, others panhandle. The difference is behavioral and a matter of degree. Beggars humbly and passively solicit donations; panhandlers accost and importune. Partly as a consequence, beggars tend to be objects of pity, whereas panhandlers often engender fear or scorn or both.[17] Consistent with these distinctions, begging tends to predominate among the traditional bums, largely because of their physical degeneration. Gypsy Bill, who claimed to be particularly good at begging, informed us, "Sparing change is easier for me than it is for a lot of guys. I don't have to hassle anybody, 'cause they just look at me and feel sorry. I just sit on my bedroll on the sidewalk and when people come by they drop some change in my hat." In contrast, it was primarily hippie tramps and redneck bums who panhandled. It was not uncommon, for example, to see Bill-Bob and a fellow redneck bum accosting passersby either in the downtown area or in the vicinity of the plasma centers and following them for half a block or more, arguing with them if they refused the request for money. Traditional tramps and the mentally ill engaged in a greater mix of begging and panhandling activities than did traditional and redneck bums. The tack they took depended on such factors as degree of sobriety, interactional capabilities, or general state of mind. An example is provided by a mentally ill woman with a shaved head, who spent most days wandering barefoot along the Drag and whose soliciting style was highly dependent on her mood. Some days she would sit quietly soliciting donations with a sign, but at other times she would scream at and chase after those who refused her requests.

Distinctions were also observed with respect to the location of the two activities. Since panhandling is more intrusive, it is typically done in areas where passersby are likely to have loose change. It is very unusual to see someone panhandling near the Sally, for instance. At the same time, they seldom go where they are particularly likely to appear out of place, such as the more expensive suburban shopping centers. In Austin, most of the panhandling occurs in the shopping area along the Drag, in the downtown night-life area, and in the supermarket parking lots in the lower-middle to lower-class neighborhoods adjacent to the downtown area.

Although an occasional beggar can be spotted on the Drag, it is the domain of the hippie tramps, who generally panhandle. On any given weekday while the university is in session, a number of them can be observed requesting money from pedestrians.[18] Shop owners on the Drag are convinced that these panhandlers scare off potential customers. As a consequence, the shop owners are continually calling on police officers to enforce the local ordinance that prohibits panhandling, but such enforcement is episodic at best.[19] The same ordinance applies to the downtown area, where most of the beggars hang out and where most of the panhandling is done by traditional tramps. While enforcement here is episodic as well, a bum or tramp who is working the area when the law is being tightly enforced is particularly vulnerable. An elderly tramp who went by the name of Boxcar Billie, for instance, was observed one Friday night, slouched against a wall by a downtown donut shop, drunk and asking passersby for spare change for a cup of coffee. When we went to municipal court on the following Sunday morning, Boxcar Billie was there for the second day in a row, having been arrested Friday night for panhandling (the city does not distinguish between begging and panhandling) and again on Saturday afternoon, less than half an hour after his release from the city jail.

Some particularly creative individuals endeavor to stay within the letter of the law while persisting in this activity. Rhyming Mike, for instance, frequently accosts passersby and offers to recite a poem for a quarter. While Rhyming Mike contends that he is not panhandling, the police take a different view and have arrested him at least once for "selling his poems."

Shotgun devised a more successful ploy for garnering donations. He stands on a downtown street corner with a sign proclaiming, "Jobs Wanted: $3/Hour and Food." Beneath this proclamation is added, "Donations accepted with thanks!" Shotgun does occasionally land a temporary job in this manner, but the bulk of his income derives from donations, and the sign is primarily a ploy for getting them. As he informed us, "You have to have the right appearance to pull this off. I know how to look the part, and that's important."

Rhyming Mike and Shotgun's techniques have an element of performance to them that goes beyond straightforward panhandling. Frequently panhandling is overlaid with such a dramatic or narrative element, transforming the encounter into one of quid pro quo, in which the solicitor offers entertainment in exchange for money. Hoyt Page, for example, who used to panhandle extensively at interstate freeway rest stops, attributed his success to his ability to tell a good tale.

An ambiguous boundary separates performing for donations from panhandling, and thus the groups of homeless who engage in public performance constitute a subset of the groups who panhandle. Traditional and hippie tramps were the only groups among the homeless whose members we observed performing, with hippie tramps predominating. Several of Rhyming Mike's acquaintances were street musicians who played the guitar and sang for spare change on the Drag during the day and, occasionally, on the city's major night-life strip in the evening. Unlike panhandlers, street singers seemed to be relatively immune to arrest, although Banjo, who had a long history of performing in public and who had come to "winter" in Austin because he thought he could sing here, decided to forego performing on the streets when he heard that police were arresting performers who did not have business licenses.

SCAVENGING

Scavenging, the third general form of shadow work, is a salvaging process that entails rummaging through discarded materials to find usable or salable items. Since its material base is the refuse of others, scavenging reflects the location of the homeless at the bottom of the social order. Many of the homeless, not surprisingly, hold scavenging in low regard, and they engage in it only as a last resort. We seldom observed scavenging among the recently dislocated, and only a few straddlers scavenged, and then only when other options were not available, such as on weekends when there was no prospect of day labor. One Sunday morning, for instance, Pat Manchester explained to us, "I couldn't sleep this morning, so I went out looking through dumpsters till I got enough cans to sell so I could buy a breakfast taco and some coffee." The traditional and hippie tramps and the redneck bums also scavenge only rarely, and it is clearly not a favored form of shadow work.

Traditional bums and the mentally ill, by contrast, tend to scavenge fairly regularly. It is the former's primary subsistence activity and the mentally ill's second most important means of survival, next to public assistance. Their patterns of scavenging are quite different, however. Traditional bums often work in a team, whereas the mentally ill engage in solitary scavenging that both reflects and reinforces their social isolation.

The most common items the homeless in Austin scavenge are aluminum beer and pop cans, which they then sell at the going rate. One forty-one-year-old traditional bum, known on the streets as Pushcart, makes almost daily rounds of the student-housing area that surrounds the university campus, pushing an expropriated grocery cart that he loads with aluminum cans he collects from dumpsters, parking lots, and the side of the road. When asked why he engaged in this activity, Pushcart replied, "I've been in the Marines, man, and I've taken too many orders too long. Scrapping for cans, there's nobody telling me what to do. I'm my own boss, and when I want to take a break or call it a day, I can."

The price paid for aluminum varies. During the course of our research, it fluctuated between 14 and 21 cents per pound at the metal recycling companies and supermarkets in Austin.[20] Several twenty-four-hour mechanical recycling stations are located in busy parts of Austin. These machines usually pay 5 to 8 cents per pound less for cans than supermarkets, but they are more accessible. On a good day, according to Pushcart, a diligent worker can collect $5 to $10 worth of cans.

Large apartment complexes, particularly those in which the relatively affluent and heavy-drinking student population resides, are a favorite hunting ground for aluminum cans. The traditional bum keeps an eye out for other items as well: clothes, magazines, broken radios, and the like. The recycling that results from this scavenging is graphically illustrated by the experiences recounted by Elbert, a forty-seven-year-old self-proclaimed "burnt-out bum" who has spent the last two years living at a charity-supported rural facility for homeless substance abusers:

> When I was on the streets I knew where to find things and I knew how to fix them. I've put together good televisions out of parts I got from dumpsters. One time I sold the junk I found in just one dumpster for more than a hundred bucks. I made a living on stuff other people threw away. . . . If I was living in Calcutta with the beggars, I could get by better than most of them, 'cause I know what to do.

Similar sentiments were voiced by a thirty-seven-year-old traditional bum who was among the homeless who traveled to the Oregon com-

munity of Antelope when the Rajneeshee cult made their much-publicized
recruiting sweep to gather voters for local elections. One night in the
winter warehouse, after he had returned disillusioned, he rambled at
length about the useful items to be garnered from student dumpsters:

> You wouldn't believe the stuff students throw away. I've found radios and
> clocks and clothes. Hell, everything I've got almost I found in dumpsters. I
> haven't bought a pair of shoes in a year and a half. A couple days ago I
> found a $65 pair of running shoes in a dumpster. And shirts—you can find
> good shirts. And pants. One time I even found a pair of pants with five bucks
> in a pocket.

As was suggested earlier, traditional bums will frequently try to sell
scavenged items to other homeless people. Indeed, the area around the
Sally functions at times as a sort of scavenger's flea market. Traditional
bums also resourcefully search through dumpsters for food. Gypsy Bill,
who, as we mentioned before, considered himself "an expert dumpster
diver," described the activity well:

> When we had the camp at Bull Creek, some of the guys would go in to TEC
> every morning and try to get out on jobs. The ones who did would come
> back in the evening and buy beer for the rest of us. My job was camp cook,
> and part of that was dumpster-diving down at Safeway. There were these
> two brothers who would help me—they'd toss me into the dumpster and I'd
> start going through junk, looking around. Bread and fruit and meat—good
> meat, just outdated was all. I'd make supper from what I found: a stew, fried
> chicken, or something! Man, between them working and buying the beer
> and me dumpster-diving and cooking dinner, we could party every night.

When traditional bums locate a good dumpster, they tend to develop
a pattern of regular usage. For instance, most afternoons about ten bums
were observed waiting patiently beside two dumpsters where a vending-
machine company tossed its unsold burritos and sandwiches. Such patterns are occasionally broken when grocery stores and restaurants decide to "clean up the area" and take measures, such as chaining the
dumpsters, to prevent dumpster-diving.[21]

We noted earlier that scavenging tends to be held in low repute by
many of the homeless, largely because of the obdurate fact that it means
rummaging through garbage. But we suspect that another reason more
homeless do not scavenge on a regular basis is that most lack the skill
to do it effectively. It is necessary not only to know where to look and
when but also to have a sense of what to look for, that is, to have good
judgment about its salability or edibility. This is what Gypsy meant
when he called himself an "expert dumpster-diver," a "craftsman" at

scavenging. Such know-how can be acquired only through firsthand experience over time, something the traditional bums have had plenty of, with 93 percent having been on the streets for more than two years.

Know-how is evident in the scavenging activities of the mentally ill, but they approach it in a more isolated or solitary manner than the traditional bums do. Jorge Herrera, for example, scavenges alone for food and change, making a regular circuit of convenience store and fast-food restaurant garbage cans and telephone booths. Similarly, we often observed a mentally ill women in her mid-thirties alone in fast-food restaurants in the university area, picking up bits of food that customers had left on the tables. The solitary survival activities of the homeless mentally ill reflect their isolation not only from each other but within the world of the homeless in general. Nonetheless, the subsistence of the homeless mentally ill in Austin, just as for the traditional bum, is contingent in part on their scavenging activities.

THEFT

The final type of shadow work engaged in by some of the homeless is theft and related criminal activities such as burglary and fencing stolen goods.[22] Although theft is almost always performed surreptitiously, we did learn indirectly that it is fairly commonplace among some of the homeless. A few confessed to having stolen this or that, as when Tom Fisk told us about his theft of a motorcycle, for which he spent thirty-seven days in jail, or when Pushcart admitted to stealing the scavenged cans of other homeless, but only when they are drunk and passed out in public. "I'll say, 'Hey, wake up! I'm gonna take your cans!' If he doesn't wake up, it's 'Sayonara.' Hey, it's happened to me. What goes around, comes around."

Some of the homeless would talk openly with each other about what they had stolen, on occasion even flaunting the stolen item. One afternoon in front of one of the plasma centers, for instance, a homeless woman who was only about eighteen showed Nona a set of earrings she had stolen and then bragged about them until Nona refocused the discussion onto her own exploits at thievery. On other occasions, homeless people would show up inexplicably with new personal possessions, such as radios and tape recorders, or with goods they would try to sell at cut-rate prices. We met a twenty-year-old man, who frequently sold joints around the Sally, one evening several blocks west of the Sally fencing what we took to be stolen goods:

We were walking toward the Sally when a street acquaintance called to us from across Congress Avenue. We crossed over and he showed us a suitcase full of freshly washed, almost new jeans and asked if we would buy a pair. He sold six pairs for five bucks each while we were hanging around. He told us he had met a guy on the street who sold him the suitcase for fifty cents. "At least I'm making honest money," he said. "And I'm not selling dope either."

More direct evidence of theft comes from the tracking sample data. Of the 697 criminal offenses for which the homeless in our sample were arrested in Austin, fewer than a quarter of the arrests were for felonies.[23] But 62 percent of these felonies involved theft and another 27 percent burglary, usually for the purpose of theft. Thus, 89 percent of all felonies for which the homeless were arrested locally were theft-related. When this finding is considered in conjunction with the corroborating finding that the age-standardized arrest rates for burglary and theft per 1,000 homeless adult males are 1.5 and 1.3 times higher than the corresponding rates for non-homeless adult males, it seems clear that theft and related criminal activity constitute a fairly salient subsistence strategy for some of the homeless.[24] This finding is unsurprising, considering the meager funds at the disposal of most of the homeless and the fact that many begin each day penniless. After all, theft is one of the few means available to the homeless for procuring cigarettes, coffee, beer, and snacks when their pockets are empty or nearly so. Moreover, opportunity for theft abounds, with convenience stores and gas stations on the corners of nearly every major intersection. Were it not for the vigilance of convenience-store proprietors and employees whenever the homeless are shopping or browsing in their stores, the incidence of theft among the homeless might be even higher.[25]

As with the other types of shadow work, theft is not chosen randomly by the homeless. Although the clandestine nature of theft made it impossible to discern fine-tuned variation across the types of homeless, several findings from the tracking data point to significant clustering and variation. For one thing, slightly fewer than a third of the tracking sample were arrested for criminal offenses in Austin, but the 248 arrested averaged nearly three arrests per person, thus suggesting patterned rather than random variation. And, using the span of contact with the Salvation Army as a proxy for length of time on the streets, we found that the homeless with local arrest records also have longer records of contact with the Sally. As is shown in Table 5.2, this pattern is reflected most dramatically in the fact that 33.5 percent of those with

TABLE 5.2   SPAN OF SALVATION ARMY CONTACT
AND LOCAL ARREST RECORDS OF HOMELESS
TRACKING SAMPLE*

Span of Salvation Army Contact	Local Arrest Records (N: 248)	No Local Arrest Records (N: 519)
1 day	18.5%	28.3%
2 days–2 weeks	13.3	29.3
2 weeks–2 months	17.7	16.8
2 months–6 months	16.9	12.9
More than 6 months	33.5%	12.7%

*$\chi^2 = 63.34$; $\alpha = .0001$.

arrest records show a span of contact with the Sally covering more than six months, in contrast to 12.7 percent of those who have not been arrested locally. Since thefts constitute the plurality of felonies committed by the homeless and since the recently dislocated average less than six months on the streets, it seems likely that theft is engaged in more often by straddlers and outsiders who are not physically incapacitated.[26] For many of these individuals, theft functions as an adaptive strategy that, like other forms of shadow work, facilitates survival in a world shorn of more conventional ways of making do.

SUMMARY

In this chapter we have examined an array of non–wage labor subsistence strategies the homeless fashion because they are excluded from existing labor markets, because participation in those markets fails to offer them a living wage, because institutionalized assistance proves inadequate, or because these unconventional strategies provide a more reliable means of survival on the streets. We have called these compensatory subsistence strategies shadow work because they are not traditionally counted as work and because they are pursued in the shadow of regular work—that is, on the sidewalks of urban America and in its back alleys and refuse receptacles. And, just as in the previous chapter we discerned variation in the pursuit of wage labor and the receipt of public assistance among the different types of homeless, so we have found here variation in the extent to which the various types of homeless engage in the different kinds of shadow work.

These observations, with those in the previous chapter, raise a number of issues that warrant discussion in order to illuminate further the subsistence activities of the homeless. The first concerns the mix of strategies employed by each type of homeless. Although it is clear that the set of subsistence strategies available to the homeless is limited, it is equally clear that each type of homeless has its own peculiar mix of strategies, such that we may speak of type-specific or personalized repertoires of material subsistence. The existence of such repertoires suggests that some degree of selectivity is exercised with respect to the strategies pursued. Yet, the use of one strategy rather than another is not merely a matter of choice. No single strategy can ensure subsistence on the streets, and no matter how strongly one subsistence activity is preferred over another, there is no guarantee from one day to the next that it will still be a viable option. Day labor is not sufficiently abundant to ensure paid work day after day, and it is virtually nonexistent on weekends. Plasma centers, too, are closed on the weekends. And Sundays are particularly bad days for begging and panhandling, because few non-homeless pedestrians are on the streets.

Survival, then, is contingent on the opportunistic fashioning and utilization of a mix of strategies. The recently dislocated and straddlers may frown on scavenging, but, as Pat Manchester discovered when he turned to dumpster-diving in search of funds for breakfast one Sunday, necessity may leave them with little choice but to engage in some subsistence activity they hold in low regard.

These constraints and uncertainties notwithstanding, what is perhaps most noteworthy is that the different types of homeless do have preferred strategies and that they pursue those more regularly than the other strategies. Such selectivity suggests both that the homeless attempt to exercise some autonomy in their lives and that material survival on the streets is more than a random or chaotic affair. Like most spheres of life, it is patterned and ordered, not solely by the network of street institutions that structure the routines and options of the homeless, but also by the preferences and idiosyncrasies of the different types of homeless themselves.

A second and related issue is why outsiders do not pursue wage labor as persistently as the recently dislocated and even the regular straddlers. The traditional tramps are somewhat of an exception to this tendency, but even their mean score for wage labor is lower than that for both the recently dislocated and the straddlers. Thus, the general tendency is that the longer the homeless are on the streets and the more they drift into the world of the outsider, the less salient wage labor becomes as a mode of subsistence for them and the more prominent become one or more forms of shadow work. What accounts for this apparent inverse relationship between time on the streets and pursuit of wage labor? Or, stated differently, why does shadow work figure more prominently in the survival of outsiders?

Two contrasting answers are possible. One, rooted in conventional wisdom, holds simply that the greater salience of shadow work among outsiders is due to a decline in work orientation, which makes them lazy and disinterested in work as traditionally conceptualized. This explanation strikes us as wrongheaded. It resonates neither with the subculture of the homeless as we came to know it nor with the nature of shadow work. As was emphasized earlier, shadow work, like all work, requires the concentration of energy and attention on the procurement of money or other material goods for personal use or exchange. It differs from other work only in that it is neither formally regulated nor sanctioned in terms of time, place, or wage. But to scavenge involves no less toil and sweat than most kinds of manual labor, and to panhandle effectively requires a certain interactional mettle and the employment of interpersonal skills and lines that are part and parcel of many kinds of sales work. Similar comparisons could be made for the other forms of shadow work.

Such observations suggest an alternative explanation: it is not a decline in work orientation per se that accounts for the greater prominence of shadow work among outsiders, but a change in orientation from the world of regular work to the world of shadow work. Most outsiders retain the incentive to work—they have no choice if they are to survive—but it is directed toward a different order of work. Moreover, it is a shift in orientation that is quite reasonable in light of the demoralizing nature of the wage labor available to the homeless. Its irregularity and low pay prevent wage labor from serving either as a reliable basis for surviving on the streets or a means off the streets. As a consequence, experience with the world of wage labor frequently leads to alienation from it, especially as familiarity is developed with the various forms of shadow work. Thus when Pat Manchester finds a dollar one morning on the way to the Labor Corner and says, "Fuck it, I'll get a cup of coffee and go donate blood," it is not so much a decline in work orientation that prompts him to forego his job-hunting as it is the realization that the attempt is unlikely to succeed and that, with a little luck, he is likely to fare better pursuing shadow work. In either case, time and energy are expended and attention is focused on making do. Unlike the middle-class working person, though, the outsider and slipping straddler, as in Pat's case, cast their bets on the world of shadow work, not because they are disinterested in regular work, but because they have lost faith in its capacity to sustain them.

It might be argued, of course, that if the homeless would only look beyond the moment to the future, if they were not so "impulse-" or "present-oriented," they would come to see the fruits of playing the wage-labor game.[27] But the issue is not so much one of orientation to time or whether the homeless are less future-oriented than those of higher status. Rather, the issue is one of articulation between the present and the future. Elliot Liebow understood this well when he wrote that the difference between black street-corner men of the 1960s and their middle-class counterparts "lies not so much in their different orientations to time as their different orientations to future time or, more specifically, to their different futures."[28] Most people of higher status see a positive articulation between their immediate present and their future. They have a strong sense that what they do today will yield a tomorrow that is just as good as or better than today. The psychiatrist Robert Coles has called this a sense of entitlement and has observed that its salience increases with movement up the status system.[29]

Clearly, such a sense is not pervasive among the homeless. Most of them have little confidence that their actions today will yield a better tomorrow for them. As we have seen, the wage labor that awaits them, if they are lucky enough to secure any, typically involves jobs that lead only to the repetition of their current plight. With this negative articulation between their immediate present and their anticipated future, it is little wonder that many drift from the world of regular work to the world of shadow work. It is not so much because they are present-oriented—although they have good reason to be so, given that their daily survival commands all the resources they can muster. Rather, it is because the tomorrows they can realistically imagine are not ones that inspire either the investment of whatever limited resources they may have scrimped to save or the adoption of lines of action that go beyond the world of shadow work. For many of the homeless, then, the repeated failure of the world of wage labor to yield a fair return on the time and energy invested pushes them into the world of shadow work. Initially, shadow work is seen primarily as a stop-gap measure, as a kind of supplemental, temporary work. In time, however, as experience and familiarity with it increase, it can become a way of life.

CHAPTER SIX

Tenuous Ties

It is approaching 9:00 on a midweek morning. Most of the homeless have been up for hours, but Nona George and Marilyn Fisch are still sleeping off a late-night drunk in a weather-beaten Oldsmobile Delta Eighty-Eight that belongs to Nona's new boyfriend. In a car next to them, Gypsy Bill and a couple of friends are smoking a morning joint before heading for Caritas. At the Labor Corner, Ron Whitaker and Pat Manchester wait together, smoking cigarettes and watching the traffic. If no day-labor employer arrives soon, they'll grab a sandwich at Caritas and then head for the plasma center. Six blocks away, on the curb across from the Red River Liquor Store, Indio and JJ sit, nursing a bottle of "Mad Dog" with three other homeless men who chipped in for the bottle.

A couple of miles away, at a fast-food restaurant near the university, Banjo, Willie Hastings, and Tanner Sutton have spent the past two hours sipping mugs of unlimited-refill coffee, reading the newspaper, and talking about mystical religious experiences they have had. In a booth at the back of the restaurant Lance McKay sits alone with three notebooks spread over the table, writing furiously and trying unsuccessfully to start a conversation with Banjo, Willie, or Tanner each time one of them walks past him to use the restroom.

Down the street from the restaurant, two homeless men we have not seen before sit on a brick retaining wall beside a convenience store, sharing a quart of beer and panhandling passersby. When we stop to chat with them, they offer us a swig from the bottle and quickly incorporate us into their conversation. They introduce themselves as Shorty and Steve. "I just got into Austin from San Antone two days ago," Shorty says, "and already I can tell I'm gonna like it. There's lotsa good people here—I can feel it. I mean, I been here just two days and already I got good friends." He seems to count us among his "good friends."

.   .   .   .

The most prevalent social-science perspective on homelessness has taken it to indicate a state of social withdrawal and isolation. Over fifty years ago the skid-row man was characterized as "a homeless and friendless person, isolated from all social contacts of intimate and personal nature."[1] Since then, various researchers have conceptualized the homeless as "incompletely socialized,"[2] "undersocialized,"[3] "fundamentally detached from social life,"[4] and "disaffiliated men."[5]

Our field observations do not corroborate this picture of the homeless, however, at least not in such a one-dimensional and stereotypic fashion. As the preceding vignette illustrates, many of the homeless spend considerable time in sociable interaction. In this chapter we focus on the social relationships among the homeless themselves. Of course, the homeless are also involved in secondary relations and interactions with members of caretaker and control agencies, as we have already seen, and in relationships with non-street intimates, especially family members, as we will discuss in Chapter 8. Street peer relationships warrant a separate discussion, however, because they are so central to the daily lives of most of the homeless. We begin this chapter by describing some of the paradoxical characteristics and associated tensions of street relationships. Then, in the second half of the chapter, we examine the various patterns of peer affiliation among the various types of homeless street people.

GENERAL CHARACTERISTICS
OF STREET RELATIONSHIPS

Peer relationships among street people are infused with a paradoxical combination of isolation and sociability. Street life is characterized on one level by easy conviviality and the quick development of friendships, as was exemplified by Shorty's comment that he had been in town only two days and had already made good friends. But that same remark indicates how social relations on the streets also tend to be characterized by superficiality and instability.

There are several reasons for this ambivalence. First of all, the quick development of friendships on the streets serves a compensatory function, as other homeless individuals provide one of the few sources of positive social validation. This function has also been recognized in the lives of marginal but domiciled black street-corner men. Writing about such men in the early 1970s, Elijah Anderson noted that "for many their most important social and psychological supports are found in the company of peers."[6] Such peer groups serve both expressive and instrumental functions. They provide an essentially nonstigmatizing reference group and a source of interpersonal self-validation. They also provide a nexus for the sharing of meager resources.

Much of the literature on skid-row men in the 1950s and 1960s focused on the formation of "bottle gangs" and the pooling of resources that enabled the men to maintain steady access to alcohol despite their shifting economic circumstances. We, too, observed a high level of "bottle gang" activity on the streets, particularly among straddlers and outsiders. We also found considerable borrowing of small amounts of money, usually two to five dollars, among close friends or "hanging buddies." And, in keeping with the moral code of "what goes around, comes around," we witnessed the sharing of modest resources with fellow street people in general.

This sharing went well beyond known peers, to include a large portion of those living on the streets. On numerous occasions we saw people share what little they had, even when it created some hardship for them. Late one Friday evening, for instance, as we sat on the curb across from the Sally talking to two men, an elderly drunk man who had arrived at the Sally too late for dinner climbed into a dumpster to search for food. Despite the fact that the two men we were with did not know him and were unlikely to pick up any extra cash until the following Monday, they talked the drunk into getting out of the dumpster and then bought him dinner at a nearby fast-food restaurant. This sort of altruism was especially notable among cigarette smokers in the Sally dinner line on Sunday evenings. Since work, and therefore money, was scarce on the weekends, many of the homeless had run out of cigarettes by Sunday afternoon. We were surprised to see how willing those who still had cigarettes were to "bum smokes" to those who had run out, often even refusing payment, even though they would later have to go without themselves. Several street people proudly pointed out this kind of behavior to us. "People look down on the homeless," Hoyt Page told us, "but there's more people willing to give you the shirt off their back down here than anywhere else."

Nonetheless, the support and self-validation provided by street peers are fragile. Street relationships are plagued with instability. One major reason is the high degree of transience among some of the homeless.[7] Their mobility is partly based on constraints related to their means of survival. Shelters, for example, frequently limit the number of consecutive nights a homeless person can stay. This strategy, ostensibly for preventing dependency, has been used for years. George Orwell discussed it in *Down and Out in Paris and London,* when he wrote of one-night limits in the "spikes," as London's men's shelters of the 1920s were called. Banjo, who had spent the past twenty years traveling as a homeless person around the United States, made a similar observation:

> You want to know why we're always on the move? I'll tell you why. The Sally won't let you stay but three nights for free in most places. After that you have to pay or you gotta leave. So you go to the next town, and it's the same thing. Three days and then you gotta pay or go. Now, how're you supposed to get a job and a paycheck in a new town in three days? See, that's what happens, and then they call us "transients." What're we supposed to do?

Of course, mobility is a result of other "push" and "pull" factors besides shelter policies. The homeless frequently become disillusioned by their experiences in a city and begin to search for ways to improve their situation. A considerable amount of street talk involves the exchange of information and speculation regarding opportunities in other cities. Those homeless who have few strong connections to a locale and who have a fairly strong wage-labor orientation are particularly susceptible to the fantasy of a move to another city as a quick fix for their problems.[8] The resulting high level of geographical instability among some of the homeless thus makes it difficult for them to form enduring relationships.

Nonetheless, although mobility impedes the development of long-lasting friendships, a substantial number of the homeless spend much of each day hanging out at various street sites with large numbers of other homeless people. This provides them with a pool of potential "buddies." A gregarious individual can almost always find someone to team up with in making his or her daily rounds. In a sense, the homeless find compensation for the dearth of enduring relationships in the easy availability of more superficial ones. They frequently seek, however, to imbue these superficial connections with the trappings of deeper relationships, as was poignantly illustrated by an encounter we had two days before Christmas of 1984. We were walking from the Texas Employment Commission office toward the university area when we ran into three homeless men who asked us to chip in on a couple of quarts of beer to drink behind a nearby convenience store. These three men had known each other for only a few hours when we encountered them, but already they talked of their close friendship and were planning to hitchhike together to St. Louis, where they said they would stay over the holidays with one of their families and, after that, find jobs and rent an apartment together. They also talked about their commitment to each other. One, a small arthritic man in his fifties who had recently witnessed a homeless person getting beaten up, talked of his fear of being a victim of a similar assault. One of the younger men assured him, "No one's gonna beat you up when I'm around. I guarantee you that." By the time we had finished the beer, however, their travel plans had disintegrated and the small group split up. One of the men went to sleep behind a retaining wall; another left to look up some friends in a hobo jungle in South Austin; and the third took off to get dinner at the Sally. This was just one of many such incidents we experienced that showed both the quick conviviality and the impermanence that seem to characterize most street relationships.

The homeless also vacillate between romanticized feelings of closeness and discounting other homeless individuals as untrustworthy and exploitative. Marilyn, for instance, spoke of street people in general as "my people" and boasted that she had "over 150 friends on the streets in Austin." She frequently asserted that "us transients stick together," and we often observed her talking with others about renting an apartment together. At other times, however, Marilyn claimed that street people could not be trusted and that she would not have been homeless if she had not tried to help some street friends after she landed a job that provided her with housing:

> I quit my waitressing job down at the Lounge [a downtown bar that catered to street people] when I got this other job doing painting and repairs for an apartment company. They gave me an efficiency apartment as part of my wages, you see. So I was there, off the streets, for ten months. I was doing good and no one but a couple of people on the streets knew where I was. Then one day there's a knock on my door and here's three old friends who've just got in from San Antone. Patty had told them where I was, which she wasn't supposed to do, and they asked if they could get showers and spend the night. Then, when I was at work, they ripped my place off and got in a fight out at the swimming pool, so I ended up losing my job and my apartment over that. That's why I'm back on the streets—'cause I tried to help some transients.

A number of other individuals expressed similar mixed and fluctuating emotions regarding their peers. Many of the homeless said that street friends helped them get by from day to day, but that they could also prevent them from getting off the streets. "If you need a couple of bucks for a cup of coffee and some smokes," Ron Whitaker explained, "that's where having friends comes in. They know you're good for it. What goes around, comes around. Sometimes you help them too." But a week after having told us this, when he had taken two part-time jobs in the hope of making enough money to get a place off the streets, Ron offered a different assessment of his peers: "Most of the guys down at the Sally have gotten used to living on the streets and are satisfied with it. One of the most important things in getting off the street is not spending time around guys like that."

Ambivalence and fluctuation were also evident when the homeless complained about friends behind their backs. For instance, Willie Hastings, Ron Whitaker, and Tanner Sutton were buddies for a couple of months, spending a good portion of their days together chatting and making various plans for the future. When we ran across one of them by himself, however, he frequently spent much of the conversation degrading his partners. One morning we encountered Willie at the fast-food restaurant near the university where he regularly hung out until the plasma center opened. Over coffee he told us:

> You don't know Tanner like I do. He's way out. You should hear the things he talks about. Weird shit! He doesn't even think he's human. Tanner's crazy and he doesn't have a future. He's gonna live on the streets till he dies—and he's gonna die young.

In a similarly disparaging vein he commented on Ron:

> Ron has no sense of who he is. He'll be whatever he needs to be. If you put him with dopers, he'll use dope. If you put him with Christians, he'll be a Christian. But he doesn't know who he really is.

Willie was not the only one of them who spoke this way. "You can't believe what Willie's telling you," Ron confided to us when we were alone with him one day:

> Forget it. He's full of bullshit. I've known him for a while now, in San Antone and Houston, different places. He's always talking shit. That's all. Like now, he's talking about riding bikes up to Dallas with Pat 'cause he says he's got some manager's job there. It's never gonna happen, man. Just more bullshit.

The skepticism that pervades street conversations and relationships is understandable, considering how many of the homeless make exaggerated identity claims and tell outrageous stories. As we will discuss in detail in the next chapter, outlandish claims and stories are commonplace on the streets. Few of the homeless accept at face value what others tell them, but they seldom directly call each other into question on even the most outrageous claims. This too is understandable. Most of the homeless have relatively little biographic knowledge of one another that can be used as a reliable basis for assessing the plausibility of such stories. Additionally, consistent with the code of "what goes around, comes around," an unspoken norm apparently prohibits biographical probing and questioning of claims. Moreover, people who challenge others' stories risk reprisal or loss of support for their own claims. It thus seems wiser and safer to discount privately rather than challenge publicly the stories and claims of others.[9] Perhaps this is why Willie and Ron expressed their doubts about each other's "bullshit" to us rather than to one another.

Although the homeless are quick to profess friendship in each other's presence, then, it is a friendship that usually diverges from working- and middle-class patterns.[10] They share an intimacy of sorts, spending large blocks of time together and sharing meager resources in the most elemental situations, but this physical intimacy is often countered by social and biographical distance. For instance, people often did not know their "sleeping buddy's" or "best friend's" name.[11] Hoyt, who worked as the monitor of the Salvation Army dinner line and was one of the most outgoing and likable street people we met, told us, "I don't remember names. I can tell you what kind of cigarettes they smoke. I can tell you how they walk and if they have yellow teeth. I can tell you what I talked to them about, but I just can't remember names. I don't even try."

In fact, the exchange of personal names was often actively discouraged. On one of the occasions when Marilyn was handing out discarded burritos in the alley she and her friends had converted into a lounging area with several old sofas and chairs, a young man thanked her by shaking her hand and introducing himself as Mark. Marilyn quickly responded, "Don't tell me your name. The first thing, I know your name, and then the police'll be coming around asking questions. I don't want to know names. I know faces." As Marilyn's admonition to Mark indicates, anonymity is not simply a symptom of the impersonal nature of street life but an adaptive strategy that promotes mutual survival.[12]

As the preceding discussion shows, peer relations on the streets are a paradoxical combination of easy sociability and fundamental suspicion. The character of such relations, however, varies significantly among the types of homeless.

VARIATION IN RELATIONSHIPS AMONG TYPES OF HOMELESS

Interpersonal relationships, whether among the homeless or others, can vary in numerous ways. In peer relationships among the different types of homeless, four dimensions of variation seemed particularly relevant. The first dimension is the *temporal span* of relationships, which can vary from an hour or a day to a span of years or even decades. The second dimension is the *number* of affiliations an individual has. This can range, obviously, from few or no relationships to a large pool of friends and acquaintances. The third dimension of contrast is *intensity,* the degree of attachment homeless individuals exhibit toward their peers. The final dimension is the *locus of affiliation* in which relationships are embedded.[13] This focuses attention on the various types of activities in which the homeless tend to develop interpersonal attachments.[14] Different types of homeless individuals, as we discussed earlier, are characterized by different patterns of adaptation and orientation to street life. In the following discussion we examine how such variation in the above dimensions is reflected in their peer affiliations.

THE RECENTLY DISLOCATED

We noted in Chapter 2 that individuals who find themselves on the streets for the first time tend to have very similar cognitive orientations to the experience. Among other reactions to their new situation, they often feel fear of the company in which they find themselves. They are quick to assert that they are not really like the others on the streets, and they tend to feel that there is something dangerous and contaminating about associating with such people. They shy away from those who extend offers of friendship, engaging primarily in fleeting conversations. This was clearly illustrated one Saturday evening after dinner at the Sally when a young man in his mid-twenties approached us and nervously explained that he had missed a ride to a small town on the outskirts of Austin where he was staying temporarily with someone he had met a few days earlier. He took a crumpled resumé out of his back pocket and went over it with us in detail, emphasizing that he was a responsible worker. "I'm just down on my luck," he said. "I've only got a dollar, but I'll give you that if you'll give me a ride out to my friend's place. Last night was the first time I've ever been in a shelter like this, and these people scare me to death."

Tony Jones, who had been on the streets for about a month when we met him, also loathed other homeless people, but with considerably more bravado. He could be readily distinguished from most Sally users by the neatness of his clothes and the disdain with which he treated others. Most of the time he refused to associate with them. When he did interact with them, it was generally to chastise them for their "laziness and heavy drinking." In our conversations with him he talked continuously about his plans to get off the streets and how different he was from the rest of the homeless.

The foregoing examples provide insight into the street relations of the recently dislocated. The brief temporal span of their relationships reflects the brevity of their time on the streets. They also know strikingly fewer street people than do most other types of homeless. This, too, is partly a result of the short time they have been on the streets, but it also stems from their active avoidance of contact. When Tom Fisk began eating at the Sally, for instance, he made it a practice to get there early, eat quickly, and leave the area as soon as possible. "I don't got any reason to be hanging around people like that," he told us. "They just mean trouble, and I got enough of that already."

Consistent with the aversion of the recently dislocated toward other street people, what bonds and contacts they do make are usually quite weak. This statement must be qualified, however, as we did observe a few recently dislocated individuals who developed fairly strong attachments to other persons on the streets. These were almost always relationships between two or three recently dislocated individuals who had similar orientations to street life and found solace in each other's company. Often the major locus of affiliation for such friendships was job-hunting for regular employment. The friendship between Tom Fisk and Sonny McCallister provides a case in point. They first met at a gas station shortly after Sonny had hitchhiked into Austin. Tom took Sonny under his wing, letting him sleep in the back seat of his car and helping him find work. When they became disillusioned with Tom's boss, who never paid them for their work, they spent several days together selling plasma and looking for permanent jobs out of the TEC office. They seldom associated with other homeless individuals and talked frequently about plans and hopes for getting off the streets. Interestingly, however, even though Tom and Sonny spent most of their time together for several weeks, we did not hear them talk about getting off the streets together. Rather, each made individual plans that did not include the other person, which bears out our finding of the weakness of interpersonal relationships among the recently dislocated.

Despite their aversion to other homeless, the recently dislocated find themselves drawn into contact with other street people by virtue of their situation. Whatever the factors that pushed them onto the streets, their former ways of handling their basic everyday needs of food, shelter, medical care, and the like are no longer available or adequate for dealing with the exigencies of street life. They find themselves stranded in an alien and frightening environment, and they must develop new means of survival. In doing so they are drawn into the web of affiliation with other homeless. They quickly learn that the best guides to the resources and strategies for getting by on the streets are other homeless people. Despite their distrust, then, the newly dislocated thus rely on other homeless to teach them the ropes. Marilyn's experience when she first found herself on the streets is illustrative:

> I was staying in Travis Park [in San Antonio] and I didn't know where to go or what to do. It was over Christmas and New Year's. There was a little church by the park and I had a blanket, so I'd go over and sleep there or out in the weeds. I spent five days just drinking water without any food. But then one day it hit me how someone had told me that if you ever get on the streets, ask a tramp and they'll tell you where to go. So I saw these two guys carrying bedrolls and I started talking to them, and they told me where to go. And that was how I learned about the Sally.

Tom Fisk provides an even more detailed example of the same pattern. When Tom first became homeless in Austin he slept on the roof of an apartment complex and managed to keep himself fed through the few dollars he earned from selling plasma and from working as a roofer. Then one day he met someone at the plasma center who told him he could get dinner free at the Sally. Tom began eating there out of necessity, despite his dislike for the other clients. But as he adapted to street life and took advantage of street-level resources, Tom was drawn into increasing contact with other homeless. Over time he began to socialize with them more, in large part simply because he was around them so much.

Even so, Tom's interactions with other street people, except for Sonny, were usually brief and superficial. Like Tony, he was suspicious of them and continued to prefer to associate with people who were not on the streets. In the evenings, rather than hanging out with others at the Sally, for instance, he frequently drove to a private hospital a few miles away where he had met a night security officer when he received treatment for tar burns on his arm. Tom would spend hours drinking coffee and talking with the security officer in the cafeteria, leaving late at night to sleep in his car, either alone or with Sonny.

The antipathy of the recently dislocated toward other homeless makes them prime candidates for jobs at the Sally, since one of the main requirements is that workers not socialize with other homeless. The administrative rationale for this regulation, as the director of social services explained to us, was to avoid partiality in the dispensing of services:

> We just can't have the workers or the women who are staying in the shelter associating with the guys on the streets. They start doing favors for their friends, or wanting favors, and that just means trouble. So that's why we have the policy. That way I don't have to chew people out all the time and things go smoother. We just don't need the friction.

Those who have been on the streets longer and have developed friends are frequently unwilling to give up these associations. As we noted earlier, Gypsy Bill refused to work for the Sally because he felt it would require him to turn his back on his friends. The recently dislocated, in contrast, are actually looking for ways to separate themselves from the other homeless. So they are often quick to accept an offer to work for the Sally, as the following episode illustrates:

> In the dinner line at the Sally this afternoon there was a man in his mid-forties, dressed in clean clothes and carrying two suitcases full of clothes and belongings. He seemed very uncomfortable as he waited in the line for dinner. Behind him was a man we frequently saw on the streets. He struck up a conversation with the newcomer, explaining how things are run at the Sally and offering to help him figure things out. The newcomer listened intently and asked a lot of questions. After about an hour Hoyt came by, taking names of those who wanted a shower that night. When he saw the newcomer, he took him off to the side and talked to him alone for a few minutes. The regular who had been talking to him turned to us and said, "Hoyt knows he's got a live one. Watch! He's gonna talk the guy into working for him. For five bucks a week and a bunk upstairs. It's a rip-off. I've been there. That's why they try to get new guys. Everybody else knows better." Sure enough, a couple of minutes later the newcomer grabbed his bags and went inside with Hoyt. When we got in for dinner the new guy was already working, setting up the tables.

Ultimately either the recently dislocated manage to rekindle or de-velop non-street relationships and tap into the resources such relation-ships make available, or they are forced into increasing association with other homeless. As time goes by, their aversion to street affiliations tends to diminish. This transition marks the movement of the recently dislo-cated into straddler status.

REGULAR STRADDLERS

Straddlers are more comfortable with street life than the recently dislo-cated, largely because they have had more time to adapt to it. But their changing behavior and cognitive orientation reflect more than simply increasing familiarity with street life. As the days and months drag on, recently dislocated individuals begin to lose sight of the world from whence they came. Thoughts about the past occur, but they are over-whelmed by the consuming character of the immediate present. More-over, as people spend time on the streets they come to see ever more clearly how it is possible to subsist in a fashion that is likely to become routinized. They find out, for example, the schedules of the various caretaker agencies. And they learn noninstitutional street-survival strat-egies, such as how to pool resources with other homeless and how to manage various types of shadow work. Considering the difficulty many of the recently dislocated experience in trying to work their way off the streets, and considering that caretaker agencies offer at least food and shelter, it is not surprising that many of the recently dislocated begin to adapt to street life. However, this is not a simple linear process of ac-culturation. Regular straddlers are still oriented, at least in part, to the conventional, domiciled world. What characterizes them most is the fluctuation in their thoughts and actions. They often talk of getting off the streets, but they are becoming ever more habituated to life on the streets. They are slipping toward outsiderhood, but they continue to make at least fleeting efforts to resist.

Whereas the newly dislocated exhibit a profound apprehension re-garding other homeless, regular straddlers evince a much more tolerant attitude toward fellow street people and are much more open to inter-action with them. Straddlers have been on the streets long enough that many of their initial fears regarding safety and survival have dissipated. They have learned ways to take care of their physical and psychological needs, at least to some degree, through institutional dependence and makeshift strategies. These adaptive behaviors lead to sustained contact with other homeless people. As individuals spend time with other homeless on a continuing basis they begin to develop acquaintanceships and friendships. Over time, in conversations in dinner lines, in shelters, and on the streets, they come to realize that at least some of the other homeless share many of their concerns and make for good company during the long hours spent marking time in their daily circuits.[15]

The development of street-based acquaintances and friendships is a key ingredient in movement into the regular straddler status. All of our major straddler informants knew a large number of people on the streets. The temporal span of their interpersonal relationships also far exceeded that observed among recently dislocated individuals. Straddlers frequently developed relationships that spanned weeks or even months. Willie, Ron, and Pat exemplify this. Each had come to Austin in early autumn from a different place, and by early October they were spending large parts of many days together, often with one or two other friends. They developed a fairly consistent routine, beginning at a fast-food restaurant where they dawdled over coffee and the morning newspaper while waiting for the plasma center to open at 8:00 A.M.; getting "bled at the blood bank" until around 11:00 A.M.; hitting Caritas or Angels House for lunch; and heading from there to a bookstore or cheap movie, or to look for odd jobs. By 3:30 P.M. they were usually back at the Sally to be at the front of the dinner line. Ron picked up several part-time jobs shortly after Halloween and no longer had time to spend with the group, but the rest of the clique continued to hang out together until Willie's disappearance in late November.

The locus of affiliation for social relationships among regular straddlers is much more rooted in street life than is affiliation among the recently dislocated. But, like the recently dislocated, these straddlers spend a substantial portion of their time together fabricating plans to get off the streets. Social relationships among them tend to be more intimate and indexed more to the norm of reciprocity than are relations among the recently dislocated. One indication of this is that unlike the recently dislocated, who devote considerable time to talking about how to get off the streets individually, regular straddlers frequently develop scenarios in which they find a consistent source of income and get off the streets together. One morning as we were sipping coffee with Willie, Ron, and Pat, for instance, Willie detailed a plan he had been working on for several days:

What we've gotta do is get this dope deal off the ground. It's like the start, man. If we can get this weed, which I think we can, then we sell it and save that money and buy some more and sell that—and then we've got enough dough together to get a place of our own and quit staying at the Sally. See, if we can get enough money together to get this pound of primo weed, and then we sell it at a good price to people we know, right? Then we get a reputation and it's like we're the people they're gonna buy from after that. And then pretty soon we don't even have to be selling the shit, we just get other guys to do that for us—on commission, right? The only problem is coming up with the money, which I'm hoping we won't even have to do, 'cause I know these guys and they know I won't fuck them over. So, what I'm thinking is, they're gonna know they can trust me and go ahead and front me the pound. That's what I'm seeing them about tonight. So, it's gonna be up to you guys then, to make sure we sell it fast as hell.

Willie's scheme never materialized, nor did anyone really seem to expect it to. It was just a fantasy that filled some time over morning coffee for several days and was then forgotten.

The fantastical character of Willie's plan points to a glaring problem in street relationships among regular straddlers insofar as they are cognitively oriented toward getting off the streets. Street-based relationships provide social and material support on the streets, but they fail to provide resources for getting off the streets. On the contrary, the daily routines on which these relationships are based tend to enmesh their practitioners increasingly in street life. Many regular straddlers are very open about their belief that association with street peers reduces their chances of getting off the streets. Ron Whitaker's comment, quoted earlier, is worth repeating in this regard: "Most of the guys down at the Sally have gotten used to living on the streets and are satisfied with it. One of the most important things in getting off the street is not spending time around guys like that." Ron's fear appears to be justified.[16] Street-based relationships do not provide the material resources necessary to exit homelessness, and their focus on daily street routines eats up time that could perhaps be put into more fruitful activities.

It is interesting to note that when straddlers do engage in activities that are at least ostensibly directed toward exiting the streets, such as securing regular work, entering a detox or rehab program, or developing church or other non-street affiliations, they almost always do so as individuals rather than with buddies. Such activities also demand a great amount of time and thereby pressure individuals to disengage from their street associates. However, such individual efforts to leave the streets are usually unsuccessful. This means that most regular straddlers who try to get off the streets and disengage from peers ultimately return to street life after their work efforts or stay in a rehab program. When they return, they either reengage with previous associates or quickly move to find new "hanging buddies."

The street-based ties of regular straddlers may fracture from the stress of other forces, such as interpersonal conflicts, which arise in most relationships but which have a more serious impact on the streets. Indeed, these straddler relationships frequently disintegrate over time. Most individuals then move on to new relationships in a pattern of serial friendship. In doing so, they expand their social contacts on the streets.

INSTITUTIONALLY ADAPTED STRADDLERS

The situation of institutionally adapted straddlers resembles that of regular straddlers in some ways and differs in others. The defining characteristic of institutionally adapted straddlers is their employment in accommodative and restorative caretaker agencies. Their affiliation with these agencies restricts their peer relationships and their opportunities for fraternizing. As we already noted, agencies that employ the homeless endeavor to limit their fraternizing with other homeless, but the effort is only partially successful, since rules regarding street associations are difficult to monitor and enforce. Many of the institutionally adapted straddlers we observed maintained at least some steady contact with peers who were still on the streets. Hoyt, for instance, left the Sally after dinner on many evenings to go to a nearby park and drink beer with a group of street friends. Similarly, after Tanner finished his morning chores cleaning the Sally shelter, he often met Willie and Ron at the fast-food spot where they hung out to "shoot the shit" over several cups of coffee.

The daily routines of the institutionally adapted straddlers do keep them somewhat apart from their street peers, though. Rather than being tied to the daily circuit of various street-based agencies like most of the homeless, institutionally adapted straddlers are oriented to the daily schedule of the specific agency where they work. They spend a large part of most days with other agency personnel, both non-street staff and others like themselves. These people constitute their primary pool of potential friends, largely because of their proximity. But it is difficult for institutionally adapted straddlers to develop strong friendships with agency staff who have not been on the streets, and who often look down on the homeless. Instead, these straddlers tend to form friendships with others from the streets. Furthermore, most of these straddlers sooner or later return to the streets, and many are aware that this is their likely fate. Street lore, firsthand experience on the streets, and the code of "what goes around, comes around" warn against turning away from homeless friends when working for a street agency. As Hoyt told us:

> There was one guy working at the Sally, oh, about a month ago, who shit on his friends, you know. He could've been helping them out, like for showers and staying in the shelter. And he could've let them in for dinner even if they'd had a drink, as long as they weren't causing trouble. But he got to thinking he was better than them 'cause he was working for the Sally. Some guys are like that. Give 'em a little bit of power, and they think they're God Almighty. But what happened was, he pissed everybody off. I mean, there was ten guys ready to dust his ass if they had the chance. And then he ended up being fired for getting drunk one night. And he was so scared about having to go out and face his old buddies that he was ready to piss his pants. So what he finally did was call a cab to pick him up at the Sally and take him to the bus station so he could get out of town.

Although some institutionally adapted straddlers try to disassociate themselves from street peers, as in this case, most of them maintain at least some social connections with people on the streets. Ultimately, then, institutionally adapted straddlers live in a world of marginal and ambivalent social relationships, neither solidly on nor off the streets.

OUTSIDERS

Outsiders, with the exception of the mentally ill, are the category of homeless people whose daily lives and cognitive orientations are most firmly based on the streets. They are also the group that has been on the streets for the longest stretch of time. Not surprisingly, these factors influence their social relationships. As we have indicated, our research revealed several subgroups of tramps and bums with fairly distinct life-style patterns. These differing life-styles are reflected in their social relationships. Our discussion of outsider relationships thus considers the relationships for each type separately, beginning with the tramp category.

Traditional Tramps   Although traditional tramps have the longest average span of time on the streets (6.1 years), they have less social involvement with street peers than any other outsider group except the mentally ill. Unlike the mentally ill, however, whose isolation stems largely from their interactional incompetence, traditional tramps deliberately pursue a solitary life-style. They speak proudly of their ability to get by without assistance from street agencies or from other homeless people. In fact, they frequently told us of their disdain for other homeless people, whom they perceived as largely incompetent and dependent. Shotgun explained the tramps' attitude:

> It's gotten tougher to be a tramp the past five or six years. These new people on the streets are giving tramps a bad name. They're too screwed up to work and they don't know how to take care of themselves. I stay away from them, 'cause they're just trouble to me. That's why I don't sleep at the Sally. I've got my own spot by a warehouse down here and as long as I keep it to myself no one's going to ruin it for me. That's what it takes, knowing how to take care of yourself. And that's where other [homeless] people can screw you. I don't need "friends" 'cause they just get you in trouble, or you end up taking care of them. It's enough just taking care of myself. . . . And friends hold you down. A tramp can't live that way. When I get ready to go, I don't need anything holding me back.

The traditional tramps' preference for solitude was evident in their drinking patterns. In contrast to most other outsiders, we observed traditional tramps on several occasions turn down the opportunity to join drinking groups. Again Shotgun provides a case in point:

> There's times I'll drink with another tramp, and sometimes I'll drink with somebody who hires me for a job, but most of the people on the streets are bums or virgins, and I ain't drinking with them. They don't know how to take care of themselves. Half the time they end up fighting and the rest of the time they end up in jail.

This disdain for most homeless people explains why traditional tramps have a fairly small number of interpersonal ties on the streets. Of course, their disinterest in street peers is counterbalanced, to a degree, by the fact that they have been homeless so long. Over the years they inevitably develop acquaintances in freightyard jungles, migratory labor camps, and other work settings. Banjo, for instance, told us that he knew carnival workers throughout the South and Midwest. "Twenty years I've been working carnivals on and off," he explained. "After a while it gets so that any carnival you work, you're bound to know somebody." Despite such acquaintances, the tramps we came to know generally traveled alone when they were not working. And although they occasionally ran into acquaintances in Austin, they were unlikely to team up with them on the streets.[17]

Hippie Tramps   The social relationships of hippie tramps make an interesting counterpoint to those of traditional tramps. Like their traditional counterparts, hippie tramps are highly mobile and view themselves as largely self-sufficient. They are much more gregarious, however, at least with those whom they perceive as members of their own group. Hippie tramps formed the most coherent subcultural group among the homeless on the streets of Austin, and their social relationships reflected their countercultural values and their sense of solidarity.

Hippie tramps routinely claimed special competence at surviving on the streets. In this regard, they saw themselves as superior to most of the homeless, especially those who relied on institutional assistance. As Gimpy Dan explained to us:

> It wouldn't be right for us to be using the Sally because we don't really need it. Not like the people down there. We can always find a place to crash—some empty building or something. And you can always sell a few joints to get a burger and some coffee. But them, they're out of it. They couldn't make it without the Sally.

Hippie tramps are not always as self-sufficient as Gimpy Dan's comment suggests. In actuality, many of them do at least occasionally use the Sally and other caretaker agencies such as Caritas, but they do not do so as regularly as most other categories of the homeless.

Hippie tramps tended to avoid interaction with other categories of street people, but they were very involved with each other. They tended to sleep in groups of three to eight people in alcoves and abandoned buildings. During the day they congregated in the area surrounding the Drag, adjacent to the university, a location ideally situated for several of their favored forms of shadow work: selling drugs to students, panhandling, and performing. Frequently in the afternoons fifteen to twenty-five hippie tramps could be found hanging out together, telling stories or conversing about three interrelated themes: past and future "Rainbows" (the annual gathering of old and new hippies), rock music, and drug-related activities. Many of them spent hours discussing "Rainbow" gatherings and Grateful Dead concerts they had been to over the years. Often they vied with each other over who had been to the most gatherings and concerts. There was undoubtedly some exaggeration, but the detail with which they recalled and corroborated these activities suggests that they were frequently telling the truth. Rumors circulated regularly among them about when and where the next "Rainbow" gathering would be held. They also spent many hours discussing various types of drugs, especially marijuana and psychedelics. This talk provided a sense of shared experiences and values that reinforced the hippie tramps' group identification. Very seldom did we hear any of them talk about getting off the streets. Rather, their orientation was toward making the most of life on the streets. In contrast to most street people, hippie tramps knew the names of their associates. They enjoyed socializing with each other and had far greater knowledge about each other's backgrounds than did the other types of homeless.

Hippie tramps drank large amounts of beer almost daily, and this activity was central to their socializing. Their drinking groups were usually made up of six to twelve regulars, perhaps supplemented by a few other street people and an occasional student or two. A drinking group typically developed when some member of the core group urged others to "circle up," an activity in which participants tossed money for beer into a circle that one of them had drawn on the sidewalk, or into someone's hat. The person who initiated the circle was responsible for collecting the money and making the run to a nearby convenience store to purchase several quarts of beer. Contribution to the "circle" was not considered essential to participation in the drinking, however. In keeping with the moral code of "what goes around, comes around," individuals who had contributed in the past or who had general credibility in the group were allowed to drink even when they had no money to chip in. Some degree of reciprocity was expected over time, but it was not tightly monitored.

In summary, then, hippie tramps are a gregarious group with a strong countercultural identity. They tend to know a relatively large number of other street people, although these acquaintances are confined to a small, permeable but relatively self-contained segment of the total homeless population in Austin. Their peer relationships are rooted in their day-to-day street activities, such as drinking, panhandling, and selling drugs, and in their frequent conversations about countercultural themes. Not surprisingly, considering their sense of common identity, their relationships are generally more intense and of longer duration than those of most of the homeless.

Traditional Bums　　As was noted in earlier chapters, traditional bums most closely approximate the popular image of the skid-row alcoholic. They are characterized by their relative lack of mobility, their alcohol dependency, and the fact that they seldom engage in regular work. They rank second only to traditional tramps in length of time on the streets, with an overall average of 4.4 years. With their considerable time on the streets and their tendency to stick around Austin, traditional bums generally had the largest number of street acquaintances of any of the homeless. Many of these relationships, however, were quite superficial, based primarily on casual contact at caretaker agencies or in drinking or sleeping groups. Over the course of several years many individuals had developed extensive networks of acquaintances in this manner. Some traditional bums also had a small number of closer friendships, a few of which they maintained for many years. The friendship between JJ and Indio, for instance, had lasted for nearly five years, and Marilyn and Nona had been relatively close friends and drinking partners for over two years. Traditional bums also exhibited a pattern of serial friendships similar to that which we observed among regular straddlers. These short-term, relatively close friendships were often terminated when one or both parties decided that the other was "more trouble than he's worth."

The main activities that brought traditional bums together were centered on either street-survival activities such as sleeping, or activities related to the purchase and consumption of alcoholic beverages. In practice, drinking and sleeping were often closely connected since group members would get together in some relatively safe place, drink until they were drunk, and then fall asleep. In the mornings they would often go their separate ways, to engage in shadow work or make the agency circuit, and then would regroup in the late afternoon or early evening to resume their drinking and "jungle up" together.[18]

These "bottle gangs" were loosely organized, consisting of a few core members and a larger number of peripheral participants.[19] The groupings exhibited a high degree of flux, tending to coalesce in the afternoons and evenings on the basis of expediency as two or three associates persuaded others to chip in on some beer or wine. Gypsy Bill frequently organized such groups to drink through the evening in his car. Marilyn and Nona participated in drinking and sleeping groups on a regular basis as well, in abandoned buildings, alleys, motel rooms, and cars.

The social relationships of traditional bums, like those of other homeless, serve important instrumental and socioemotional functions in their daily lives. The instrumental function that has received the most attention is that of ensuring access to alcohol. Any given individual street alcoholic may lack money to buy beer or wine, so the pooling of resources increases the odds of getting the alcohol they desire.[20]

A second important instrumental function of street relationships for traditional bums, and the one they themselves seemed to mention most often, is protection. Traditional bums are frequently alcoholic, physically decrepit, and older than other homeless, and therefore they are at relatively high risk of victimization. Furthermore, the threat of arrest looms for them whenever they are drunk in public. Being in a group reduces the risk of being victimized and lowers the chances of being arrested, since more sober members of the group are likely to warn and even hide inebriated members from the police.[21] "If you get drunk alone, you're asking for it," Marilyn told us, "but as long as you're with some people, no one's going to bother you." Furthermore, when trouble does develop friends may step in to help, as we witnessed in the following incident:

> We had been sitting on the curb drinking with JJ and Indio for about an hour when the police came by around 9:00 P.M. and told us to move on. We went down the block and walked up an alley in the direction of the Sally. JJ explained to us that he and Indio were our friends and that they would protect us if anyone jumped us in the alley. He said that they would grab sticks and come to our defense. Then he stopped by a car that was pulled up by some bushes, using the car as partial cover while he urinated. What he had not seen was that three men were sitting in the car. One of them jumped out, brandishing a tire iron, and looked as though he was going to attack JJ, but Indio quickly intervened. "Get the hell away from their car, you dumb son-of-a-bitch!" he yelled at JJ, who zipped up his pants and moved back. "What the hell are you doing pissing by their car?"
>
> "Just get him the fuck outta here," the fellow who had stepped out of the car responded. We quickly walked down the alley. When we got out of earshot of the car, Indio explained, "If I yell at JJ, then they figure his friends are gonna keep him in line. So they don't have to do something. Sometimes I have to do that when the cops come by too. If I didn't cuss him out, they'd take him to jail.

The strategy Indio used to protect JJ in this incident is indicative of an underlying problem when traditional bums try to defend each other. Although they may occasionally be able to use their wits to protect their friends, as Indio did in this case, they often lack the physical strength to protect each other. Nonetheless, a substantial amount of conversation among them is devoted to promises of mutual protection. Despite the empirical weakness of such claims, they are seldom called into question.

In summary, in comparison to other types of homeless individuals, traditional bums tend to have substantially more acquaintances, gleaned from their long tenure on the streets. Most of their associations are relatively superficial, but that can be a pragmatic adaptation for those whose lives on the streets are largely centered on alcohol consumption.

Redneck Bums   As we discussed earlier, redneck bums constitute what we suspect is a southwestern variant of the broader bum category. Members of this group are similar to traditional bums in relative immobility and heavy use of alcohol, but they are younger, have been on the streets for a shorter period of time, and are more regularly involved in various forms of shadow work. The redneck bums we observed had a tightly knit social network, consisting of a group of fifteen to twenty men who were called the James Gang, after one of their dominant members. They hung out together across the street from the Sally in a used car lot and alley where they had negotiated with the car-lot owner to protect his cars in exchange for being able to set up a large lean-to against the back wall of the office. The group had access to a few amenities by virtue of this arrangement. An extension cord strung from inside the building provided the lean-to with electricity, and the men had free access to water spigots and hoses in the lot, which they used to take showers. Rednecks bums were very protective of their turf, ostensibly because of their responsibility to the lot owner. They seldom allowed homeless people who were not members of their group to enter the lot or even to walk on their side of the street unchallenged. On several occasions we witnessed individuals being beaten up because they had unknowingly crossed into the redneck bums' territory. Not surprisingly, most of the homeless feared and avoided the redneck bums.

The James Gang frequently partied late into the night, annoying those who slept in cars near the Sally. Gypsy Bill complained to us, "You just can't get to sleep with all the racket they make." Other homeless at the Sally had different complaints, such as that made by one young man from Arkansas: "They think they can just take what they want. Like the way they come over here and try to take women to the car lot." We also observed this. As an evening party wore on, members of the gang would cross to the Sally side of the street and try to lure women back to the car lot by offering them alcohol and marijuana. Marilyn, who was particularly vulnerable to offers of alcohol, frequently went with them even though she often protested when sober that they had robbed her numerous times when she was drunk. She was also at least occasionally abandoned by them in unsavory circumstances after their evening bacchanalia, as in one instance when she was arrested after being discovered drunk and naked at the edge of the car lot. Hostile sentiments toward the James Gang were a common topic of discussion at the Sally, and when their camp was destroyed by a fire in the late winter the rumor spread that the place had been torched by people who were striking back at the gang.

Although redneck bums formed a fairly tightly knit social group, they were prone to violent confrontations among themselves, as is exemplified in the incident discussed in Chapter 2, in which the gang leader kicked Bill-Bob in the groin for having taken a beer from his six-pack while they were drinking in a plasma-center parking lot. Despite their sometimes violent interactions, however, redneck bums remained a relatively cohesive subgroup of the homeless and maintained a distinctive group identity.

The Mentally Ill   The homeless mentally ill can be distinguished from other types of homeless not only by their cognitive and emotional difficulties but also by their survival repertoires and social patterns, both of which stem largely from their mental illness. The mentally ill were the most consistently isolated individuals we encountered on the streets.[22] This observation was corroborated by several of our informants. Hoyt, for instance, felt sympathetic toward those whom he perceived as mentally ill, commenting, "They just don't have any snap, you know, and no one wants to be around someone like that—or if they do, it's 'cause they want to rip them off." Furthermore, most of the mentally ill homeless seldom initiated interactions with other street people. Jorge Herrera, for instance, had spent twenty years on the streets of Austin, and yet he told us that he had no friends on the streets, and we never saw him in the company of another homeless person. He virtually never initiated interactions with other homeless, and they avoided him as well, undoubtedly because his wild, matted hair, filthy appearance, and frequent convulsions suggested to others that he would be a troublesome and perhaps dangerous companion.

Not all the mentally ill homeless were as reclusive as Jorge, but even the more talkative ones generally failed in establishing sustained friendships, largely because of their interpersonal styles. Lance McCay, for instance, regularly tried to lure other people into conversations. Once he had their attention, however, he overwhelmed them with self-absorbed tirades that allowed them no chance to talk. People quickly tired of interacting with him once they realized that he constantly demanded attention. Other mentally ill individuals put their street peers off by talking obsessively about bizarre and violent experiences. For example, the main topic of conversation of one heavily tattooed man in his early thirties was evil forces, which, he claimed, had deformed his body when he was living with a "group of people in New York who kept the spirits of murdered children around because it made them horny." Such talk unnerved other homeless, who understandably perceived him as potentially violent.

Just as most of the homeless tend to avoid those whom they perceive as mentally ill, so many of the mentally ill hold a fairly disdainful attitude toward other street people. Lance, for instance, spoke loudly and frequently about how "fucked up" the other homeless were and how much they "get on my nerves." Similarly, a mentally ill woman who claimed to be an extraterrestrial being told us that she found human beings in general to be "repulsive, ugly creatures." These individuals, then, are frequently isolated from their street peers not only because of interactional problems but also by virtue of their attitudes toward their peers.

The homeless mentally ill in Austin conducted their lives largely in the same geographical and institutional space as many of the other homeless, but they were socially disconnected from other street people. In fact, the mentally ill homeless were social outsiders in a double sense, being outside conventional society and outside the social world of the other homeless as well.

SUMMARY

In this chapter we have examined the social relationships the homeless develop with their street peers. We have seen that these relationships are plagued by contradictory characteristics. Quick and easy conviviality and an ethos supporting the sharing of modest resources are counterbalanced by chronic distrust of peers and fragility and impermanence of social bonds. These characteristics reflect the impoverished social world of the homeless, a world in which they are largely dislocated from the primary bonds of family and are forced to live their private lives in caretaker facilities and public places, frequently in the presence of large numbers of strangers. In such a milieu the development of quick friendships with anonymous others may be a highly functional survival strategy. At the same time, however, the milieu itself undermines the long-range potential of such social bonds. Residential instability frequently results in separation. The easy availability of superficial friends can undermine motivation to work through conflicts and develop deeper friendships. And although homeless friends can facilitate survival on the streets, they may be an impediment to getting off them. Such contradictory forces result in ambivalent relationships.

The character and extent of peer relations among the homeless are not simply a result of their environment, however. Their relationships are mediated by the various cognitive and behavioral orientations of the different types of homeless individuals. The recently dislocated tend to exhibit a strong aversion to other homeless people. They neither identify with them nor want to be around them. Nonetheless, as they adapt to the institutional matrix of street life in order to survive, they find themselves in the company of their street peers. In time, as the recently dislocated slide, both cognitively and behaviorally, into straddler status, they tend to lose their antipathy for other homeless people and begin to identify with them. The liminal nature of the straddler status, however, pulls them in two directions. On the one hand, they are drawn toward their peers as co-participants in the life of the streets. On the other hand, they are periodically wrenched away from such affiliations by their desire to extricate themselves from street life and their belief that to do so requires avoiding association with street peers. Straddler life is characterized in many ways by the behavioral and cognitive vacillation between these two social poles.

The social patterns of outsiders, by and large, are far less filled with conflict than are those of the recently dislocated and straddlers. The primary reason for this is that outsiders have adapted more completely to street life. With the partial exception of the mentally ill, outsiders have developed relatively stable material, psychological, and social patterns of adaptation. For most outsiders these patterns include the acquisition of a large number of peer relationships. We have noted variations in the character of peer networks among the various types of outsiders. Traditional tramps prefer to "go it alone." In contrast, hippie tramps are highly social, although they tend to restrict their associations to others who share their countercultural values and experiences. Traditional bums frequently have one or two close associates at any given time and fairly extensive street networks, albeit loosely coupled ones, which they tap on a regular basis in order to secure alcoholic beverages and protection while drinking and sleeping. Redneck bums compose a much more tightly knit social network than do their traditional counterparts. They define themselves as a social group separate from the other homeless, much as the hippie tramps do, but they are far more hostile and predatory in their interactions with the other homeless. Finally, the homeless who are seriously mentally ill lack the requisite interactional skills, and frequently the motivation, to develop social relationships with their street peers. Of all the homeless, they are clearly the most isolated socially.

In concluding this chapter it is useful to consider how our findings compare to other research on social relations among the homeless. As we noted at the outset of the chapter, the dominant social-science perspective on homelessness has portrayed it as a process of social disaffiliation and isolation. This theory, which puts social relationships—or, more accurately, the lack of them—at the center of homelessness, became especially well established during the 1960s and early 1970s. Evidence for this view came primarily from survey research that found that skid-row men had less stable employment and fewer connections with their families than did men who were not on skid row. However, this research seldom explored the potential alternative street-level forms of affiliation of the homeless. During this same period a contrasting perspective on social relationships among the homeless developed. Based on participant observation, this research paid close attention to the ongoing lives of the homeless and found that they exhibited a considerable degree of attachment to and interaction with their peers.[23] Clearly, our findings are far more consistent with these latter studies.

Although in the 1980s homelessness has been one of the most widely researched social problems, far less attention has been paid to social relations than in earlier research. However, several studies that have considered this aspect of street life have found a consistently higher level of affiliation among the homeless than the disaffiliation model would suggest.[24] Besides providing a strong empirical critique of the perception of the homeless as "retreatists,"[25] these findings have revealed considerable range in the variety and extent of social ties among the homeless and in the effects of those ties on the well-being of homeless individuals.[26] Consistent with our findings, these studies demonstrate that street peer relationships do indeed provide many of the homeless with emotional, material, and informational support,[27] but that such support is essentially accommodative rather than curative. Although "social ties yield a sense of personal efficacy," as one set of observers have noted, "they cannot resolve the severe impoverishment of homelessness."[28]

While these studies have documented considerable affiliation among the homeless, then, they have also found that the street ties of the homeless are in many ways weaker and less efficacious than those of domiciled citizens. The reasons for the tenuous nature of social ties among the homeless are not to be found in their psychological status as social isolates or retreatists, however. Rather, as we have shown in this chapter, the fragility of social bonds on the streets stems primarily from the precarious social circumstances under which those bonds are formed and maintained. More specifically, their tenuousness is rooted in large part in the survival value of weak ties in resource-depleted contexts. Since nearly all homeless street people are impoverished materially and socially in terms of access to others who can bail them out or attend to their immediate needs, it makes little sense in most cases to develop intimate, enduring relationships with street peers. There are exceptions, of course, as in the case of JJ and Indio. But for most of the homeless, quickly developed but ephemeral relationships that have the trappings of friendship are frequently the most adaptive, in that they expand rather than limit both subsistence opportunities and resource pools. This conclusion suggests that weak or tenuous ties among the homeless are not necessarily indicative of social pathology or asociality, but instead are often highly functional.[29]

When looked at from this angle, many of the homeless seem to exhibit a surprisingly high level of gregariousness and social resilience as they strive to develop what social relationships their circumstances permit. This resilient ability to adapt to impoverished circumstances is characteristic of the homeless in many realms of activity. It is reflected in the creativity with which they fashion shadow-work strategies in order to survive materially on the streets, as we discussed in the previous chapter. It can also be seen in the ways that they adapt psychologically to life on the streets, as we will see in the following chapter.

CHAPTER SEVEN

Salvaging the Self

To be homeless in America is not only to have fallen to the bottom of the status system; it is also to be confronted with gnawing doubts about self-worth and the meaning of existence. Such vexing concerns are not just the psychic fallout of having descended onto the streets, but are also stoked by encounters with the domiciled that constantly remind the homeless of where they stand in relation to others.

One such encounter occurred early in the course of our fieldwork. It was late afternoon, and the homeless were congregating in front of the Sally for dinner. A school bus approached that was packed with Anglo junior high school students being bused from an eastside barrio school to their upper-middle- and upper-class homes in the city's northwest neighborhoods. As the bus rolled by, a fusillade of coins came flying out the windows, as the students made obscene gestures and shouted, "Get a job." Some of the homeless gestured back, some scrambled for the scattered coins—mostly pennies, others angrily threw the coins at the bus, and a few seemed oblivious to the encounter. For the passing junior high schoolers, the exchange was harmless fun, a way to work off the restless energy built up in school; but for the homeless it was a stark reminder of their stigmatized status and of the extent to which they are the objects of negative attention.

Initially, we did not give much thought to this encounter. We were more interested in other issues and were neither fully aware of the frequency of such occurrences nor appreciative of their psychological consequences. We quickly came to learn, however, that this was hardly an isolated incident. The buses passed by the Sally every weekday afternoon during the school year; other domiciled citizens occasionally found pleasure in driving by and similarly hurling insults at the homeless and pennies at their feet; and, as we have seen, the hippie tramps and other homeless in the university area were derisively called "Drag worms," the police often harassed the homeless, and a number of neighborhoods took turns vilifying and derogating them.

Not all encounters with the domiciled are so stridently and intentionally demeaning, of course, but they are no less piercingly stigmatizing. One Saturday morning, for instance, as we walked with Willie Hastings and Ron Whitaker along a downtown street, a woman with a station wagon full of children drove by. As they passed, several of the children pointed at us and shouted, "Hey, Mama, look at the street people!" Ron responded angrily:

> "Mama, look at the street people!" You know, it pisses me off the way fucking thieves steal shit and they can still hold their heads high 'cause they got money. Sure, they have to go to prison sometimes, but when they're out, nobody looks down on them. But I wouldn't steal from nobody, and look how those kids stare at us!

The pain of being objects of curiosity and negative attention are experienced fairly regularly by the homeless, but they suffer just as frequently from what has been called "attention deprivation." In *The Pursuit of Attention,* Charles Derber commented that "members of the subordinate classes are regarded as less worthy of attention in relations with members of dominant classes and so are subjected to subtle yet systematic face-to-face deprivation."[1] For no one is Derber's observation more true than for the homeless, who are routinely ignored or avoided by the domiciled. As previously noted, pedestrians frequently avert their eyes when passing the homeless on the sidewalk, and they often hasten their pace and increase the distance between themselves and the homeless when they sense they may be targeted by a panhandler. Pedestrians sometimes go so far as to cross the street in order to avoid anticipated interaction with the homeless. Because of the fear and anxiety presumably engendered in the domiciled by actual or threatened contact with the homeless, efforts are often made at the community level, as we saw earlier, to regulate and segregate the homeless both spatially and institutionally. Although these avoidance rituals and segregative measures are not as overtly demeaning as the more active and immediate kinds of negative attention the homeless receive, they can be equally stigmatizing, for they also cast the homeless as objects of contamination. This, too, constitutes an assault upon the self, albeit a more subtle and perhaps more insidious one.

Occurring alongside the negative attention and attention deprivation the homeless experience are an array of gestures and acts that are frequently altruistic and clearly indicative of goodwill. People do on occasion give to panhandlers and beggars out of sincere concern rather than merely to get them off their backs. Domiciled citizens sometimes even provide assistance without being asked. One evening, for instance, we found Pat Manchester sitting on a bench near the university eating pizza. "Man, I was just sitting here," he told us, "and this dude walked up and gave me half a pizza and two dollar bills." Several of the students who worked at restaurants in the university area occasionally brought leftovers to Rhyming Mike and other hippie tramps. Other community members occasionally took street people to their home for a shower, dinner, and a good night's sleep. Even Jorge Herrera, who was nearly incoherent, appeared never to wash or bathe, and was covered with rashes and open sores, was the recipient of such assistance. Twice during our field research he appeared on the streets after a brief absence in clean clothes, shaved, and with a new haircut. When we asked about the changes in his appearance, he told us that someone had taken him home, cleaned him up, and let him spend the night. These kinds of unorganized, sporadic gestures of goodwill clearly facilitate the survival of some of the homeless, but the numbers they touch in comparison to those in need are minuscule. Nor do they occur in sufficient quantity or consistently enough to neutralize the stigmatizing and demeaning consequences of not only being on the streets but being objects of negative attention or little attention at all.

In addition to those who make sporadic gestures of goodwill, thousands of domiciled citizens devote occasional time and energy to serving the homeless in an organized fashion in churches, soup kitchens, and shelters. Angels House kitchen was staffed in part by such volunteers, and their support was essential to the operation of the kitchen. Yet the relationship between these well-meaning volunteers and the homeless is highly structured and sanitized. The volunteers typically prepare sandwiches and other foods in a separate area from the homeless or encounter them only across the divide of a serving counter that underscores the distance between the servers and the served. Thus, however sincere and helpful the efforts of domiciled volunteers, the structure of their encounters with the homeless often underscores the immense status dif-

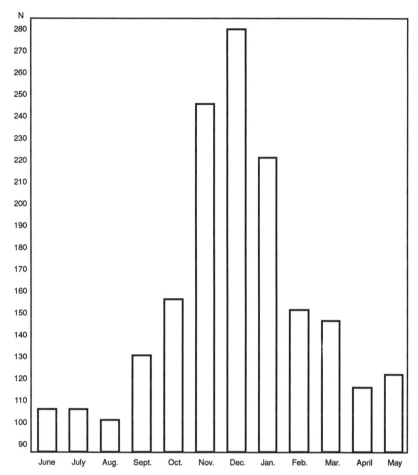

Figure 7.1. Newspaper Stories on Homelessness by Month in *New York Times Index*, 1975–1989

ferences and thereby reminds the homeless again of where they stand in relation to others.

Gestures of goodwill toward the homeless and the kinds of attention they receive are not constant over time. Instead, they tend to follow an annual cycle, with sympathetic interest increasing with the first cold snap in the fall and reaching its zenith during the Christmas holiday season. This pattern is clearly seen in Figure 7.1. Based on a frequency count of newspaper stories on the homeless across the country, the figure reveals a dramatic increase in the number of stories as the Thanksgiving/Christmas holiday season approaches. Moreover, once Christ-

mas passes, coverage declines precipitously.[2] This same pattern was seen
in Austin in the activities both of the media and of many community
residents. At times this expression of holiday concern reached almost
comical dimensions. One Thanksgiving Day, for instance, the homeless
were inundated with food. In the morning several domiciled citizens
came to the Labor Corner to hand out sandwiches, and a few gave away
whole turkeys, assuming they would be devoured on the spot. The Assembly of God Church served a large meal around noon, and the Salvation Army served its traditional Thanksgiving meal in midafternoon.
At one point in the early afternoon the Sally officials appeared to be
worried that only a few people would show up for the meal. Newspaper
and television reporters lingered around the Sally much of the afternoon, taking pictures and interviewing both officials and street people
for stories that would be aired that evening or would appear in the
morning newspaper.

After Christmas, charitable interest in the homeless declined dramatically. The public span of sympathy seemed to have run its course. Thus,
except for a two- to three-month period, the homeless tend to be recipients only of negative attention, ignored altogether, or dealt with in a
segregated and sanitized fashion that underscores their stigmatized status.[3]

The task the homeless face of salvaging the self is not easy, especially
since wherever they turn they are reminded that they are at the very
bottom of the status system. As Sonny McCallister lamented shortly
after he became homeless, "The hardest thing's been getting used to the
way people look down on street people. It's real hard to feel good about
yourself when almost everyone you see is looking down on you." Tom
Fisk, who had been on the streets longer, agreed. But he said that he
had become more calloused over time:

> I used to let it bother me when people stared at me while I was trying to
> sleep on the roof of my car or change clothes out of my trunk, but I don't
> let it get to me anymore. I mean, they don't know who I am, so what gives
> them the right to judge me? I know I'm okay.

But there was equivocation and uncertainty in his voice. Moreover, even
if he no longer felt the stares and comments of others, he still had to
make sense of the distance between himself and them.

How, then, do the homeless deal with the negative attention they receive or the indifference they encounter as they struggle to survive materially? How do they salvage their selves? And to what extent do the webs of meaning they spin and the personal identities they construct vary with patterns of adaptation? We address these questions in the remainder of the chapter by considering two kinds of meaning: existential and identity-oriented. The former term refers to the kinds of accounts the homeless invoke in order to make sense of their plight; the latter refers to the kinds of meaning they attach to self in interactions with others.

MAKING SENSE OF THE PLIGHT OF HOMELESSNESS

The plight of human beings brought face-to-face with the meaning of their existence by suffocating social structures, unanticipated turns of events, dehumanizing living conditions, or the specter of death has been a long and persistent theme in both literature and philosophy. Underlying this strand of writing, generally discussed under the rubric of existentialism, are two consistent themes: that the quest for meaning, while an ongoing challenge in everyday life, is particularly pressing for those individuals whose routines and expectations have been disrupted; and that the burden of finding meaning in such disruptive moments rests on the shoulders of the individual.[4] From this perspective, meaning is not an essence that inheres in a particular object or situation, but a construction or imputation; and the primary architects of such constructions are human actors. The burden of infusing problematic situations with meaning is heavier for some actors than for others, however. Certainly this is true of the homeless, with their pariah-like status, limited resources, and the often demeaning treatment they receive.

How do the homeless carve out a sense of meaning in the seemingly insane and meaningless situation in which they find themselves? Are they able to make sense of their plight in a fashion that helps to salvage the self?

Some are able to do so and others are not. Many of the homeless invoke causal accounts of their situation that infuse it with meaning and rescue the self; others abandon both concerns by drifting into the world of alcoholism or into an alternative reality that is in this world but not of it and that is often treated as symptomatic of insanity by those not privy to it. Of the two lines of response, the first is clearly the most pronounced.

INVOKING CAUSAL ACCOUNTS

By causal accounts we refer to the reasons people give to render understandable their behavior or the situations in which they find themselves. Such accounts are essentially commonsense attributions that are invoked in order to explain some problematic action or situation. Whether such accounts seem reasonable to an observer is irrelevant; what is at issue is their meaningfulness to the actor.

These explanatory accounts are seldom new constructions. Rather, they are likely to be variants of folk understandings or aphorisms that are invoked from time to time by many citizens and thus constitute part of a larger cultural vocabulary. This view of causal accounts accords with the contention that culture can best be thought of as a repertoire or " 'tool kit' of symbols, stories, rituals, and world views which people use in varying configurations to solve different kinds of problems."[5] These stories, symbols, or accounts are not pulled out of that cultural tool kit at random, however. Instead, the appropriation and articulation process is driven by some pressing problem or imperative. In the case of the homeless, that predicament is the existential need to infuse their situation with a sense of meaning that helps to salvage the self. In the service of that imperative, three folk adages or accounts surfaced rather widely and frequently among the homeless in Austin in their conversations with us and each other. One says, "I'm down on my luck." Another reminds us, "What goes around, comes around." And the third says, "I've paid my dues."

"I'm down on my luck"   The term *luck,* which most citizens invoke from time to time to account for unanticipated happenings in their lives, is generally reserved for events that influence the individual's life but are thought to be beyond his or her control.[6] To assert that "I'm down on my luck," then, is to attribute my plight to misfortune, to chance. For the homeless, such an attribution not only helps to make sense of their situation, but it does so in a manner that is psychologically functional in two ways: it exempts the homeless from responsibility for their plight, and it leaves open the possibility of a better future.

Exemption from personal responsibility was a consistent theme in the causal accounts we overheard. As Willie Hastings asserted aggressively in discussing with Ron Whitaker and us the negative attention heaped on all of us just a few minutes earlier by the children in the passing car:

Shit, it ain't my fault I'm on the streets. I didn't choose to become homeless. I just had a lot of bad luck. And that ain't my fault. Hell, who knows? Those kids and their old lady might get unlucky and wake up on the streets someday. It can happen to anyone, you know!

Ron chipped in:

Yeah, a lot of people think we're lazy, that we don't give a shit, that this is what we want. But that sure in hell ain't so—at least not for me. It wasn't my fault I lost my job in Denver. If I'd been working down the street, maybe I'd still be there. I was just at the wrong place at the wrong time. Like Willie said, some people just ain't got no luck!

Sonny McCallister, Tom Fisk, Tony Jones, Tanner Sutton, and Hoyt Page would all have agreed, in large part because their recently dislocated or straddler status makes them take street life less for granted than the outsiders do and therefore prompts them to try to explain their situation. But why invoke luck? Why not fix the blame for their plight on more direct, tangible factors, such as family discord, low wages, or being laid off? Not only are such biographic and structural factors clearly operative in their lives, as we will see in the next chapter, but reference to them can also exempt people from personal responsibility for their plight. After all, it was not Tony Jones's fault that he lost his job as a security guard at a Chicago steel mill when the plant cut back. Yet, although he referred to this event as the one that triggered his descent onto the streets, he still maintained that he was primarily the victim of "bad luck" rather than less mysterious structural forces that clearly intruded into his life. Apparently, he felt that had he chanced to work at a different job or in a different factory, his fate would have been different.

The same logic is evident in Hoyt's efforts to make sense of his situation. His biography is strewn with a host of factors not of his own doing, such as having been orphaned and not having received proper attention for a learning disorder, which could have been woven into a responsibility-free account for being homeless. Yet, he too often said that he was simply "down on my luck."

This tendency to cling to the luck factor in lieu of structural or biographic accounts of homelessness does not stem from ignorance about these other factors or from false consciousness regarding their causal influence. As we will see in the next chapter, the homeless often name structural and biographic factors when discussing the reasons for their homelessness. But the bad-luck account more readily allows for the possibility of a better day down the road. The victim of bad luck can become the recipient of good luck. "Luck changes," as we were frequently reminded. So, too, do structural trends and biographic experiences, but perhaps not so readily or positively from the standpoint of the homeless. Luck is also more fickle and mysterious, and its effects are supposedly distributed more randomly across the social order than are the effects of most structural trends. For good reason, then, some of the homeless cling to the luck factor.

Yet, the lives of most homeless are devoid of much good fortune, as is clear from the biographies of virtually all of our key informants. Why, then, do some of the homeless talk as if good luck is about to come their way? The answer resides in two other frequently invoked causal accounts that are intertwined with the luck factor: "What goes around, comes around," and "I've paid my dues."

"What goes around, comes around"   We saw in an earlier chapter that insofar as there is a moral code affecting interpersonal relations on the streets, it is manifested in the phrase, "What goes around, comes around." But the relevance of this phrase is not confined solely to the interpersonal domain. It is also brought into service with respect to the issue of meaning in general and the luck factor in particular.

Regarding the former, the contention that "what goes around, comes around" suggests a cyclical rather than linear conception of the process by which events unfold. This circularity implies, among other things, a transposition of opposites at some point in the life course. Biblical examples of such transpositions abound, as in the New Testament declarations that "The last shall be first and the first last" and "The meek shall inherit the earth." Although few homeless harbor realistic thoughts of such dramatic transpositions, many do assume that things will get better because "what goes around, comes around."

This logic also holds for luck. Thus, if a person has been down on his or her luck, it follows that the person's luck is subject to change. Hoyt, among others, talked as though he believed this proposition. "Look," he told us one evening over dinner and a few beers at a local steak house:

> I've been down on my luck for so damn long, it's got to change. . . . Like I said before, I believe what goes around, comes around, so I'm due a run of good luck, don't you think?

We nodded in agreement, but not without wondering how strongly Hoyt and others actually believed in the presumed link between luck and the cyclical principle of "what goes around, comes around." Whatever the answer, there is certainly good reason for harboring such a belief, for it introduces a ray of hope into a dismal situation and thereby infuses it with meaning of the kind that helps keep the self afloat.

"I've paid my dues"   This linkage is buttressed further by the third frequently articulated causal account: "I've paid my dues." To invoke this saying is to assert, as Marilyn Fisch often did in her more sober moments, that "I deserve better" after "what I've been through" or "what I've done." The phrase implies that if there are preconditions for a run of good luck, then those conditions have been met. Thus, Gypsy Bill told us one afternoon that he felt his luck was about to change as he was fantasizing about coming into some money. "You may think I'm crazy," he said, "but it's this feeling I've got. Besides, I deserve it 'cause I've paid my dues." A street acquaintance of Gypsy's, a man who fancied himself as "a great blues harmonica player," broke in:

> Yeah, man, I know what you mean. I was playing the blues on Bleeker Street once when Jeff Beck comes by and tells me I'm the best blues harmonica player he's ever heard. "Where do you live?" he asks me. And I tell him, "Here on this sidewalk, and I sleep in the subways." And he asks me, "What do you want from me?" And I tell him, "Nothing, man. A handshake." And he reaches into his pocket and pulls out a hundred-dollar bill and gives it to me 'cause I had it coming! I know the blues, man. I live them. I sleep on the fucking street, paying my dues. That's why no one plays the blues like me!

He then pointed to the knapsack on his back and asked if we knew what was in it. We shook our heads, and he said, "My jeans, man. I fucking pissed in 'em last night, I was so drunk. That's what I'm saying: I know the blues, man! I've paid my dues."

So a streak of good luck, however fleeting, or anticipation of such a streak, albeit a more sustained one, is rationalized in terms of the hardships endured. The more a person has suffered, the greater the dues that have been paid and the more, therefore, a run of good luck is deserved. Perhaps this is why some of those with the longest stretches of time on the streets, namely, outsiders, were heard to assert more often than others that "I've paid my dues." As Shotgun explained in one of his moments of sobriety, "I been on the streets for about fifteen years. . . . I've rode the boxcars and slept out in the wintertime. That's how you pay your dues." Yet, many outsiders do not often invoke this phrase. The reason, we suspect, is that they have been down on their luck for so long that their current fate seems impervious to change and they have therefore resigned themselves to life on the streets. Those who assert that they've paid their dues, however, invoke the phrase in service of the luck factor and the corollary principle of what goes around, comes around. And for good reason. Together, these accounts both exempt the homeless from responsibility for their plight and hold the door ajar for a change in luck.

AVENUES OF ESCAPE: ALCOHOL AND ALTERNATIVE REALITIES

Not all homeless attend to the existential business of making sense of their situation by invoking conventional folk understandings. Some individuals may have been on the streets too long or have endured too many hardships, experienced too many frustrations, and suffered too many insults to the self to bother any longer with the accounting process. Instead, they gradually drift down alternative avenues for dealing with the oppressive realities of street life and the resultant brutalization of the self. These avenues, while stigmatized by the larger culture, are often consonant with the subculture of street life itself. One such avenue is alcoholism; the other involves the creation or adoption of alternative realities frequently associated with mental illness.

The suggestion that some of the homeless drift into alcoholism and mental illness as a consequence of the hopeless and demeaning situation in which they find themselves runs counter to the tendency to treat these conditions as precipitants of homelessness or at least as disabilities that increase vulnerability to becoming homeless.[7] That this presumed causal connection holds for some of the homeless is no doubt true, but it is also true that alcoholism and mental illness sometimes function as means of coping psychologically with the traumas of street life. Clearly, they do not guarantee literal escape from the streets, but they can serve as insulation from further psychic assaults and thereby create illusions of personal autonomy and well-being. How often this process occurs is unclear, but that it is not an infrequent occurrence we are certain.

Evidence of this process is most pronounced with respect to the use of alcohol and drugs. This is clearly seen when we consider the mean scores for alcohol use among the different types of homeless in the field sample, as shown in Table 2.2. Recalling that a mean score of 0 indicates infrequent use or engagement, whereas a score approaching 2 indicates frequent use, a mean score of .23 for the recently dislocated suggests that relatively few of the homeless are chronic alcoholics when they first hit the streets. Furthermore, the hippie tramps and traditional and redneck bums have the highest mean scores for alcohol use (1.33, 1.67, and 2.00, respectively), making it appear that the general tendency is for alcohol use to increase during the drift toward outsiderhood. Since outsiders have been on the streets much longer than the recently dislocated, it also follows that alcohol use is in part a function of time on the streets. Thus, the longer the time on the streets, the greater the probability of chronic alcohol use. The same general tendency also holds for drug use, although not quite as strongly.

Evidence of this tendency for substance use to escalate with increasing time on the streets also comes from our key informants. Hoyt is an avowed alcoholic, but he reminded us a number of times that he did not come to the streets as a chronic alcoholic. Instead, his "drinking problem," as he referred to it, developed over the course of eleven years on and off the streets. He began with drugs, primarily marijuana and speed, but gradually came to use alcohol more heavily because it was cheaper and "didn't get you into as much trouble with the law." During the past several years, he has used alcohol almost exclusively and has recently come to the realization that he has "a serious drinking problem" that must be attended to if he is to get off the streets permanently. Marilyn's experience with alcohol is similar. As she explained one morning over coffee:

> I didn't have much of a drinking problem before I landed on the streets. But I found it all so depressing. And everybody else was drinking and asking me to drink. So I said, "Why not?" I mean, what did I have to lose? Everything was so depressing. Drinking sure couldn't make it any worse!

Her claim of gradually increasing levels of drinking was substantiated by our frequent contacts with her for over two years. When we first met her Marilyn, like many of the homeless, was a spree or binge drinker, but as time passed the period between the sprees became shorter and her drinking became more chronic, all of which was manifested in her increasingly emaciated, weathered, and scarred physical appearance.[8] The experiences of Shotgun, Gypsy, Nona George, and JJ and Indio, as well as other outsiders we met, are all quite similar: increasing use of alcohol with the passage of time, resulting eventually in apparent physiological and psychological dependence.

Why this drift toward alcohol? Reasonable explanations are not hard to come by. One is subcultural. Drinking is, after all, one of the more salient features of street life, and, as Marilyn found, there is often normative pressure to join in either by sharing what one has or by drinking a portion of what has been offered. Boredom is another explanatory factor. Idleness is also a salient characteristic of street life, as the one thing many homeless have to fritter away is unscheduled time. But the explanatory factor that was most often cited by the homeless we came to know is psychological. In a word, it is escape—not so much from boredom as from the travails and miseries of street life, or from the past, or perhaps from both. Hoyt often noted how his reach for the bottle was driven by the need to escape the moment, to get away from the wretchedness and humiliation of his current experience. Shelters, he told us, activated this urge more than anything else:

> You're in there, with lotsa people you don't know. They look like shit and smell like it, too. And they remind you of where you are and who you are. It ain't pleasant. So you begin to crave a drink.

Hoyt was also aware that the drive to drink was sometimes prompted by the need to escape thoughts of the past. He told us once of a former street friend in Dallas who initially drank to obliterate the pain he experienced whenever he thought about the daughter he had lost through divorce:

> He did what a lot of us do when you think about something like that or about where you are now. You think about it and you get pissed off about it and you get drunk and forget about it. At least for a while, and then you start all over. It's just a cycle, a vicious cycle.

Hoyt, JJ, Indio, Nona, Marilyn, Gypsy, and others were all caught in this vicious cycle. Most were not ignorant about what they were doing, but they knew that they were ensnarled in a "catch-22" of sorts. On the one hand, there was awareness of both the physiological and the psychological hazards of chronic drinking; on the other hand, alcohol was often seen as the only avenue for escaping the traumas of the past or present and the meaningless of it all. "At times," as Hoyt once put it, "it seems like the only way out."

Viewed in this light, drinking clearly functions for some of the homeless as adaptive behavior that provides a psychological antidote to the pains of existence. For the chronic drinkers, to be sure, it is an adaptive behavior that has gotten out of control. But it did not begin that way for all of them. Much of the drinking behavior on the streets, including that which has gone awry, thus constitutes a variant of behaviors Erving Goffman has called "secondary adjustments," ways in which individuals who find themselves trapped in demeaning social contexts attempt to stand "apart from the role and the self" implied. They are "undertakings that provide something for the individual to lose himself in, temporarily blotting out all sense of the environment which, and in which, he must abide."[9]

Like much of the drinking that occurs on the streets, some of the behaviors and verbalizations customarily read as symptomatic of mental illness can be construed as forms of adaptive behavior. Undoubtedly, some of the homeless who might be diagnosed as mentally ill were that way prior to their descent onto the streets, but others evince symptoms of such illness as a result of the trauma of living on the streets. The symptoms we refer to are not those of depression and demoralization, which are understandably widespread on the streets,[10] but more "bizarre" patterns of thought and behavior that are less prevalent but more conspicuous.[11] These include auditory and visual hallucinations, that is, hearing or seeing things to which others are not privy; conspiratorial delusions, such as the belief that others are talking about you or are out to get you; grandiose delusions, like the belief that you have extraordinary powers, insights, or contacts; and the public verbalization of these hallucinations and delusions as well as audible conversations with others not present. Such beliefs and behaviors suggest an alternative inner reality that is neither publicly shared nor fully accessible to others and is therefore "out of this world." Although such alternative realities frequently invite both folk labels of "nuts" and "crazy" and clinical labels of schizophrenia and paranoia, they may often be quite functional for some individuals who find themselves in a demeaning and inhumane context in which they are the frequent objects of negative attention or attention deprivation. After all, if you are rarely the recipient of any positive attention or are ignored altogether, creating and retreating into a private reality that grants you privileged insights and special status may be more adaptive than it appears at first glance.

Certainly this appeared to be the case with Tanner Sutton, the badly burned and disfigured Sally street employee who was preoccupied with the occult and higher forms of consciousness and who claimed to be a "spiritually gifted person" with "special mystical powers" that enabled him "to read people," live in "many different dimensions of space," and "look into the future when humans will be transformed into another life form." Taken at face value, such claims appear to be outlandish and perhaps even symptomatic of psychosis. Even some of Tanner's street associates regarded him as "far out," as we saw earlier. Yet Tanner was able to function quite resourcefully on the streets, as was evidenced by his ability to discharge his duties at the Sally. Moreover, however weird or bizarre Tanner's claims, to evaluate him in terms of their veracity misses the point. Tanner's biography and the context in which he found himself make the issue one not of verisimilitude but of psychological functionality. For Tanner, as for others who appear to have lodged their self in some alternative reality, that reality provides a psychological alternative to the material world in which they find themselves, thus insulating them from further psychic assaults emanating from that world and providing an alternative source of self-regard.

Such secondary adjustments, albeit psychological ones, are not fashioned in a highly conscious and intentional manner. Instead, they are drifted into unwittingly over a period of time in much the same way some of the homeless drift into chronic alcohol use. Evidence of this drifting process was clear in the life histories of both Tanner and Lance McCay. Lance's case is particularly revealing: he was admittedly and visibly mentally ill at the time we met him, but his behavior became increasingly bizarre over the two-year period we maintained contact with him. More often than not, such changes seemed to be triggered by an abbreviated visit home, after which he could be seen ranting and raving about his parents, incessantly talking to himself and engaging in more delusional thinking. It seemed clear to us that such outbursts were in large part defensive reactions to feelings of abandonment and exclusion that were magnified by the attention deprivation he experienced on the streets. Not only did we rarely see him conversing with others who were physically present, but other people made a point of avoiding him. In response, Lance retreated into his inner world. That world consisted of conspiratorial thoughts and behaviors, as when he wrote to his mother that he was considering moving to Billings, Montana, where "people won't be prejudiced against me because they won't even know me," as well as grandiose delusions, such as his claim to be "a writer like Hemingway."

Such statements and claims may appear to be strikingly outlandish at first glance, but their strangeness dissipates when they are put in context.[12] For example, it seems less odd that Lance's talk and behavior were peppered with examples of paranoia and delusional thinking when it is remembered that he was frequently rejected and excluded. Moreover, these two sets of observations were linked together in a kind of interactive, self-fulfilling dynamic: the longer Lance was on the streets and the more he experienced rejection and exclusion, the more pronounced his conspiratorial and delusional thinking became and the more bizarre he appeared.[13]

The point is that the bizarre patterns of thought and behavior exhibited by Tanner and Lance, among others, and commonly taken as symptomatic of mental illness can be understood, in part, in terms of their psychological survival value. This is not to suggest that individuals like Lance are not mentally ill in a clinical sense. But to frame their mental functioning and the realities they identify with solely in that fashion is to gloss the extent to which these alternative realities can function as adaptive shields against the painful realities of street life and thereby render superfluous the need to account for that existence in terms of conventional folk understandings. Like alcohol, then, bizarre, alternative realities can provide psychological escape from a brutalizing world out of which physical escape seems unlikely.

CONSTRUCTING IDENTITY-ORIENTED MEANING

However the homeless deal with the issue of existential meaning, whether by stringing together causal accounts borrowed from conventional cultural vocabularies or by seeking refuge in alcohol, drugs, or alternative realities, they are still confronted with establishing who they are in the course of interaction with others, for interaction between two or more individuals minimally requires that they be situated or placed as social objects.[14] In other words, situationally specific identities must be established. Such identities can be established in two ways: they can be attributed or imputed by others, or they can be claimed or asserted by the actor. The former can be thought of as social or role identities in that they are imputations based primarily on information gleaned from the appearance or behavior of others and from the time and location of their action, as when children in a passing car look out the window and yell, "Hey, Mama, look at the street people!" or when junior high school students yell out the windows of their school bus to the homeless lining up for dinner in front of the Sally, "Get a job, you bums!" In each case, the homeless in question have been situated as social objects and thus assigned social identities.[15]

When individuals claim or assert an identity, by contrast, they attribute meaning to themselves. Such self-attributions can be thought of as personal identities rather than social identities, in that they are self-designations brought into play or avowed during the course of actual or anticipated interaction with others.[16] Personal identities may be consistent with imputed social identities, as when Shotgun claims to be "a tramp," or inconsistent, as when Tony Jones yells back to the passing junior high schoolers, "Fuck you, I ain't no lazy bum!" The presented personal identities of individuals who are frequent objects of negative attention or attention deprivation, as are the homeless, can be especially revealing, because they offer a glimpse of how those people deal interactionally with their pariah-like status and the demeaning social identities into which they are frequently cast. Personal identities thus provide further insight into the ways the homeless attempt to salvage the self.

What, then, are the personal identities that the homeless construct and negotiate when in interaction with others? Are they merely a reflection of the highly stereotypic and stigmatized identities attributed to them, or do they reflect a more positive sense of self or at least an attempt to carve out and sustain a less demeaning self-conception?

The construction of personal identity typically involves a number of complementary activities: (a) procurement and arrangement of physical settings and props; (b) cosmetic face work or the arrangement of personal appearance; (c) selective association with other individuals and groups; and (d) verbal construction and assertion of personal identity. Although some of the homeless engage in conscious manipulation of props and appearance—for example, Pushcart, with his fully loaded shopping cart, and Shotgun, who fancies himself a con artist—most do not resort to such measures. Instead, the primary means by which the homeless announce their personal identities is verbal. They engage, in other words, in a good bit of identity talk. This is understandable, since the homeless seldom have the financial or social resources to pursue the other identity construction activities. Additionally, since the structure of their daily routines ensures that they spend a great deal of time waiting here and there, they have ample opportunity to converse with each other.

Sprinkled throughout these conversations with each other, as well as those with agency personnel and, occasionally, with the domiciled, are numerous examples of identity talk. Inspection of the instances of the identity talk to which we were privy yielded three generic patterns: (1) distancing; (2) embracement; and (3) fictive storytelling.[17] Each pattern was found to contain several subtypes that tend to vary in use according to whether the speaker is recently dislocated, a straddler, or an outsider. We elaborate in turn each of the generic patterns, their varieties, and how they vary in use among the different types of homeless.

DISTANCING

When individuals have to enact roles, associate with others, or utilize institutions that imply social identities inconsistent with their actual or desired self-conceptions, they often attempt to distance themselves from those roles, associations, or institutions.[18] A substantial proportion of the identity talk we recorded was consciously focused on distancing from other homeless individuals, from street and occupational roles, and from the caretaker agencies servicing the homeless. Nearly a third of the identity statements were of this variety.

Associational Distancing   Since a claim to a particular self is partly contingent on the imputed social identities of the person's associates, one way people can substantiate that claim when their associates are negatively evaluated is to distance themselves from those associates.[19] This distancing technique manifested itself in two ways among the homeless: disassociation from the homeless as a general social category, and disassociation from specific groupings of homeless individuals.

Categoric associational distancing was particularly evident among the recently dislocated. Illustrative is Tony Jones's comment in response to our initial query about life on the streets:

> I'm not like the other guys who hang out down at the Sally. If you want to know about street people, I can tell you about them; but you can't really learn about street people from studying me, because I'm different.

Such categorical distancing also occurred among those individuals who saw themselves as on the verge of getting off the street. After securing two jobs in the hope of raising enough money to rent an apartment, Ron Whitaker indicated, for example, that he was different from other street people. "They've gotten used to living on the streets and they're satisfied with it, but not me!" he told us. "Next to my salvation, getting off the streets is the most important thing in my life." This variety of categorical distancing was particularly pronounced among homeless individuals who had taken jobs at the Sally and thus had one foot off the streets. These individuals were frequently criticized by other homeless for their condescending attitude. As Marilyn put it, "As soon as these guys get inside, they're better than the rest of us. They've been out on the streets for years, and as soon as they're inside, they forget it."

Among the outsiders, who had been on the streets for some time and who appeared firmly rooted in that life-style, there were few examples of categorical distancing. Instead, these individuals frequently distinguished themselves from other groups of homeless. This form of associational distancing was most conspicuous among those, such as the hippie tramps and redneck bums, who were not regular social-service or shelter users and who saw themselves as especially independent and resourceful. These individuals not only wasted little time in pointing out that they were "not like those Sally users," but were also given to derogating the more institutionally dependent. Indeed, although they are among the furthest removed from a middle-class life-style, they sound at times much like middle-class citizens berating welfare recipients. As Marilyn explained, "A lot of these people staying at the Sally, they're reruns. Every day they're wanting something. People get tired of giving. All you hear is gimme, gimme. And we transients are getting sick of it."

Role Distancing   Role distancing, the second form of distancing employed by the homeless, involves a self-conscious attempt to foster the impression of a lack of commitment or attachment to a particular role in order to deny the self implied.[20] Thus, when individuals find themselves cast into roles in which the social identities implied are inconsistent with desired or actual self-conceptions, role distancing is likely to occur. Since the homeless routinely find themselves being cast into or enacting low-status, negatively evaluated roles, it should not be surprising that many of them attempt to disassociate themselves from those roles.

As did associational distancing, role distancing manifested itself in two ways: distancing from the general role of street person, and distancing from specific occupational roles. The former, which is also a type of categorical distancing, was particularly evident among the recently dislocated. It was not uncommon for these individuals to state explicitly that they should "not be mistaken as a typical street person." Role distancing of the less categoric and more situationally specific type was most evident among those who performed day labor, such as painters' helpers, hod carriers, warehouse and van unloaders, and those in unskilled service occupations such as dishwashing and janitorial work. As we saw earlier, the majority of the homeless we encountered would avail themselves of such job opportunities, but they seldom did so enthusiastically, since the jobs offered low status and low wages. This was especially true of the straddlers and some of the outsiders, who frequently reminded others of their disdain for such jobs and of the belief that they deserved better, as exemplified by the remarks of a drunk young man who had worked the previous day as a painter's helper: "I made $36.00 off the Labor Corner, but it was just nigger work. I'm twenty-four years old, man. I deserve better than that."

Similar distancing laments were frequently voiced over the disparity between job demands and wages. We were conversing with a small gathering of homeless men on a Sunday afternoon, for example, when one of them revealed that earlier in the day he had turned down a job to carry shingles up a ladder for $4.00 an hour because he found it demeaning to "do that hard a work for that low a pay." Since day-labor jobs seldom last for more than six hours, perhaps not much is lost monetarily in foregoing such jobs in comparison to what can be gained in pride. But even when the ratio of dollars to pride appears to make rejection costly, as in the case of permanent jobs, dissatisfaction with the low status of menial jobs may prod some homeless individuals to engage in the ultimate form of role distancing by quitting currently held jobs. As Ron Whitaker recounted the day after he quit in the middle of his shift as a dishwasher at a local restaurant:

> My boss told me, "You can't walk out on me." And I told her, "Fuck you, just watch me. I'm gonna walk out of here right now." And I did. "You can't walk out on me," she said. I said, "Fuck you, I'm gone."

The foregoing illustrations suggest that the social identities lodged in available work roles are frequently inconsistent with the desired or idealized self-conceptions of some of the homeless. Consequently, "bitching about," "turning down," and even "blowing off" such work may function as a means of social-identity disavowal, on the one hand, and personal-identity assertion on the other. Such techniques provide a way of saying, "Hey, I have some pride. I'm in control. I'm my own person." This is especially the case among those individuals for whom such work is no longer just a stopgap measure but an apparently permanent feature of their lives.

Institutional Distancing   An equally prevalent distancing technique involved the derogation of the caretaker agencies that attended to the needs of the homeless. The agency that was the most frequent object of

these harangues was the Sally. Many of the homeless who used it described it as a greedy corporation run by inhumane personnel more
interested in lining their own pockets than in serving the needy. Willie
Hastings claimed, for example, that "the major is money-hungry and
feeds people the cheapest way he can. He never talks to people except
to gripe at them." He then added that the "Sally is supposed to be a
Christian organization, but it doesn't have a Christian spirit. It looks
down on people. . . . The Salvation Army is a national business that
is more worried about making money than helping people." Ron
Whitaker concurred, noting on another occasion that the "Sally here
doesn't nearly do as much as it could for people. The people who work
there take bags of groceries and put them in their cars. People donate
to the Sally, and then the workers there cream off the best." [21] Another
straddler told us after he had spent several nights at the winter shelter,
"If you spend a week here, you'll see how come people lose hope. You're
treated just like an animal."

Because the Salvation Army is the only local facility that provides
free shelter, breakfast, and dinner, attention is understandably focused
on it. But that the Sally would be frequently derogated by the people
whose survival it facilitates may appear puzzling at first glance, especially given its highly accommodative orientation. The answer lies in
part in the organization and dissemination of its services. Clients are
processed in an impersonal, highly structured assembly line–like fashion. The result is a leveling of individual differences and a decline in
personal autonomy. Bitching and complaining about such settings create psychic distance from the self implied and secure a modicum of
personal autonomy. [22] This variety of distancing, though observable
among all of the homeless, was most prevalent among the straddlers
and outsiders. Since these individuals have used street agencies over a
longer period of time, their self-concepts are more deeply implicated in
them, thus necessitating distancing from those institutions and the self
implied. Criticizing the Sally, then, provides some users with a means
of dealing with the implications of their dependency on it. It is, in short,
a way of presenting and sustaining a somewhat contrary personal identity.

Thus far we have elaborated how some of the homeless distance
themselves from other homeless individuals, from general and specific
roles, and from the institutions that deal with them. Such distancing
behavior and talk represent attempts to salvage a measure of self-worth.

TABLE 7.1   TYPES OF DISTANCING, BY TYPE OF
HOMELESS *

Types of Homeless	Categoric Distancing[a] (N: 16)	Specific Distancing[b] (N: 23)	Institutional Distancing[c] (N: 23)
Recently dislocated	68.8%	—	8.7%
Straddlers	12.4	60.9%	43.5
Outsiders	—	34.8	47.8%
Mentally ill	18.7%	4.3%	—

* $\chi^2 = 41.88$, df = 6, P <.001.

[a] Comments or statements coded as categoric distancing include those indicating dissociation or distancing from such general street-role identities as transient, bum, tramp, or drifter, or from other street people in general.

[b] Comments or statements coded as specific distancing include those indicating dissociation from specific groupings of homeless individuals or from specific survival or occupational roles.

[c] Comments or statements coded as institutional distancing include those indicating dissociation from or disdain for street institutions, such as the Salvation Army or soup kitchens.

In the process, of course, the homeless are asserting more favorable personal identities. Not all homeless individuals engage in similar distancing behavior and talk, however. As is indicated in Table 7.1, which summarizes the foregoing observations, categorical distancing tends to be concentrated among the recently dislocated. Among those who are more firmly entrenched in street life, distancing tends to be confined to distinguishing themselves from specific groups of homeless, such as novices and the institutionally dependent, from specific occupational roles, or from the institutions with which they have occasional contact.

EMBRACEMENT

Embracement connotes a person's verbal and expressive confirmation of acceptance of and attachment to the social identity associated with a general or specific role, a set of social relationships, or a particular ideology.[23] So defined, embracement implies that social identity is congruent with personal identity. Thus, embracement involves the avowal of implied social identities rather than their disavowal, as in the case of distancing. Thirty-four percent of the identity statements were of this variety.

Role Embracement   The most conspicuous kind of embracement encountered was categoric role embracement, which typically manifested itself by the avowal and acceptance of street-role identities such as tramp and bum. Occasionally we would encounter an individual who would immediately announce that he or she was a tramp or a bum. A case in point is provided by our initial encounter with Shotgun, when he proudly told us that he was "the tramp who was on the front page of yesterday's newspaper." In that and subsequent conversations his talk was peppered with references to himself as a tramp. He said, for example, that he had appeared on a television show in St. Louis as a tramp and that he "tramped" his way across the country, and he revealed several "cons" that "tramps use to survive on the road."

Shotgun and others like him identified themselves as traditional "brethren of the road" tramps. A number of other individuals identified themselves as "hippie tramps. When confronted by a passing group of young punk-rockers, for instance, Gimpy Dan and several other hippie tramps voiced agreement with the remark one made that "these kids will change but we'll stay the same." As if to buttress this claim, they went on to talk about "Rainbow," the previously mentioned annual gathering of old hippies which functions in part as a kind of identity-reaffirmation ritual. For these street people, there was little doubt about who they were; they not only saw themselves as hippie tramps, but they embraced that identity both verbally and expressively.

This sort of embracement also surfaced on occasion with skid row—like bums, as was evidenced by Gypsy Bill's repeated references to himself as a bum. As a corollary of such categoric role embracement, most individuals who identified themselves as tramps or bums adopted nicknames congruent with these roles, such as Shotgun, Boxcar Billie, Gypsy Bill, and Pushcart. Such street names thus symbolize a break with their domiciled past and suggest, as well, a fairly thoroughgoing embracement of life on the streets.

Role-specific embracement was also encountered occasionally, as when Gypsy would refer to himself as an "expert dumpster diver." Many street people occasionally engage in this survival activity, but relatively few pridefully identify with it. Other role-specific survival activities embraced included panhandling, small-time drug-dealing, and performing, such as playing a musical instrument or singing on a street corner for money. "Rhyming Mike," as we have seen, made his money by composing short poems for spare change from passersby, and routinely referred to himself as a street poet. For some homeless individuals, then, the street roles and routines they enact function as sources of positive identity and self-worth.

Associational Embracement   A second variety of embracement entails reference to oneself as a friend or as an individual who takes his or her social relationships seriously.[24] Gypsy provides a case in point. On one occasion he told us that he had several friends who either refused or quit jobs at the Sally because they "weren't allowed to associate with other guys on the streets who were their friends." Such a policy struck him as immoral. "They expect you to forget who your friends are and where you came from when you go to work there," he told us angrily. "They asked me to work there once and I told them, 'No way.' I'm a bum and I know who my friends are." Self-identification as a person who willingly shares limited resources, such as cigarettes and alcohol, also occurred frequently, particularly among self-avowed tramps and bums.

Associational embracement was also sometimes expressed in claims of protecting buddies. As was noted in the previous chapter, JJ and Indio repeatedly said they "looked out for each other." When Indio was telling about having been assaulted and robbed while walking through an alley, JJ said, almost apologetically, "It wouldn't have happened if I was with you. I wouldn't have let them get away with that." Similar claims were made to one of us, as when two straddlers said one evening after an ambiguous encounter with a clique of half a dozen other street people, "If it wasn't for us, they'd have had your ass."

Although protective behaviors that entailed risk were seldom observed, protective claims, and particularly promises, were heard frequently. Whatever the relationship between such claims and action, they not only illustrate adherence to the moral code of "what goes around, comes around," but they also express the claimant's desire to be identified as a trustworthy friend.

Ideological Embracement   The third variety of embracement entails adherence to an ideology or an alternative reality and the avowal of a personal identity that is cognitively congruent with that ideology. Banjo, for example, routinely identifies himself as a Christian. He painted on his banjo case "Wealth Means Nothing Without God," and his talk is sprinkled with references to his Christian beliefs. He can often be found giving testimony about "the power and grace of Jesus" to other homeless around the Sally, and he witnesses regularly at the Central Assem-

TABLE 7.2   TYPES OF EMBRACEMENT, BY TYPE
OF HOMELESS*

Types of Homeless	Categoric Embracement[a] (N: 16)	Specific Embracement[b] (N: 23)	Ideological Embracement[c] (N: 23)
Recently dislocated	—	10.0%	7.7%
Straddlers	5.1%	35.0	46.1
Outsiders	87.2	45.0	30.8
Mentally ill	7.7%	10.0%	15.4%

* $\chi^2 = 21.11$, df = 6, P < .05.
[a] Comments or statements coded as categoric embracement include those indicating acceptance of or attachment to street people as a social category or to such general street-role identities as bum, tramp, drifter, or transient.
[b] Comments or statements coded as specific embracement include those indicating identification with a situationally specific survival role, such as dumpster diver or street performer, or with a specific social-relational role, such as friend, lover, or protector, or with an occupational role.
[c] Comments or statements coded as ideological embracement include those indicating acceptance of a set of beliefs or ideas, such as those associated with a particular religion.

bly of God Church. Moreover, he frequently points out that his religious beliefs transcend his situation on the streets. As he told us once, "It would have to be a bigger purpose than just money to get me off the streets, like a religious mission."

A source of identity as powerful as religion, but less common, is the occult and related alternative realities. Since traditional occupational roles are not readily available to the homeless as a basis for identity, and since few street people have the material resources that can be used for construction of positive personal identities, it is little wonder that some of them find in alternative realities a locus for a positive identity. As we noted earlier, Tanner Sutton identifies himself as a "spirit guide" who can see into the future, prophesying, for instance, that "humans will be transformed into another life form."

Like mainstream religious traditions and occult realities, conversionist, restorative ideologies such as that associated with Alcoholics Anonymous provide an identity for some homeless people who are willing to accept AA's doctrines and adhere to its program. Interestingly, AA's successes seldom remain on the streets. Consequently, those street people who have previously associated with AA seldom use it as a basis for identity assertion. Nonetheless, it does constitute a potentially salient identity peg.

We have seen how the personal identities of the homeless may be derived from embracement of the social identities associated with certain stereotypic street roles, such as the tramp and the bum; with role-specific survival activities, such as dumpster-diving; with certain social relationships, such as friend and protector; or with certain religious and occult ideologies or alternative realities. We have also noted that the use of embracement tends to vary across the different types of homeless. This can be seen more clearly in Table 7.2, which shows that categoric embracement in particular and embracement talk in general occur most frequently among outsiders and rarely among the recently dislocated.

FICTIVE STORYTELLING

A third form of identity talk engaged in by the homeless is fictive storytelling about past, present, or future experiences and accomplishments. We characterize as fictive stories that range from minor exaggerations of experience to full-fledged fabrications. We observed two types of fictive storytelling: embellishment of the past and present, and fantasizing about the future.[25] Slightly more than a third of the identity statements we recorded fell into one of these two categories.

Embellishment   By *embellishment* we refer to the exaggeration of past *or* present experiences with fanciful and fictitious particulars so as to assert a positive personal identity. Embellishment involves enlargement of the truth, an overstatement of what transpired or is unfolding. Embellished stories, then, are only partly fictional.

Examples of embellishment for identity construction abound among the homeless. Although a wide array of events and experiences, ranging from the accomplishments of offspring to sexual and drinking exploits and predatory activities, were embellished, such storytelling was most commonly associated with past and current occupational and financial themes. The typical story of financial embellishment entailed an exaggerated claim regarding past or current wages. A case in point is provided by a forty-year-old homeless man who spent much of his time hanging around a bar boasting about having been offered a job as a Harley-Davidson mechanic for $18.50 per hour, although at the same time he constantly begged for cigarettes and spare change for beer.

Equally illustrative of such embellishment was an encounter we overheard between Marilyn, who was passing out discarded burritos, and a homeless man in his early twenties. After this fellow had taken several burritos, he chided Marilyn for being "drunk." She yelled back angrily, "I'm a sheetrock taper and I make 14 bucks an hour. What the fuck do you make?" In addition to putting the young man in his place, Marilyn thus announced to him and to others overhearing the encounter her desired identity as a person who earns a good wage and must therefore be treated respectfully. Subsequent interaction with her revealed that she worked only sporadically, and then most often for not much more than minimum wage. There was, then, a considerable gap between claims and reality.

Disjunctures between identity assertions and reality appear to be quite common and were readily discernible on occasion, as in the case of a forty-five-year-old straddler from Pittsburgh who had been on the streets for a year and who was given to substantial embellishment of his former military experiences. On several occasions he was overheard telling about "patrolling the Alaskan/Russian border in Alaskan Siberia" and his encounters with Russian guards who traded him vodka for coffee. Since there is no border between Alaska and Siberia, it is obvious that this tale is outlandish. Nonetheless, such tales, however embellished, can be construed as attempts to communicate specifics about the person and the person's sense of self. Additionally, they focus a ray of positive attention on the storyteller and thereby enable him or her to garner momentarily a valued resource that is typically in short supply on the streets.

Fantasizing   The second type of fictive storytelling among the homeless is verbal fantasizing, which involves the articulation of fabrications about the speaker's future. Such fabrications place the narrator in positively framed situations that seem far removed from, if at all connected to, his or her past and present. These fabrications are almost always benign, usually have a Walter Mitty/pipe dream quality to them, and vary from fanciful reveries involving little self-deception to fantastic stories in which the narrator appears to be taken in by his or her constructions.[26]

Regardless of the degree of self-deception, the verbal fantasies we heard were generally organized around one or more of four themes: self-employment, money, material possessions, and women.[27] Fanciful constructions concerning self-employment usually involved business schemes. On several occasions, for example, Tony Jones told us and others about his plans to set up a little shop near the university to sell leather hats and silver work imported from New York. In an even more expansive vein, two straddlers who had befriended each other seemed to be scheming constantly about how they were going to start one lucrative business after another. Once we overheard them talking about "going into business" for themselves, "either roofing houses or rebuilding classic cars and selling them." A few days later, they were observed trying to find a third party to bankroll one of these business ventures, and they even asked us if we "could come up with some cash."

An equally prominent source of fanciful identity construction is the fantasy of becoming rich. Some of the homeless just daydreamed about what they would do if they had a million dollars. Pat Manchester, for instance, assured us that if he "won a million dollars in a lottery," he was mature enough that he "wouldn't blow it." Others made bold claims about future riches without offering any details. And still others confidently spun fairly detailed stories about being extravagant familial providers in the future, as Tom Fisk did when he returned to town after a futile effort to establish himself in a city closer to his girlfriend. Despite his continuing financial setbacks, he assured us, "I'm going to get my fiancée a new pet monkey, even if it costs a thousand dollars. And I'm going to get her two parrots too, just to show her how much I love her."

Fanciful identity assertions were also constructed around material possessions and sexual encounters with women. These two identity pegs were clearly illustrated one evening among several homeless men along the city's major nightlife strip. During the course of making numerous overtures to passing women, two of the fellows jointly fantasized about how they would attract these women in the future. "Man, these chicks are going to be all over us when we come back into town with our new suits and Corvettes," one exclaimed. The other added, "We'll have to get some cocaine too. Cocaine will get you women every time." This episode and fantasy occurred early in the second month of our fieldwork, and we quickly came to learn that such fantasizing was fairly commonplace and that it was typically occasioned by "woman-watching," which exemplifies one of the ways in which homeless men are both deprived of attention and respond to that deprivation.

One place homeless men would often watch women was along a jogging trail in one of the city's parks adjacent to the river. Here on warm afternoons they would drink beer and call out to women who jogged or walked along the trail or came to the park to sun themselves. Most of the women moved nervously by, ignoring the overtures of the men. But some responded with a smile, a wave, or even a quick "Hi!"

Starved for female attention, the homeless men are quick to fantasize, attributing great significance to the slightest response. One Saturday afternoon, for example, as we were sitting by the jogging trail drinking beer with Pat Manchester and Ron Whitaker, we noticed several groups of young women who had laid out blankets on the grassy strip that borders the trail. Pat and Ron were especially interested in the women who were wearing shorts and halter tops. Pat called out for them to take their tops off. It was not clear that they heard him, but he insisted, "They really want it. I can tell they do." He suggested we go over with him to "see what we can get," but he was unwilling to go by himself. Instead, he constructed a fantasy in which the young women were very interested in him. Occasionally the women glanced toward us with apprehension, and Pat always acted as though it was a sign of interest. "If I go over there and they want to wrap me up in that blanket and fuck me," he said, "man, I'm going for it." Nonetheless, he continued to sit and fantasize, unwilling to acknowledge openly the obdurate reality staring him in the face.[28]

Although respectable work, financial wealth, material possessions, and women are intimately interconnected in actuality, only one or two of the themes were typically highlighted in the stories we heard. Occasionally, however, we encountered a particularly accomplished storyteller who wove together all four themes in a grand scenario. Such was the case with the straddler from Pittsburgh who told the following tale over a meal of bean stew and stale bread at the Sally, and repeated it after lights-outs as he lay on the concrete floor of the winter warehouse: "Tomorrow morning I'm going to get my money and say, 'Fuck this shit.' I'm going to catch a plane to Pittsburgh and tomorrow night I'll take a hot bath, have a dinner of linguine and red wine in my own restaurant, and have a woman hanging on my arm." When encountered on the street the next evening, he attempted to explain his continued presence on the streets by saying, "I've been informed that all my money is tied up in a legal battle back in Pittsburgh," an apparently fanciful amplification of the original fabrication.[29]

Although both embellished and fanciful fictive storytelling surfaced rather frequently in the conversations we overheard, they were not uniformly widespread or randomly distributed among the homeless. As is indicated in Table 7.3, embellishment occurred among all the homeless but was most pronounced among the straddlers and outsiders. Fantasizing, on the other hand, occurred most frequently among those who still had one foot anchored in the world they came from and who could

TABLE 7.3   TYPES OF FICTIVE STORYTELLING,
BY TYPE OF HOMELESS*

Types of Homeless	Embellishment[a] (N: 39)	Fantasizing[b] (N: 31)
Recently dislocated	2.6%	45.2%
Straddlers	42.1	32.2
Outsiders	50.0	9.7
Mentally ill	5.3%	12.9%

* $\chi^2 = 24.35$, df = 3, P < .001.

[a] Comments or statements were coded as embellishment if they entailed the elaboration and exaggeration of past and present experiences with fictitious particulars. See note 25 for criteria used for determining the fictive character of comments and stories.

[b] Comments or statements were coded as fantasizing if they entailed future-oriented fabrications that placed the narrator in positively or strangely framed situations. See note 25 for criteria used for determining the fictive character of comments and stories.

still envision a future, and it occurred least often among those individuals who appeared acclimated to street life and who tended to embrace one or more street identities. For these individuals, especially those who have been on the streets for some time, the future is apparently too remote to provide a solid anchor for identity-oriented fictions that are of this world. It is not surprising, then, that it is also these individuals who exhibit the greatest tendency to drift into alternative realities, as did a thirty-three-year-old black female who claimed to be "the Interracial Princess," a status allegedly bestowed on her by "a famous astrologer from New York."

We have elaborated three generic patterns of talk through which the homeless construct and avow personal identities. We have seen that each pattern of this identity talk—distancing, embracement, and fictive storytelling—contains several varieties, and that their frequency of use varies among the types of homeless. Categoric role and associational distancing and the construction of fanciful identities occur most frequently among the recently dislocated, for example; whereas categoric embracement and embellishment tend to manifest themselves most frequently among the outsiders. Overall, then, many of the homeless are active agents in the construction and negotiation of identities as they interact with others. They do not, in other words, passively accept the social identities their appearance sometimes exudes or into which they are cast. This is not to suggest that the homeless do not sometimes view themselves in terms of the more negative, stereotypical identities frequently imputed to them. One afternoon, for example, we encountered Gypsy stretched out on a mattress in the back of his old car. Drunk and downhearted, he muttered glumly:

> I've just about given up on life. I can't get any work and all my friends do is keep me drunk. Crazy, just crazy—that's all I am. Don't have any desire to do anything for myself. This car is all I've got, and even it won't work. It's not even worth trying. I'm nothing but an asshole and a bum anymore.

But on other occasions, as we have seen, Gypsy was not only more cheerful but even managed to cull shreds of self-respect and dignity from his pariah-like existence. Moreover, we found that self-deprecating lamentations like Gypsy's were relatively rare compared to the avowal of positive personal identities. This should not be particularly surprising, since every human needs to be an object of value and since the homeless have little to supply that sense of value other than their own identity-construction efforts.

SUMMARY

All animals are confronted with the challenge of material subsistence, but only humans are saddled with the vexing question of its meaning. We must not only sustain ourselves physically to survive, but we are also impelled to make sense of our mode of subsistence, to place it in some meaningful context, to develop an account of our situation that does not destroy our sense of self-worth. Otherwise, the will to persist falters and interest in tomorrow wanes. The biblical prophets understood this well when they told us that "man does not live by bread alone." The homeless appear to understand this existential dilemma, too, at least experientially; for while they struggle to subsist materially, they confront the meaning of their predicament and its implications for the self. These concerns weigh particularly heavily on the recently dislocated, but they gnaw at the other homeless as well—sometimes when they drift off at night, sometimes when they are jarred from sleep by their own dreams or the cries of others, and often throughout the day when their encounters with other homeless and with the domiciled remind them in myriad subtle and not-so-subtle ways of their descent into the lowest reaches of the social system and of their resultant stigmatized status.

In this chapter we have explored the ways the homeless deal with their plight, both existentially and interactionally, by attempting to construct and maintain a sense of meaning and self-worth that helps them stay afloat. Not all of the homeless succeed, of course. The selves of some have been so brutalized that they are abandoned in favor of alcohol, drugs, or out-of-this-world fantasies. And many would probably not score high on a questionnaire evaluating self-esteem.[30] But the issue for us has not been how well the homeless fare in comparison to others on measures of self-esteem, but that they do, in fact, attempt to salvage the self, and that this struggle is an ongoing feature of the experience of living on the streets.

The homeless we studied are not the only individuals who have fallen or been pushed through the cracks of society who nevertheless try to carve a modicum of meaning and personal significance out of what must seem to those perched higher in the social order as an anomic void. Other examples of such salvaging work have been found in mental hospitals, concentration camps, and among black street-corner men.[31] In these and presumably in other such cases of marginality, the attempt to carve out and maintain a sense of meaning and self-worth seems especially critical for survival because it is the one thread that enables those situated at the bottom to salvage their humanity. It follows, then, that it is not out of disinterest that some people find it difficult to salvage their respective selves, but that it results instead from the scarcity of material and social resources at their disposal. That many of the homeless are indeed able to make some culturally meaningful sense of their situation and secure a measure of self-worth testifies to their psychological resourcefulness and resolve, and to the resilience of the human spirit.

Considering these observations, it is puzzling why most research on the homeless has focused almost solely on their demographics and disabilities, to the exclusion of their inner lives. Perhaps it is because many social scientists have long assumed that the issues of meaning and self-worth are irrelevant, or at least of secondary importance, in the face of pressing physiological survival needs. This assumption is firmly rooted in Abraham Maslow's well-known hierarchy of needs, which holds that the satisfaction of physiological and safety needs is a necessary condition for the emergence and gratification of higher-level needs such as the need for self-esteem or for a positive personal identity.[32] This thesis has become almost a cliché in spite of the fact that relevant research is scanty and ambiguous at best. Our finding that concern with both existential and identity-oriented meaning can be readily gleaned from the talk of homeless street people, clearly some of the most destitute in terms of physiological and safety needs, provides an empirical counter-point to this popular assumption. Moreover, our observations suggest that the salience of such cognitive concerns is not necessarily contingent on the prior satisfaction of physiological survival requisites. Instead, such needs appear to coexist, even at the most rudimentary levels of human existence. The homeless we came to know clearly evidence such concerns.

PART THREE

Dynamics of Homelessness

CHAPTER EIGHT

Pathways to the Street

In the preceding chapters, which examined how the homeless negotiate street life materially, socially, and psychologically, we alluded to some of the factors accounting for the plight of our key informants and their counterparts. But we have yet to tackle head on the question of the causes of homelessness. Do the life experiences or biographies of the homeless contain factors that account for their descent onto the streets, or are they victims of forces beyond their control? And why did so many of them appear in the mid-1980s, rather than the 1970s or 1960s?

The question of the precise number of homeless on the streets of urban America has of course generated considerable debate. But there is no disputing the dramatic proliferation in their numbers in virtually every American city in the 1980s. As we noted earlier, Austin's Salvation Army served over 100 percent more homeless in 1985 than in 1979. And it was not because of the generation of a pseudo-issue or the lack of other pressing issues that the city appointed two successive task forces on homelessness during the 1980s.[1] Rather, it was to deal with the real problems posed by the mounting numbers of homeless on the city's streets. Where did they come from, and why? What was going on in Austin as well as in other cities across the country that fueled this proliferation of homelessness? And why do some individuals rather than others find themselves on the streets? Why Tony Jones, Hoyt Page, Tanner Sutton, Marilyn Fisch, Gypsy Bill, Lance McCay, and the others we came to know in varying degrees of intimacy? Did they all take the same path to the streets, or did they travel there along a multitude of interconnected pathways? What, in short, are the precipitants of homelessness?

We address these questions in this chapter by exploring two interconnected but fundamentally different sets of factors. One encompasses large-scale, structural trends that place masses of individuals at risk of becoming homeless; the other concerns biographic or individual-level factors that push some of those at risk over the edge and onto the streets. We begin with an extended discussion of the structural sources of homelessness. Pursuit of these broader, supraindividual factors necessitates that we leave the ground a bit, but we will reestablish contact with Austin and the homeless we know best as we proceed.

THE STRUCTURAL ROOTS OF HOMELESSNESS

Structural factors refer to social arrangements and trends that affect the probability that specific events or life trajectories will be experienced. By narrowing or expanding life chances and opportunities, they facilitate or constrain individuals' options.

Two sets of structural factors are repeatedly mentioned in most discussions of the roots of homelessness. One set concerns the scope and sources of residential dislocation; the other concerns the nature and sources of economic dislocation.

RESIDENTIAL DISLOCATION

Homelessness is above all else a problem of residential dislocation. If all Americans had relatively permanent access to a safe, decent, and sanitary place of residence, then clearly homelessness would not be such a pressing national problem. This core linkage is appropriately reflected in the titles of a number of recent books on homelessness—in James Wright's *Address Unknown* and Peter Rossi's *Without Shelter,* for example—as well as in the burgeoning literature on the scope and causes of residential dislocation.[2] All of this literature points in varying degrees to the interplay of three dislocating trends: deinstitutionalization, decline in the nation's stock of low-income housing, and inflation in the cost of housing in general.

Deinstitutionalization   As the ranks of the homeless expanded in the early 1980s, the search for a principal cause of this pressing social problem initially focused on the social experiment called deinstitutionalization. This term refers to the well-meaning but misguided attempt to reduce inpatient populations of institutions for the mentally ill by releasing or channeling them into more humane, community-based residential facilities.[3] At the end of 1955, the peak year of institutionalization in the United States, 558,922 patients resided in state and county mental hospitals. By the end of 1980, that figure had declined to 137,810, a 75 percent decrease in the number of institutionalized mentally impaired.[4]

Since the community absorption phase of this process was never successfully implemented,[5] and since the majority of the growing legions of homeless were initially thought to be mentally ill, a causal link was quickly made between deinstitutionalization and homelessness. Indeed, by the mid-1980s there appeared to be an emerging consensus on this point. Thus, a 1985 *Time* essay referred to the homeless as "the remnants of a grand and noble experiment."[6] A *Newsweek* cover story titled "Abandoned" referred to the homeless as "America's cast-offs—turned away from mental institutions and into the streets."[7] And a *People* magazine essay asserted rather matter-of-factly that "probably the greatest contributors to the size of the homeless population . . . are state mental hospitals."[8]

The same connections were being made in local contexts as well. One observer in Houston claimed that no less than "half of [the city's] homeless population are former mental patients."[9] And in Austin, where the rate of chronically mentally ill outpatients per 100,000 residents was considerably higher than for any other major Texas city,[10] a series of local newspaper articles left the distinct impression that the city's streets had become the dumping grounds for growing numbers of discharged mental patients.[11]

This characterization of the streets of urban America as open asylums was not merely a media creation, but was buttressed by pronouncements and research reports issuing from the psychiatric establishment. One such report, for example, based on examination of ninety homeless individuals treated in the psychiatric wing of New York's Bellevue Hospital, concluded that "the streets, the train and bus stations, and the shelters have become the state hospitals of yesterday."[12] These initial investigations were flawed in three respects. They were not based on samples systematically selected to yield a representative cross-section of homeless individuals.[13] They tended to infer prior institutionalization from current diagnostic assessments that are themselves highly suspect.[14] And they were historically nearsighted in that they overlooked the fact that deinstitutionalization had been going on for more than a quarter of a century and that the bulk of it had taken place by the middle of the 1970s. National figures on the pace of deinstitutionalization show that 87 percent of the decline in the resident population of mental hospitals between 1955 and 1980 had occurred by the end of 1975, with most of it taking place between 1965 and 1975.[15] Since then the decline has been relatively insubstantial. The same pattern is evident in Texas: 87 percent of the decline in the population of its state hospitals had occurred by 1975.[16]

If deinstitutionalization were a major cause of homelessness, then the ranks of the homeless should have swelled considerably in the first half of the 1970s. Since they did not, and since the rate of increase in the homeless population during the 1980s far exceeds the rate of deinstitutionalization during the same period, it would appear that the presumed causal linkage between deinstitutionalization and homelessness has been grossly exaggerated. That this is indeed the case is indicated by a number of more systematic and broad-based surveys of the homeless.[17] These studies show that although the number of homeless previously institutionalized in mental hospitals is not insubstantial, especially when compared to the incidence of institutionalization in the population in general, the deinstitutionalized constitute a much smaller proportion of the homeless than was initially presumed.[18]

This pattern was also strikingly evident in Austin. In fact, with only 10.8 percent of the tracking sample having been institutionalized in psychiatric facilities just before their descent onto the streets, it appeared that the contribution of deinstitutionalization to homelessness in Austin was even lower than in most cities.[19] Moreover, even when deinstitutionalization is a precipitant of homelessness, as it was for Jorge Herrera and Lance McCay, its influence often turns out to be indirect or at least modified by other factors. Lance's case is illustrative. Although he has been in and out of the state's mental hospital system, his homelessness must also be ascribed to the difficulties between him and his parents that have ruled out their Houston home as a place of permanent residence for him. Jorge's situation is less clear, but he did tell us on a number of occasions that he has had no contact with his family since he left the Austin State Hospital some twenty years ago.

When such observations are merged with the other findings regarding the relationship between deinstitutionalization and homelessness, three conclusions seem inescapable: that the number of individuals whose path to the street was through asylum doors has been exaggerated; that

deinstitutionalization typically operates in conjunction with other factors rather than alone; and that deinstitutionalization has functioned as
a minor rather than a major precipitant of homelessness.

Decline in the Stock of Low-Income Housing   As the pace of deinstitutionalization slowed in the second half of the 1970s, the gap between
the number of poverty-level renters and the number of affordable rental
units available to them was beginning to widen considerably. This gap,
which continued to expand throughout the 1980s, resulted in part from
the increase in the number of Americans living in poverty in the early
1980s, which increased the demand for low-income housing.[20] But what
changed in American cities in the 1980s was not merely the need for
low-cost housing, which, like poverty, has always been with us, but the
shrinkage in the supply of such housing. That shrinkage did not occur
overnight, of course, but it came to a head during the first half of the
1980s because of the intersection of two trends: decline in the actual
stock of low-income housing, and inflation in the cost of such housing.

Evidence of the first trend is plentiful. The federal government's housing
surveys, reports issued by homeless advocacy groups, and independent
housing researchers all report virtually the same conclusion: the nation's stock of low-income housing has been decimated over the past
twenty years. Between 1973 and 1979 alone, 91 percent of the nearly
one million housing units renting for $200 per month or less nationally
disappeared from the rental market.[21] In New York City alone, over
310,000 units of low-income housing were estimated to have been lost
between 1970 and 1983.[22] Since this decimation of the low-income rental
market escalated throughout the 1980s, the National Coalition for the
Homeless estimated that about half a million low-income units were
being lost annually by the second half of the decade.[23]

A sizable proportion of this loss can be accounted for by the even
more thoroughgoing disappearance of the housing most relevant to the
homeless historically—the single-room occupancy (SRO) hotels that had
dotted America's skid rows since the turn of the century and provided
the housing of last resort for itinerant workers and others. As the skid
rows of most major cities have gradually declined,[24] so have the bulk
of SROs. It is difficult to determine exactly how many SROs have disappeared nationally, but a number of local studies indicate that the loss
has been substantial. In Los Angeles, for example, more than half of the
SRO units were demolished between 1970 and 1985.[25] During roughly
the same period, New York City lost an estimated 87 percent of its SRO

units.[26] And in Chicago, where the most systematic research on SRO decline has been conducted, 81 percent of the city's stock was lost between 1960 and 1980.[27] In light of these and other such findings, estimates of the loss of around a million SRO rooms nationally between 1970 and 1980 seem quite reasonable.[28]

This precipitous decline in the existence of low-income housing units was coupled with a rise in the number of low-income renter households, increasing at an alarming rate the shortfall of low-income units available. In 1975 in New York City, the vacancy rate for SROs and other low-priced rentals was around 26 percent, but by 1981, just as the homeless began to appear in greater numbers on the streets of New York and other large cities, the vacancy rate had dropped to zero.[29] By the second half of the 1980s, about twice as many low-income families were seeking housing as there were affordable units available, with the number of very low-income renter households exceeding the number of available units nationally by 94 percent.[30]

The disappearance of increasing numbers of low-income housing units—2.5 million units since 1980, according to some estimates[31]—can essentially be ascribed to the conjunction of governmental indifference and such market forces as gentrification and abandonment. The former was clearly reflected in the withering of governmental support of housing programs for the poor during the Reagan administration. When housing starts for all HUD lower-income housing programs declined from around 183,000 units in 1980 to an estimated 28,000 in 1985, one observer contended that not only was the Reagan administration waging war on housing programs for the poor, but it was also seeking to reverse "the federal government's 50–year old commitment to such programs."[32] Clearly, the federal government did little during the 1980s to curtail the loss of millions of low-cost housing units through the market processes of abandonment, arson, and central-city redevelopment and gentrification, let alone to replace them.[33] The operation of a number of these forces is captured by an extensive examination of the disappearance of much of Chicago's SRO housing. "What made the demise of skid row housing inevitable in Chicago and other large cities," the authors note, was "the policy of wholesale land clearance adopted by redevelopment agencies and supported by local growth coalitions. The modest revenue of the SRO hotels could not compete against the financial promise of commercial redevelopment plans backed by the threat of condemnation under the municipal police power of eminent domain. Owners sold their buildings, and thousands of SRO hotel units were destroyed, their tenants displaced and dispersed throughout the city. Although large-scale clearance seldom ushered in the real-estate boom its proponents claimed it would, it did succeed in destroying most skid row housing."[34]

These processes of land clearance and redevelopment were initiated in Chicago long before homelessness became a problem in the 1980s. But these same processes, fueled by gentrification and governmental in-difference, were at work in virtually all major cities in the country in the 1980s. Austin was no different.

As we noted earlier, the redevelopment and gentrification of Austin's downtown transformed much of the central city's marginal space into prime space, thereby defining as off-limits the traditional haunts of the city's down-and-out and increasing the prospect of their public visibility as their numbers increased. But these market processes did far more than push the homeless into greater contact with the domiciled com-munity; they also devoured increasing portions of the city's limited housing stock for the poor. A graphic case in point was the demolition in 1984 of the city's only remaining SRO-like hotel in the downtown area. Its demise was inevitable once downtown revitalization and the resultant real-estate speculation became preoccupations in the first half of the 1980s, even though it provided temporary shelter for 72 percent of the recipients of emergency housing assistance in 1982. As one ob-server remarked just after the hotel was leveled, "The property it was on is just too damn valuable commercially, and even for taxes. It just had to go."

The same factors also appeared to operate in the case of some of the low-income housing in the black and Mexican-American communities just east of the city's downtown. Until 1984, when the city's largest public housing project was closed as a result of a variety of factors, the city operated about 1,900 public housing units that accommodated some 5,000 tenants.[35] Within a year the number of units available had dwin-dled by more than 300, now housing fewer than 4,000 tenants and leaving nearly 1,000 people on the waiting list for low-rent public hous-ing.[36] Thus, in Austin in the mid-1980s, as throughout the country, the demand for low-income housing was intensified by the destruction of existing units. Moreover, the supply in Austin was expected to dwindle even further as the low-income minority communities east of the down-town were targeted for further development. According to one notable community figure, who was dismayed by the redevelopment/gentrifica-tion process, "[T]he marketplace left to its own devices over time will eat up East Austin and once again force a mass migration of the two [minority] communities."[37]

These market processes affected the actual size of the city's homeless population only indirectly. Since fewer than 10 percent of the homeless were local residents and three-quarters of the homeless were Anglo, it is clear that relatively few locals were pushed onto the streets by forces at work in the local housing market.[38] What those market forces did do, however, was make it well-nigh impossible for the many homeless drifting into town to find housing, particularly of the SRO variety. Not only was the stock of such housing virtually nonexistent, but low-cost housing in general was becoming increasingly scarce because of the city's inflationary housing market.

Inflation in the Cost of Housing   At the same time that the nation's stock of low-income housing was vanishing, the mismatch between the cost of housing and income was growing. This gap was especially glaring among renters, particularly those with low income. Between 1970 and 1983, rents increased an average of 192 percent throughout the country, while tenant income increased only 97 percent.[39] During that same period, rent increased from one-fourth of income to nearly one-third for the average American renter.[40] In comparison, the mortgage paid by the average American homeowner in 1983 was only around one-fifth of income.[41]

But such averages can be misleading, since the rent-to-income ratio is not the same for all income groups. In 1983, for example, 89 percent of all households earning less than $10,000 paid 25 percent or more of their incomes for housing, whereas only 3 percent of those with incomes of $50,000 or more had that high a ratio.[42] Moreover, as income plummets in the lowest reaches of the socioeconomic order, the rent burden seems to increase almost exponentially. One of the most compelling studies of the connection between homelessness and the rent-to-income ratio found that by the mid-1980s, 82 to 97 percent of all low-income unsubsidized renters in eight major cities exceeded the maximum recommended "affordable" ratio of 30 percent, and that 52 percent of all of these renters paid more than 60 percent of their income to rent.[43] Not only do such figures represent a dramatic increase in the rent burden among low-income Americans since the mid-1970s, but the burden continued to grow throughout the 1980s, with over three million poverty-level renter households paying more than 70 percent of their income to rent by 1985.[44]

The situation in Austin was in fact worse than in many cities, as can be readily seen by comparing it to other cities in terms of an index of housing affordability. Using the common three-to-one income-to-housing-cost ratio as the baseline standard for the index and setting it at 1.0, any figure below that baseline indicates an affordability problem. For Austin in 1984 the index registered 0.68, the lowest of Texas's six major cities and considerably lower than the state index of 0.83 and the national index of 0.91.[45] In the mid-1980s, as a result of this gap between income and housing prices, 55 to 60 percent of Austin households could not afford the most inexpensive new home.[46]

The rental market, too, was plagued by an affordability crisis. The city's median rent skyrocketed from around $150 per month in 1976 to around $450 in 1985.[47] And this was not for a lavish, spacious apartment. Rather, the $450 might rent at best an 800-square-foot apartment in a fairly new complex. Using the three-to-one income-to-housing-cost ratio, rent of such a modest unit required the tenant to earn roughly $1,350 per month, or around $16,200 annually.[48]

Thus the conventional rental market was also out of reach of many Austinites, particularly those in the East Austin minority neighborhoods where well over a quarter of the population was earning less than $9,000 a year.[49] Most of these individuals were not literally living on the streets, however. During the time of our research, as was already noted, only a small proportion of the city's street homeless were local residents. Many of the local minority residents were, however, hanging by a thread, living in substandard subsidized housing, doubling up with relatives or friends, and receiving occasional emergency housing assistance. Certainly many of these individuals were vulnerable to becoming homeless, given the juxtaposition of their marginal economic situation and the city's housing affordability crisis, but relatively few had yet to suffer the indignity of finding themselves on the city's streets.

For those homeless individuals whose thread had already snapped elsewhere and who drifted into town in the first half of the 1980s, the prospects of finding housing were even more dismal. Not only did the city lack any SRO-like housing, but the rental market was hopelessly beyond their reach, even if they found work. Moreover, few had relatives or friends with whom they might double up. Whatever their reasons for coming to Austin, then, clearly the rumor of affordable housing was not among them. In fact, not one homeless person with whom we conversed ever mentioned housing as a factor that had pulled them toward Austin, or anywhere else, for that matter. For the homeless living in or passing through Austin in the first half of the 1980s, then, the city's housing situation functioned not as a precipitant of their homelessness but as a factor contributing to its persistence.

But before they came to Austin did some kind of residential trauma, such as eviction or an increase in rent, push them onto the streets? Perhaps. But if such dislocating events did figure prominently among the factors precipitating their homelessness, they were rarely mentioned. Only nine of the sixty-three individuals with whom we discussed the reasons for their homelessness named such sources of residential dislocation. This is not to suggest that decline in the availability of low-cost housing in the cities from which they came did not contribute to their homelessness. It is our sense, however, that this housing problem was seen by the homeless as a universal constant that functioned as taken-for-granted context. Moreover, the low-cost housing shortfall invariably operated in conjunction with other factors that the homeless we came to know tended to mention more frequently. One set of such factors concerned their economic situation.

ECONOMIC DISLOCATION

Whatever the supply and cost of low-income housing, its accessibility is dependent in part on the economic situation of those in need of such housing. If income keeps pace with the cost of housing, then the structural basis for homelessness is not so robust. If, however, housing costs escalate much more rapidly than income, as occurred nationally between the mid-1970s and mid-1980s, then the incidence of homelessness is likely to increase dramatically. A thoroughgoing understanding of the structural roots of homelessness thus requires consideration of this income shortfall and its sources.

Unemployment and the Rumor of Work   Throughout the ages, massive increases in the number of homeless have been associated with some variety of socioeconomic transformation. More often than not, as we noted in Chapter 1, economic disintegration has been the dislocating force that not only has pushed people onto the streets, but also onto the road in search of greener pastures; whereas the rumor of economic opportunity in another locale has provided the pull or lure. History is replete with examples of this double-edged process,[50] and it was clearly operative for the thousands of homeless who lived in or passed through Austin in the first half of the 1980s.

The vast majority came in search of work. As we saw earlier, 85 percent of the over six hundred individuals in the tracking sample who came directly from out of state or from another Texas city indicated that they came to Austin in hopes of finding work, which was rumored to be plentiful. Indeed, this rumor attracted a number of our key informants to Austin: Tony Jones from Chicago via Baton Rouge and Houston; Ron Whitaker from Denver; Tanner Sutton from Houston; Pat Manchester up from San Marcos; Tom Fisk down from Killeen; and Hoyt Page from Dallas. Other factors may have figured in the decisions of some of them to come to Austin, to be sure, but the hope of finding work was prominent.

Many of the homeless newcomers did indeed find work. But it was rarely of a kind to enable them to escape the streets. The regular work market, as we have seen, was not responsive to the employment needs of the homeless, and the day-labor market seldom provided jobs that paid a living wage for more than a few days running. Nonetheless, the rumor of work, fueled by the local construction boom, ensured that a steady stream of homeless would find their way to Austin in the first half of the 1980s.

We know what attracted them to Austin, but what set them adrift in the first place? For many, unemployment appears to have been a central factor, as nearly 98 percent of the tracking sample claimed to have been out of work at the time of their initial contact with the Sally. This figure may at first glance appear inflated, but we suspect it is fairly accurate. Most of these individuals presumably would not have come to Austin if they already had regular work that paid a living wage. The figure is also supported by the widespread unemployment we observed in the field, the extensive use of various forms of compensatory shadow work among all but the recently dislocated, and the fact that 51 percent of the 63 homeless with whom we discussed the reasons for their being on the streets named unemployment as a central factor.

The plight of a substantial proportion of the local homeless, then, was triggered in part by unemployment. Moreover, it is clear that their unemployment was more persistent than that experienced by other Americans in the first half of the 1980s. The average length of unemployment in the United States in 1983, for example, was 20 weeks;[51] for the homeless checking into the Sally for the first time it was 23 weeks. The median number of weeks unemployed was considerably less, 8 weeks to be exact. Still, nearly 30 percent of the homeless had been unemployed for 15 weeks or longer at the time of their arrival in town.

In contrast, only 2 to 4 percent of the national civilian labor force were unemployed that long during the same period.[52]

Given the pervasiveness of unemployment among the homeless in general and its persistence among so many of them, it is little wonder that many were attracted to Austin by the rumor of work. But why did so many people, particularly relatively young men, find themselves out of work, as conventionally conceived, at some point in the late 1970s or early 1980s?

The answer lies in part in the dramatic increase in U.S. unemployment during the first part of the 1980s. In 1979 the national unemployment rate was 5.8 percent. By 1982 the rate had jumped to 9.7 percent, the highest since before World War II. The 1983 rate of 9.6 percent was only slightly lower, but by mid-year the number of unemployed had begun to decline, and by 1985 the rate for the nation as a whole was 7.2.[53] But the damage was done: millions of Americans had been cut loose from their occupational moorings and set adrift.

The reasons for unemployment during this or any other period can be quite varied. They include being fired, becoming disabled, quitting a job, moving to be with relatives, termination of a job, and being laid off.[54] Most of these factors were operative in the work histories of the homeless coming to Austin. This can be seen in Table 8.1, which provides information pertaining to the most recent job experiences of some of the homeless prior to their initial contact with the Texas Employment Commission, whether in Austin or some other Texas city. When individuals registered with TEC, they were asked a series of questions about their work experiences, skills, and interests. When asked about their most recent job experiences, 228 of the 348 homeless in our tracking sample with TEC contact provided some information about one or more of their three most recent job experiences. In response to the query regarding the reasons for termination of their most recent jobs, the modal response was that the jobs ended or that the respondents were laid off.

Both these factors were found in the life histories of many of our street informants. Tony Jones was laid off from his job as a security guard at a steel mill in Chicago "when the plant cut back." Ron Whitaker lost his job as a short-order cook in "a greasy spoon" in Denver when the restaurant closed. At the time Ron was clearly on the margins, sharing a $5.00-per-night room "with five other guys" in an SRO hotel. But he had a job and was paying for a roof over his head. Pat Manchester found himself unemployed and on the road to Austin when his job as a construction laborer was terminated because the project was in

TABLE 8.1   JOB EXPERIENCE OF HOMELESS BEFORE INITIAL
TEC CONTACT

	Most Recent Job	2nd Most Recent	3rd Most Recent	Total
Type of job:	(N: 228)	(N: 191)	(N: 129)	(N: 548)
General laborer (construction; warehouse loading; oil field)	30.7%	24.6%	24.0%	27.0%
Service (dishwashing; janitorial; nursing home)	21.5%	29.8%	24.0%	25.0%
Factory work and vehicle operation	20.6%	16.8%	20.2%	19.2%
Craft/skilled work (building trades; mechanics)	19.3%	16.2%	15.5%	17.3%
Sales and clerical	5.7%	6.8%	7.8%	6.6%
Military	2.2%	5.8%	8.5%	4.9%
Hourly wage:	(N: 197)	(N: 164)	(N: 110)	(N: 471)
Median	$4.90	$4.50	$4.82	$4.74
Mode	$5.00	$3.35	$5.00	$5.00
$3.35 or less	15.2%	17.0%	15.5%	15.9%
$3.36 to $5.00	43.7%	47.0%	46.4%	45.4%
More than $5.00	41.1%	36.0%	38.1%	38.6%
Duration of job:	(N: 218)	(N: 181)	(N: 124)	(N: 523)
Median	6.5 mos.	8.7 mos.	11.6 mos.	8.9 mos.
Mode	1 mo.	1 mo.	3 mos.	1 mo.
6 mos. or less	50.0%	41.8%	40.3%	44.9%
7 to 12 mos.	23.4%	27.1%	15.3%	22.8%
13 to 24 mos.	15.6%	10.5%	16.9%	14.1%
More than 24 mos.	11.0%	20.4%	29.4%	18.2%
Reason for job termination:	(N: 219)	(N: 182)	(N: 120)	(N: 521)
Laid off/job ended	44.3%	35.2%	35.8%	39.2%
Fired	9.1%	3.9%	3.3%	5.9%
Quit	21.0%	35.2%	30.8%	28.2%
Other	25.6%	25.8%	30.0%	26.7%

financial trouble. And even Indio, who had been on the streets much longer, recalled that his drift into chronic homelessness was caused in part by his dismissal from a brickyard where he "had worked for years." In all, nine of our twenty key informants said that having been laid off because of cutbacks or shutdowns or having been released because of the temporary nature of their jobs either helped to push them down the path toward homelessness or accounted for their descent.

Other factors also figure prominently in the loss of regular work among the recently dislocated, as is shown in Table 8.1. Being fired is not one of them, however, as it accounts for only 6 percent of the reasons given by the homeless for the loss of recent jobs. But a sizable number, between 25 and 30 percent, do admit to quitting those jobs. It might be argued that this propensity for some individuals to walk away from existing jobs, especially with no other job in hand or with the prospect of homelessness staring them in the face, is indicative of an unstable work orientation peppered with considerable indifference and irresponsibility. But few of those who take this path do so in the belief that they are acting irresponsibly or that they will be unemployed indefinitely. Instead, they often quit the jobs they have because those jobs provide neither a living wage nor the promise of a better life. As is indicated in Table 8.1, their most recent regular jobs tended to be low-status, low-wage, unskilled laboring and service jobs congregated at the bottom of the occupational structure. The median wage for these jobs was about $4.75 per hour, with 61 percent paying $5.00 or less.

It is these jobs, and particularly those at or below the minimum wage of $3.35 per hour, that people are most likely to quit. Pat Manchester explained it simply: "If you can't make it on what you're getting paid, you might as well look for something else." Thus, one recently dislocated man we met in the Sally dinner line explained that he had just hitchhiked into town after quitting a job in Dallas because he "couldn't make a go of it." He was working for minimum wage at a restaurant, "mainly sweeping floors and washing dishes." Since that did not provide him with sufficient income to rent an apartment alone, he "pooled some money with two other guys," who were also on the margins, and found a cheap one-bedroom apartment. "The problem" was that the apartment was rented only to him, so when the landlord found out about the other two guys, she got "pissed off and kicked 'em out and said she was gonna raise the rent." Based on "what I was making," he said, "there was no point sticking around. So I split for Austin."

This rationale for quitting a regular job was fairly standard, with the exception that some individuals came from much further away via a more circuitous route. A fellow we met once while working a day-labor job provides a case in point. He told us he was from Alabama, but that he had left there almost a year earlier with his wife and child because he "couldn't find any work." After he had made an abortive effort to find work in Corpus Christi, his wife and child returned to Alabama, and he "moved around a bit," finally landing in a small town northwest of Austin "working part-time for a fellow who gave me a place to stay." But "the hours were short and the pay was poor," so he decided to leave and "hitchhiked to Austin" in hopes of finding something better.

Such accounts, in conjunction with the job descriptions and wage data presented in Table 8.1, tell us that many of the jobs the homeless quit are hardly the kinds worth keeping. Such jobs can best be thought of as stopgap measures that keep the worker off the streets, but only for a while and not by much. To quit these bottom-rung jobs is not so irrational as it might appear, especially when it is done in hopes of securing a better job elsewhere. The cost, of course, is a bout with homelessness that may become chronic. But this cost appears to be worth the risk when there are rumors of work that pays a better wage some-place down the road.

These observations suggest that for some individuals homelessness is but one element in an overall subsistence pattern that includes menial, low-wage employment, followed by a stint of homelessness prompted by the search for more lucrative work, followed again by low-wage work that functions as a stopgap measure.[55] This pattern is consistent with the relatively brief duration of the most recent jobs held by some of the homeless prior to their first TEC contact. As is shown in Table 8.1, the median length of time these jobs were held was 8.9 months, with about 45 percent of them held for 6 months or less and only about a third of them lasting for more than a year. Given the fact that 30 percent of these jobs were quit, in conjunction with the rationales of-fered for walking away from them, it seems reasonable to assume that some proportion of these jobs were not only followed by homelessness but also preceded by it, thus linking homelessness and low-wage em-ployment together in a highly episodic fashion.

In addition to being laid off or fired, or quitting, the homeless seeking work at the TEC attributed their unemployment and subsequent home-lessness to a number of other work-related experiences. These factors are lumped together in Table 8.1 in the catch-all "Other" category, but they are not insignificant, since they include nearly 27 percent of the reasons given for job termination. Although catch-all categories are usually mute about their contents, the accounts of the homeless are loud and clear and point often to the job-ending impact of illness and injury. Tanner Sutton's experience is illustrative. For several years prior to finding himself on the streets, Tanner was gainfully employed as a janitor at a university in Beaumont, Texas. He worked at that job consistently for three years, he told us, and never thought seriously of quitting, especially since he was married at the time. Then he began to experience "physical problems" that were connected to bad burns he had suffered years earlier. The physical problems were sufficiently debilitating that he was forced to work less and less. Eventually he lost the job. His application for SSI was denied and his "marriage turned sour." He and his wife eventually separated, and he "hit the road," drifting from one Texas town to another in search of steady work. "No one would hire me," he told us. He ended up at the Austin Sally, working for $5.00 a week plus room and board. There are clearly several interacting dimensions to Tanner's story, but the present point is that a debilitating illness put him out of work and on the path to the street.

Gypsy Bill's path to the street was littered with a number of the same factors, including a disabling back condition that ruled out most kinds of work. A disabling injury also accounted for Marilyn's first bout with homelessness. She was living in San Antonio at the time, working as a waitress and "just managing to stay off the streets." Then one night after work she was hit by a car, broke an ankle, and was "put out of work." With no savings and no one to fall back on, Marilyn soon found herself broke and living on the streets.

We have explored the relationship between unemployment and homelessness in the preceding pages, noting, first, the extraordinarily high proportion of homeless who came to Austin in search of work; second, the link between their joblessness and national unemployment trends; and, third, the immediate reasons they gave for their unemployment—namely, being laid off, quitting, and illness or injury. We have seen that the jobs they lose or leave prior to becoming homeless—whether for the first time, as in the cases of Tony, Tanner, and Marilyn, or the second or third time, as with Marilyn and Pat—are low-wage, low-status, bottom-of-the-barrel jobs. They are jobs that are typically just a notch above the day labor that awaits the homeless, if they are lucky. Yet, they enable some people to stay off the streets, if all goes well. That is their upside. Their downside is that they leave many individuals dangerously on the edge economically. The question thus arises: What factors accounted for the conspicuous increase in the numbers of unemployed and economically marginal individuals in the early 1980s? There is little question but that the homeless come primarily from these ranks,[56] but what led to this proliferation of vulnerable individuals?

Deindustrialization, Job and Income Polarization, and Governmental Cutbacks   Dramatic changes in the occupational and economic fortunes of hundreds of thousands of individuals across a nation invariably signal a deep, large-scale transformation in the nation's socioeconomic structure. Initially, the guardians of the state or the beneficiaries of such change often seek to explain away its more deleterious outcroppings by focusing on the presumed imperfections of the victims themselves or on some narrow institutional policy that has gone awry. Such attributions are self-serving in that they deflect attention from the structural roots of the problem and thereby exempt certain decisionmakers and large-scale institutional processes from responsibility. In time, however, the linkage between that problem and deeper structural changes becomes transparent.

Evidence of this skewed attributional process can be seen clearly with respect to the problem of homelessness. Initially, attention was focused on the failed policy of deinstitutionalization and on the disabilities and presumed pathologies of the homeless, as we will soon see. More recently, the structural factors of deindustrialization, job and wage polarization, coupled with government cutbacks have been identified as the primary sources of economic marginality that rendered growing numbers of Americans vulnerable to homelessness in the 1980s.

Deindustrialization is the cover term that surfaced in the early 1980s to capture the dramatic shift in the national economy from a manufacturing to a service base.[57] Several dimensions of this economic transformation are pertinent to homelessness. First are the thousands of plant closings or cutbacks that occurred in the 1970s and 1980s because of capital flight, shutdowns, and disinvestment,[58] and that resulted in the loss of hundreds of thousands of reasonably well-paying manufacturing jobs. Although the exact number of jobs lost through these processes is not known precisely, there is consensus that the number is staggering. One study, which found that 30 percent of the plants in existence in the United States in 1969 had closed by 1976, estimated that "runaways [transfer of plants to other sites], shutdowns, and permanent physical cutbacks short of closure may have cost the country as many as 38 million jobs."[59] Another study concluded that over 16 million manufacturing jobs were lost between 1976 and 1982 because of plant closings,[60] and a congressional examination of the consequences of such structural unemployment reported that "in the past few years, millions of American workers have lost their jobs because of structural changes in the U.S. and world economies. Some of them—especially younger workers with skills in demand or the right educational background—have little trouble finding new jobs. Others—hundreds of thousands a year—remain out of work for many weeks or months, or even years."[61]

What proportion of this latter group ended up on the streets is unknown, but there is good reason to presume that it is considerable. As is noted in Table 8.1, nearly 45 percent of the 228 homeless who provided TEC with information regarding their most recent job indicated that they were laid off that job. No more than 20 to 25 percent of those jobs were in the manufacturing sector, and most were probably not with large firms or companies. Nonetheless, being laid off was clearly connected to the experience of homelessness for many of them.

Insofar as these "victims" of plant, office, or store shutdowns and cutbacks found new jobs, they seldom entailed an advance in status and income. More typically, the new jobs involved a step downward or, at best, stasis. At the national level, it is estimated that at least 50 percent of the 11.5 million workers who lost their jobs between 1979 and 1984 because of plant shutdowns, relocations, and layoffs and who subsequently found new jobs were earning less than they had before.[62] And at the local level, we have seen how many of the homeless who came to Austin in search of work had previously moved laterally from one low-level, low-paying job to another.

Underlying both of these tendencies is the second relevant aspect of the deindustrialization process: a proliferation of low-wage service jobs and a corresponding increase in the number of temporary and part-time workers. It is estimated that 94 percent of the jobs created between 1970 and 1984 were in the service sector and that most of them paid considerably less than the manufacturing jobs they replaced.[63] During roughly the same period (between 1975 and 1985), the number of temporary and part-time workers also increased dramatically, to compose nearly 28 percent of all U.S. workers by 1985.[64] One consequence of both of these trends, in conjunction with the decline in manufacturing jobs, is the polarization of jobs and income.[65] Jobs, in other words, have become increasingly concentrated at both ends of the wage scale, with the result that not only has the bottom broadened but that the wages paid at this level are increasingly inadequate to make ends meet, especially in a period in which the cost of housing spiraled upward in comparison to income.

Had the federal government during the Reagan years acted to tighten the "safety net" that was set in place during the New Deal and expanded throughout the 1960s, the social misery that resulted from deindustrialization and income polarization might have been muted and the descent of many might have been halted before they reached the streets. Instead, the government during the Reagan years, and especially during the first term, snipped away at the safety net as if it were intent on overseeing its unraveling. First, the minimum wage remained fixed at $3.35 per hour throughout the 1980s. The result was that by the end of the decade its purchasing power had dropped to its lowest level since 1955, and a person working full-time, year-round was earning less than $7,000, nearly 40 percent below the poverty line for an urban family of four.[66] Although most adult workers earn more than the minimum wage, it can function as a threshold for setting wages. Thus, as indicated in Table 8.1, only 16 percent of the jobs the homeless worked prior to checking into the TEC were at or below the minimum wage, but 45 percent fell between that and $5.00 per hour, which is still a poverty-level wage in most urban areas.

The government also did nothing to stem the affordable-housing crisis. As we have already noted, federal support for low-income housing, both in terms of subsidies and construction, declined appreciably, and the Reagan administration had no effective housing policy.[67] Even more to the point, there was a corresponding erosion of funds for public assistance programs such as AFDC (Aid to Families with Dependent Children), food stamps, and unemployment compensation. Programs targeted at low-income families were slashed, for example, by some $57 billion in the 1981–1985 period.[68] Even the Social Security Administration's disability programs were cut: nearly half a million disabled recipients were lopped from the rolls in the early 1980s through tightened eligibility standards.[69] Although about 40 percent were eventually reinstated upon appeal, some who were not and who were unable to find work or could not hold a job because of their disability were pushed along the path toward homelessness. Gypsy Bill provides a vivid example. With a severely hunched back and accompanying physical problems that disqualified him from most work, he was eligible for Supplemental Security Income (SSI) payments, which he received for a number of years. That, coupled with the few dollars he made working part-time in a restaurant and that which his wife brought home, enabled him and his wife to stay off the streets. Then, in the fall of 1982, he was "axed from the rolls," as he put it, and that seemed to trigger his descent to the streets. Gypsy was reinstated on SSI three years later, following his third appeal, but by then he was divorced, had grown accustomed to street life, and did not seem to know what else to do or where to turn.

Lance McCay was also cut from SSI rolls and subsequently reinstated, but the experience did not affect him in the same way it did Gypsy. Lance was already homeless at the time he lost his SSI benefits, so the erosion of that support could not have provided the initial push toward the streets. It did, however, make it even more improbable that Lance would get off the streets, and it compounded his difficulties in surviving on them.

It is our sense that public-assistance cutbacks like those experienced by Gypsy and Lance typically interacted with other factors and processes to push people along the path toward homelessness or to keep them on the streets. Although these cutbacks may sometimes have functioned as a triggering mechanism, as they did for Gypsy, they alone cannot be held responsible for the proliferation of homelessness in the 1980s. The pervasive, transformative processes of deindustrialization, job and wage polarization, urban redevelopment and gentrification, and the decline of affordable housing were already at full throttle by the beginning of the decade. Thus, the cutbacks and indifference of the Reagan administration did not produce the problem of homelessness but contributed to it by reinforcing broader structural trends and by exacerbating their immiserating consequences (e.g., unemployment, low wages, poverty) by unraveling rather than strengthening the federal government's "safety net." Put metaphorically, the cracks at the bottom of the socioeconomic structure were widened rather than narrowed or repaired, thus increasing the likelihood that the worst off would fall through, onto the streets.

Considering the historical conjunction of governmental indifference and cutbacks with the previously discussed structural forces that marginalized or dislocated masses of individuals both residentially and economically, it is not surprising that increasing numbers of individuals found themselves living on the streets in the 1980s. What is surprising, though, is that only a relatively small proportion of the masses of individuals whose lives were altered by these forces experienced homelessness, at least at any given time. Since the number of individuals who find themselves living on the economic margins is considerably greater than the number of people who are homeless at the same moment, the puzzling question arises as to why some people become homeless when others who appear equally vulnerable from a structural standpoint do not. To answer that question, we consider the biographic factors associated with homelessness.

BIOGRAPHIC DETERMINANTS OF HOMELESSNESS

Anyone who consults with agency personnel who have contact with the homeless, listens to media discussions of the problem, peruses the social science literature on homelessness, or talks with the homeless themselves will quickly discern a host of answers to the question of why some individuals become homeless rather than others who seem equally at risk. Although the answers may vary considerably in terms of the specific locus of blame, such as mental illness, alcohol, wanderlust, or marital discord, nearly all of them constitute variants of four explanations regarding the biographic roots of homelessness. One is voluntaristic; a second emphasizes the disabilities or pathologies of the homeless; the third focuses on the absence of family support; and the fourth points to the role of bad luck. In the remainder of this chapter we will examine each of these explanations as well as how some of the factors suggested by these explanations often interact in a spiraling, dynamic fashion.

VOLUNTARISM

The voluntaristic explanation holds that people are on the streets largely by choice. Homelessness is regarded as a life-style that has been selected rather than forced upon someone. The question of why masses of individuals would opt for life on the streets is sidestepped in deference to the notion that, except in the rarest circumstances, people have options and are therefore partly responsible for the situation in which they find themselves.

Such voluntaristic reasoning often has considerable currency within the political arena, in part because it exempts political decisionmakers and the structures and trends with which they are associated from direct responsibility for some of the problems confronting them. Thus, it is not surprising that Ronald Reagan favored this voluntaristic explanation of homelessness during his presidency. "One problem we've had," he explained when commenting on this problem in 1984, "is the people who are sleeping on grates, the homeless who are homeless, you might say, by choice."[70]

This voluntaristic theme can be found in some social science discussions of homelessness,[71] and it resonates, as well, with some agency personnel who work with the homeless. The Benedictine brother in charge of Angels Kitchen, for one, likened the homeless to wayward souls who "are on a pilgrimage . . . in quest of a better life," thereby suggesting that for many people homelessness is a voluntary undertaking.[72] Some of the city police held a similar, although less charitable, view, attributing homelessness not to social forces, personal problems, or bad luck, but to ill-considered choice. In the words of one officer, "They have chosen their life-style" and are "content to be the way they are."

When we turn to the homeless themselves, however, we find little support for this voluntaristic explanation. It is not one of the favored or frequently articulated reasons the homeless give for being on the streets. As is indicated in Table 8.2, only 6.3 percent of the homeless with whom we discussed the reasons for their plight alluded to factors suggestive of personal choice, and fewer than 3 percent of all the reasons given fell into this category.[73] But even if a greater proportion explained their homelessness by reference to voluntaristic assertions, we would be skeptical about attributing great explanatory power to these claims alone.

The reasons for our skepticism are threefold. First, voluntaristic attributions were typically made by outsiders who have been on the streets for an extended period of time, such as Shotgun, Gimpy Dan, and Rhyming Mike. This suggests that such accounts may be subcultural artifacts or at least reflective of some level of acceptance of the situation. In this regard, it is worth recalling that not only did a sizable portion of our street sample give some indication of embracing their street identities, but that those who did so were mostly outsiders. The point is that voluntaristic accounts proffered by homeless who have spent appreciable time on the streets may tell us more about their current orientation than about their cognitive state before they landed on the streets.

Moreover, even if the recently dislocated attributed their homelessness to choice, it would be difficult to assess accurately the meaning of such assertions without an understanding of the range of options available. Homelessness may indeed be a matter of so-called choice for some people, but perhaps only when the few available alternatives are no more palatable than life on the streets. To the extent that this is true,

TABLE 8.2   REASONS GIVEN BY HOMELESS FOR THEIR
HOMELESSNESS

	Reasons (N: 146)	Individuals (N: 63)
Structural	34.3%	68.2%
1. *Residential dislocation*	6.1	14.2
a. Increase in rent; eviction, etc.	3.4	7.9
b. Deinstitutionalization	2.7	6.3
2. *Economic dislocation*	28.1	53.9
a. Unemployment	21.9	50.8
b. Pay too low	4.1	9.5
c. Cut in benefits	2.1	4.8
Biographic	65.7	79.4
3. *Personal choice; wanderlust*	2.7	6.3
4. *Disabilities/pathologies*	15.8	26.9
a. Mental illness	3.4	7.9
b. Drinking problems	6.2	14.3
c. Drug problems	1.4	3.2
d. Physical disability	2.1	4.8
e. Criminal activity	2.7	6.3
5. *Family problems*	39.7	66.6
a. Marital discord; separation; divorce	11.6	26.9
b. Unstable, troubled family life	14.4	33.3
c. Grew up in orphanage or foster care	10.3	23.8
d. Death of spouse or parents	3.4	7.9
6. *Accidents/bad luck*	7.5%	17.5%

the choice is of the lesser of evils and takes on a rather different meaning than if it were made in the face of more attractive options. Thus, to attribute homelessness to choice without an understanding of the context in which that choice is made is to engage in an insidious form of victim-blaming.[74] For all of these reasons, both empirical and theoretical, we find the voluntaristic explanation of little value in understanding the biographic roots of homelessness.

DISABILITIES AND PATHOLOGIES

A more popular and pervasive explanation focuses on personal disabilities or pathologies that are thought to render some individuals particularly vulnerable to homelessness. The homeless have long been regarded as individuals who are functionally crippled in one or more ways.
In earlier times, they were characterized as inadequately socialized individuals who withdrew from the larger social order.[75] More recently,
the disabilities that have been the focus of much research and discussion
include mental illness, alcoholism and drug addiction, poor physical
health, and a record of criminal behavior.[76] The basic argument is that
individuals with one or more of these disabilities are the ones most
susceptible to homelessness because they "are least able to negotiate
successfully the labor and housing markets, to use the welfare system,
or to obtain support from family, kin, and friends."[77]

The erosion of support networks, especially familial ones, is regarded
as particularly critical in the determination of homelessness. A person
does not become homeless, it is argued, "simply because he or she is an
alcoholic or mentally ill, but because these disabilities exhaust the patience or resources otherwise available in one's social network."[78] In
other words, "those with chronic mental illness, severe alcoholism, and
criminal records do not make good housemates and are eased out from
under the protective wing of their relatives and friends."[79]

Structural factors, such as the decline of inexpensive housing, are not
dismissed or glossed. Rather, they are seen as expanding the ranks of
the extremely poor and thereby placing greater numbers of individuals
at risk of becoming homeless. But among these destitute individuals,
the disabled are regarded as "the most vulnerable" to homelessness.[80]
Although such structural factors may be regarded as preconditions,
homelessness is still seen as "the consequence of various personal pathologies and failings."[81]

How helpful is this argument in explaining the biographic sources of
homelessness? The answer depends on what is counted as evidence of
predisposing disabilities. If any trace or mention of one or more vulner-
ability-producing disabilities is counted, without taking into account
whether the disabilities preceded or followed the onset of homelessness,
then, given the disabling nature of street life itself, the count of such
disabilities should be strikingly high. And that, indeed, is what most
research finds.

In study after study the homeless are reported not only to be riddled with disabilities, but the incidence of disability among them is considerably higher than among the domiciled population. This relationship appears to hold, whatever the disability. In Chicago, for example, it was found that the incidences of psychiatric hospitalization, of alcoholism, of poor health, and of contact with the criminal justice system tended to be much higher among the homeless than among either the general adult population or the domiciled extremely poor.[82] This same pattern surfaced in Austin, where 10.8 percent of the tracking sample had been institutionalized for mental illness one or more times, in contrast to less than 0.26 percent of the state's adult male population.[83] A similar disparity is evident when we turn to criminal behavior. The arrest rates for the homeless in Austin for major property offenses were significantly higher than for the general local male population, with the differences being particularly pronounced for burglary and theft.[84] And their arrest rate for misdemeanors was nearly five times higher. Although most of the crimes for which the homeless were arrested were relatively minor,[85] they were still arrested at a significantly higher rate than the general adult male population, thus suggesting in the minds of some observers greater proclivity toward criminal behavior.

There are, then, abundant communications and behaviors on the streets that can easily be counted as indicative of disability or dysfunction. The immediate question, however, is not whether the homeless are more disabled than the domiciled adult population, but whether those disabilities precede the onset of homelessness and can thus be construed as causal precipitants. This is a tough question to answer because there is relatively little directly relevant research. Virtually all of the disability research has been conducted during the experience of homelessness rather than before. As a result, it is difficult, if not impossible, to determine whether disabilities are a cause rather than a consequence of homelessness. Nonetheless, the general tendency has been to presume such a causal connection.

Such a presumption strikes us as highly questionable. First of all, to argue in the absence of longitudinal or panel data that the disabilities identified are among the primary determinants of homelessness is empirically premature. Such an inference is especially dubious when the disabilities in question can also have been produced by the experience of homelessness itself.[86] Not only is homelessness a highly disabling condition, as we have noted repeatedly, but many of the behaviors and communications counted as symptomatic of disability may be better understood as behavioral and psychological adaptations to the trying exigencies of street life. We have already seen in previous chapters how excessive alcohol consumption, predatory criminal behavior such as theft, and even seemingly psychotic thought patterns frequently develop as adaptations to the arduous and often brutalizing nature of street life. Yet these contextual adaptations can mimic behavioral or psychological dysfunction and can thus be misread not only as symptoms of pathology but as precipitating disabilities.

This is not to suggest that the path to the street is never paved with preexisting disabilities. Indeed, a good number of the homeless in our field sample with whom we had the opportunity to discuss the reasons for their homelessness pointed to such disabilities. One institutionalized straddler who was working in an alcohol rehab facility on the outskirts of town told us that he used to "work steady as a mechanic and had a wife and son until about fifteen years ago when my drinking started getting out of control." Shortly thereafter, he said, "I left my wife and son and hit the streets." A self-proclaimed bum who had been on and off the streets for some three years also attributed his homelessness to alcohol. "Alcohol is the secret," he told us. "My problem is that I can get off the streets, but I can't stay off them. This damn bottle licks me every time." And among our key informants, Hoyt, Nona George, Shotgun, and JJ mentioned a drinking problem as a precursor of their homelessness; Tanner and Gypsy Bill alluded to physical problems; and Lance and Jorge pointed, both verbally and behaviorally, to deinstitutionalization and mental illness.

The role of such predisposing disabilities is also indicated in Table 8.2, which shows that 27 percent of the homeless from whom we gathered such information noted that one or more disabilities figured in the process by which they became homeless, and that these disabilities constituted 16 percent of all the reasons given for being homeless. These figures, although not insubstantial, are not as robust as those reported in a number of other studies, thus indicating that the role of preexisting disabilities as a precipitant of homelessness may have been overstated, at least for the homeless in Austin. The reason for the discrepancy between our findings and those of some other studies resides, we suspect, not so much in differences between the homeless in Austin and those elsewhere, but in what is counted as a predisposing disability. For us the key is whether the disability preceded the onset of homelessness; in most other research no distinction is made between predisposing and consequential disabilities.

The role of disabilities as precipitants of homelessness is also muted by the finding that they seldom provide the only push down the path toward homelessness. Instead, they are typically coupled with other factors, particularly the absence of familial support.

LACK OF FAMILIAL SUPPORT

That the family figures somehow in the process by which individuals become homeless is clearly indicated in Table 8.2, which shows that around two-thirds of the individuals with whom we discussed the reasons for their homelessness mentioned family-related problems and that these accounted for almost 40 percent of all of the reasons given. Indeed, family-related problems were mentioned by more of the individuals in our sample, and more frequently, than any other category of reasons for homelessness.

A correlation appears to exist, then, between family problems and homelessness. But what kinds of family contexts or relationships enhance the prospect of homelessness? Here there are three related yet distinct arguments.

The first was clearly stated by a local alcohol rehab counselor who insisted that "a lot of the homeless have just worn their families out, especially by the time they get to us." This may be true for the long-term alcoholic homeless served by that rehab facility. But most of the homeless do not fall into that category. Nonetheless, the view articulated by the rehab counselor has been applied to the homeless in general. As we noted earlier, one popularized version of the disability thesis holds that it is not disabilities per se that account for homelessness, but disabilities that make some individuals too burdensome and costly to keep around the house, thus resulting in their being nudged out the door. This image of the homeless portrays them as troublesome members of otherwise intact and relatively healthy families. As one proponent of this view puts it, "[M]any of the homeless have simply worn out their welcome with parents, other kin, and friends, who after an extended period of support, patience, and shared resources, are exhausted."[87]

The second argument regarding the link between family and homelessness focuses on troubled families rather than problem-riddled individuals. The basic proposition is that the family situations of many homeless are so dysfunctional and abusive that they have sought refuge on the streets. From this vantage point, the homeless are not so much troublesome rejects as voluntary disaffiliates or "domestic refugees."[88]

The third argument holds that the key factor making some individuals more vulnerable than others to homelessness is the lack of familial support, not because it has been withdrawn but because there was none to begin with. Whereas most people are thought to have a family support system they can activate in times of personal crisis, those who become homeless are seen as not having any such buffer. As the head of one of the local caretaker agencies put it, "A lot of people today don't have a back-up. They don't have anyone to fall back on in times of need, and I think that's why we have homelessness." When pressed a bit about "times of need," he elaborated:

> Sure, a lot of these people are victims of hard times. But the bottom line is that they have no one to fall back on when experiencing hard times. And that's why we're here: to give people something to fall back on when they need it.

Varying degrees of support for each of the foregoing arguments can be found in the biographies of our key informants and in the field sample more generally. Evidence for the worn-out welcome thesis is particularly pronounced among the chronically mentally ill. Lance McCay provides a vivid case in point. We noted earlier that although Lance came from an intact family of considerable financial means, his contact with them consisted of short, periodic visits, usually during some holiday. When he returned to the streets of Austin after one of these short stays, he would usually have a cache of gifts and a wad of money. But these gifts seemed to represent "guilt payments" to a troubled son more than a realistic effort to provide basic support, as Lance seemed to recognize, at least subconsciously. He had no illusions of receiving more basic stable support from his family and became quite angry, slamming his fists on the table and yelling, when we asked if he might be able to live with his parents. "Out of the question!" he yelled. "I don't want to stay in Houston! I hate the mother-fucking place! It just makes me mad and I don't want to talk about it." Our impression from this and other encounters with Lance, as we suggested earlier, was that such hostile outbursts were largely defensive reactions to genuine feelings of parental rejection.

Such rejection and the resultant withdrawal of familial support were evident among a number of other homeless mentally ill, as well as among a few non–mentally ill homeless. Illustrative of the latter is the case of a straddler whom we met stumbling drunkenly with his backpack through an alley. As we walked with him, he lamented:

I called my mother in New York a few days ago to see if she would help me out. But she just told me she's not going to accept collect calls from me any more. She said, "Leo, I used to believe in you, but not any more. I'm not going to give you anything from now on. You're going to have to work for it."

These examples clearly indicate that some of the homeless find themselves on the streets because they have exhausted either their families' resources or their willingness to help, largely because of unrelenting and burdensome disabilities such as alcoholism and mental illness. All of this is consistent with the worn-out welcome thesis, of course. But when we probed deeper into the biographies of our street informants we found a more complex picture that suggests that the other two arguments are closer to the mark for many of the homeless.

This observation is clearly supported by consideration of the types of family problems listed in Table 8.2. There we see that 27 percent of the homeless with whom we discussed the reasons for their plight mentioned marital discord, and 33 percent indicated that their unstable family situations contributed to their homelessness. Taken together, then, a significant number spoke of factors indicative of familial dysfunction and turbulence, and these factors constituted more than a quarter of all the precipitating reasons given.

These findings square with the experiences of many of our key informants as reflected in some of their explanations for homelessness in general, as well as their own situation. Banjo, for example, told us that "most of the time homelessness begins with family problems." Clearly this was the case with Gimpy Dan, who ran away from home at the age of thirteen in order to escape family chaos and confusion. Sonny McCallister also came from such a turbulent family situation that he ran off as a teenager:

My dad never did love my mother very much. When I was fourteen, things got pretty bad at home. Fifteen, they got worse. And then at sixteen, my parents got a divorce. My mom moved down to Coxey and stayed with a friend, but it got too bad for me—too mixed up. You was supposed to go to church all the time and to Christian school. Phooey on that! I moved in with my dad, then back with my mom, then back with my dad—just jumping back and forth. My mom kept pushing me to go to Christian church and when I moved back with my dad, he started saying this and that, saying I was just acting too crazy and he was going to put me in a mental institution. So I said I'm not going to go and I took off for two or three weeks to California. And then I came back and stayed with my dad and everything started going haywire again. So he finally sent me to a mental institution. But they only kept me for a month 'cause they could see it was the family that was crazy. So when I got out I took off.[89]

Just as some of the homeless are refugees from dysfunctional families, others are flotsam from shipwrecked marriages. In fact, Willie Hastings repeatedly insisted that "at least 40 percent are running from a bad marriage." Willie's estimate was not far off for our twenty key informants, as marital discord figured prominently in the process by which Tony Jones, Hoyt, Tanner, Shotgun, Gypsy Bill, and Indio became homeless. Clearly it was not the only factor leading to their homelessness, but it was contributory in each case. As Hoyt reminded us:

> I've had some problems ever since I was a kid. But things got really bad after my wife and I got a divorce. I was so shocked and disoriented then that I hit the road. I didn't know what else to do, and I sure didn't have no one to fall back on.

Hoyt had been orphaned at an early age and then shuttled between relatives' homes and institutional facilities: first an orphanage, then a juvenile correctional facility, and finally the army. When Hoyt and his wife divorced after six years of marriage, he had no one to turn to for either financial or psychological assistance. His grandparents and an aunt and uncle who had raised him until he was sent to an orphanage had died, and he knew no other family members who might give him a hand. Hoyt, then, had literally no one to fall back on.

The fact that experiences like Hoyt's were fairly common takes us to the third argument regarding the link between family and homelessness: that many individuals have no family to turn to when they find themselves unemployed, short of cash, victims of benefit cuts, or otherwise in need. Again, Table 8.2 is instructive, as we see that 24 percent grew up in orphanages and foster care facilities, and 8 percent lost their parents. The biographies of many of our key informants are illustrative. Like Hoyt, Tanner and Nona were orphaned and bounced from one institutional care facility to another. "I was orphaned as a baby," Tanner explained, "and as a kid they just moved me around from one group home to another." Nona George's parents both died when she was an infant, and she was raised in boarding facilities run by the Bureau of Indian Affairs. "The people there didn't give a shit about me," she told us. "I didn't even know I had a birthday until I was thirteen and they decided to give a party for me. And they say I got two brothers, but I never met them. They were sent somewheres else." In such cases, it makes little sense to speak of individuals being rejected by their families because of personal disabilities or disaffiliating because of family discord, for Tanner, Nona, and Hoyt never really had families at all.

An even larger number of our informants spent a portion of their childhood away from their parents, in foster homes or other institutional care facilities, largely because of family instability.[90] The experiences of Tom Fisk and Willie Hastings provide concrete examples. Tom's mother was an alcoholic, and his father left home when he was seven years old. A pattern of short stays at home interspersed with foster care had begun even before his parents were divorced:

> When I was about six years old I went to my first foster home, before my parents got divorced. I stayed six months in each one, except for the last two. I ended up spending around a year, a year and a half in the last two of them. We'd only be at the house with our mom for like maybe a month. I could never figure it out. I mean, after a while, when you've been sent away from home and you go back and then your mom, she kicks you out and then during the time you're gone she's whining and everything else, wanting to see you—then when you go home and see 'em and nothing works right, what's the purpose in it? After a while I kinda figured, "Well, hell, I'm not wanted here anyways."

Ultimately, Tom dropped out of high school and joined the army, hoping to find a more stable environment.

Willie Hastings's childhood seems even more chaotic and dysfunctional than Tom's. Willie's parents divorced when he was six years old. His father was given custody of Willie and his younger brother because their mother worked in a "disreputable" bar and was judged to be an unfit parent. When Willie was seven his father married a woman whom Willie remembers as a vicious tyrant: "Man, I wouldn't do nothing wrong, but she would get pissed and beat me with her spiked-heel shoes. I've got scars on my back to prove it." When Willie was nine his father beat him so badly that he was hospitalized, and when he was released he was sent to a Methodist children's home. He told us:

> That was the best thing that ever happened to me. They really cared about me there. They taught me how to cook and how to play the piano. But then when I was fourteen they sent me back to my father, who forced me into being a child prostitute.

Like Tom Fisk, when Willie turned eighteen he joined the army to get away from home, and he never returned, largely because of the unpleasant memories and the fact there was really nothing to return to in the way of support.

In each of these cases, as well as that of Sonny's, we see a highly conflictual and unstable family that turned Tom, Willie, and Sonny into what has been termed domestic refugees. But it is not so much the bouts of familial disaffiliation that we find interesting as it is the unsupportive and turbulent family contexts from which escape was ultimately sought and to which there was little interest in returning. When these features of the families in question are combined with the economic marginality of each family, we see that Tom, Willie, and Sonny simply had no viable family to fall back on.

The same is true of a number of other homeless who lost their families, or at least their parents, at critical junctures in their lives, leaving them vulnerable to homelessness. Ron Whitaker, for example, was left alone when his parents were killed in an auto accident during his senior year of high school. Since he had "no other close relatives," a social worker suggested that he be placed in foster care. But Ron objected, insisting that he wanted to stay put so he "could finish high school." He did, too, and then he joined the army. When he was discharged three years later, he had no family to which to return, so he drifted until he landed in Denver. It was after losing his job there that he wound his way to the streets of Austin. There is reason to assume that, had his parents not been victims of an auto accident, Ron's recent life trajectory would have taken a different turn. The same holds for a local homeless fellow whose mother died when he was a senior in high school. After that, he said, "my life took a shit. My father moved to California. We didn't get along, so I stayed here. I quit school and started working as a painter's helper. When things got slow I was let go. I didn't make enough to save anything. So here I am!"

Like Hoyt, Nona, and Tanner, who were orphaned at an early age, or Tony Jones, Shotgun, Gypsy Bill, and Indio, who were divorced shortly before hitting the streets, or Sonny, Tom, and Willie, who were the casualties of dysfunctional families, still others, like Ron Whitaker, who lost his parents at a particularly untimely moment, find themselves without any hint of familial support at critical junctures in their lives. In all of these cases we see the same link between family and homelessness, a link that points to a seemingly inescapable conclusion: many of the homeless are on the streets because they have no viable familial support network to tap when they are victimized by one or more of the structural forces discussed earlier or by some other misfortune. And the reasons for this void have little to do with the moral decay emphasized by some caretaker personnel. Nor does the worn-out welcome thesis appear to be empirically on target. Rather, insofar as we can believe the recollections and accounts of the homeless we came to know, many found themselves on the streets because they had never been associated with relatively stable and supportive familial networks. Some of them, including both orphans and children from troubled homes, were essentially state-raised youths who first experienced homelessness after they turned eighteen and were no longer eligible for institutional support. Some ran off before then, whereas others joined the military in their late teens and faced the prospect of homelessness after being discharged.[91] And still others were left without support when their parents died unexpectedly. To attribute homelessness to personal disabilities in these and other such cases is not only to engage in victim-blaming, but it is to obfuscate the family dynamics that render some people especially vulnerable to homelessness.

Family ties or relations are not so dysfunctional or disarticulated for all of the homeless, of course. One-third of the homeless with whom we discussed the reasons for their situation did not mention familial factors, and some maintained quite amiable contact with their families. Banjo, for instance, wrote weekly letters to his mother, who lived in Arkansas, and hitchhiked to visit her from time to time. Rhyming Mike kept in less regular touch with his parents but said he was welcome to return home to California anytime. Furthermore, family ambivalence does not preclude all contact and support. Many of the homeless who were on poor terms with their families called or wrote to them at least occasionally. For the majority of the homeless, however, family relationships appeared to be nonexistent, weak, or, at best, highly ambivalent. Moreover, most of the homeless come from families that are quite marginal economically and are therefore not in a position to offer much financial support. Familial income supplements, as we noted in Chapter 4, were relatively minuscule among the homeless we came to know. Unlike most Americans, then, many of the homeless come from families that have little economic or emotional support to offer in times of need, whether that need is occasioned by structural forces, personal disabilities, or just plain bad luck.

BAD LUCK

A final biographic factor mentioned by some of the homeless as a precipitant of their plight is an unanticipated twist of fate, misfortune, or accident—that is, a stroke or run of bad luck. We have already seen that some of the homeless invoke the luck factor to make sense of the obdurate fact that they are on the streets and that such an attribution makes good sense psychologically. But is there empirical substance to the claim that they are "down on their luck?"

The answer depends on what is counted as bad luck. If losing a job because of a plant closing, industry-specific slow-down, or general economic downturn counts, then clearly many of the homeless who came to Austin were victims of bad luck. But far more individuals find themselves out of work for reasons not of their own doing than actually become homeless. So if bad luck is a precipitating factor, other forms than structural victimization must be operating as well.

When we turn to less systemic, structural misfortunes that reflect how we normally think about bad luck, such as an automobile accident or severe work-related injury, we find that some of the homeless are indeed victims of such bad luck and that these personal misfortunes sometimes provide the initial nudge down the path toward homelessness or the final push over the edge. Consider the case of a straddler from Dayton, Ohio, who suffered a job-related accident that triggered his descent onto the streets. He was "living from hand to mouth, but making it as a painter's helper." Then "everything hit the shits," he told us:

> I fell off a three-story scaffold while on the job. I busted up my back and landed in the hospital for a couple of weeks. When I got out, the guy I worked for had hired somebody else. I had no job, no place to go, and not much money. I got in a fight with some guy I didn't even know and was thrown in jail for a few days. When they released me I headed for Houston. I'd gone there once before with a painter from Dayton. I didn't find no work there, so I hitched a ride over here.

When we first met him, two weeks after his arrival in town, he was still jobless, nearly penniless, and continuously bemoaning the work-related accident he had suffered several months earlier. "If only I hadn't fallen off that damn scaffolding I'd still be making it," he said time and time again.

Such hard luck also figured prominently in the biography of Tiny, the thirty-two-year-old Mississippian who left for Texas with his fiancée in search of work after he had lost his job in an industrial tubing plant. They got as far as Kansas, where Tiny suffered a final push: his pickup engine blew up. He had only enough money to send his fiancée back to Mississippi, so he abandoned the pickup and continued, via "thumb," his trek to Austin where, he had heard, work was plentiful. Before "the engine blew," he told us, he was "on the road looking for work." Now he was literally on the streets. An unanticipated occurrence proved to be the final precipitant.

Bad luck such as this laced the biographies of many of our informants. The particulars varied—an automobile accident, stolen belongings, a work injury, a car breakdown—but the result was always an initial or final push onto the streets. Although only 18 percent of the sixty-three informants with whom we discussed the reasons for their homelessness told us about such misfortunes, we suspect that they figured prominently in the process by which most of the homeless we came to know ended up on the streets. Like the low-income-housing shortfall that hangs over homelessness like an enormous dark cloud, strokes of bad luck, we suspect, are so commonplace that they are often taken for granted and therefore are not articulated.

To invoke bad luck as a contributing factor in the process by which people become homeless seems strikingly incongruous with causal thinking in the social sciences, with its emphasis on rational processes and well-defined causal models. With the exception of Christopher Jencks's analysis of income inequality in America, which argued heretically that "income also depends on luck," strokes of luck, be they bad or good, are rarely discussed as determinants of life chances.[92] Yet to dismiss bad luck as a determinant of homelessness is not only to ignore what some of the homeless tell us, but it is to gloss over real experiences that do help to determine the path or trajectory on which some individuals find themselves.

Everyone encounters bad luck at some point, of course. But its effects are not the same for all of its victims. For most individuals a minor automobile accident or a dying car engine leaves them unsettled for a day or two; for a few others it alters their life course. What accounts for the difference? Why are some individuals more vulnerable to strokes of bad luck than others? The answer lies in part in the individual's economic and social situation. Most people can absorb a run of bad luck without being thrown off course. Most of the homeless, however, had been so marginally situated, both economically and socially, that they did not have the resources to parry an encounter with bad luck. In short, many, and perhaps most, of the homeless are individuals who were particularly vulnerable to bad luck, not so much because of personal disabilities or incompetencies, but because of their already marginal existence. There is, then, a sense in which the claim "I'm down on my luck" is a faithful description of what many of the homeless have in fact experienced.

SUMMARY

In this chapter we have sought to identify and elaborate the array of factors that account for the homelessness of our informants and their counterparts. Pursuit of this objective has entailed examination of two interacting sets of factors: broad, macro-level structural trends, and biographic or individual-level factors. Exploration of the structural precipitants of homelessness took us beyond the homeless living in or passing through Austin in the mid-1980s to an examination of the factors that fueled the proliferation of homelessness nationally. Two considerations prompted us to step beyond the confines of Austin and take this more expansive view. First is the fact that only a small percentage of the city's homeless in the mid-1980s were local residents. An understanding of the growth of Austin's homeless population was thus contingent on an understanding of the sources of homelessness elsewhere. This tack was also prompted by a second and even more basic consideration: homelessness was a mounting national problem throughout the 1980s, a problem that touched virtually every community of any size. To have focused only on local determinants would have been to ignore the broader context in which the local problems are embedded.

In order to attain a more historically contextualized understanding of the roots of homelessness, then, we began by considering broad structural factors that affect the probability that certain events will be experienced by some aggregation of people, and by then returning to Austin to see whether these structural trends and arrangements were operative there. What we found is hardly surprising from a sociological standpoint: the driving structural dynamic underlying homelessness, both locally and nationally, involves a decline in the availability of low-cost housing and a concomitant decrease in actual income or its purchasing power. To paraphrase one set of observers, homelessness is rooted structurally in the gap that has widened for increasing numbers of individuals between the cost of subsistence needs, particularly housing, and the availability of economic resources to meet those needs.[93]

The widening of this gap, as we have seen, can be traced to the confluence of several structural-level trends, coupled with governmental indifference and cutbacks that exacerbated rather than muted the effects of those trends. The trends in question include a dramatic shrinkage in the nation's stock of low-cost housing; a corresponding increase in the cost of housing; a growing mismatch between the cost of housing and income, particularly for low-income renters; deindustrialization, which fueled a proliferation of low-wage service jobs, and the resultant job and income polarization; and escalating unemployment rates in the early 1980s. The historical conjunction of these trends with the federal government's failure to stem the affordable-housing crisis and to keep in good repair the "safety net" that was put in place during the New Deal and expanded during the 1960s resulted in the increasing marginalization of growing numbers of Americans, many of whom were pushed to the very brink of homelessness.

Exactly how many of those structurally at risk of becoming homeless actually fell through the widening cracks of the socioeconomic structure and onto the streets is unknown. What is known is that not all of those at risk of becoming homeless suffer that fate, at least not simultaneously. The reason is that individual-level effects of macro-level social forces are seldom experienced in the same way by all individuals, or even by those in similar social situations. A thoroughgoing understanding of the determinants of homelessness thus requires identification of those factors that render some people more vulnerable than others who appear equally at risk from a structural standpoint. In order to address this issue we turned from a structural to an individual level of analysis and to the biographies of our homeless informants.

Three sets of biographic factors surfaced, in varying degrees, in the accounts our informants provided as to why they became homeless. One had to do with various personal disabilities, such as mental illness and alcoholism; another with the lack of family support; and the third with bad luck. Of the three, family-related problems that undermined the prospect of support in times of need were the most frequently mentioned, as they peppered the biographies of the vast majority of the homeless with whom we had the opportunity to discuss the reasons for their descent onto the streets. Indeed, the absence of "real" family support was the one factor that seemed to knit together the biographies of most of our informants.

That homelessness is somehow linked to the absence of familial support in times of personal need and crisis makes both sociological and experiential sense. Sociologically, the family is regarded as the primary agent of socialization and as the institutional buffer between the larger world and the individual. Although evidence has been mounting in recent years that the family is also a crucible of tension and conflict, the

norm of familial assistance remains very strong. Most of us have, indeed, been the recipients of emotional or material support from our
families. The homeless, as we have seen, have had far more urgent occasion than most of us to solicit such familial support. But such support
was rarely forthcoming for most of them. Absence of a helping familial
hand thus appears to be a necessary condition for homelessness.

The difference between the homeless and the domiciled, then, is not
just that the homeless have been the victims of impersonal structural
forces or strokes of bad luck that have pushed them down the path
toward the streets, but that they have not been the beneficiaries of the
kind of familial support that most people take for granted in times of
personal crisis. Some of the homeless have no doubt worn out their
welcomes because of their burdensome disabilities. But the vast majority of the homeless we came to know either came from families so marginalized that they had nothing to give or had no family at all.

Taken together, these observations make clear that the sources of
homelessness reside in neither purely structural nor individual factors,
but in the interaction of the two. Yet that explanation still does not
fully capture the way the structural and biographic factors we have
identified interact in the lives of the homeless themselves. When we turn
to their life histories, it becomes strikingly evident that although homelessness results from the confluence of various misfortunes, that confluence does not just happen mysteriously. Rather, one misfortune or
problem triggers or exacerbates another, which, in turn, leads to yet
another until the individual is forced onto the streets.

In some instances the downward spiral begins with the loss of a job,
which then puts added pressure on an already strained marriage, which,
in turn, culminates in divorce or separation. Without a steady source of
income, a place to stay, or a family to turn to, the victim becomes homeless. That was the path to the streets traveled by Tanner, Tony Jones,
and Indio. Gypsy took a similar route, but in his case the process was
initiated by a cut in government assistance. For others, the process was
triggered by the death of a spouse or parents, coupled with several strokes
of bad luck and the failure to find steady work that paid a living wage.
This was the road to homelessness initially traveled by Marilyn and
Ron Whitaker. And for still others, the path to the streets began in
turbulent, often dysfunctional families that left them on their own to
deal with the structural victimage and bad luck they would suffer later
on, as was the case for Hoyt, Willie Hastings, Banjo, Gimpy Dan, Tom
Fisk, Sonny McCallister, and Nona. For some, like Shotgun and JJ,

excessive alcohol consumption was the initial precipitant, but often heavy drinking and streams of thought and behavior suggestive of mental illness followed rather than initiated the downward spiral.

There are, of course, still other pathways to the streets. Any number of factors can trigger homelessness: eviction, an increase in rent, deinstitutionalization, discharge from the military, a cut in pay or general assistance, and so on. These factors can also interact in a multitude of ways, thus yielding different pathways to the streets. And differences in local circumstances may yield differences in typical or modal pathways in different cities.

For the homeless in Austin, the modal pathway entailed some kind of economic dislocation, usually loss of job; the absence or erosion of familial support; migration in search of work; and failure either to find a job that paid a living wage or to find affordable housing in the city of destination. Whatever the predominant pathway to the street in any given city, however, we suspect that in all cities they are the product of interaction among structural and biographic factors that takes the form of a downward spiral in which one factor triggers or exacerbates another until the traveler has fallen onto the streets. This not only makes good sense sociologically, but it also captures the experience of the homeless we came to know.

CHAPTER NINE

Homeless Careers

Throughout this book we have made use of our typology of homeless street people, documenting variation among the types along a number of behavioral and cognitive dimensions, including work strategies, social relationships, and the construction of existential and identity-oriented meaning. In attending to these concerns we may have proceeded at times as though homelessness were a static condition. Clearly this is not the case. Some of those who suffer homelessness manage to extricate themselves fairly quickly, whereas others become chronically mired in street life. Still others develop a pattern of episodic homelessness. And a few, after having been homeless for years, get off the streets permanently. Over time, then, individuals may move from one category in our typology to another as they adapt to life on the streets or attempt to extricate themselves from it.

In this final chapter we examine the contingencies and dynamics that influence the temporal patterns of life on the streets. In doing so we invoke the concept of homeless careers. In everyday discourse the term *career* is associated with occupational trajectories or with professions or callings demanding certified training. Sociologists have used the term more broadly, however, to refer to the temporal organization and sequencing of activity in almost any sphere of social life. Thus, at the individual level, we can talk about the careers both of incumbents of conventional occupations and of individuals engaged in deviant pursuits such as drug-dealing or homosexual prostitution.[1] The career concept can also be useful in analyzing nonoccupational arenas of social life.[2] Although the homeless lack careers in the conventional sense of the term, their life histories on the streets are clearly amenable to the types of analysis sometimes conducted with respect to nonoccupational activities and routines. The utility of this type of career analysis is three-fold: it focuses attention on specific stages of development; it emphasizes sequential movement between stages; and it calls attention to the factors that influence movement from one stage to another. We are interested in the career paths common among the homeless and in the contingencies that affect movement along these paths from one type to another.[3] We begin this chapter by outlining these possible trajectories, focusing attention on the more common sequences, and then we turn to an elaboration of the dynamics and contingencies that influence movement along the various career paths. Throughout the discussion we draw on pertinent findings and observations from the previous chapters.

HOMELESS CAREER PATHS

The varieties of homelessness conceptualized in our typology and the possible paths incumbents of those typological positions might take are charted in Figure 9.1. The best place to begin our examination is with the recently dislocated, since their dislocation represents the initial phase of homelessness.

The potential career paths of recently dislocated individuals lead in two directions: one toward early extrication from homelessness, and the other toward increasing immersion in street life. The cases of the three recently dislocated men we have followed throughout the book clearly illustrate these different trajectories.

First, consider Tom Fisk. Once Tom became homeless he was unable to find a way off the streets. Despite his almost constant preoccupation with finding a steady job and a place to stay, his efforts to do so were consistently ineffective. Instead, he drifted toward increasing dependence on street institutions and into problems with the police that stemmed from his impoverished condition.

Tony Jones's trajectory stands in striking contrast to Tom's. Like Tom, Tony exhibited a strong aversion to the homeless condition. Unlike Tom, however, Tony was quickly able to land a reasonably good semi-skilled job, rent an apartment, and develop at least some degree of security off the streets.

Sonny McCallister's experience fell between those of Tom and Tony.

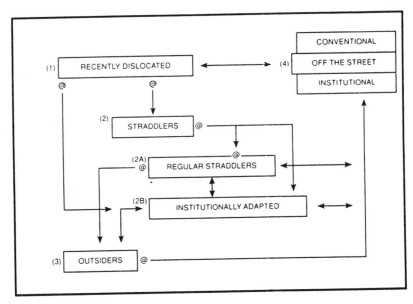

Figure 9.1. Diagram of Homeless Careers

Sonny was able to find a way off the streets, but not through the world of regular work. Instead, Sonny went to live with an older man who had befriended him on the streets near the Sally for largely sexual motives. Although Sonny, like Tony and unlike Tom, was now off the streets, his dependence on his friend's fondness for him suggested that Sonny might well find himself homeless again in the not-so-distant future, and perhaps ultimately involved in a cycle of episodic homelessness.

These three cases do not exhaust the potential paths of the recently dislocated. Other possibilities noted in Figure 9.1 warrant discussion. Two of these possibilities entail attachment to institutions or agencies that provide a place to stay. The recently dislocated may be institutionalized, for instance, through incarceration in penal facilities or through stays in mental hospitals or detox facilities. Each of these alternatives provides a possible route off the streets, albeit one that is seldom selected voluntarily. As previously discussed, some recently dislocated individuals may volunteer to take jobs in agencies, such as the Salvation Army's transient lodge, that provide services for the homeless. A final logical possibility, although not one we observed directly, is that some homeless individuals may swiftly succumb to serious mental illness and sink into outsiderhood without ever passing through a distinct liminal phase.

Among the recently dislocated who remain on the streets, we have noted a gradual progression toward liminality, with several possible career paths traveled by the regular straddlers. The movement at this stage, however, is seldom as rapid as movement among the recently dislocated. Indeed, some individuals remain regular straddlers for years before experiencing significant change in their life histories. Like the recently dislocated, regular straddlers can take various paths. One entails extrication from street life and return to conventional society. This was the direction in which Willie Hastings appeared to be heading as he became friends with members of the Central Assembly of God Church. Big Dan, one of the church elders, was so impressed by Willie's interest in the church that he found a job for him, and the church promised to help him secure an apartment. Willie seemed ready to accept both offers of help, but he disappeared mysteriously from the streets of Austin a few days before he was to begin his job.[4]

A second possibility for regular straddlers is to move into institutional positions in the agencies they frequent. Tanner Sutton's case exemplifies this trajectory. Tanner had been homeless for nearly two years when he arrived in Austin. Over two months during which he sometimes slept at the Sally, he became friends with several of the workers there. Those connections ultimately resulted in a job for him cleaning the men's shelter and passing out dinner tickets.

Two other possibilities exist for regular straddlers. One is movement off the streets via institutionalization—again, particularly in penal facilities and mental hospitals. Finally, straddlers may gravitate toward some type of outsiderhood, in which they frequently find subcultural peer support and, as we have seen, may develop identities at variance with conventional society.

Outsiders are the final category or stage in our typology, but the term does not necessarily indicate a terminal stage in the careers of the long-term homeless. Although some of the homeless who slip into outsiderhood become permanently anchored to the streets, three other possibilities exist. One is that an outsider may move into a position as an institutional straddler, as was illustrated by Hoyt, who, while trying to overcome his drinking problems, went to work at the Salvation Army. A second path, which outsiders share with those already mentioned, is institutionalization in penal facilities and mental hospitals.

A third and final possibility entails movement off the streets and back into conventional society. Although this career turn appears to be quite infrequent, it is nonetheless important both empirically and theoretically, sensitizing us to the fact that even long-term homeless individuals cannot be written off definitively. Occasionally we heard of a street person who had managed to mend bridges with family members and go to live with them, much as William Kennedy's homeless protagonist, Francis Phelan, does in the bestselling novel *Ironweed*. And a few others finally manage after years on the streets to find employment and, often with support of AA or various service agencies, "work themselves off the streets." During the course of our field research we met three such individuals, including a fifty-one-year-old man who had been on the streets of Austin for twelve years, from the age of twenty-nine to forty. After over a decade on the streets he became committed to the AA program and, through the help of several service agencies, ultimately became a counselor in a local detox facility.[5]

It is important to bear in mind that there is neither a definitive path nor any necessarily terminal stage in homeless careers. The material circumstances in which the homeless find themselves and their adaptive responses to those circumstances are changeable. Although being anchored in a particular stage, especially one of the later ones, is fairly common, considerable movement occurs, especially in the early stages, but potentially at any stage.

There is also considerable looping in the career trajectories of the homeless. Their career paths are frequently filled with movement ostensibly toward extrication from street life, followed by return to the streets and increasing physical, social, and psychological engulfment in homelessness. As Ron Whitaker told us succinctly, "My problem is not getting off the streets, it's staying off them." One common pattern in homeless careers, then, is episodic homelessness.[6]

The possibility of episodic homelessness is faced both by those whose movement off the streets is via institutionalization and those who return to domiciled civilian life. As we noted earlier, rehabilitative agencies often fail in their official mission of enabling homeless individuals to develop a life permanently off the streets. This aspect of homeless careers has received substantial attention over the years, primarily stemming from the prevailing view of homelessness as an individual pathology and the concomitant interest in rehabilitation programs, especially for alcoholism. Far less attention has been paid to the experiences of the homeless in their attempts to get off the streets without the help of institutional services. Here, too, the homeless frequently face a vicious circle, for reasons we will examine in the next section.

Ultimately there seem to be five possible career trajectories for the homeless. Some have only brief careers on the streets. Others sink into a pattern of episodic homelessness. A third career entails permanent embeddedness in a liminal plateau, typically in an institutional niche that provides a place to stay that is not on the streets, but yet remains outside conventional society. A fourth career leads to chronic, unrelieved homelessness. And a final possibility involves permanent, or at least relatively long-term, extrication from street life and return to conventional society after years, or perhaps even a decade or more, of homelessness.

DYNAMICS AND CONTINGENCIES INFLUENCING HOMELESS CAREERS

Having identified the various career paths, we turn to the question of how to account for these different trajectories. Why, for example, did Tony and Sonny extricate themselves from the streets, albeit with different risks of returning, whereas Tom seemed to be slipping toward straddler status and perhaps eventual outsiderhood? What accounts for the fact that some career paths are much more commonly traveled than others? And how is it that occasionally an outsider can find his or her way off the streets while so many recently dislocated become trapped in episodic homelessness? To answer these questions, we consider four sets of factors that influence movement over time in the street careers of the homeless: personal resource deficits, institutional factors, group-based ties, and cognitive factors.

PERSONAL RESOURCE DEFICITS

The first and perhaps the most visible constraint on the lives of the homeless consists of the various resource deficiencies they suffer. There are four categories of such deficits: mental and physical disabilities, lack of human capital, lack of material resources, and lack of social margin.

Disabilities   One standard finding in virtually all research on the homeless is their high level of disability compared to the domiciled population.[7] As was noted in the previous chapter, not only are an inordinate number of the homeless thought to be mentally ill, in poor health, alcoholic, criminally inclined, and interactionally incompetent, but these disabilities are often posited as the proximate causes of homelessness. We think this presumed causal linkage between disabilities and homelessness is exaggerated, but it is clear that such disabilities, whether they are causes or consequences of homelessness, are likely to impede efforts to get off the streets. Many of the men we saw at the Sally sick bay, for example, were unable to work because they had been injured on day-labor jobs. We also saw some individuals become mentally disoriented while living on the streets, although, for reasons previously discussed, we would hesitate to label their disorientation as mental illness. We observed that criminal arrest and conviction, too, often resulted from the condition of homelessness itself and the secondary adaptations individuals developed to survive on the streets. Several of our informants were arrested on numerous occasions, for example, for panhandling or sleeping in unauthorized places. We have also seen that the consumption of alcohol, and with it the risk of alcoholism, increases with time on the streets. Each of these disabilities obviously makes extrication from the streets more difficult. Tom with his arrest record, Gypsy Bill with his severely deformed back, Tanner with various debilitating physical ailments, Nona George, JJ, and Indio with their drinking problems, and Jorge Herrera and Lance McCay with their mental disabilities are all cases in point.

Lack of Human Capital   The second resource deficit among the homeless can be thought of in terms of what social scientists studying the labor process call human capital: acquired attributes that enhance an individual's value in the work force, such as education, occupational skills, or work experience. The homeless living in and passing through Austin were relatively impoverished in terms of these attributes.

First, consider education. Our data on the educational status of the homeless come from two sources: the Salvation Army and the Texas Employment Commission. The Sally data show that 10 percent of the homeless had only an elementary school education, 74 percent had some high school, and 16 percent had some level of postsecondary training. The TEC data indicate that 49 percent of the homeless had completed high school only, and another 18 percent had some postsecondary education, for a total of 67 percent with a high school degree or better. This figure is a bit surprising, considering the presumed connection between homelessness and educational deficiencies and the fact that the proportion of all Texans with a high school or college degree is only 10 percent higher (77 percent, as of the 1980 census).[8] Nonetheless, the percentage of homeless individuals without a high school diploma is nearly twice that of the overall U.S. adult population.

The work experience of the homeless presents an even more dismal picture. As we saw in Chapter 4, few of the homeless have work experience and occupational skills that can be used to secure jobs beyond the lower level of the secondary labor market. Four-fifths of the homeless who registered at the Salvation Army in Austin identified themselves as blue-collar workers (in comparison with 44 percent of the overall U.S. male work force), with the majority being unskilled laborers. An additional 12 percent identified themselves with lower-level jobs in the service sector, primarily in food service. Furthermore, few of the homeless we met had recent steady employment, thus putting them at a competitive disadvantage even when they apply for the kinds of jobs they have held in the past. Those who did have more valued skills or recent work experience often found it easier to locate regular employment. Tony's skills as an appliance repairman, for instance, enabled him to secure a job fairly quickly. Considering their low level of human capital and the contemporary labor market, however, the prospects for most of the homeless seem grim.

Vocational training programs geared toward unskilled workers have not had much success in helping the homeless secure stable employment. Consequently, the programs often engender disillusionment in the homeless who participate. We first realized this on a Thanksgiving Day after eating dinner at the Assembly of God church. A hearing-impaired man in his early twenties, who had just returned from the Rajneeshee commune in Antelope, Oregon, asked if he could get a ride with us back downtown right after dinner so that he could go "can picking" to make enough money to buy a new hearing-aid battery. Another young man at the table told him, "Man, if you really want to make some money, you oughta go down to TEC and tell 'em you want to get on the JPTA [Job Partnership Training Act] thing. They're gonna get me a job learning body work in a paint and body shop." The hearing-impaired man responded:

> I'm tired of that training stuff. I got trained by CETA to be a mechanic, but then I could never get a job. And then I went to Goodwill Industries and they taught me furniture repair, but I couldn't ever get a job at that either. I don't need more training, I need a real job. 'Course, if they want to offer me some work, I ain't gonna turn 'em down.

Lack of Material Resources   The problems the homeless face as a result of disabilities and lack of human capital are compounded by their lack of material resources. The homeless not only lack shelter—their most obvious material deprivation—but, as was discussed in Chapter 4, they are usually deprived of a host of other material resources, such as clean clothes, access to facilities to maintain personal hygiene, private and public transportation, personal tools for skilled and semi-skilled labor, and a telephone. The lack of these trappings of conventional life inhibits their efforts to find work and stable housing and frequently causes them to be perceived as potentially difficult and unreliable employees.

Even though some of the homeless go to great lengths to act as solid, stable employees when they get jobs, they often fail, as we noted earlier, for the daily exigencies of their lives interfere with their on-the-job performance. Because they have trouble finding places to sleep during the day, they may show up exhausted for the swing or graveyard shift; if they cannot hitch a ride in time, they may arrive on the job late; and if they become ill, they may be unable to get to a phone to call in sick. Furthermore, the strategies they develop to deal with these problems often backfire. Both Tom and Gypsy tried to keep a rattletrap car running so they would have transportation to work. But neither could afford to keep a car inspected, licensed, and insured. Over time each of them accumulated numerous tickets and ended up spending time in the city jail to pay off their fines. Willie's makeshift strategy similarly backfired during his stint at a fast-food restaurant. Since the Sally was not available for daytime sleeping, Willie slept in an abandoned building, thus putting himself at risk for being arrested and victimized.

The extreme difficulty of pulling oneself up by one's bootstraps is one of the bitterest pills the homeless have to swallow. As Hoyt lamented, "Man, once they get you down, they'll never let you up. You just don't have a chance no matter what you do."

Lack of Social Margin   Some individuals do manage to get off the streets, by taking maximum advantage of whatever resources and strengths they have. Sonny, for instance, capitalized on his youth and his willingness to engage in a homosexual liaison with an older man, and Tony made it off the streets on the basis of his work skills.

As we have seen, however, it is usually difficult for the homeless to capitalize on their meager assets unless they are granted a degree of leeway when they show up late, or they miss work for a day. Jacqueline

Wiseman noted the importance of such leeway, or "social margin," as she termed it, in her examination of the lives of skid-row alcoholics. "Social margin," she wrote, "is compounded of the goodwill of people within the actor's ambit of influence, and the time, credit, or money they are willing to devote to assist him should the need arise."[9] Social margin has a tremendous influence on the amount of deviant or idiosyncratic behavior an individual is allowed to exhibit. Whereas individuals with a wide band of social margin find it easy to secure a loan from a friend or get excused for missing several days at work, those without it rarely have any one to turn to for a loan, and their accounts of their absences are less likely to be believed.

The width of a person's social margin is determined primarily by his or her social relationships and what others know about them. By the time an individual hits the streets, he or she usually has little, if any, social margin left. Indeed, Wiseman observes that the phrase "my luck ran out" refers largely to the "dramatic disappearance of social margin."[10] Evidence of this was abundant among the homeless in Austin, many of whom had unsuccessfully sought financial assistance from family and friends to get themselves established in a residence. As we discussed in the previous chapter, this was not due so much to the homeless having alienated other members of their families as it was to the simple fact that most of them came from impoverished or disintegrated families that themselves had little social margin. Tom Fisk told us the same thing we heard from others time and again: "My family can't help me. They're almost in as bad shape as I am." Street peers have little social margin to share, and employers, even when they hire the homeless, may be unwilling to grant them much room for error.

Some individuals hide their homelessness in the hope that they will be able to get a job and avoid stigmatization. Unfortunately, this subterfuge may work against a person who does get a job, since the employer cannot be apprised of the personal problems that may cause poor performance.

Ultimately the person may be forced to divulge that homelessness in order to explain frequent tardiness, soiled clothes, or other problematic behavior. In some cases an individual may have built up sufficient social margin with an employer to offset the revelation of their homelessness. On his third day in a row of showing up late for his breakfast shift as a dishwasher at a local pancake house, for instance, Ron Whitaker admitted his situation to his boss. As he related the incident later:

I told her, "You can do what you want about it, but I'm gonna tell you the truth. I'm staying at the Salvation Army until I get enough money to rent a place. I lied about it on my application because I didn't think you would give me a job. And I've been late because there's no bus to get me here on time. You can fire me for lying, but now I'm telling you the truth." I really thought she would fire my ass, but instead she told me I was a good worker and she'd swing by the Sally to pick me up in the morning. So now I got a steady ride.

Such honesty is not always rewarded, however. When Willie offered a similar explanation to the night manager of a fast-food restaurant where he was working, he was fired on the spot. Willie recalled, "The night manager said, 'I'm not having any bums working here. You can pick your check up on Friday. Now get out!' " The bottom line is that a homeless person, in this as in so many other situations, is stuck between a rock and a hard place, unable to get a job without having some social margin and unable to obtain social margin without a respectable biography and the resources necessary to maintain an adequate performance.

The cases of the relatively few homeless who do manage to acquire a degree of social margin while on the streets are highly instructive regarding the dynamics of street careers. Social margin for the homeless comes primarily from two sources: private individuals, and street agencies that provide what Wiseman has referred to as "institutional margin."[11]

A few homeless receive social margin and support from domiciled individuals who offer them a place to stay in return for work. In other cases, sexual expectations are attached to the proffering of individual support. As one woman in her early twenties explained to us at the detox facility, "I used to hang out in the bars and look for some guy to pick me up and take me home. Most of the time they'd let me stay with them at least a few days. Sometimes longer. As long as I gave them what they wanted, no problem." The social margin in such situations is very precarious, because it is dependent on the continuing need or interest of the near-stranger who is offering it. Consequently, such social margin can be easily lost, toppling the individual back onto the streets.

INSTITUTIONAL FACTORS

The primary sources of institutional margin are the caretaker agencies that extend official sponsorship to some of the homeless, with the expressed aim of helping them get off the streets. And sometimes they succeed. Two of the alcoholism counselors we came to know at the detoxification and rehabilitation facilities were themselves formerly homeless and had been helped by alcoholism treatment programs and other agencies to deal with their drinking problems and to find steady employment and stable private housing. But, more often than not, these agencies fail in their restorative mission. For each success story we encountered we found a host of counterexamples. Why? Part of the answer lies in the fact that some of the homeless, especially outsiders, are difficult to reintegrate into conventional society. Some of them struggle with alcoholism, and others suffer from physical, mental, or emotional impairments that reduce their ability to support themselves.

Such disabilities undoubtedly account for the persistence of chronic homelessness in some cases, but it seems less adequate for explaining the inability of caretaker agencies to assist the majority of unimpaired homeless individuals who have not yet become outsiders. In these cases the failure of caretaker agencies is rooted in the ways in which their organizational structure and proximate goals undermine the realization of their restorative ideals. Three sets of factors seem to produce this situation: the ultimately accommodative emphasis of most caretaker agencies, the bureaucratization and decentralization of services, and problems associated specifically with rehabilitation programs. We address each of these in turn.

As we noted in Chapter 3, although many agencies proclaim an official goal of rehabilitating the homeless, often the bulk of their energy goes into providing accommodative services. The Sally and Angels House exemplify this situation. Despite their avowed interest in helping the homeless leave the streets, neither agency expends much of its energy and resources in pursuit of this goal.[12] In an effort to legitimate their services some agencies may exaggerate how much routine energy they actually allocate to this goal. In practice, however, most caretaker agencies busy themselves with the task of helping the homeless survive from day to day. One result, as we have noted before, is that as the homeless develop routines based on the availability of services, they become accommodated to street life rather than directed toward disengagement.

A second set of problems arises from the bureaucratic nature of most of the agencies that deal with the homeless. Our discussion in Chapter 4 of the operation of agencies that dispense transfer payments and benefits is pertinent here. Many of the barriers we discussed there exist in other agencies as well. The distribution of specialized agencies throughout the city, for instance, is an endemic problem for social services, as is the rigidity of rules and schedules that frequently ignore the special needs of specific disadvantaged populations, such as the homeless. Agency appointments and service times, for instance, are often inflexible. To keep an appointment with one agency an individual may have to forego contact with another. The person must choose between a job interview and a shower, or a medical appointment at the evening clinic and a bed at the Sally. Many agency services also require scheduling far in advance—a difficult task for the homeless, whose personal lives and routines are centered so much in the present. Far too often, analyses of the lower classes have blamed the victim in this regard by focusing on their presumedly disabling "present orientation" or inability to delay gratification.[13] Agency personnel, too, often complain that the homeless are unwilling to plan ahead or wait their turn. Our experiences on the streets, however, suggest that the real issue for the homeless is often their desperate need for some sort of immediate assistance, which tends to focus both energy and attention on the problems at hand and thus on the present. This was driven home to us on numerous occasions.

Once, for example, while visiting at a small charity at the edge of Austin, we encountered a twenty-one-year-old woman who had been living for nearly a week, with her two small children, in her unemployed brother's car. The weather had turned cold and the young woman was trying desperately to find more suitable shelter for herself and her children. The agency from which she sought help did not provide shelter services, and since the woman was adamant that she would not stay at the Salvation Army since she did not want to "be around that kind of people," the agency worker called Caritas to see whether they could assist her. The person he spoke to at Caritas informed him that the woman might be able to get help from them in the future, but she would have to show up no later than 7:00 A.M. in order to be sure of seeing a counselor that day. The Caritas representative stressed the importance of arriving early to get on the waiting list and that even then the possibility of assistance was highly uncertain. "We'll talk to her," the counselor said, "but we can't promise anything."

When she found out that Caritas could not provide immediate assistance, the young woman turned her attention to the upcoming night rather than making plans for getting to Caritas the following day. "I can't worry about that right now," she said despondently. "I've got to figure out where we're going to sleep tonight."

On another occasion, one evening in the Sally dinner line, two middle-aged men told us that they had been next in line for interviews at the food-stamp office but at the last minute had decided to leave. "See, the thing is," they explained:

> this was just an interview to get an interview. They wouldn't give us any food stamps today. And we hadn't eaten since this morning at Caritas. So we decided since we're broke that we better hightail it down here for dinner. If we'd waited for our interviews, we'd never have made it here in time. And we wouldn't get the food stamps for two weeks anyway.

Caught in similar circumstances, it is unlikely that even middle-class persons would be much concerned with anything beyond their immediate situation. Lacking sufficient resources to deal with immediate needs, then, is likely to force the individual into a "present orientation." Although that orientation may bewilder service providers, it is often highly adaptive for the homeless, as the above observations suggest.

The perspectives of many social service workers and their homeless clients are frequently quite discordant in other ways as well.[14] From the agency's perspective, clients often seem difficult and unfairly demanding. This was evident in the complaint of one angry caseworker at a food-stamp office:

> A lot of people expect you to bend over backwards for them. You wouldn't believe it, what they expect you to do. We've got our rules to follow, but they just won't listen. It's like just because they're in bad shape we owe them something no matter what they do. But it doesn't work like that. If they don't do their part, there's nothing I can do for them.

From the standpoint of the homeless the situation often appears quite different. Some homeless individuals try to meet the demands agencies place on them and simply become confused when they are unable to do so. This is especially likely to happen when the homeless person is confronted with agency expectations that were developed with domiciled clients in mind. One thirty-year-old man we came to know, for instance, was befriended by the pastor of a downtown church. The pastor gave him the name and phone number of a counselor at a vocational rehabilitation program. When the homeless man called, the counselor was not in his office. "So they asked for my name and number to call me back," he explained. "What do I do then? I said, 'That's okay, I'll call him back later.' And every time I call back, he isn't in. Guess all I can do is keep calling."

Sometimes confusion and feelings of futility give way to angry outbursts. Lance McKay recounted a particularly frustrating encounter with a counselor at a halfway house for former mental patients:

> He's been telling me I could move in when they got an opening. So now they've got one and he tells me I have to have a job before they let me move in. I got so mad I couldn't help myself. I just started screaming at him, "What do you mean, get a job before I move in? Nobody'll give me a job until I have a place to live, for Chrissakes! Fuck you, I'm taking off for Montana!"

The upshot is that the homeless are often disillusioned with social service and charity agencies; they believe, as Marilyn put it, "They won't help a tramp." This alienation is especially evident in relation to caretaker agencies geared toward rehabilitation or restoration.

Street-based restorative agencies, as we discussed in Chapter 3, are in the business of trying to help the homeless recover from the problems that are presumed to account for their homelessness and/or prevent them from extricating themselves from the streets. The majority of these agencies' programs primarily aim at changing the attitudes, behaviors, and self-identity of their homeless clientele. In attempting to help the homeless, however, such restorative programs often unwittingly impose several barriers that reduce the prospects of the homeless getting off the streets. These include a bias in the criteria that determine who will and who will not receive assistance; agency beliefs that conflict with client identities and thereby prevent many individuals from taking advantage of available services; and fertile soil for the development of secondary adjustments on the part of both agencies and clients that unintentionally produce accommodation among the homeless to a street-based existence.

One obvious way selectivity criteria bias rehabilitation programs is through the kinds of services that receive funding. Since the majority of services directed toward helping the homeless extricate themselves from the streets are focused on alcohol and, more recently, drug abuse, a large portion of available resources are allotted to those who admit to having such problems. Other services that might better address the problems the majority of the homeless perceive themselves as having, such as simple economic insecurity, are reduced by the amount of available resources channeled into substance-abuse programs.

A second way that selectivity bias operates is in the development of admission guidelines. Staff members and administrators often give preference to those who appear to be sincere about overcoming substance abuse problems. As one counselor we spent time with put it, "What we're looking for is people who can and will work the program." This is defined in terms of two characteristics: an appropriate biography, and a willingness to see oneself from the agency's therapeutic perspective and to participate in treatment. An appropriate biography would include a recent history of substance abuse, along with employment potential. But perhaps more important from the agency's perspective is that the individual display a sincere desire to overcome "his problem with alcohol or drugs." The official daily routines in treatment facilities are usually geared toward some type of work activity, which is seen as useful in rehabituating "disorganized individuals" to productive lives, and participation in AA-style meetings to help them overcome their substance abuse.

The focus on substance abuse and its treatment provides rehabilitation facilities with their operational perspective and with a general body of information and associated techniques for dealing with the homeless in these settings. The operational perspective provides a blueprint for managing the homeless by identifying a specific underlying problem and its most appropriate treatment. One major problem undermining the success of substance-abuse programs for the homeless, however, is that the majority of the clients do not embrace the operational perspective on which the agency's program is based. In fact, many individuals in these programs have quite negative views of them. There are several reasons for this attitude.

First of all, the homeless individual seldom enters a rehabilitation program without ambivalence. Most of the homeless are forced into these programs through desperate circumstances. When brought to court on a charge of public intoxication, some individuals offer to enter a program in order to avoid spending time in jail, much as McMurphy in Ken Kesey's *One Flew Over the Cuckoo's Nest* sought asylum in a mental hospital to avoid prison time. Many others seek out rehabilitation programs when they need a respite from the physical stresses and deprivations of street life. As we noted before, we first met Shotgun on a snowy day in late December when he was wandering the streets in search of a program that would take him in out of the cold. A counselor at a detox center, who was himself a former street person, emphasized such basic physical motivation for seeking treatment:

> You have to see the shape these guys are in when they enter detox to believe it. Staph infections, worms, ulcers, all kinds of things. You name it, they've got it. Fire ant bites from sleeping out—I mean, bites so bad you wouldn't believe it. We spend more time nursing them back to health than anything

else. . . . There's guys out there who would die—literally—if they couldn't use us to get off the streets now and then.

Many of the homeless thus view participation in rehab programs as a last-ditch effort to survive. A large number do not perceive themselves as having substance-abuse problems, and an even larger number have little faith in the agencies' promises of success, feeling that they place too much emphasis on the voluntary component of their problems and not enough on external factors. Nonetheless, in order to gain access to the facilities and services, they often present at least a facade of openness to the agency's ideology.

Second, rehabilitation facilities exhibit many of the operational dynamics of total institutions, such as prisons and mental hospitals. These facilities have been described as "forcing houses for changing persons,"[15] since they seek to impose alternative identities on their clients. Whereas the AA philosophy explicitly rejects the efficacy of forcing AA on individuals, most substance-abuse programs demand participation in meetings. AA and other such programs have demonstrated their power in assisting many alcoholics and drug addicts to regain control of their lives, but they are less effective with a captive, frequently hostile population.

Many of the homeless we met in these facilities were unwilling to "admit" they were powerless over their lives and to accept that a "Higher Power" could restore them to sanity—the first two steps of the AA program. Instead, they "worked the program" only as much as necessary to keep in the staff's good graces. Often they seemed to do so more to obtain amenities such as free cigarettes, coffee, or donuts than to deal with their "problem." This was clearly illustrated one evening when we attended an open AA meeting at one facility. As described in our field notes:

The meeting began at 7:00 P.M. and lasted about an hour and a half. The director of client services opened the meeting by complaining about the men's apparent lack of interest in going to extra meetings off grounds. A man sitting next to us mumbled to his friend, "Shit, all we do is go to meetings."

After asking whether there were any AA birthdays to be announced (no one responded), the director introduced two speakers who talked for half an hour each about their experiences. One of the speakers was an ex-biker who came wearing his "colors"; the other, his girlfriend, was a self-proclaimed ex-prostitute and former mental patient at the state hospital who had spent some time on the Austin streets. Each of them gave a rambling drunkalogue that did not seem to catch the interest of many of the men, who spent much of their time getting coffee and donuts from a nearby table. A couple of the men dozed, and one had to be awakened twice because he was snoring.

When the meeting was over half a dozen men went into the restroom to smoke cigarettes and expound on the meeting outside the earshot of the staff. "Can you believe the way that bitch talked?" exclaimed a man who had known the woman speaker on the streets. "Like she's got her shit together, right? Christ, every guy I know's had a piece of her ass—and they didn't pay for it neither, I'll tell you that. I bet she's had more kinds of VD than everybody in this place combined. What bullshit, getting her to come here and talk!"

Other men voiced similar sentiments and complained about the program in general. As they were leaving the restroom one of the men proclaimed, "I've had about all I can take of this place. I'm gonna stay till Friday for my ten bucks and then get the fuck out."

Finally, the negative assessment of rehabilitation facilities by many of the homeless is reinforced by the agencies' rigid, bureaucratic rules. Most facilities place severe restrictions on personal freedom. Especially during the early weeks of the program, individuals are not allowed to "go off grounds" or to socialize with people outside. Daily life is often regimented, with not only work and meals but AA-style meetings, sleeping, and religious services tightly scheduled. Furthermore, progress in "the program" is judged in large part by the degree of acceptance of the often quite arbitrary rules and staff decisions. Complaining is seen as an indication of resistance to rehabilitation. A counselor at the facility where we observed the preceding AA meeting explained when we asked him about homeless clients' complaints about restrictions: "The problem with most of these guys is that they don't want to work the program. It's that simple. The program works if you work it, but lots of these guys don't even try." [16]

Clients pointed to the self-serving nature of such explanations. One man who had been in several different facilities around the state explained:

> Of course they're going to say that we don't work the program, otherwise things look bad for them, right? But what I'm saying is that the program doesn't work. Maybe for some guys, but not many. . . . Most guys finish the program and, bam! they're back on the streets—not because they want to be, but because the programs don't help them once they're out.

A state of chronic tension between staff and clients thus seemed endemic to the agencies we observed.

In the final analysis, caretaker agencies that at least ostensibly provide support services for the homeless fall into three groups. The first group is composed of welfare agencies focused on disadvantaged clients in general rather than just the homeless. As we have seen, the homeless find it difficult to gain access to these services. Indeed, one consistent finding of research has been the underutilization of such services by the homeless, and some social scientists have recommended aggressive advocacy of these services as a partial solution to the problems of the homeless.[17] Others, however, have suggested that the problem of access to these agencies is often intentionally structured to restrict their utilization by qualified individuals.[18]

The second group is made up of caretakers, such as the Salvation Army and most shelters, that are keenly aware of the need for programs that help the homeless get off the streets but that direct the bulk of their resources toward providing accommodative services. The third group, and the one to which we have devoted most attention here, is composed of those agencies that seek to rehabilitate the homeless. These organizations are highly significant in the careers of many of the homeless, although seldom in the way that the official ideology would suggest. Not many individuals manage to extricate themselves from homelessness by following agency plans. A few use the facilities and programs as springboards off the streets in ways the agencies themselves do not sanction, such as when two clients "elope" with their modest savings from the program and attempt to set up an apartment on their own. Some others develop attachments to agency staff and become so useful in the day-to-day operations that they stay on for long periods in niches within the agencies as maintenance and clerical workers. But the majority use the programs primarily as rest stops at which to recover from the strains and deprivations of life on the streets. In the long run, then, social services often seem more effective in facilitating accommodation to street life than in helping individuals get off the streets permanently.

STREET-BASED TIES

The third set of street-level factors that influence the careers of homeless individuals are the social ties they develop with each other. In Chapter 6 we examined the kinds of street relationships, noting how they develop over time. As we discussed in that chapter, most research on street-based social ties has found that they perform a number of social, psychological, and instrumental functions. We too have observed these functions. But we have also observed that they tend to undermine the prospect of disengagement. As individuals make street friends and become increasingly involved with them, they often become more committed to the street-based activities out of which their friendships have grown. While they may still have a strong desire to get off the streets, their day-to-day behavior revolves more around the activities they share with their homeless associates than around efforts to get off the streets. This is not a smooth transition for many of the homeless, however, but often provokes ambivalence, frustration, and inconsistent behavior.

It is not at all surprising that street relationships should strengthen individuals' street attachments. The situations in which relationships are developed and maintained include many adaptive street activities, such as bottle-gang drinking, "hitting" the plasma center, and dumpster-diving. These activities tend to engage people in continuing involvement on the streets and take time and energy away from efforts they might otherwise make to get off the streets.

Our field notes are peppered with dozens of cases in which individuals' plans to look for work were scuttled when they ran into friends and acquaintances with alternative proposals of how to spend the day. Late one spring afternoon, for instance, we encountered a thirty-eight-year-old man from Florida who had told us the previous night that he was "hell-bent on getting a steady job" the next day. When we ran into him, however, he was drunk and sitting on the hood of an old car with several other men. Although we did not confront him about his change of plans, he felt compelled to offer an account. "I really was going to hunt for a job today, but what can I say?" he told us. "I ran into my best buddies and I got drunk. I couldn't let them get drunk by themselves, could I?" Similarly, despite frequent efforts to stay sober, Marilyn admitted to us, "I just can't say no when it comes to friends and drinking." And on several occasions we witnessed her succumb to peer pressure to drink after she had struggled for several days to stay sober.

Street-based ties not only increase the pressure to drink, but they also generate commitment to the activities in which the relationships are grounded, as is reflected in the sanctions that may result from withdrawal from such activities. Three kinds of sanctions or penalties are particularly salient. First, the individual risks social rejection by those who expect him or her to participate in peer-group activities. Second, the person is threatened with the possibility that others will withdraw their material support—a particularly distressing consequence for the many homeless who rely on others for minor but daily material support. And, third, since a sense of both self and morality is based in part on these relationships, their disruption may cast doubt on an individual's sense of moral selfhood. To violate the expectations of peers is to deny a projected self-image and thus to throw that lived identity into question. These unintentionally acquired side bets or commitments exert strong pressure toward maintaining street life and relationships as the primary point of reference and most important priority.

Many of the homeless we met recognized that street ties both make street life easier and mire them deeper in homelessness. As we noted in Chapter 6, numerous informants attribute their continuing homelessness in part to the influence of their peers. This leads to a profound and enduring ambivalence in their street relationships, an ambivalence that varies among the different types of homeless. It is a relatively small problem for the recently dislocated, who shy away from street ties. It is, however, a particularly salient dilemma for straddlers, since they have developed a substantial number of street acquaintances but have not yet acquired stable street identities. Straddlers often feel that they have to make a choice between street friends and getting off the streets. In actuality their view is unrealistically one-sided, since eliminating street ties is no guarantee of extrication from homelessness. Nonetheless, straddlers tend to vacillate in a predictable fashion between their perceived choices. For a while they "hang" with friends on the streets. Then they become disillusioned with street life and their associates and turn their attention and energy toward efforts to get a steady job and a place to stay. When their efforts to find steady work and get off the streets fail, they return to "hanging out," often with new street associates who take the place of the ones they abandoned.

The lives of most of our key straddler informants exemplify this cyclical pattern. Ron Whitaker, for instance, became part of a street clique soon after coming to Austin from Denver. Within six weeks, however, he had withdrawn from the clique and was putting all his energy into working two part-time jobs. During this period he distanced himself from his street associates, speaking negatively about "the men who stay at the Sally" and particularly about his old friends, whom he derided as "fuck-ups with nothing better to do with themselves." Three weeks later, however, he had exhausted himself trying to work the two jobs simultaneously, frequently with no place to sleep. He quit the jobs and returned to the Sally. Since his old buddies were angry at him, he found a new set of associates, whom he spent most of his time with until he slipped out of Austin a few weeks later.

Despite their best intentions, then, straddlers are seldom successful in getting off the streets permanently. From a coolly rational point of view, it may seem unwise to give up street friends and their support for the uncertain chance of making it off the streets. Straddlers, however, often feel so strong a desire to extricate themselves that it outweighs such calculations. And some do eventually work their way off the streets, whereas others end up moving toward more consistent street involvement.

Outsiders, with the exception of the mentally ill, who frequently lack the ability to establish social ties, have by and large resolved this conflict in favor of street life and associates. They have become habituated to their daily routines and relationships and seldom engage in serious endeavors to extricate themselves. They therefore seldom confront the nagging dissonance that is an ongoing feature of the straddler's world.

COGNITIVE FACTORS

The final set of factors that influence the careers of the homeless is that of their cognitive orientations. These orientations are closely related to the three sets of factors we have examined so far. They develop largely in response to the problematic material and social conditions of the homeless, and they frequently reinforce their homelessness.

One major cognitive dilemma that impedes the life chances of the homeless is their inability to formulate concrete plans of action directed toward getting off the streets. Usually when we asked individuals about ways they might extricate themselves, they answered with vague generalities: they would work steadily, save money, and get a place. But they were seldom able to elaborate specific plans they would be able to implement. One morning, for instance, we met Tom Fisk at a roofing job. Since his boss had not been paying him, Tom had stopped at the plasma center to earn some money for breakfast and cigarettes before work. As we stood there, waiting for his boss to arrive, Tom confided, "See, the thing is, I don't know if he's fucking with me or not. Maybe the apartment manager hasn't paid him for that last job we did, I don't know. What I think is I should get another job, but where? All's I really know is that I've got to do something, 'cause this whole weekend I just sat in my car."

Such anxious preoccupation with trying to formulate a concrete plan was particularly common among the recently dislocated. Straddlers struggled with this problem too, but not as consistently. Rather, they tended, as we just saw, to move back and forth between endeavors to get off the streets and relative acceptance of street life. In shifting into a street mode, so to speak, they could find a reprieve from the frustrations of trying to get off the streets. The cognitive orientation of straddlers is strikingly different in these two situations. When it comes to getting off the streets, their plans—like those of the recently dislocated—tend to be either vague and general or implausible, such as starting a business, winning a sweepstakes, or writing a bestseller. By contrast, they have a large body of knowledge that enables them to develop concrete and effective plans for getting by on the streets. Pat Manchester's experience is illustrative. He originally intended to get a steady job shortly after coming to Austin. But he found it harder to locate work than he had anticipated, and as time went by he became increasingly familiar and comfortable with the structure and routines of street life in Austin. As he told us one day as we waited in line for lunch at Angels House:

> Once you get into the life, it's easy to stay in it. I get up in the morning and I plan my day: breakfast at the Sally, get a sandwich at Caritas, lunch at Angels, sell blood for some money, and then hit the library or a dollar movie. You get used to living like that and you don't think about doing anything else. It's just too easy—if you don't mind waiting in lines. 'Course, if you do manage to get a few days' work and some money, then you start thinking, "Wouldn't it be great to get enough money to get a place to stay?" But most of the time you don't think about it.

Understandably, then, many of the homeless feel far more effective in negotiating life on the streets than they do in managing to get off them. It is not just that they are able to formulate clear plans for one but only vague plans for the other. The very rhythm of street life itself militates against long-range planning. As we have emphasized before, it demands a focus on the present: on the next meal, the next night's shelter, enough money to make it through the day.

Outsiders tend to take homelessness for granted and to exhibit the least concern with getting off the streets. Their daily routines and inter-actions are rooted most completely and consistently in street life. Escape from homelessness does not seem a pressing issue for them, and their attempts to get off the streets are usually minimal. Banjo, for instance, kept a daily schedule very similar to that described by Pat Manchester. In fact, occasionally they spent their days together. But, unlike Pat, Banjo seldom turned his attention to getting off the streets.

The fact that some existential dilemmas are more sharply felt by those who have been on the streets a relatively short time raises an interesting issue. Many researchers have suggested that the problems and depriva-tions of the homeless increase with the length of time they are on the streets.[19] Our experience, however, leads us to argue that although this may be true for certain types of problems, especially physical ones, other social and psychological problems (and even subjective perception of physical problems) may decrease in severity as an individual moves toward chronic homelessness. Perceived deprivation and social psychological anxiety are closely related to reference group and expectations, the effectiveness of behavioral repertoires, and sense of personal identity. All of these are more problematic for those who have recently hit the streets than for those who have been there for several years, have developed street-based relationships, and have become knowledgeable about and acclimated to street life.[20]

The inability of the homeless to establish concrete plans of action for getting off the streets stems in large part from the fact that street life is filled with a host of double binds. Lance McKay's situation, mentioned earlier in this chapter, is a case in point: he could not gain admission to a halfway house unless he had a job, but he could not get a job unless he had a verifiable home address. Our field notes are filled with observations of individuals in similar circumstances. These seemingly irresolvable dilemmas have a profound impact on the cognitive orientations of the homeless.

Take, for instance, the case of Eddie and Tiny, to whom Willie introduced us one winter night when we slept at the Sally warehouse. Eddie was a tall, emaciated man in his mid-fifties, although he looked perhaps a decade older. Tiny, whom we introduced earlier, was thirty-one years old, although he could easily have passed for forty-five. They had been pouring concrete foundations for a building contractor until the cold and rainy weather shut down the operation. When they were laid off their boss paid them one hundred dollars each. They desperately wanted to save the money so that they could rent an apartment, but Eddie had gotten concrete burns on his feet, and they were worried that he would get an infection if they stayed at the Sally warehouse, which lacked running water and sanitary facilities, so they paid for a motel room. Eddie explained:

> The only thing we could do was get a motel room for a week. And that cost a hundred and sixty dollars, which meant we only had forty bucks left for food. So there went our savings and now we're back here, broke and outta work. What we wanted to do was put our money in the bank, or send it to Tiny's fiancée to save it for us—you know, just keep a little for cigarettes and stuff and send her the rest so we couldn't spend it. But then my feet got burned, and we had to deal with that.

Eddie and Tiny were deeply disappointed because their work efforts had ultimately cost them as much as they had made. They struggled to keep each other's spirits up by constantly talking about how they were certain to find jobs again soon, but their optimism was difficult to sustain.

The consistent experience of irresolvable dilemmas ultimately takes its toll on the homeless. Faced with failure after failure in their attempts to find steady employment and work their way off the streets, they may come to view their situations as hopeless. The profound demoralization that frequently accompanies such a realization can have serious behavioral consequences. The combination of stress and hopelessness may serve as a rationale for blowing resources built up through hard work and frugality. One twenty-nine-year-old man we met at the Sally, for instance, came to Austin with a job lead and hopes of renting an apartment. He started work the day he arrived in town and worked the next ten days without a day off. But then the bottom fell out:

> The boss gave me a check one night and said there wasn't any more work. I got $325 in pay that day. And I told myself, "I'm saving this for an apartment." But that was on a Monday, and I didn't find anything but a one-day job the rest of the week. When I came here I was thinking everything was ironclad, and then it fucked up on me. And next thing I knew, I was drinking over in a club on the Eastside. I stayed drunk for three days and blew my whole check.

Similarly, Hoyt observed, "A lot of guys don't even know what's happening. They know how they used to live and what they used to have, but it's not like that any more. Nothing works right. And they think about it and they get depressed, so they get drunk and forget about it. It's just a cycle."

A second common response to hopelessness among the homeless is to slip into a state of despondent paralysis. Faced with what they have experienced as nothing more than catch-22s and dead ends, they lose their motivation. We witnessed slips into lassitude in many of our key informants. During February, when Tom was staying near the Sally and trying to figure out how to piece his car together and get a job, he spent days at a time in depression, sitting in his car reading old *Argosy* and *Field and Stream* magazines. Pat Manchester and Ron Whitaker frequently exhibited similar behavior for days or weeks on end, and one week in March Gypsy Bill refused to leave his car except to use the Sally restroom.

Such paralysis is often accompanied or followed by increased identification with street life. Over time the homeless person's resistance to the social role in which he or she has been cast breaks down and ultimately he or she may become engulfed in it. Role engulfment results from the cumulative social psychological impact of street experiences and the labeling of the homeless as defective and therefore to be excluded from conventional employment opportunities and social support.[21] Role engulfment prevents individuals from distancing themselves from their role.[22] Restricted options, derogatory labeling, and pervasive stigmatization become increasingly difficult for some homeless to overcome or deny. This gradual shift in self-identification, which we detailed in Chapter 7, coincides with an acceptance of street life and thus provides relief from the struggle to maintain an identity that transcends the present social situation. At the same time, street peers may come to provide "a haven of self-defense and a place where the individual deviator can openly take the line that he is at least as good as anyone else."[23]

Up to this point we have considered the homeless on the streets and the ways that such cognitive factors as an inability to plan concretely and a sense of hopelessness may impede their chances of escaping the streets. But it is also important to examine how homelessness and the cognitive orientations it fosters affect the experiences of those who manage to get off the streets. Past research on skid-row habitués has noted that a substantial period of homelessness often makes it difficult to reintegrate into the domiciled world even when the opportunity presents itself.[24] The person who has been on the streets often lacks common experiences and a sense of belonging with the domiciled. As one skid-row observer noted, the formerly homeless man may desire companions with whom he can talk of his past experiences, such as "living in institutions . . . fooling the authorities, panhandling, and general Skid Row adventures."[25] His new workmates may have little experience or interest in such activities, however, and may wish to talk about issues more pertinent to their own lives. As a result, the formerly homeless individual may be quite insecure and lonely in their company.

Furthermore, habits developed in response to street experiences may cause cognitive discrepancies in life off the streets. The easy willingness to blow off a day of work in order to spend time with peers, a characteristic quite common among straddlers and the long-term homeless, must now be resisted. Even sexuality may prove to be a source of difficulty in reintegrating into domiciled society, as we learned from the detox counselor who had been on the streets for over a decade:

When you're on the streets, you have the same needs and the same desires as everybody else. Just 'cause you're on the streets doesn't mean you're not going to feel things like sexual needs. And there's no women around, not really. And you've got these feelings and you're gonna take care of them. You've got to do that. And say you're drunk and horny and there's only another guy around. Well, it's just natural you're gonna turn to him. And he may want it as much as you do. Nobody talks about it much, but I know it happens because I've been there. But then, if you get off the streets, you start wondering about yourself. You try to figure it out. Did I do that because I like it or was it just circumstances? And if you didn't have enough on your mind before, now you've got to worry about this. It's just one more thing people can put you down for. I try to spend time talking to guys about this. A lot of them don't want to face it, but it's still in the back of their minds.

Extricating oneself from street life, then, can be a difficult and painful process, especially for the chronically homeless. Just the thought of it may engender fear and resistance. Again, the detox counselor put it well:

After a while the streets are all you know. And you may think about getting back in society and what that would be like, but you don't really know. And it scares you when you really think about trying to do it—fear of the unknown, and of not being able to make it. That's what stops a lot of guys from even trying. Or they'll start to get situated in a job and an apartment and then they'll get scared and blow it and go back to the streets where they don't have to worry about blowing it.

The cognitive factors influencing the careers of the homeless include an inability to form specific plans for extrication, a tendency to focus narrowly on street routines, confusion and demoralization brought on by the double binds of street life, role engulfment, and unfamiliarity and discomfort with conventional social life. Each of these factors tends to mire individuals deeper in homelessness. Since each of these cognitive dilemmas is firmly connected to street life, to transcend them would entail transcending lived experience. This is a crucial point, for researchers on homelessness have traditionally treated the behavioral and cognitive adaptations discussed in this chapter from a middle-class perspective, seeing them as bad habits and fatalistic attitudes that must be overcome in order to be able to take advantage of opportunities for mobility. As we have documented in this chapter, however, to judge the behaviors and cognitions of the homeless by standards outside their world is to distort their meaning. Although the cognitive factors we have discussed in this section may impede the chances of the homeless for getting off the streets, they are usually contextually rational, and sometimes even healthy, responses to the dilemmas the homeless face in their daily lives.

SUMMARY

In concluding this chapter we want to draw out the connections between the four sets of constraining factors and homeless careers. First we address several general issues, then we focus on a number of specific empirical observations and, finally, we examine a number of social-policy implications of our findings.

To begin with, it is important to recognize that although our discussion has separated the various constraining factors into distinct categories for analytic purposes, they actually occur simultaneously, interact with each other, and frequently blur into one another. Together they compose a holistic web in which the homeless are ensnared by multiple strands. This helps explain why disengagement from homelessness is often so difficult. Successful extrication involves cutting through a complex of interrelated entanglements that include a mix of resource deficiencies, institutional dynamics, social ties, and cognitive factors. What is at issue here is neither just the "vulnerability-enhancing disabilities" that have been the focus of so much research nor various exogenous factors that may propel an individual into homelessness. The state of homelessness itself creates problems that impose new barriers to extrication.

One of the oppressive consequences of this web of constraints is that the homeless generally find only a narrow band of career alternatives available to them. By and large they face career moves that reinforce their marginality rather than reduce it. Even when they are able to overcome some constraints, they tend to be kept in place by others. An individual may land a steady job that holds potential for getting off the streets, as did Willie Hastings and Pat Manchester, for instance, but other factors may undermine the person's ability to keep the job. Similarly, even when individuals do manage to find shelter off the streets, as Marilyn did for several months, their meager material resources and social margin render them highly vulnerable to falling back onto the streets. No doubt this is a major reason for the high levels of episodic homelessness noted by other researchers.[26]

Another general observation is that the same adaptations that enable the homeless to adjust to street life also tend to limit their search for opportunities for extrication. In particular, as we have seen, institutional, social, and cognitive accommodations to homelessness may be both rational and functional for street life, but they deflect attention and energy from efforts to get off the streets. This dilemma is recognized by many of the homeless themselves, although they are often unsuccessful in resolving it.

We have noted two major career transitions among the homeless: from recently dislocated to straddlers, and from straddlers to outsiders. We now turn to two sets of empirical observations about these transitions. The first concerns the intervals between them, and the second addresses the issue of extrication.

Familiarization with street life begins soon after an individual becomes homeless, but the shift in status from recently dislocated to straddler may take as much as half a year on the streets. This is because straddler status requires an increasing immersion in street-based patterns of association and survival that results in a resetting of cognitive and behavioral priorities. This, in turn, leads to periodic dissipation of the desire to get off the streets. This fluctuation in concern with extrication is the central distinction between the recently dislocated and straddlers, and it results only from increasing time and experience on the streets.

The transition from straddler to outsider generally appears to take even longer than the shift from recently dislocated to straddler. This is because individuals are capable of maintaining the ambivalent orientation of straddlers for considerable lengths of time and are therefore slow to move from simple acceptance of street life to actual identification with it. Most straddlers resist engulfment, and few of them who have been on the streets for less than two years exhibit strong identification with the role of homeless street person.

The foregoing observations suggest a general proposition: the longer a person is on the streets, the more difficult extrication becomes. The reasons for this flow from the constraining factors we have examined. The personal resources at an individual's disposal diminish over time. Personal possessions, such as tools and clothes, are likely to be sold, pawned, or lost. It becomes progressively more difficult to maintain a car. Work history and skills become more remote. And the possibility of physical disability increases. As personal resources diminish, homeless individuals become more dependent on caretaker agencies and their homeless peers, who provide street-based support, both material and social. The result of these considerations is that the homeless shift their focus from extrication to survival on the streets. Ultimately, if they succumb to role engulfment, they may lose even the desire to leave the streets.

A corollary of this proposition is that the longer someone is on the streets, the more difficult it is for rehabilitative caretaker agencies to assist that person in extrication. As a consequence, the long-term homeless are particularly prone to using rehabilitation programs as rest stops and to be involved in a revolving-door pattern of service use. We do not, however, intend to suggest by this that disengagement from the streets is impossible for the long-term homeless. On the contrary, we occasionally saw seemingly chronically homeless individuals manage to escape the streets. Such examples underscore the mutability of street careers. Nonetheless, such career trajectories appear to be the exception rather than the rule and to require not only acquisition of resources but also an identity transformation. These considerations perhaps help to explain why participation in Alcoholics Anonymous seems to be common among formerly long-term homeless individuals who have made it off the streets.

This brings us to the implications of our findings for social policies intended to alleviate homelessness in the United States. The first, and in many ways most basic, implication is that homelessness will be alleviated only when sufficient resources are allocated to the problem of economical marginality in our society. As we saw in Chapter 8, broad structural forces in American society over the past several decades have operated to reduce housing and other material support for the poor. And in this chapter we have detailed how the resource deficits of the homeless often interact to enmesh them ever more deeply in homelessness over time. It follows that any effective social program dealing with the homeless will have to address the issue of extreme inequality and poverty in American society.

The second policy implication pertains to the dangers of institutionalization of emergency services for the homeless. This is a difficult issue. Emergency service programs provide desperately needed assistance for those who find themselves on the streets, but, as we have seen in this and earlier chapters, they do little more than facilitate accommodation to a destitute existence. They are largely incapable of providing the homeless with the support necessary to get off the streets. Crisis housing for those who are now on the streets is clearly essential, yet we agree with one observer's cautionary statement that "there is also the danger that a shelter 'industry' may develop that acquires a strong stake in the permanent existence of what should rightly be construed as temporary emergency measures."[27]

A third implication that follows from the previous two is that any serious attempt to alleviate the problem of homelessness in the United States must move beyond a perspective based on individual pathology. Such perspectives, as we have suggested throughout the book, tend to blame the victim and thereby misperceive the nature of homelessness. To focus on treating the homeless without changing the sociopolitical and economic context in which they are embedded is to perpetuate a revolving-door policy that uses resources inefficiently, results in repeated failures, and engenders alienation and hopelessness among the homeless.

A fourth implication stems from the finding that homeless street people differ in the degree to which they are anchored in street life behaviorally, socially, and cognitively. Clearly, those who are recently dislocated are likely to be relatively amenable to social service assistance and to be easier to "rescue" from the streets. Similarly, the homeless who fall into the straddler category are probably likelier candidates for being helped off the streets than are outsiders. Implicit in these typological distinctions is a triage approach to dealing with the problem of homelessness at the individual level. Additionally, these distinctions suggest that programs for the homeless that are based solely on differences in their demographics and disabilities will have a lower overall rate of success than they would if they took into account the way differences in patterns of adaptation can affect the prospect of getting off the streets.

Finally, considering the difficulty of effecting permanent extrication from the streets, we need to recognize that measures aimed at preventing homelessness by reducing the number of Americans in such desperate circumstances will be both more effective and more humane than waiting to assist them until they have fallen onto the streets.

Epilogue

In this book we have presented a case study of homeless street people in Austin, Texas, in the mid-1980s. In the first section of the book we observed that street homelessness was distinguished not only by residential dislocation but by attenuation of familial support and a loss of conventional role-based dignity and sense of moral worth. We then developed a typology of homeless street people based on a range of significant behavioral and cognitive variations. In the second section of the book, we turned our attention to the daily routines of the homeless in Austin. Utilizing the typology developed in Part One, we examined the material subsistence strategies, peer relationships, and attempts to salvage a positive identity and sense of meaning on the streets. We also considered the context of street life in Austin, describing the variety of organizational responses and operational perspectives that affect the daily routines of the homeless. Throughout this section we sought to provide the reader with a multiperspectival account of homelessness, albeit one that gave priority to the perspectives of the homeless themselves. In the final section of the book we turned to an examination of the pathways that had led individuals in our study to homelessness and to the common factors in their street careers. Our analysis has emphasized the constraints on the routines and movements of the homeless and the resourceful ways they negotiate those constraints and their environment more generally.

In attempting to put the behaviors, experiences, and perspectives of the homeless in context, we have produced a document that, like all case studies, is necessarily historically situated. Such studies capture social processes and actors in configurations of relationships and perspectives at a specific time. But social configurations change. The situation of the homeless in Austin was far from static even during the course of our fieldwork: neighborhood animosity closed Angels House; the escalating debate over relocation of the Salvation Army pushed the issue of homelessness to the forefront of public consciousness and led to greater public scrutiny of the homeless and their daily routines; the Texas Employment Commission closed its day-labor operation; the Labor Corner was relocated by the city and heavily patrolled by the police; the price of aluminum cans increased substantially, raising the potential profits to be made from collecting cans, but also increasing the competition for them; and the city's economy began to decline dramatically, particularly in building and construction. All these changes had their effect on the daily routines and prospects of Austin's homeless. Furthermore, as we have endeavored to emphasize, homeless individuals changed over time as well. During the course of our research, we saw some individuals extricate themselves from the streets, others become more enmeshed, and still others cycle through phases of episodic homelessness.

In light of the seemingly fluid character of both the organizational context and the careers of the homeless themselves, we thought it appropriate to conclude by considering how the context and lives of the homeless have changed since we completed our research in 1986. With that in mind, we returned to the streets of Austin in late December, 1989, and early January, 1990. Our objectives were twofold: to glimpse the changes in the context of street life in Austin; and to learn what we could about the homeless with whom we had spent considerable time nearly half a decade earlier, especially the twenty key informants whom we had come to know best.

ECOLOGICAL AND INSTITUTIONAL CHANGES

During the period of our research, homelessness became an increasingly high-profile social problem in cities across the country. As a result, many individuals and groups became aware of the plight of the homeless and began to seek ways to help them. In Austin, as in other cities, churches either increased their support for services provided by street agencies such as Caritas, Angels House, and the Salvation Army or developed direct services of their own. For instance, a few churches in Austin started meal and church-service programs. Some disintegrated rapidly; others have remained in operation for several years. These programs are appreciated by many of the homeless, but they are essentially accommodative in nature and, as a consequence, have little long-range impact.

At about the time we left the field, a wave of advocacy for the homeless began to swell in Austin. This activism was led in part by domiciled local activists and in part by several homeless individuals. The results of this advocacy are difficult to assess. Activists have mobilized many of the homeless for several protests and have organized a Street People's Advisory Committee (SPAC) that has been officially recognized by the city and has been consulted about some city policies and services, but most of the homeless we talked to on the streets in the winter of 1990 seemed to have only marginal interest in SPAC's activities.

Some of the homeless did speak highly, however, of a new organization that goes by the acronym HOBO (Helping Our Brother Out). Founded by a group of lawyers who have worked with several members of the Street People's Advisory Committee to develop a variety of services, HOBO provides legal aid, counseling, some meals, and clothing. Like most street-level organizations, HOBO provides a number of basically accommodative services. But it has also developed a transitional housing program that utilizes a broad range of governmental and private forms of support. Unfortunately, the agency can provide for only a small fraction of what staff members see as the deserving poor. As the director of HOBO told us, "We do our best to provide transitional housing, but we can help only 5 percent of the people who could qualify for our help." Our sense is that even this low figure is an overly optimistic assessment.[1]

Probably the most striking change in Austin's street scene occurred in early 1988 when, despite vigorous protests from downtown merchants, Austin's new Salvation Army opened about six blocks from its previous location. Spurred in part by recommendations from the city's task force, the new Sally expanded its services in ways that enable some of the homeless to manage street life better. Twenty-four-hour-a-day laundry and shower facilities make it possible for them to address hygiene and clothing needs on a more regular basis than before. Storage lockers are available at a nominal charge, giving people a way to protect their belongings. A message center and mail service are provided, so that prospective employers and other members of the domiciled world can contact them. The sleeping quarters are vastly better—bright, clean, and air-conditioned—than they were in the "big room" and the warehouse. At the old shelters, users slept on floor mats, often without blankets; today they sleep in bunks with bedding that is washed daily. The new facility includes nearly two hundred beds for homeless single men, nearly seventy beds for women and families, and quarters for formerly homeless employees. In addition, an open courtyard underneath the building is available for shelter day and night.

Another major change in the Sally's operations is a dramatically increased interface with state and local government agencies. The Texas Employment Commission now runs a day-labor operation out of the Sally, thus eliminating the need for the homeless to walk across town in the early morning to look for work. The new facility houses a twenty-bed medical clinic for ill men, with medical personnel provided by the Health Department. The Sally also provides office space for an office of the Veterans Administration, for Alcoholics Anonymous and Narcotics Anonymous meetings, and for counseling services provided by the county. Social services have also expanded dramatically from the days in the earlier facility when the Sally employed only one social worker. Now there are five full-time social workers, four of whom are funded by the city. Pressure from the city has even prompted the Salvation Army to provide meeting space for SPAC, which has been one of the Sally's most vocal critics.

The expanded facility and increase in services have required a larger maintenance and support staff. The operation now employs seven maintenance workers instead of one, and more cooks and kitchen helpers than before. All totaled, thirty-one street people now work for the Sally.

Salvation Army officials are understandably proud of the new facility and programs, especially after the shortcomings of the previous facility and the hard battle waged over a new location. Nonetheless, they recognize a deficiency in their current operations. "There is only one thing missing now," said the former major, who continues to spend many of his days at the Sally even though he retired in June of 1988, not long after the new building opened. "That shortcoming is transitional housing. We just don't have the resources to provide medium-length housing as people get their feet on the ground and try to work their way back into regular lives."[2]

Of course, not all the homeless feel as excited about the new Sally as the major and other full-time staff do. One day we ate lunch at the Sally and then spent some time in the area, talking to people about the differences between the old and the new facilities. One of the people with whom we spoke was a forty-five-year-old man originally from Parkersburg, West Virginia, whom we found wrapped in an overcoat and hiding from the cold wind in an alcove by Caritas, a block and a half from the Sally. The man, who introduced himself as Robert, had been on the streets of Austin for nearly four years. As he sucked on salted sugared peanuts he could not chew because he had long since broken his dentures and had been unable to get them replaced, he told us about his experiences at the new Sally operation:

> Actually, for me and some of the other guys like me, things were better in the old place as far as sleeping goes. See, 'cause in the old place you could stay as long as you needed to, but now they put a limit of one week a month on it. And that means I've got to find someplace else to sleep for the whole rest of the month. A lot of the time you can sleep out somewhere, but in weather like this [temperatures in the teens and twenties] you gotta find an inside spot. I was staying in a park restroom with some other people for a while, but they locked it last week. A couple of nights I couldn't find anything, so I slept down in the bull pen,[3] but finally I found an apartment complex with an unlocked boiler room. I been staying in there for a week, but the way my luck's been going, they'll probably lock it up.

Those familiar with both the old and the new Salvation Army facilities have no doubt that the accommodative services are much improved. Yet, as Robert's comments illustrate, some of the needs of the homeless are still unmet or, at best, are attended to only in part.

KEY INFORMANTS

When we visited Austin in late December of 1989 to see what we could learn about the lives of our informants since the summer of 1986, we initially attempted to locate people by hanging out at the Sally and making institutional rounds. This strategy did not work, as we saw few familiar faces. Occasionally a person remembered some of the people we were asking about, but no one had seen any of them recently.

Our next strategy was to talk to Salvation Army staff and to examine their records for the past year. Staff members failed to recall many of the people we were seeking, and they had no news about those they did remember. The agency's records provided some, albeit sketchy, information about only two of our key informants. Gypsy Bill had spent five nights at the Sally during the previous February, but his file contained no other information. Tom Fisk had also stayed at the Sally for two nights in late October. According to his file, he was passing through Austin on his way from Los Angeles to Florida. When we had last heard from him, two and a half years earlier, he had been living in Ocala,

Florida, and was planning to get married to a woman he had met there. From his file it seems likely that in the autumn of 1989 he was traveling alone.

Our attempts to find Marilyn Fisch and Nona George on the streets were particularly frustrating. Several people said they had seen one or both of them in the past months, but they could not tell us where we might locate them. After looking unsuccessfully for two days, we went to the police department, where an officer who had assisted us in collecting the tracking sample searched the police records for information. He found an August, 1985, incident report in which Marilyn had charged a homeless Hispanic man with trying to rape her in the early morning as she slept in a vacant lot in the downtown area, but there was no record of contact with her since we last spoke with her in the summer of 1986. Considering her rather voluminous incident and arrest record prior to that and the fact that she had appeared in very poor health when we last saw her, it made us uneasy that the police had no more recent contact with Marilyn. Nona, however, had been arrested for public intoxication in late May of 1989 at a local McDonald's. Judging from the location of her arrest, the officer suggested that she might be staying in a camp in a small wooded area between the railroad tracks and a major street in south Austin.

The next morning, in near-record-breaking cold weather, we bought coffee and donuts and headed for the camp. It was easy to find from the road because the members of the camp had set up a Christmas display on a small bridge nearby. They had hung several tattered wreaths and tinsel chains on the bridge and posted two signs, one proclaiming "Happy Birthday, Jesus!" and the other announcing "Your Help Appreciated." Two men layered in clothes stood by the bridge, waving at passersby. When we asked them if they knew Nona, they pointed us toward two campfires about fifty yards up the hill in the woods. We followed the trail to a sprawling campsite consisting of two large tents, a couple of dozen plastic garbage bags bursting with used clothing, a few boxes of cooking utensils, and a small pile of cans of food. Nona was sitting with eight men around the larger campfire, most of whom were drinking sixteen-ounce beers in the cold morning. Wrapped in a dirty ski jacket, Nona sat close to the fire with the smoke blowing in her face, which was noticeably more wrinkled than when we had last seen her. Her hair was matted and filled with sticks and leaves. It took her a minute to recognize us, but once she did, she asked for a cup of our coffee and warmed to telling us about her life since she had last seen us. "I've been okay," she told us, "just staying around here for a couple of years now. I don't go to the Sally any more, or anything like that. I just hang out here with these guys."

"Yeah, we take care of Nona," one of the men chimed in. "We make sure nothing happens to her. Like now, she's got the best sleeping bag we've got."

"Why don't you tell my feet that?" Nona replied jokingly. "They got so cold last night I still can't feel them." She then resumed her story of the past several years. "I finally had to quit working at all, because I've been so sick. I been in the hospital a bunch of times for emphysema, and I've lost some fingers." She took off a glove and held up her right hand, on which two fingers had been cut off at the first knuckle. "One night we were drinking down at the motel and everybody was drunk and I tried to break up a fight, but I ended up with my fingers slammed in the door. So I went up to Brackenridge to get them taken care of, but then they got infected, so they had to cut them off. After that I quit trying to break up fights."

"Yeah, Nona, but that don't mean you don't still start them," one of the men put in.

"Only when I'm drunk," Nona answered. "My temper gets away from me then."

"Sure," he responded, "and you're drunk a lot."

"Yeah, that's true," Nona said, shaking her head resignedly.

When we asked Nona if she could tell us anything about Marilyn, she perked up again. "You mean you haven't heard? Mom isn't a tramp any more! She and her man got jobs and got off the streets a couple of years ago. Yeah, she's working at the motel restaurant now—what's it called?"

No one could remember the name of the motel, but one of the men fished through his wallet and found a scrap of paper with Marilyn's name and a telephone number on it.

Soon the two men who had been standing down at the bridge, waving to passersby, showed up at the campfire. "Not bad, not bad," one of them said with a smile, "a guy just came by and gave us a pecan pie and five bucks." He sat down by the campfire and grabbed a beer. "Now it's someone else's turn to go out to the 'Wall.'"

Over the course of the next several days we found that members of the camp subsisted primarily on such donations and that the 'Wall' was almost always manned during daylight hours. We also witnessed the strength of group members' resolve to maintain their independence from local caretaker agencies. As the temperatures plummeted to record-breaking lows they stubbornly hung on at the camp, refusing to seek shelter at the Sally. In fact, even after a concerned Austin resident came by and offered to put them up in a motel until the weather warmed, several of the men refused to go.

On the day we found Nona, we called the telephone number we had been given for Marilyn. Much to our delight, Marilyn answered the phone. "Yeah, I've been off the streets ever since November of 1986," she informed us, offering to give us her story if we came by the motel coffee shop the next morning.

When we arrived the next morning she was standing behind the counter, wearing a clean dress and a white sweater, with an attractive haircut and a pair of prescription glasses, which she had always sorely needed. We could not help but think of the last time we had seen her on the streets, stumbling drunk and ill up the sidewalk on an August afternoon in 1986, her face swollen almost out of recognition. Considering her condition then, we would not have been surprised to have learned that she had soon died. But here she was before us, sober and in apparently good health.

After exchanging greetings, we sat for the next several hours at the counter of the coffee shop, listening to Marilyn tell us about the changes in her life since we had last seen her:

Yeah, I been working here for thirteen months now. I work a split shift, in the morning as a waitress and then as a cook in the evening. And I got me a place and a car and two dogs and four parakeets. It's a lot different than back when you knew me before, but the strange part's how I got off the streets. I got off the streets because I got TB. Well, if it hadn't been for that, nothing would of happened. But my Higher Power was looking out for me, I guess, without my even knowing it.

See, one day that winter [1986] while we was staying in a camp toward the river, Smitty—we'd been married for nine or ten months by then—gave me ten dollars to go get some Thunder Chicken. We was all drunk down there and I guess I was the soberest, so I got to go. And on my way to the liquor store, I had to pee, so I went down an alley behind a dumpster, and I pulled down my pants, but the police came by and arrested me for that and took me to jail. Then when they got me to jail, they said, "You're coughing so much, you must have pneumonia."

So they took me to Brackenridge Hospital and when they checked me out they found out that I had TB. I was so bad that they sent me by ambulance all the way to San Antonio to the chest hospital. They said I was on the verge of dying when I got there, but I got better in just four months. They called me the "miracle girl" because they hadn't ever seen anyone as sick as me get well so fast.

But the funny thing was that there wasn't anybody on the streets who knew what had happened to me. And Smitty was so drunk that it was four days before he figured out that I hadn't come back with the wine. Then he went looking for me 'cause he thought I'd run off with his money, but he couldn't find me anywhere and he started getting worried. And finally one of the workers at Caritas told him, "Marilyn's in the hospital in San Antone and she's so sick she may die."

And Smitty prayed, "God, if you'll let Marilyn live, I won't ever drink again." And then he went into detox, and when I came back to Austin, we went through a halfway program together and neither of us has had a drink since. Now we go to AA meetings all the time and we go around and pick up other people who don't have cars to get there by themselves.

'Course, there's lotsa people out there who won't go to AA. And I understand, 'cause when you're on the streets it's hard to quit drinking. Like, I was always trying, but then everyone's saying, "Come on, Mom, have a beer," or "Have some wine," and you try to keep away from it, but there's nothing else to look forward to. You can't stay sober on the streets, you just can't. And that's what's happened to Nona. And Debby. Remember Debby? Well, she died on the streets last year from drinking. And Crystal—that's Streeter's old girlfriend—well, she was on a long drunk and she had a stroke. Now she's been in a coma up at Brackenridge for months. And then Bill-Bob was diagnosed as having cirrhosis of the liver and now he's gone back to live with relatives in East Texas, but it's too late. His liver's already shot.

She paused and shook her head. "I'm lucky I made it out—and I know it."

Marilyn went on to talk about the help AA meetings have been to her and how she has gone to several meetings where she has shared the story of her life as an alcoholic:

You know me, I've always loved to ratchet-jaw anyway. And then a while back a woman from England was in Texas and she heard about me, so she called and asked me if she could do an interview. So I said "sure" and she did that and published it in England, I guess. And she said she was going to try to get me on the "Oprah Winfrey Show," but I don't know nothing more about that except that I'd like to go.

Marilyn had clearly come a long way since her days on the streets. However, her life was not problem-free. Her job, although steady, did not pay much, and it provided no sick leave or medical coverage:

If something happens to me, it's all out of my pocket—and I don't make that much to begin with. Smitty works laying foundations, but sometimes he's out of work too. So we never really get ahead, and sometimes we're just hanging on, hoping for our Higher Power to pull us through.

But then you look around, and there's always someone doing way worse than you are. And we try to help out when we can. I go see Nona and take her some food and some money for cigarettes and beer. Right now I'm planning to take her and the guys some dinner: hot turkey, stuffing, and sweet potatoes. They're gonna need it in this weather.

She nodded toward the window and the frigid dawn beyond. "I don't forget where I come from," she concluded. "I was a tramp too long to ever forget that."

Our continuing efforts through the week to locate other key informants met with little success. We contacted several individuals whom we knew had periodic interactions with Jorge Herrera, but none of them had seen him in the past year. We searched the police records for any information on him, but to no avail. Whether he was taken in by an individual or organization, or left town, or died without being found or identified, we simply do not know. Finally, on the last day of our return field visit, after saying goodbye to Nona at her campsite in the late afternoon, we caught a glimpse of Lance McKay walking briskly down the sidewalk of a busy four-lane street. His face was pursed in a troubled scowl and he was carrying a briefcase, much as he had done in the past. By the time we were able to turn around and head back toward where we had seen him, he had disappeared. Since he had not shown up in the Sally files for the previous year, we assume he has some relatively stable housing, but that is all we can surmise.

In sum, then, we were able to acquire varying degrees of information about six of our twenty key informants. Furthermore, as we might have expected, all but one of the six informants were outsiders. The more mobile homeless and those with shorter street careers presumably moved on from the Austin street scene—whether to more stable housing in Austin, to institutionalization, or to other cities, we do not know.

CONCLUSION

Our return to the streets of Austin in the winter of 1989–90 reaffirmed and clarified a number of earlier observations and impressions. We discuss them here not only to highlight a number of the central themes of the book but also because we believe they have implications for how we think about aspects of social life more generally.

The first observation pertains to the transient and dynamic nature of life on the streets. We have noted repeatedly the high level of transience among Austin's homeless, not only in terms of mobility but also in terms of changes in their street careers. This transience was made patently clear upon our return to Austin, as we saw few of the homeless we had known earlier and we were unable to locate fourteen of our key informants. This was also indicated by the changes in the ecology of street life that had occurred since we left the field. Although several of the major services remained in their previous locations, many others had shifted sites. New services, such as HOBO, and new interaction or hanging nodes, such as Nona's campsite, had become important features of the street subculture. As we spent time on the streets during our visit, we were struck that despite our detailed knowledge of the streets just a few years earlier, we had much to learn anew.

Perhaps none of these changes should surprise us, for change is one of the constants of social life. To quote the early Greek philosopher Heraclitus, it is not possible to step twice into the same river. Thus, if another set of researchers were to take to the streets of Austin now, their findings would clearly be somewhat different from ours, at least in terms of names and faces and the ecology of street life. Yet, beneath the surface currents of change, certain features of social life persist.

This takes us to our second thematic observation: street life may at first glance appear to be a shifting, anomic sinkhole, but patient and systematic study reveals that it is highly patterned. This theme was underscored during our visit when we found that despite the changes in faces and context, the day-to-day lives of the homeless appeared to be much the same in the first week of 1990 as in 1984 and 1985. The reasons for the persistence of life-style and routine among the homeless are not hard to fathom. One has to do with the fact that even though services for the homeless in Austin have expanded and become more centralized, they remain essentially accommodative. Additionally, the underlying structural precipitants of homelessness, such as the lack of affordable housing and jobs that pay a living wage, continued to plague Austin as well as the nation. Such unresolved structural problems curtail the opportunities of those on the streets to find a way off them and enforce their dependency on street-level agencies and shadow work, thus ensuring that the basic rhythms and routines of street life remain much the same.

The homeless are not merely pawns in this process, responding lockstep to the structural and organizational constraints they encounter. Rather, they contribute to the production and reproduction of the order of street life by indexing many of their behaviors to such moral codes as "what goes around, comes around," by the social ties they form, and by the sheer necessities of survival. They do not do so because they are all willing players. On the contrary, evidence of resentment and resistance is abundant in the talk, laments, and behaviors of many of them, from the scowls and tirades of Lance, to the disruptive behaviors of Nona, to the determination she and her friends evinced to go it alone, to the emergence of street-level protest organizations like the Street People's Advisory Committee. Nonetheless, the struggle to subsist at the lowest reaches of society, to make do from one day to the next with minimal resources, almost always ensures a semblance of routine and order, however alien it may appear to those higher in the social structure. Street life among the homeless in urban America in the late twentieth century is but another historical example of this process of orderly accommodation among those clinging to the margins. But it is a precarious order, because commitment to it is based on necessity rather than ideology, except perhaps for some of the outsiders for whom homelessness has become a way of life.

Our third observation pertains to the distorted, stereotypic characterization of the homeless that results when viewing them in a decontextualized fashion and focusing on their disabilities and imperfections. To view them in this fashion is a logical extension of the ascendance and power of what Michel Foucault has called the examiner's "normalizing gaze." It is a gaze that takes the reigning conceptions of normality as its baseline and then "compares, differentiates, hierarchizes, homogenizes, and excludes" with little regard for the peculiarity of the context of the objects of examination.[4] The outcome of such a gaze when applied to the homeless is twofold: it pathologizes them as individuals, and it medicalizes their condition. They are, in short, seen as individuals who are primarily crippled and disabled and thus in need of medical curatives, rather than as individuals trying to cope as well as they can with the direst of circumstances. Clearly both characterizations have empirical substance. But, as we have argued throughout the book and as the street career of Marilyn underscores, to focus on disabilities is to produce a distorted characterization in much the same way a make-up mirror distorts the face of its user, magnifying only the blemishes and imperfections.

In our attempts to understand the homeless we have been struck far more by their normalcy than by their pathology. Up close and in context, they are remarkably like most of us in their basic needs, their dreams and desires, their interpersonal strategies, and their proclivity to account for their situation in a fashion that attempts to salvage the self. There are differences, to be sure, but they are not so much qualitative as nuanced and at times exaggerated. Moreover, in most instances, these differences do not flow from frailties of character but are rooted in the profoundly dismal situation in which the homeless find themselves. Confronted with a similar set of circumstances, the behaviors, cognitions, and faces of most citizens would, no doubt, be much the same.

A fifth thematic observation follows: preoccupation with individual disabilities deflects attention from what we have come to think of as "disabling situations" or contexts. The point is that the disabilities or pathologies we tend to associate with individuals are not always so much attributes of individuals as attributes of disabling situations. If the presumably troubled individual is removed from the disabling context or the context is repaired, the disabilities often disappear or at least lose salience. Hoyt Page and Marilyn, among others, mentioned this repeatedly with respect to drinking, and Marilyn's most recent change in lifestyle provides a dramatic illustration of this dynamic.

Marilyn's transformation and the way it came about also informs a sixth theme that has run throughout the book: that many of the homeless are indeed down on their luck, and a change in luck can sometimes produce a dramatic change in life situation. Had Marilyn not been hospitalized after having been arrested for urinating in public, it is quite likely that she would still be on the streets and perhaps even be dead. But the fortuitous event of the arrest set in motion a series of corollary events that led to Marilyn's current domiciled situation. Not all homeless individuals are able to make the most of such changes in fortune or luck, of course. But some, like Marilyn, have the resolve to make the best of whatever situation comes along. Were they unable to do so, many would not have survived as long as they have on the streets.

Considering the frequency with which our homeless informants invoked the luck factor when discussing their life trajectory and considering the fact that seemingly insignificant twists of fate frequently triggered dramatic changes in circumstance, as in Marilyn's case, it appears that the homeless are particularly vulnerable to fortuitous events or happenings. At first glance, such an impression might seem particularly troublesome for sociological analysis, with its emphasis on structural determination and the nonrandomness of social processes and experiences. But it is our sense that although the occurrence of fortuitous events may be randomly distributed across social groupings, the consequences of such occurrences are not. Rather, some individuals are more vulnerable to unanticipated happenings because they have so little to hold them on course once they suffer such turns of fate. Such is the case, we suspect, with most of the homeless.

The poverty of their circumstances may render many of the homeless particularly vulnerable to twists of fate, but it does not follow that their spirits are equally fragile. On the contrary, what has impressed us most about the homeless we came to know and whose stories we have endeavored to tell is their resourcefulness and resilience. Confronted with minimal resources, often stigmatized by the broader society, frequently harassed by community members and by law enforcement officials, and repeatedly frustrated in their attempts to claim the most modest part of the American dream, they nonetheless continue to struggle to survive materially, to develop friendships, however tenuous, with their street peers, and to carve out a sense of meaning and personal identity. To emphasize this is not to romanticize the homeless and their lives but simply to recognize the many ways they confront their often brutalizing circumstances.

But let us not make too much of their resourcefulness and resilience. For the existence of the homeless, no matter how strong their resolve, is an indictment of American society. In the final analysis, then, it should be of little comfort to learn that human beings can in many ways withstand and adapt to the conditions the homeless face. It is, however, a national tragedy and disgrace that they should be forced to do so, whether they number two hundred and fifty thousand or three million.

Notes

CHAPTER ONE

1. The lower estimate cited is based on HUD calculations (Housing and Urban Development, 1984); the higher estimate comes from Hombs and Snyder (1982), but without any indication of the basis for that estimate. For critique of these estimates, as well as counter-estimates based on different procedures, see Burt and Cohen (1989a), Freeman and Hall (1986), and Rossi (1989a). For critical and useful overviews of several of these estimates, see Barak (1991) and Appelbaum, who concludes "that the problem of counting the homeless is, in a practical sense, intractable" (1990: 13). The reason for the ambiguity and debate resides in large part in the nature of the homeless population. It is a recently emergent special population for which few, if any, reliable estimation parameters have been established. Even more significantly, although shelter counts can be conducted easily, it is unclear what proportion of homeless on any given night reside in shelters rather than on the streets. This uncertainty stems from the fact that life on the streets does not lend itself to standard census-style counts, even though many researchers, including the U.S. Bureau of the Census, have proceeded in this fashion. Additionally, many of the homeless are quite transient, which makes it even more difficult to reach a reasonable reckoning. For these reasons, as well as others, counting the homeless has been an inexact enterprise. Nevertheless, numerous counts have been conducted and, as might be expected, the estimates often vary widely.

2. See, for example, Braudel (1982), Lofland (1973), and Sjoberg (1960) for descriptions of homelessness in the preindustrial city; Beier (1985), Mayhew (1985), and Ribton-Turner (1887) for discussions of the early to middle industrial period; and London (1907), Orwell (1933), and Rose (1988) for treatments of nineteenth- and early twentieth-century homelessness in England.

3. See, for example, Baxter and Hopper (1981), Housing and Urban Devel-

opment (1984), Institute of Medicine (1988), Morse et al. (1985), Ringheim (1990a), Roth et al. (1985), and Wright (1989).

4. Rossi (1989a: 48).

5. This quote is taken from Bahr and Caplow's influential definition of homelessness as a condition of disaffiliation (1973: 5). We say our conceptualization is "partly consistent" with theirs because, although we concur that the homeless frequently suffer attenuated familial ties, we find Bahr and Caplow's definition somewhat vague and empirically unfounded. It suggests that the homeless are highly atomized and socially disconnected individuals. As we will discuss in detail in a latter chapter, our research has revealed, among other things, that many of the homeless are actually linked in a fairly active way to an interconnected network of social structures, albeit those are frequently different structures from those to which domiciled individuals are attached.

6. Payne (1958: 391).

7. Guest ([1916] 1958: 391–92).

8. Frost (1964: 18).

9. Lasch (1977).

10. In fact, one consistent finding in disaster research has been that familial bonds are heightened during and following disasters. See Bolin and Trainer (1978) and Drabek and Key (1983).

11. See Banton (1965) for discussion of basic roles, and Hughes (1945) for a treatment of master statuses.

12. This can be seen clearly in public opinion polls. A January, 1989, *New York Times*/CBS News telephone survey of 1,533 people nationwide revealed that 87 percent attributed homelessness, at least in part, to the unwillingness of the homeless to work and that 90 percent thought it resulted in part from drug and alcohol abuse. Other factors noted as contributing to homelessness included the failings of local governments and the domestic policies of the Reagan administration (Oreskes and Toner, 1989). A 1987 telephone survey of a random sample of 293 residents of Nashville found that although 59 percent pointed to structural forces as a significant cause of homelessness, a sizable percentage thought that individualistic factors were also important. Thus, work aversion was believed to be a cause by 45 percent, alcoholism by 45 percent, mental illness by 53 percent, and personal choice by 37 percent (Lee et al., 1990). It is clear from both surveys that although citizens tend to hold a number of causal beliefs simultaneously about homelessness, some of which are contradictory, the personal disabilities and inclinations of the homeless figure prominently in the causal thinking of a majority of domiciled citizens.

13. Public-opinion surveys of beliefs about the homeless have tended to treat the homeless in generic terms. It is our sense, however, based on fieldwork in Austin and Tucson, that attitudes toward and beliefs about the homeless often vary significantly depending on the gender and marital and family status of the homeless individuals. This will be shown more clearly in Chapters 3 and 7.

14. This distinction between the worthy and unworthy homeless parallels a distinction made with respect to the poor in Western history, especially since the decline of feudalism and the evolution in England of what came to be known as the Poor Laws. The British Poor Laws of 1834, for instance, inaugurated the

doctrine of less eligibility, the theory that controlled the approach of the British government to the relief of destitution through the nineteenth century and into the twentieth century. Among other things, it classified the poor into four types: (1) the aged and truly impotent; (2) children; (3) able-bodied females; and (4) able-bodied males (Waxman, 1983: 83). The last group was regarded as the most morally defective and undeserving of support. This classification of the poor into deserving and undeserving categories is also suggested by Matza's (1966a, 1966b) distinction between the reputable and the disreputable poor.

15. Marin (1991), in an essay poignantly titled "The Prejudice Against Men," has noted this tendency as well. The concept of "span of sympathy" as used here is borrowed from Coser (1969) and will be discussed in greater detail in Chapter 7.

16. Although women and children constitute a higher proportion of the homeless population today than in the skid-row era, research has consistently found that the majority of the homeless continues to be made up of unattached adult males (Burt and Cohen, 1989a, 1989b; Momeni, 1989; Rossi, 1989a).

17. Sjoberg (1960: 204).

18. Lofland (1973: 40).

19. Lofland (1973: 42). For an interesting observational account of the homeless in London and Paris during the preindustrial period, see Holmes (1966).

20. See Beier (1985), Cohen and Sokolovsky (1989), and Gilmore (1940).

21. Beier (1985: 4).

22. Beier (1985: 4–7).

23. See Chambliss (1964) and Foote (1956). During this period and most succeeding eras, the terms *vagrancy* and *homelessness* have been used nearly synonymously, although vagrancy explicitly denotes the lack of a visible means of support in addition to a lack of residence.

24. Foote (1956: 615).

25. Chambliss (1964: 70). In other countries as well, vagrancy statutes have originated in state efforts to enforce low-wage labor. See, for instance, Huggins's (1985) detailed treatment of the rise of vagrancy statutes in the Pernambuco province of Brazil.

26. Chambliss (1964).

27. Luther (1860: 3). During this period a literature of roguery developed that presented an exaggerated picture of organized crime among vagrants. For a substantial edited collection of this literature from the Elizabethan period, see Salgado's *Cony-Catchers and Bawdy Baskets* (1972); and for an overview of this literature, albeit one that tends to accept this distorted perspective, see Chandler (1974). The literature of the period also tended to paint the homeless as antisocial tricksters, describing even mentally ill vagrants as frauds. The "Tom O'Bedlam man" was a literary character who feigned to have been a patient at St. Mary of Bethlehem, the major English lunatic asylum in late medieval and early modern times. Such fakery undoubtedly existed, but in fact the hospital administrators encouraged many of Bethlehem's inmates to beg in order to pay their way. Most of the era's mentally ill received no treatment or support but existed precariously in the public domain. For a more thorough discussion of Tom O'Bedlam men, see Beier (1985).

28. Beier (1985: 18).

29. As the informed reader will recognize, these forces parallel many of the structural factors contributing to homelessness today. Such factors will be treated in detail in Chapter 8.

30. Beier (1985: 159).

31. Beier (1985: 151).

32. Beier (1985: 161–64).

33. Rothman (1971: 31).

34. Rossi (1989a: 17). A modernized version of this strategy, sometimes cynically referred to as "Greyhound therapy," was used in New York during the Great Depression (Crouse, 1986) and has been a feature of social policy in some communities during the current wave of homelessness as well (Farr et al., 1986: 269).

35. The first almshouses in the colonies were established in Boston in 1643 and in New York City in 1735 (Hirsch, 1989).

36. This observation is supported by numerous historical studies, including Allsop (1967), Caton (1990), and Wallace (1965).

37. Bruns (1980: 8).

38. Monkkonen (1984: 5).

39. Bruns (1980: 14). See also Edge's *The Main Stem* (1927), a novel from this period; Flynt's chronicle, *Tramping with Tramps* (1899); and the historical studies in Monkkonen (1984).

40. Hoch and Slayton (1989: 29).

41. Anderson (1923: 3).

42. Anderson (1923: 191).

43. Anderson (1923: 161).

44. Bruns (1980: 10).

45. Quoted in Allsop (1967: 110).

46. Diesel locomotives, not needing to take on water for steam, made fewer stops and thus reduced the number of opportunities to catch a train.

47. Wallace (1965: 22).

48. Cited in Wallace (1965: 22).

49. For discussions of this transformation, see Hoch and Slayton (1989: 89–93) and Cohen and Sokolovsky (1989: 53–56).

50. Bendiner (1961: 180).

51. The story of the homeless children of the Depression years has been told by Thomas Minehan (1934).

52. Hoch and Slayton (1989: 76).

53. Crouse (1986).

54. Wallace (1965: 22).

55. Wallace (1965: 22–23).

56. The average age of skid-row men was consistent across a number of the period's studies, including those of Bahr and Caplow (1973), Bogue (1963), and Wallace (1965).

57. Bahr (1973: 91).

58. Bogue (1963: 84).

59. Vander Kooi (1973) and Bahr and Caplow (1973).

60. Bahr (1973: 67–80).

61. Among the studies showing that most skid-row men were not alcoholics were Bogue (1963), Caplow et al. (1958), and Blumberg et al. (1973). As Bahr concluded (1973: 103) after reviewing an array of such studies: "Although perhaps one man out of every three skid-row men is a problem drinker, for whom drinking is the dominant activity of life rather than an avocation, most skid-row men are not problem drinkers."

62. Bahr (1967a) and Bogue (1963).

63. Bahr (1967a) and Rubington (1971).

64. Bahr (1967a). The effects of these market processes with respect to homelessness today are noted in Chapters 3 and 8.

65. Bahr (1967a: 41) and Rubington (1971). For a more thorough empirical analysis of the decline of skid rows in the United States, see Lee (1980).

66. The array of factors accounting for this recent surge in homelessness is discussed in Chapter 8.

67. Studies from around the country in the 1980s have documented a mean age among the homeless of between 33 and 37. See, for instance, Baumann et al. (1985), Brown et al. (1983), Caulk (1983), Robertson et al. (1985), Rossi (1989a), and Roth et al. (1985).

68. See Burt and Cohen (1989a: Table 3.6, 45–47) for descriptive data from around the country.

69. Burt and Cohen (1989a: Table 3.6, 45–47).

70. Rossi (1989b: 65).

71. This is also revealed by a sampling of major research studies on the homeless during this period. See, for instance, Baumann et al. (1985), Burt and Cohen (1989a), LaGory et al. (1989), Lee (1989), Robertson et al. (1985), Roth et al. (1985), and Rossi et al. (1987).

72. In addition, of course, there are discussions of the causes of homelessness, which focus primarily on extreme poverty and the decline in affordable housing (see Barak, 1991: chapter 3; Hope and Young, 1986: chapters 5–7; Ringheim, 1990a; Ropers, 1988: chapter 3; Rossi, 1989a: chapter 7; and Wright, 1989: chapter 3). But discussions of the homeless themselves have focused almost exclusively on demographics and pathologies. See, for example, Institute of Medicine (1988), Lamb (1984), Momeni (1989), Rossi et al. (1987), Rossi (1989a), and Wright (1989). We return to this point in Chapter 8.

73. Geertz (1983: 57–58).

74. The low estimate cited here comes from Baumann et al.'s research (1985); the high estimate was made by the Austin–Travis County Health Department (1984); and the figure of 1,300, which includes both unattached homeless street people and homeless children and families, was issued by the city's Task Force on the Homeless in its final report (City of Austin, 1986). For a discussion of these estimates and an attempt to adjudicate among them, see Baker and Snow (1989).

75. See Denzin (1989a) and Klapp (1964) for discussion of social types.

76. See Lincoln and Guba (1985: 199–202).

77. This terminology was developed in a study of the world of heroin users conducted by Gould et al. (1974).

78. Gould et al. (1974: xxv).

79. Interviewing by comment means attempting to elicit information from an informant by making intentional statements rather than by asking a direct question. Comments can vary, just as questions do, in the degree to which they are focused or unfocused and in their level of specificity or generality, ranging from general and commonplace statements of puzzlement or bewilderment such as "I don't get it" or "I don't understand" to statements that cast others into a specific identity or role such as "He sure looks like a greenhorn" or "I didn't think you were a regular Sally user." For a discussion of interviewing by comment as a supplementary data-gathering technique, the rationale and logic underlying its use, and the variety of forms comments can take, see Snow et al. (1982).

80. See Campbell and Fiske (1959), McGrath et al. (1982), and Webb et al. (1981).

81. Denzin (1989b: 236–37).

82. Denzin (1989b), Douglas (1976), McGrath et al. (1982), and Webb et al. (1981).

83. McCall and Simmons (1969: 29).

84. See, for example, Anderson (1976), Harper (1982), Liebow (1967), and Whyte (1943).

85. This somewhat uncomfortable but necessary aspect of the buddy-researcher role was similarly noted by Liebow (1967: 253), who comments, "I was not always on the giving end and learned somewhat too slowly to accept goods or let myself be treated to drinks even though I knew this would work a hardship on the giver."

86. Liebow also made a conscious effort not to be too noticeably different from his companions. "While remaining conspicuous in speech and perhaps dress," he wrote, "I had dulled some of the characteristics of my background. I probably made myself more accessible to others, and certainly more acceptable to myself" (1967: 225).

87. Regarding his use of this role with young street-corner men in Boston, Whyte (1943: 304) similarly observed, "I learned that people did not expect me to be just like them . . . in fact, they were interested and pleased to find me different, just so long as I took a friendly interest in them."

88. Even though the researcher was released before his two homeless friends were freed, the fact of being arrested and jailed with them proved to be a critical turning point in our fieldwork. Until that occasion, which occurred toward the end of our second month in the field, some of the homeless looked on us with suspicion. A few even had us typed as proselytizing Christians or as "narcs" who were out to bust them for selling drugs. But shortly after the arrest and jailing, the word spread that we were all right, and our rapport with many of the homeless increased immeasurably. It was almost as if we had unwittingly negotiated an important rite of passage.

89. One of the problems hampering research on the homeless has been the difficulty of securing reasonably accurate estimates of their institutional contacts and careers. Institutions that have a broader constituency than the homeless rarely track their clients in a systematic fashion. This is one reason why it

has been difficult to document the presumed relationship between deinstitution-alization and homelessness. Additionally, institutions seldom separate the records of the domiciled from those of the undomiciled. Consequently, research on the institutional contacts of homeless individuals has been limited primarily to interviews on streets or in shelters. Such research has been plagued by three problems. First, the samples are typically nonrepresentative and nonrandom; second, shelter personnel may inflate their constituency estimates in order to make their appeals more compelling; and, third, little effort has been made to validate respondents' self-reports or estimates, whether they come from the homeless or from agency personnel. The tracking strategy represents an attempt to circumvent these problems.

90. Austin is peculiar in having only one shelter. A state report on home-lessness throughout Texas indicated, for example, that Dallas and Forth Worth each had seven shelters, San Antonio four, and Houston over thirty (Texas Health and Human Service Coordinating Council, 1985). And a report by the U.S. Conference of Mayors (1985) indicated that St. Louis, which is only slightly larger than Austin, had twenty-three shelters in 1983.

91. For a critique of lone-ranger research, see Douglas (1976). This is not to say, however, that high-quality research has not been achieved by some individual researchers. For good examples of this style of research, see Anderson (1976), Liebow (1967), Spradley (1970), Whyte (1943), and Wiseman (1970).

92. For discussions of this chronic tension from various points of view, see Merton (1972), Pollner and Emerson (1983), and Rosaldo (1989).

93. Merton called this the "serendipity" component of research: "the discovery, by chance or sagacity, of valid results which were not sought for" (1968: 157). We would extend the notion of serendipity to include the discovery of novel data sources. Such fortuitous observations provide the occasion not only for "developing a new theory or for extending an existing theory," as Merton emphasized (1968: 158), but for also probing deeper into little-explored social and psychological terrain.

94. Cultural domains refer to categories of meaning, events, and problems that constitute the social world and life-style of the homeless (e.g., alcohol, drugs, food, sleeping and shelter, social relationships, work). For a further discussion of the concept of cultural domains, see Spradley (1980: 88–99).

95. Data entries are single pieces of information relevant to any single focal setting, cultural domain, or homeless individual. The data entries, extracted from the field notes, varied from a single sentence to several pages in length and were assigned to one or more of the coding categories.

96. Statistical generalization refers to the enumeration of frequencies for randomly selected samples. This is the more conventional meaning of generalization, but it is not the only one. Yin (1984), for example, distinguishes between statistical generalization and theoretic or analytic generalization, and Stake (1978) speaks of "naturalistic generalization." For an incisive critique of the notion of generalization as conventionally conceived, see Lincoln and Guba (1985).

97. This is what Yin (1984) has in mind when he refers to analytic or theoretic generalization, which, he contends, is one of the rationales for case studies.

98. This is essentially a paraphrase of Geertz's rationale for doing ethnographic research (1973: 13–16).

99. See Van Maanen for a brief discussion of this issue (1988: 65, 72).

100. See Rosaldo (1989).

101. See, for example, Clifford and Marcus (1986) and Denzin (1989a).

102. This is true of all ethnographic writing. "What we call our data," as Geertz (1973: 9), among others, has noted, "are really our own constructions of other people's constructions of what they and their compatriots are up to."

103. See Agar (1986: 17–19) for an elaboration of this conception of ethnography.

CHAPTER TWO

1. Social scientists routinely construct typologies, but usually without articulating the process or the criteria that are used. We attempt in this chapter to be somewhat more clear about how we have proceeded in typologizing the homeless. In the course of our efforts in that direction, we have run across only a handful of works that discuss typologizing analytically. Among the few that do so, we have found particularly instructive those by Lofland and Lofland (1984: 91–97), McKinney (1966; 1970: 235–69), Sjoberg and Nett (1968: 248–56), and Spradley (1980).

2. For a clear and richly illustrated discussion of taxonomic and componential analysis in the context of fieldwork, see Spradley (1970; 1980, especially 112–39). Also see Werner and Schoepfle (1987: 72–108).

3. James (1932: 11–13).

4. Our understanding and application of the concept of subculture is informed primarily by the observations of Fine and Kleinman (1979), Hall and Jefferson (1976), Kornhauser (1978: 1–20), Liebow (1967), Rubington and Weinberg (1981: 257–60), Suttles (1968), Waxman (1983), and Willis (1977). A reading of these and other works suggests that the subculture concept is simultaneously one of the most overworked and most controversial concepts in sociology. Nonetheless, it is constantly invoked, we suspect, because of the heterogeneity of social life in the modern world and because it facilitates an understanding of certain systems of action in ways that other available concepts do not. Certainly that is part of the rationale for our use of the concept in trying to make sense of life on the streets.

5. This conception of subculture as not just cognitive and ideological but heavily behavioral, residing in the responses of social actors to forces in their daily lives, is particularly consistent with cultural studies both in Great Britain (Centre for Contemporary Cultural Studies, 1982; Hall and Jefferson, 1976; Willis, 1977) and in the United States (Giroux, 1983; McLaren, 1988; MacLeod, 1987). One notable feature of this work is its emphasis on and frequent ethnographic attention to the ways that subcultural accommodation and opposition are manifest in behavior.

6. That subcultures can exist without recognizable value orientations and should thus be construed as limited or incomplete is consistent with Liebow's (1967) characterization of the subculture of black street-corner men as a "shadow

culture," Suttles's (1968) analysis of slum subculture, Kornhauser's (1978) critique of cultural approaches to delinquency, Waxman's (1983) reassessment of cultural perspectives on poverty, and Fine and Kleinman's (1979) attempt to rescue the subculture concept and enhance its analytic utility. As Fine and Kleinman (1979: 7) correctly note, "Values (or world views, themes, or folk ideas) . . . do not exhaust cultural content." Thus, to focus on value orientation, as has traditionally been done, deflects attention from the behavioral, artifactual, and interactional aspects of subculture.

7. Anderson (1923, 1931, 1940).

8. The titles of some of the most prominent books on skid row and its homeless inhabitants graphically illustrate this contention. See, for example, Bahr and Caplow's *Old Men Drunk and Sober* (1973), Pittman and Gordon's *Revolving Door: A Study of the Chronic Police Case Inebriate* (1958), Spradley's *You Owe Yourself a Drunk* (1970), Wiseman's *Stations of the Lost: The Treatment of Skid Row Alcoholics* (1970), and, in England, Archard's *Vagrancy, Alcoholism and Social Control* (1979). A sense of the preoccupation with alcohol as a defining feature of homeless men can also be gleaned from perusal of back issues of the *Quarterly Journal of Studies on Alcohol*. See, in particular, Bahr (1969), Jackson and Connor (1953), Rooney (1961), and Rubington (1968).

9. As was noted in note 61 of Chapter 1, only around a third of skid-row residents were regarded as "problem drinkers." Interestingly, research on the homeless of the 1980s reports a parallel finding. In a review of fifteen studies with self-report data on alcohol use among these homeless, for example, 32.7 percent were counted as having problems with alcohol (Rossi, 1989a: 156). The dynamics of drinking on the streets will be explored in subsequent chapters.

10. For discussion of this point, see Becker's (1960) analysis of the relation between "side bets" and commitment.

11. The number or proportion of homeless falling into each typological category should not be construed as representing the typological distribution of unattached homeless adults living in or passing through Austin. Indeed, we can make no claims about the precise distribution of types among the homeless in Austin, since the figures for the field sample were derived, not through random sampling, but through maximum variation sampling, as was described in Chapter 1. We are, however, reasonably confident that we have discerned the range of types and their defining characteristics.

12. Ages given for informants are from the time of first contact with them.

13. Turner (1969, 1974).

14. Turner (1969: 95).

15. See, for example, the ways the concept is used by Becker (1963), Camus (1946), Merton (1972), and Wilson (1965).

16. Turner (1974: 232–33).

17. The classic sociological articulation of this trichotomy was provided by Anderson (1923).

18. Quoted in Bruns (1980: 11).

19. Spradley (1970).

20. Harper (1982).

21. Quoted in Harper (1982: 24).

22. Given their mean age of thirty-one, it is clear that most hippie tramps were too young to have been flower children in the late 1960s. But membership in the initial cohort of a life-style is not necessary for subsequent identification with it. Obviously, most hippie tramps have picked up some of the characteristics of the hippie life-style through a process of association and identification with a handful of homeless who had already adapted it to the exigencies of street life.

23. The police were well aware of her tendency to change her name and in fact listed several of her aliases at the top of her file.

24. We are very much aware of the ambiguity and debate associated with the concept of mental illness (see, for example, Eaton, 1986; Goffman, 1967, 1971; Sarbin, 1969; Scheff, 1966; Sedgwick, 1982; and Szasz, 1961). Indeed, we considered the possibility of describing the individuals who fell into this category as "outcasts," since they are clearly treated as such by other homeless. Nonetheless, we retained the concept of mental illness because the term is used on the streets and because it has been a pervasive feature of the public and media-promulgated image of the homeless—albeit a misguided and overstated one, as we will discuss later. Rather than sidestepping the issue of mental illness among the homeless, then, we thought it best to tackle it directly. In a later chapter we will address the presumption of pervasive mental illness among the homeless and the corollary issue of the relationship between deinstitutionalization and homelessness.

25. We exclude substance abusers from the mentally ill category for two reasons. First, although substance abuse may be rooted in part in personality disorders, neither the abuse nor the underlying disorder is typically associated with mental illness as conventionally conceived. Second, the line between substance abuse and nonpathological use is not always easy to discern, especially among groups such as the homeless. The exclusion of the depressed from the ranks of the mentally ill may engender even greater opposition, particularly from those who approach mental illness in an abstract, decontextualized fashion. But we think such exclusion is warranted in light of the brutalizing and depressing nature of street life itself. Moreover, the use of scales such as the Global Assessment Scale (GAS) and the Center for Epidemiologic Studies Depression Scale (CES-D), to assess depression among the homeless seems to guarantee that a high incidence will be found given the questions asked, such as "Do you feel unhappy about the way your life is going?" and "Do you feel discouraged or worried about your future?" (see Burt and Cohen [1989a]; LaGory et al. [1990]; and Rossi [1989a], among others, for examples of the application of such scales). Aside from confirming the obvious—that life on the streets can be terribly depressing, especially for the less resilient—applications of these scales are suspect because they fail to address whether the measured depression is an artifact of homelessness or an artifact of mental illness, an issue to which we will return in later chapters. A recent governmental evaluation of research using these scales among the homeless concluded that because of these considerations their findings may be highly suspect (General Accounting Office, 1988: 36–37).

26. Some might object to our decision to classify a person as mentally ill

only if two of three field indicators were present, on the grounds that it is "overly strict" (Wright, 1988: 183). Such an inclusion rule is strict, to be sure, but we believe that cross-validation of measures yields more valid findings. This is not only in keeping with the previously discussed principle of triangulation, but it is also consistent with the folk directive that two medical opinions are always better than one. The danger of this more rigorous operationalization of mental illness on the streets is that the actual incidence of such illness may be underestimated. But we thought the risk worth taking, because of the difficulty of distinguishing truly symptomatic communications and behaviors from those that are contextual adaptations subject to being misread as indicative of mental illness. We were also sensitive to the fact that psychiatric diagnostic work is itself a judgmental enterprise (Snow et al., 1988: 193) often prone to misdiagnosis (Lipton and Simon, 1985; Ropers, 1988: 153–55)—particularly, we suspect, in the direction of false positives in nonclinical settings, such as the streets, and among marginal populations, such as the homeless.

27. This assumption is articulated clearly in the work of Goffman (1961a, 1967, 1971) and is summarized by Eaton (1986).

28. For a general discussion of this issue, see Plog and Edgerton (1969) and Eaton (1986).

29. Edgerton (1969: 57).

30. The 10 percent figure should not be read as an accurate count of the number of mentally ill on the streets of Austin. Recall that our ethnographic sampling strategy was to discern the diversity and characteristics of types of homeless, and not the number in each category. The tracking data bearing on this issue, which we will discuss in a later chapter, suggests a somewhat higher figure.

CHAPTER THREE

1. Even the Salvation Army did not have enough toilet facilities for its overnight clients. Off the recreation room, where most of its homeless clients slept, was a single toilet, which could be in use for ten minutes at a time. As a consequence, many, if not most, relieve themselves outside. "What the hell else are they to do?" Hoyt asked us rhetorically.

2. "Jungle" is an old hobo term still in use among today's homeless. It refers to camping spots used by several homeless individuals or groups.

3. Some of these risks speak for themselves; others—mean-spirited citizens and probing surveyors—may require explanation. In some communities, the homeless have been the object of brutal attacks by domiciled citizens. One of the most notorious incidents of such violence occurred in Santa Cruz in the fall of 1984, when there was a rash of assaults on homeless transients—dubbed "trolls" because some of them slept under bridges. The activity was referred to as "troll busting" and spawned the sale of several thousand "Troll Busters" t-shirts with a caricature of a drooling, drunken transient covered by a red circle and a slash (*Los Angeles Times,* October 26, 1984). Rumors of fraternity brothers assaulting hippie tramps were common in Austin, although we never wit-

nessed such attacks. Whatever the frequency of such assaults, they do constitute a risk associated with sleeping rough.

Having one's sleep interrupted by probing survey researchers is also a real risk, although obviously not a terribly dangerous or common one. Nonetheless, in a number of cities throughout the country, researchers have conducted street surveys of homeless in the dead of night in order to reduce the possibility of double-counting persons as they move about later in the day and in order to ascertain the ratio of homeless sleeping rough to those using shelters. Whatever the methodological utility of such a procedure, it raises ethical questions that have been glossed for the most part by both researchers and granting agencies. Are not the hours between 10:00 P.M. and 8:00 A.M. generally regarded as a period in which citizens are not to be disturbed unless the contact has been prearranged or there is an emergency? If so, then why are the homeless not extended the same courtesy domiciled residents take for granted? Would granting agencies fund research to conduct telephone interviews with domiciled citizens at 3:00 A.M.? Although disrupting slumbering or half-awake homeless in the early morning, shining a flashlight in their eyes and then asking them a battery of questions, may be a minor indignity compared to their other sufferings, why heap additional indignities upon them? Perhaps the use of such questionable procedures for studying some populations is as good a measure as there is of how they are actually regarded by both researchers and the general public.

4. The use of the library by the homeless for purposes for which it was neither designed nor intended created problems for the library staff that prompted them to introduce measures to control the ways the homeless used the facility. As the associate director of the city's libraries related:

> A great many of them do use our facilities, but it isn't a big problem now, because we have a list of untolerated behaviors that the security guard gives them. It does seem, though, that more street people run afoul of the rules, especially bathing or washing clothes in the restrooms and sleeping. The central library has a sign outside prohibiting people to bring bedrolls inside, mainly because we're afraid of flea infestation. The ACLU wasn't pleased with this because they felt it discriminated against street people because they are the only ones who have bedrolls, but they didn't take us to court. We've taken out some of the larger seats we have too, but we haven't gone as far as Dallas. In Dallas they removed all but the straight-backed chairs in their new public library.

The homeless continued to use the library, of course, as many still saw it primarily as a refuge from the elements and a place to catch up on their sleep. But pursuit of such ends was made more difficult by the regulations. So it is not surprising that "more street people ran afoul of the rules" and that the police were occasionally called to attend to the rule violators, as in the case of one informant who was arrested nearly a dozen times because of his penchant for using the library as a place to sleep rather than read. For an illustrative commentary on the appropriation of public facilities and spaces by the homeless of an earlier era, see Love (1956).

5. There is a tendency in some historical and fictionalized accounts of the homeless of earlier eras, particularly of the hoboes and tramps of the first third of this century, to romanticize their life-styles (see, for example, Anderson, 1931;

Bruns, 1980; Kennedy, 1983). But this derived in no small part from a parallel tendency among many hoboes themselves. The characterizations of more recent waves of homeless persons, by contrast, tend in the direction of pathologization rather than romanticization. This is partly because many of the homeless of the second half of this century, including the 1980s, have indeed been riddled with disabilities and partly because the discernment of these presumed pathologies has been the focus of much of the research. Yet we suspect that aspects of the life-style of some of these homeless can also engender romantic characterizations in the minds of some observers, particularly those who find oppressive the weight of their everyday lives and who therefore yearn at times to get away from it all. The image of a presumably responsibility-free homeless person following his or her whims and impulses thus strikes a responsive chord. The daily life of the typical homeless person, however, is much more constrained than meets the eye at first glance, as we will see shortly.

6. Operating perspectives are "perspectives in action" rather than "perspectives of action," as discussed in Chapter 1; that is, they are anchored in what an organization actually does rather than in its proclamations or official objectives. To paraphrase Becker's (1970: 49) observations regarding the relationship between values and individual behavior, operating perspectives may approximate but seldom fully embody organizational ideals. This is because operating perspectives typically arise through ongoing resolution of tensions between idealized functions and situational exigencies.

7. Gans (1962: 142).

8. For discussion of such facilities for the down-and-out, see Hoch and Slayton (1989), McSheehy (1979), Siegal (1978), and Wiseman (1970).

9. The Salvation Army made an arrangement with the state whereby the Army would house parolees who had no place to stay upon release.

10. Baffled by the refusal of some homeless to use shelters on cold winter nights, New York City's Mayor Koch, among others, surmised that it must be because "they are not in full possession of their faculties" (*Time,* February 4, 1985). Such judgments are consistent with the tendency of many public officials at all levels of government to sidestep important issues regarding the homeless by invoking the rubric of mental illness. We will return to this point in a later chapter.

11. The Sally's shower facilities, like the entire physical plant, were outdated and over-used. There were too few showers, and there was seldom enough hot water. Consequently, a queue system was established, with homeless men at the bottom. The lines were typically long, and there was no guarantee that a warm shower awaited those who stayed in line. The only other "free" showers in the Austin area were near the jogging trail along the river and at the Central Assembly of God Church, on the outskirts of town and available only on Sundays. Most of the homeless men went for weeks without much of a chance to "really clean up." Ron Whitaker complained continuously about not being able to shower often and about not having "any goddamn clean clothes to change into" when he was lucky enough to take a shower. The YMCA had shower facilities, but they charged several dollars a shot, so few homeless used the "Y." Willie Hastings would use a gay bath in town on occasion. "For $8.00," he

told us, "you can get in there for most of the day and take a shower and a sauna and sleep in the 'orgy room' without anyone bothering you, since everyone's at work during the day." Most of the homeless, though, including Willie, went for weeks on end without bathing.

12. During the early part of our research, Caritas also gave vouchers for rooms at an old downtown hotel. The hotel, which was a landmark of sorts, was leveled for reasons consistent with the revitalization of the downtown, a process we return to later in the chapter.

13. In her ethnographic study of a soup kitchen in an eastern city, Glasser (1988) argues that such facilities provide supportive and accepting "humanized" environments in which the homeless can relax and interact. As the comparison between Angels House and Caritas makes clear, although some soup kitchens are relatively accepting, others are highly critical, strict environments.

14. Not only was Angels' mission of spiritual regeneration foiled, but eventually so was its mission of providing physical sustenance. At the end of the summer of 1985, Angels House was closed, in part because neighborhood animosity became more vociferous and in part because the city's Task Force on Homelessness was not supportive of Angels' plight. In the letter the director of Angels sent to the task force explaining the closure, he commented exasperatedly, "Even Jesus knew when he wasn't wanted."

15. For a more thorough discussion of the health problems of the homeless in Austin, see Baumann et al. (1985) and Snow (1989: 58–64). For detailed and systematic assessment of the health condition of the homeless across the country, see Brickner et al. (1985), Drapkin (1990), Institute of Medicine (1988), and Wright and Weber (1987).

16. See Baumann et al. (1987).

17. Our calculations suggest that the total cost of medical treatment for the homeless in this hospital in 1984 was about three million dollars. This constituted between a quarter and a third of the hospital's "bad debt" for that year. The bulk of the remainder of the debt was attributable to another group of indigents—"illegal aliens." Hospital officials speculated that this indigent population may pose an even greater financial burden for the hospital than do the homeless as traditionally conceived.

18. The corresponding figures for the state population of institutionalized males in 1984 are strikingly different: 44 percent were hospitalized for less than 30 days, and around 25 percent were institutionalized for three months or longer. Comparisons of diagnoses and of primary type of commitment also reveal significant differences, thus suggesting that the state mental hospital experiences of the homeless and nonhomeless are remarkably different (see Snow et al., 1986a).

19. The finding that only 16 percent of the tracking sample had contact with the Texas mental health system suggests an incidence of mental illness among the homeless in Austin that is much lower than has been found in most other cities. Indeed, some estimates of the incidence of mental illness among the homeless have been in the 75 to 90 percent range (Arce et al., 1983; Bassuk, 1984; Lipton et al., 1983), although the modal estimate appears to fall in the 25 to 35 percent range (see General Accounting Office, 1988; Rossi, 1989a; Wright, 1988). How

are these varying estimates reconciled? That is a question that has generated considerable discussion (General Accounting Office, 1988; Piliavin et al., 1989; Snow et al., 1986a, 1988; Wright, 1988). Our own position, as suggested in the previous chapter and elaborated in Chapters 7 and 8, is that the general tendency has been to overestimate the incidence of mental illness on the streets.

20. For a description and analysis of skid-row rescue missions, see Anderson (1923), Bogue (1963), McSheehy (1979), Rooney (1980), and Wiseman (1970).

21. This revolving-door pattern seems to be an almost universal feature of street life for the homeless with chronic drinking problems: see Archard (1979); Bahr and Caplow (1973); Pittman and Gordon (1958); Spradley (1970); Wiseman (1970).

22. Nels Anderson, in his work on the homeless of the 1920s, described two types of private employment agencies in Chicago during that period: "commission agencies" that charged employers or employees or both, and "commissary agencies" that charged nothing for finding jobs but made their money on boarding houses for the men they hired (1923: 112–14). The Labor Pool/Bunkhaus operation profitably combines the two types.

23. This complaint is actually more valid for women joggers than males. As we will discuss in more detail later, one of the favored afternoon activities of some of the younger homeless men is to hang out along the jogging trail near the river, calling out to women as they jog or walk by. The women either ignore the calls and taunts or nervously acknowledge them as they pass. In either case, the encounters are uncomfortable for the women and prompt numerous calls to City Hall.

24. Social Policy Advisory Committee Task Force on Transients (1983).

25. For a detailed examination of the evolution and career of this community dispute and the way the homeless were framed, see Worden (1987).

26. This is another striking example of what was dubbed in the 1980s as the "NIMBY" (Not in my backyard) phenomenon, a knee-jerk, defensive reaction by neighborhood residents to the proximate location of facilities for "undesirables." Halfway houses, group homes, and restitution centers, as well as shelters and soup kitchens, have been common objects of NIMBY mobilization. The NIMBY response to the Sally in Austin was hardly endorsed by all citizens; some, including the editors of the local newspaper, found it quite troubling. As one of their editorials asked rhetorically, " 'Sally': What Kind of Place Is Austin?" (*Austin American-Statesman*, July 28, 1985). One answer is that it is not all that different from many other places that responded in a similar fashion to the homeless, including Queens (*New York Times*, June 7, 1985), Cambridge (*Austin American-Statesman*, January 16, 1986), Wichita Falls (*Austin American-Statesman*, December 13, 1987), Galveston (*Austin American-Statesman*, November 30, 1985), and Tucson (Hostetler, 1986). Underlying opposition to homeless encroachment in these as well as other communities were the same kinds of beliefs and fears that were so pronounced in Austin.

27. These figures, although generated rather haphazardly, are quite consistent with the arrest profile of the homeless we tracked through the police department. Those findings show that nearly 80 percent of the arrests are for

misdemeanors, with 51 percent of all arrests being substance-related. The nature and derivation of this data will be discussed in more detail in Chapter 5.

28. The second task force was constituted by the city council in April, 1985. Its primary mission was to find a suitable location for the beleaguered Salvation Army. Once that was accomplished, nearly six months later (largely because of the financial goodwill of an investor-developer who sat on the task force), attention was turned to studying what steps might be taken to ameliorate the situation of the homeless in the community. A *Final Report* was issued some nine months later. Its recommendations begin with basic services and culminate in transitional housing (City of Austin, 1986). The recommendations were quite reasonable from the vantage point of those interested in the plight of the homeless, but taken together they were expensive, especially for a city in the throes of an economic downturn. Nonetheless, a number of the recommendations were incorporated into the design and organization of the new Salvation Army. For an informative examination of the operation and composition of the task force—it included, among others, several developers and four individuals who had fought the Sally over previous sites—see Worden (1987, especially chapters 5 through 7).

29. This same orientation was emphasized by Bittner (1967) and Wiseman (1970) in their observations on police work on skid row.

30. Chief of Police (August 3, 1983), Memorandum to City Manager.

31. Bittner (1967: 709).

32. Other studies have pointed to harassment in police work with the homeless (Aulette and Aulette, 1987; Barak, 1991: 75–99).

33. It is worth noting that 66 percent of the arrests of homeless in our tracking sample took place within the four police sectors that converge in the downtown area west of the interstate freeway.

34. The public/private dichotomy is the more conventional way of categorizing urban space. Private spaces are those areas to which access is legally restricted to owners, renters, and invited guests. Public spaces, exemplified by parks, malls, streets, and sidewalks, are legally accessible to all citizens (see Goffman, 1963a, and Lofland, 1973, for a more detailed discussion of this distinction). Such a distinction may be of some utility to the ordinary domiciled citizen, but it is of little value to the homeless, for, by definition, private spaces are almost always closed to them. Nor does the concept of public space address their needs. After all, are parks fully public if a city ordinance prohibits the homeless from sleeping in them? Are sidewalks public if the police mobilize on behalf of business interests to drive the homeless from the streets, as was attempted along the Drag and Sixth Street?

35. This distinction is developed by Duncan (1983) in his discussion of "the tramps' clarification and use of urban space." Our discussion draws on and extends Duncan's analysis.

36. See Bogue (1963: 61–62), Duncan (1983: 92–93), Dunham (1953: 30), and Wiseman (1970: 66–67).

37. As is emphasized by those who take a constructionist approach to the analysis of space (Duncan, 1983; Ericksen, 1981), the value of space does not inhere in the space itself. Rather, it is imputed to it on the basis of its uses or

significance. Consequently, the value of space is subject to change as its use and meaning change. Additionally, we would emphasize, consistent with those who take a more political-economy approach to the analysis of space (Castells, 1983; Feagin, 1988; Logan and Molotch, 1987), that since different sets of actors often attach different meanings to the same unit of space, its definition is often embroiled in community conflict and is ultimately a political issue.

38. See Feagin (1986), Logan and Molotch (1987), and Smith (1983).

39. The bar frequented most often by some of the homeless was closed in the spring of 1985. Its epitaph, featured in the *Austin American-Statesman* (March 5, 1985), provides a sense of the scope of the downtown redevelopment from the vantage point of one of the bar's customers: "The Lounge, which one long-time customer described as the last of the skid-row bars on lower Congress Avenue, has closed. 'Big business is taking over downtown,' lamented the customer, who was there when the bar served its last beer at 4 P.M. Sunday. The Lounge, on the east side of Congress in the 200 block, lost its lease in the wake of the renovation of downtown. Two years ago, the Breezeway and Punch's Lounge were closed on the block."

40. We think these processes have changed the nature of police work somewhat with respect to the homeless and the down-and-out. Previous research on the police on skid row emphasized their "peacekeeping" function (Bittner, 1967; Wiseman, 1970). The police still serve this function in part, but, as we have noted, their encounters with the homeless seem to have become more complex and conflictual, involving frequent harassment and arrest.

41. Duncan (1983: 94).

42. Following Wilson (1975) and Hunter (1985), it might be argued that the problem of homelessness, from the vantage point of domiciled citizens, is not so much the existence of the homeless as their public visibility, which makes them likely "symbols of incivility" (Hunter, 1985) and thereby produces or intensifies a sense of "urban unease" (Wilson, 1975).

43. Lyn Lofland (1973) has argued that the potential chaos and unpredictability of urban life is reduced by two kinds of order: the appearential, which allows citizens to identify others on the basis of their clothing, hairstyle, markings, and the like; and the spatial, which allows citizens to identify others on the basis of expectations about what kinds of people should be found in one place rather than another. Lofland's thesis is that the historical trend of urban life has been away from the appearential basis of order and toward the spatial, as is indicated by the increased spatial segregation of both activities and persons. If this is indeed the case, then it is no wonder that the spread of the homeless is viewed with such concern by some citizens, for their increasing numbers in areas traditionally reserved for other citizens implies a rupture of the spatial bedrock on which the urban order rests.

44. Their near-universality is suggested by the array of interactional contexts in which they are found to be operative, ranging from work settings (Dalton, 1959; Roy, 1957), to residential neighborhoods (Gans, 1962; Suttles, 1968), to prisons and asylums (Goffman, 1961a; Irwin, 1970) to peer groups and gangs (Anderson, 1976; Whyte, 1943).

45. See Cohen and Felson (1979).

46. For a more thorough discussion of these findings, see Snow et al. (1989).

47. Gouldner (1960).

48. How do such moral codes arise? They are never purely individualistic constructions, nor are they determined solely by structural forces, survival requisites, or broad, overarching value orientations. Instead, they are conjunctural entities that emerge out of the confluence of structural, cultural, and situational constraints. In street life, they arise at the intersection of the kinds of organizational, political, and ecological constraints we have elaborated, and they are intertwined with strands of culturally salient values that are relevant to making do on the streets. Moral codes, then, are emergent, collective, and negotiated understandings that give rise to a kind of interactional order in a specific context.

CHAPTER FOUR

1. Hughes (1958: 43).

2. Barton (1981: 49).

3. Marx's thoughts on work and the labor process are strung throughout most of his writings, but see in particular his early manuscripts (1932) and his essay titled "Wage Labor and Capital" (1849).

4. Anderson (1923: 121).

5. As noted in note 12 in Chapter 1, surveys of cross-sections of Americans indicate that a sizable proportion subscribe to this sentiment. Such negative, stereotypic beliefs about the homeless were commonplace in other eras as well (see Bahr, 1973: 39–86). Although some research suggests that there has been an increase in the public's willingness to blame homelessness on external factors rather than individualistic ones (Lee et al., 1990), the belief that many homeless are lazy remains widespread.

6. *Austin American-Statesman* (August 2, 1985).

7. Cited in a Associated Press release reported in an article in the *Austin American-Statesman* (March 21, 1981).

8. Each occupation was coded according to the *Dictionary of Occupational Titles* (U.S. Department of Labor, 1977) and then collapsed into one of the standard occupational categories used by the U.S. Bureau of the Census and the Department of Labor and found in most discussions of the U.S. work force.

9. The white-collar/blue-collar division, although useful for some purposes, has become increasingly misleading over the years, as jobs previously classified fairly neatly in one category or the other have become more difficult to classify in terms of these traditional categories. For a discussion of the classificatory problems, see Hodson and Sullivan (1990: 47–49).

10. This occupational distribution is consistent with Baumann's August, 1984, street survey of homeless in Austin. Of the 182 who provided work-related information, 78 percent indicated recent jobs that were either semi-skilled or unskilled (Baumann et al., 1985).

11. The secondary labor market consists of low-status, low-paying, and highly routinized jobs held by semi-skilled and unskilled nonfarm laborers and service workers.

12. This resource deficit is neither peculiar to the homeless in Austin nor to the homeless of the 1980s. Research on the homeless of Chicago, for example, shows that the homeless of the 1980s, as well as of earlier times, tend to be congregated at the bottom of the occupational structure in terms of both skills and work experiences. Rossi's study found that around 75 percent of the jobs held most recently by the 700-plus homeless interviewed were semi-skilled or unskilled. For instance, 37.3 percent were general laboring jobs, around 21 percent were service jobs, and 15.9 percent involved newspaper sales (Rossi, 1989a: 135–37). The job profile of the homeless studied by Bogue thirty years earlier was strikingly similar, with around 78 percent of recent jobs falling into the unskilled, semi-skilled, and service categories (Bogue, 1963: 176). Bahr and Caplow's (1973: 38–39) examination of the occupational distribution of earlier skid-row habitués in six major cities also revealed a low skill level among them, with the vast majority employed in unskilled labor and service work.

13. The state and national male work forces are used as the basis for comparison because the tracking sample from which these work data on the homeless were derived is predominantly male.

14. The determination of whether a given job listing was available to a homeless person was based on several criteria. Job listings were included if they did not require more than three months' experience or any formal training; a driver's license or personal transportation; local references or a stable work history; or possession of tools for use on the job. Jobs distant from the Salvation Army were included as available, despite the difficulties the homeless might have in arranging transportation.

15. Baumann's survey (Baumann et al., 1985) of homeless street people in Austin in August, 1984, reports that two-thirds (of 498) said they came to Austin looking for work. Although this is somewhat fewer than we found, it still represents a substantial majority. Other research in Sunbelt and western cities also indicates that the in-migration of homeless is prompted more by the search for work than by any other single factor (Brown et al., 1983; Robertson et al., 1985).

16. Caplowitz (1967: 15).

17. Day-labor agencies were a standard feature of skid rows, as has been documented by Bahr (1973), Bogue (1963), and McSheehy (1979). Wright (1989: 93) has recently argued that the "disappearance of day labor outlets has been no less complete" than the disappearance of SRO housing in skid-row areas. This appears to be an overgeneralization, however, as it was the case neither for Austin nor for the cities examined in the Southern Regional Council's 1988 report, *Hard Labor*. See also Wiegand's (1990) discussion of day labor use among the homeless in Nashville.

18. TEC had three agency offices within the city. Each used to operate a day-labor service, but that changed in the early 1980s when a decision was made to centralize day labor in the downtown office. According to that agency's manager, this decision was prompted by the belief that people looking for more "normal jobs" were avoiding these other offices because of "their fear of the transients." He stressed that "day laborers are an unsavory and sometimes obnoxious group and we felt it would be best to get them all in one place." More-

over, "there is a tremendous amount of filth associated with these people—beer cans and wine bottles and trash. We were afraid we were going to lose our leases on the other two buildings because of them. We own this building, so we decided to have the whole day labor here in the same place."

19. Liebow (1967: 40).

20. The Labor Pool was an exception to this tendency, as we noted earlier. Since it acted as the mediator between employers and laborers, it made employer contributions and extracted the standard deductions.

21. The vulnerability of the homeless to unscrupulous employers was highlighted when legal authorities discovered a forced-labor ranch in the Texas hill country near Austin in the mid-1980s. During the trial of the ranch owner, his son, and the ranch foreman, witnesses testified that laborers for the ranch had been recruited from among the homeless on the streets of San Antonio and by picking up hitchhikers. Over a period of a year and a half, about a hundred and twenty laborers were recruited. Several were tortured for not working hard enough, and at least one was brutally tortured in taped sessions and then was murdered (see Hathcock, 1986). The homeless are particularly vulnerable because they are often willing to take the dregs of work, they are unlikely to take legal action against exploitation, and many do not have friends and loved ones who would search for them extensively if they were missing.

22. This attitude has been noted by other observers of homelessness. In their overview of homelessness in America in the 1980s, Hope and Young (1986: 200) relate that "many of the wandering new poor we have met in our travels expressed the conviction that they would surely find that good job—it was only a matter of keeping on trying."

23. Gouldner (1960: 171).

24. What we here call institutional labor is an integral aspect of the operation of holding institutions, such as prisons and asylums, as well as of in-house rehabilitation programs. For a discussion of such work in prisons, see Mitford (1974: 207–35); for asylums, see Goffman (1961a); and for skid-row alcohol rehabilitation agencies, see Wiseman (1970: 174–76, 252–53).

25. These comments are remarkably similar to those recorded by Wiseman in her analysis of work therapy in the skid-row missions she studied in the late 1960s (Wiseman, 1970: 174–81). Apparently, the philosophic underpinning for the structure and organization of such rehabilitation work has changed little over the years.

26. This is also consistent with Wiseman's earlier (1970) findings.

27. Other marginal populations have been found to make similar use of such facilities in inclement weather. See Brown (1987).

28. This was verified late one afternoon as one of us was standing in the Sally dinner line. A van from the agency Willie had been telling us about was seen cruising the area, with the driver stopping to talk to small clusters of men about entering its program.

29. Goffman refers to such positions as "discrepant roles" in that they place the incumbents in highly liminal situations (1959: 141–66).

30. Wiseman (1970).

31. For a succinct overview of transfer programs, see Hope and Young (1986:

201–10). For more detailed discussions of such programs, particularly as they pertain to poverty, see Danziger and Weinberg (1986), Ellwood (1988), Katz (1986), and Stein (1971). For a critical analysis of the social-control functions of such programs, see Piven and Cloward (1971).

32. These findings are quite consistent with those of the Baumann study, which found that only 2 percent of the Austin street homeless interviewed counted public assistance as their major source of income (Baumann et al., 1985: 126).

33. A 1985 state report on homelessness in Texas indicated that residency requirements pose a serious problem for the homeless statewide. The report notes that "the residence requirements for state-funded programs, whether based on federal, school district, . . . county, city, or catchment area . . . guidelines are restrictive and make it difficult for the homeless to qualify for services. By their nature, residence requirements most adversely affect the homeless who are transient, migrant workers, and undocumented aliens" (Texas Health and Human Service Coordinating Council, 1985: 20).

34. The decentralization of public services has been recognized on the local and state levels in Texas, as well as elsewhere, as one of the central dilemmas confronting both the homeless and the social-service system. See the City of Austin (1986) task force report on the homeless, and the Texas Health and Human Service Coordinating Council's (1985) report on homelessness in Texas. For a compelling account of the problems faced by homeless families due to the decentralization of public services, see Kozol (1988).

35. Sjoberg et al. (1966: 329).

36. Sjoberg et al. (1966: 330–32).

37. Substantiation of the bureaucratic hassles and frustrations associated with seeking public assistance comes in part from surveys of the homeless elsewhere. A survey of a sample of homeless in New York City revealed, for example, that 54 percent failed to receive assistance because the application process was too confusing and lengthy, and another 20 percent just could not deal with the bureaucratic hassle of the whole process. Another 16 percent indicated that they were ineligible for assistance because they had neither an address nor proper identification. See the report of the Human Resources Administration of the City of New York in U.S. House Committee on Government Operations (1985).

38. He did "blow it" promptly. A few weeks after he had received that sizable check, we met him near the university and gave him a ride downtown. When he jumped into the car, he proudly showed us a leather briefcase he was carrying, as well as a number of expensive pens and other "clerical supplies," as he called them. At times Lance fancied himself as a business executive, and the briefcase functioned as a kind of identity marker. As he exclaimed, "Lots of business executives don't have a briefcase that costs this much." He was right, too, for he had purchased the briefcase from an expensive downtown leather shop for nearly $400. The briefcase and "clerical supplies" were all he had left to show for the check.

39. In her analysis of American families in the twentieth century, Bane (1976: 42–44) reported that a majority of young adults between the ages of 18 and 24 now live with their parents until marriage, and that a substantial proportion do

the same while in college. In addition to providing bed and board (surely a form of indirect financial assistance) for their offspring beyond high school, parents also often give or lend money, even to their married children.

40. As we will see in a subsequent chapter, and as has been widely documented, the bulk of the homeless come from poverty-level backgrounds. See, in particular, Rossi (1989a).

41. Research in Phoenix (Brown et al., 1983), Los Angeles (Ropers, 1988), and Ohio (Roth et al., 1985) clearly showed this to be the case. In Los Angeles, for example, 68 percent of the 236 homeless who provided information on their employment status indicated that they were either working (20 percent) or looking for work (48.5 percent) (Ropers, 1988: 43).

42. See, in particular, Brown et al. (1983: 44–46) and Rossi (1989a: 108–14).

43. The Urban Institute cross-sectional national survey of 1,704 homeless revealed that around 20 percent received AFDC, General Assistance, or SSI (Burt and Cohen, 1989a: 43). See also Ropers (1988: 36–37) and Rossi (1989a: 108–14).

44. See Burt and Cohen (1989a: 43) and Robertson et al. (1985: 53–55), as well as Marin (1991).

CHAPTER FIVE

1. Although textual discussions of work do not always specify the criteria used to distinguish it from nonwork, three criteria can be culled from most such discussions: remuneration, regulation, and enumeration. Thus, work as conventionally conceived is an activity for which an individual is paid; time, place, and rate of pay are regulated; and it can be enumerated or counted by local, state, and federal governments. These criteria result in a rather "limited set of activities and roles that are deemed legitimate ways of making a living" (Miller, 1981: 133). This narrow focus has begun to expand in recent years, however, with the growing recognition, due in part to the feminist movement, that non-occupational tasks such as housework and volunteer activities also constitute work, as do various illegal enterprises, such as prostitution, fencing, numbers-running, and drug-dealing, which are typically described as "deviant work." Still, the focus of most textual discussions of work is on jobs, occupations, and professions (Hodson and Sullivan, 1990; Miller, 1981; and Ritzer and Walczak, 1986).

Moreover, since so much of what we know about conventional work is based on government statistics, it is understandable that some students of work and labor processes emphasize state regulation as the key factor in their conceptualization (Lozano, 1983; Portes and Walton, 1981).

2. The concept of shadow work is borrowed from the philosopher, historian, and social critic Ivan Illich (1981). Illich uses the term for unpaid work that is a necessary requisite for and complement to productive and consumptive activity, such as housework, grocery-shopping, and commuting. We use the term somewhat differently, to refer to unpaid subsistence activities. We do so for several reasons. For one thing, it resonates with the obdurate fact that the

subsistence strategies engaged in by the homeless take place in the shadow of regular work. Additionally, it is consistent with the adaptive and behavioral thrust of our conceptualization of the subculture of street life. And, finally, we find *shadow work* preferable to a number of kindred terms. Some labor economists and students of informal sector activity in the Third World have used the term *nonmarket work* to encompass "all work not performed for wages, profits, or rents, including housework and even commuting work" (Uzzell, 1980: 42). But not all shadow work is nonmarket work. As we shall see shortly, some types of shadow work exist only within a market context, but the market is neither officially regulated nor sanctioned. Instead, it is an ephemeral one that exists outside the dominant economic system and thus constitutes part of the "shadow economy" (for a brief discussion of the shadow economy, see Hodson and Sullivan, 1990: 332–36). Another cognate cover term is *hustling work* (Miller, 1981). This term is too broad for our purposes. It encompasses not only what we have called shadow work but other kinds of work that are typically sanctioned and linked to fairly well-defined markets. Even more troublesome, hustling is not peculiar to shadow work but can be relevant to almost any kind of work. Like the panhandler or scavenger, the professional athlete, hot dog vendor, secretary, and floor trader can all hustle. For all these reasons, then, we find the term *shadow work* the most conceptually suitable and resonant cover term for the array of unpaid subsistence strategies engaged in by the homeless.

    3. Wiseman (1970: 27).

    4. Hopper et al. (1985: 194). Although Hopper and his associates correctly argue that the makeshift activities we call shadow work figure prominently in the life-style and subsistence of the homeless, neither they nor other students of the homeless of the 1980s have examined these activities in a detailed and systematic fashion. To be sure, a handful of survey studies have asked the homeless about their income sources and have found that a number of activities we call shadow work (e.g., panhandling, selling cans, selling plasma) are engaged in by many of the homeless (Baumann et al., 1985: 124–26; Brown et al., 1983: 44–46; Burt and Cohen, 1989a: 43; Robertson et al., 1985: 53–54; and Rossi, 1989a: 108–14). But substantial discussion of these findings is rare (for an exception, see Wiegand, 1990).

    Moreover, when the homeless are asked about their sources of income, the phrasing of the questions often elicits the most important sources, rather than how they interact or are used in combination. The findings of two studies that asked the question about income sources in two different ways are particularly revealing in this regard. When asked in Phoenix how they "usually supported themselves," 17 percent of 184 homeless indicated some form of shadow work, with another 46 percent pointing to a combination of means, 70 percent of which included shadow work. All totaled, it was found that nearly 56 percent had engaged in shadow work (Brown et al., 1983: 45). In the August, 1984, street survey in Austin, the homeless were asked not only about income sources but also about their relative importance. Relatively few pointed to shadow work as their most important source of income (only 9 percent), but it was the second most frequently listed source of income for 53 percent of the 117 homeless respondents (Baumann et al., 1985: 124–26).

A final confounding problem with the way income sources have been pursued by survey procedures is that the questions are typically followed by a fixed list of choices that rarely encompasses the full range of shadow work. Even if the responses are open-ended, it is likely that some of the criminal and more stigmatizing forms of shadow work will not be mentioned by all who have engaged in them. These considerations, then, give good reason to presume that shadow work is a more important means of subsistence among the homeless than some of the research would have us believe.

5. It is important to keep in mind that the distinction between junk and reasonably attractive personal possessions is largely subjective. As symbolic interactionists have reminded us, the meaning of an object resides in its use or function in a given situation (Blumer, 1969). Thus, what is defined as junk and what as nonjunk is likely to vary not only from person to person but also from one situation to the next. To the homeless, what is seen as a worthy personal possession one day may be redefined as a salable item or a piece of junk the next day.

6. For an interesting and relevant discussion of garage sales, see Herrman and Soiffer (1984). They note that although the motives underlying garage sales can be quite varied, often they function as an adaptive survival strategy when times are difficult economically. For a recent analysis of estate sales and auctions, see Smith (1989).

7. We have no clear idea how common situations such as Tom's are, but we know that the selling of automobile parts is commonplace, at least in Austin. It is worth noting that it is not particularly in the interests of the police to impound these cars: nearly all of them are old, battered clunkers, often hard to impound because they are up on blocks without tires. Consequently, the cars frequently are allowed to sit for some time before police action is taken.

8. We neither observed nor learned of more expensive drugs being sold by regular straddlers to homeless individuals. Some of the homeless might be interested in obtaining such drugs, but most lack the money to buy them. It is also important to note that our research was conducted in 1984 to 1986, before "crack," a relatively new and cheap form of cocaine, was available, at least on the streets of Austin.

9. Writing of sex and prostitution in the nineteenth century, Tannahill observes that "the girls who became prostitutes in [this] century usually did so because they needed the money. At one end of the scale there was the independent-minded career woman who knew that, without any capital other than herself, only prostitution and the stage offered the prospect of making a good living; at the other, the young widow or unmarried mother able to earn little but almost certain to be separated from her child if she applied for the parish relief that would save them both from starvation" (1980: 357–58). Although the character of prostitution may have changed somewhat since the Victorian era, the economic impetus still remains prominent, as Miller's (1986) study of the survival strategies of underclass women in Milwaukee makes clear. Financial considerations also figure heavily in the process of entering male prostitution, but other contextual factors are operative, too, as research on male prostitution demonstrates (Calhoun, 1988; Luckenbill, 1985).

10. Such distancing techniques are not peculiar to the homeless but have also been observed among domiciled male prostitutes (Calhoun, 1988; Reiss, 1961).

11. What Marilyn failed to add was that all the women she mentioned were quite young—in their late teens to early twenties—and physically more attractive than their older and more weathered counterparts, thus making them especially vulnerable to sexual exploitation. Yet such exploitation has its upside on the streets, since it can enhance the physical safety and material survival of the women involved. That Marilyn understood this well is indicated not only by her observations but also by the fact, as was noted in Chapter 3, that she, too, was involved in a series of monogamous relationships. She may have found these relationships objectionable at one level, but she was keenly aware of their survival value.

12. Titmuss (1971: 115).

13. Titmuss (1971: 124).

14. The plasmapheresis program, as it has operated over the years, is objectionable not only because of its exploitative character but also because it can function as a conduit for the transmission of communicable diseases. This negative, albeit unintended, function has become the focus of increasing public concern as the AIDS epidemic has spread.

15. This distinction is not commonplace in the literature, where *begging* and *panhandling* tend to be used interchangeably. However, we find it useful to distinguish between the two because our observations in Austin and Tucson indicate that solicitation of money in public places can be arrayed on a continuum, from quite passive gestures or postures intended to elicit sympathy to more aggressive, harassing overtures. For empirically grounded discussions of begging in different contexts, see Wiseman (1970: 30–32) on begging among skid-row alcoholics in a U.S. city in the 1960s, Archard (1979: 39–44) on begging among the same sort of folk in Great Britain, and Gmelch and Gmelch (1978) on begging among Irish tinkers. The latters' analysis comes closest to hinting at the distinction between begging and panhandling. For a more popular discussion of begging that is particularly apropos of today's homeless, see *Time*'s cover story titled "Begging in America: To Give or Not to Give?" (September 5, 1988). Note that much of the activity described as begging in the above works is actually characterized by the aggressive accosting we associate with panhandling.

16. In a recent study of panhandling in Tucson, consisting of field observations and interviews with eighty panhandlers, embarrassment was found to be a powerful impediment. As the study reported, "[T]he most consistent finding regarding how panhandlers felt about panhandling is that it doesn't come easily, and that it is not an enjoyable activity . . . it was repeatedly stated that panhandling is 'embarrassing' and that it takes 'courage and nerve' " (Costello et al., 1990: 31). In her ethnography of skid-row alcoholics, Wiseman also found that shame and embarrassment impeded panhandling. As one of her informants explained, "I can't do it, I just can't. It makes me feel so low. I'd rather do without or even steal. At least, if you steal, you have your self-respect" (1970: 30).

17. Evidence of both fear and scorn surfaced during our observations of panhandling in Austin. Fear showed in the aversion of the targets' eyes, the hastening of their pace, and the expansion of the lateral distance between the panhandler and themselves. Scorn was also reflected at times in the angry and hostile comments of some passersby, such as "Get lost, you lazy bum."

18. Observation of these encounters shows that the panhandler does not petition in an indiscriminate and unskilled fashion. Indeed, we sensed a kind of target hierarchy among some panhandlers, with the unattached being preferred over the coupled, mixed couples preferred over same-sex couples, and women over men. It is also clear that some panhandlers are more skilled than others, judging from differences in their respective "takes."

19. Such ordinances sprang up in a number of cities in the late 1980s. Seattle, for example, passed a law making "aggressive begging" punishable by up to ninety days in jail and a $500 fine. Portland and Minneapolis passed similar ordinances. And in New York City, where begging and panhandling were prohibited on the subways, former Mayor Koch waged a verbal war against panhandling. Fueling this apparent national anti-panhandling movement were the fear and scorn we noted earlier, along with growing citizen impatience with being continuously accosted (*Time*, January 11, 1988; September 5, 1988). But the constitutionality of such ordinances has been challenged, as when a federal district judge overturned the New York City ordinance (Baker, 1990; *Time*, February 12, 1990).

20. Texas did not have a container law at the time of our research. For the homeless, this was both a blessing and a curse. The price paid for cans is much higher where there is a container law (typically 5 to 10 cents per can), but cans are not discarded as frequently in those states. Our conversations with homeless who have lived in container-law states suggest that collecting cans is somewhat more viable and lucrative, overall, in states like Texas that do not have such laws. Recently the price of aluminum has increased nationwide, encouraging more people to save and collect cans and thus reducing the number of cans the homeless can scavenge.

21. Just as measures have been taken to curtail panhandling throughout the country, so scavenging has been targeted for control. In the fall of 1984, Fort Lauderdale passed an ordinance making it illegal to take garbage from a dumpster without the written permission of the owner. And one of the city's commissioners went so far as to suggest that rat poison be used as a topping for garbage to discourage scavenging (*Time*, March 11, 1985: 68). Similar ordinances have been considered in Santa Barbara, among other cities (*Los Angeles Times*, December 13, 1984).

22. As defined by the Federal Bureau of Investigation, theft involves "the unlawful taking, carrying, leading or riding away of property from the possession or constructive possession of another. Examples are thefts of bicycles or automobile accessories, shoplifting, pocket-picking, or the stealing of any property or article that is not taken by force and violence or by fraud." Burglary, in contrast, involves "the unlawful entry of a structure to commit a felony or a theft." (See any recent edition of the FBI's *Uniform Crime Reports in the United States*, Washington, D.C.: U.S. Government Printing Office.)

23. Two hundred and forty-eight of 767 homeless in the tracking sample were arrested in Austin on one or more occasions during the twenty-seven-month period between January 1, 1983, and March 31, 1985. The data extraction for this phase of the research was confined to this period because the Austin police department's individual records were not fully entered into the computer until January 1, 1983, and because we began this portion of the research in March, 1985. If any of the 767 tracking cases had an arrest contact with the Austin police during the period, a computer match was made and the relevant data became part of the pool of crime data on the homeless in Austin. For a more detailed discussion of these data, see Snow et al. (1989).

24. In order to place the arrest data on the homeless in a broader and more meaningful context, data were also compiled on the arrests for all domiciled adult males in Austin over the same twenty-seven-month period. Since domiciled adult males greatly outnumber the homeless, it was necessary to control for population size. We also controlled for age. The resultant age-standardized arrest rate per 1,000 homeless and non-homeless for burglary was 44.45 and 28.35, respectively, and 125.56 and 95.62 for theft.

25. The comparatively high arrest rate for theft should not be read as indicative of heightened criminal tendencies among the homeless. Not only is the age-standardized arrest rate for crimes of violence (murder, rape, assault, robbery) among the homeless one-half that for the domiciled male population (11.98 compared to 23.59), but nearly 50 percent of all thefts are for shoplifting of cigarettes, small quantities of food and drink, and occasionally calculators and other such items that are then sold on the streets or in pawn shops. These additional findings suggest that the homeless are not so much serious and dangerous criminals as deprived individuals who sometimes turn to theft in the absence of the financial resources and discretionary income most citizens take for granted. In assessing arrest statistics on the homeless, it is also important to keep in mind that research on crime and the criminal-justice system suggests that the marginal are more likely to be subjected to police scrutiny. See, for example, Black (1976: 51).

26. This presumes, of course, that higher rates of arrest among the homeless with longer stretches of time on the streets are not merely a function of greater exposure to the police. Although we certainly acknowledge this as a possibility, we think that the greater frequency of arrest among the homeless who have been on the streets for more than six months results in part from the observed fact that some of them do engage in more criminal behavior because such behaviors—panhandling, begging, and theft—have become more salient aspects of their survival repertoires. These individuals are more likely than others to catch the attention of the police and to have higher arrest rates.

27. This line of reasoning has been prominently featured in an array of attempts to account for the persistence of poverty. It is a central component of Lewis's "culture of poverty" thesis (1966), which posits a strong present orientation, or the inability to defer immediate gratification and plan for the future, as both a cause and an effect of poverty. It is at the core of Banfield's effort of some twenty years ago to explain the plight of the inner city and its inhabitants in his controversial *The Unheavenly City* (1968). And it is evident in var-

ious recent neoconservative tracts that attribute poverty and inner-city "pathologies" to the confluence of aspects of Lewis's culture-of-poverty argument and various dysfunctional "liberal" social policies, as exemplified by Gilder's *Wealth and Poverty* (1981) and Murray's *Losing Ground: American Social Policy, 1950–1980* (1984). Although such works have received a wide hearing, particularly in recent years, they are not without their critics. Thus, see Valentine (1968) and Waxman (1983) for constructive critiques of Lewis's work, and Wilson (1987), Ellwood (1988), and Katz (1989) for reasoned and well-documented counterpoints to the arguments of Banfield, Gilder, and Murray, among others.

28. Liebow (1967: 64–65). This was also a central finding of Stinchcombe's (1964) study of rebellious youth in a California high school. Adolescents who expected to become manual workers in the next labor cohort and who therefore saw no clear relation between what they were doing in school and their future occupational prospects were the ones most inclined toward rebellious behavior. Stinchcombe thus concluded that "the future, not the past, explains adolescent rebellion" (1964: 6).

29. Coles (1977).

CHAPTER SIX

1. Sutherland and Locke (1936: 37).
2. Dunham (1953).
3. Pittman and Gordon (1958).
4. Levinson (1963).
5. Bahr (1970, 1973); Caplow et al. (1968).
6. Anderson (1976: 31). Also see Liebow (1967).
7. The transience of many of the homeless in Austin is indicated in several pieces of our tracking data. Just under 10 percent claimed Austin as their current residence, with 39 percent indicating that they came from other Texas communities and the remaining 52 percent claiming out-of-state residence. Moreover, at the time of their initial Salvation Army contact, 87 percent indicated that they had been in Austin for less than a month.

Studies of the homeless in a number of other cities have also found considerable transience. As is indicated in Table 1.3, the vast majority of homeless in the mid-1980s in San Antonio, El Paso, Phoenix, Los Angeles, Portland, and Nashville were from out of state. The only city in the table that had even marginally more locals than transients is Birmingham, with 51 percent of the homeless there claiming to be from the area. All these cities are located in the South, Southwest, or Far West. When we turn to the homeless in midwestern and northeastern cities, the incidence of mobility appears less striking. Research in Chicago, for instance, found that 72.3 percent of the homeless surveyed had lived there for ten years or more (Rossi, 1989a: 126). But even research in that part of the country points to considerable mobility. A statewide study of homelessness in Ohio, for example, found that although nearly 64 percent had lived in the county in which they were interviewed for more than a year, another 31 percent were fairly recent arrivals, having lived there for six months or less.

Slightly more than a third of these recent arrivals claimed to be from another state, and a fifth from another community within the state (Roth et al., 1985: 37–38). Taken together, these findings indicate that, in spite of considerable variation in the incidence of transience among the homeless across cities, with the lowest incidence occurring in the northeastern quadrant of the country, some of the homeless are quite mobile. The key word here is "some," since not all of the homeless are equally transient, a point to which we will soon return.

8. Perhaps these considerations help explain the higher incidence of mobility among the recently dislocated and the straddlers in Austin. As is noted in Table 2.2, the segments of the homeless population in Austin with the highest mean scores for interstate and intercity mobility are the recently dislocated, straddlers, and tramps. The transience of the tramps, who have the highest mean scores for mobility, follows from the value they place on "keeping on the move."

9. It might be argued that the tendency not to challenge the claims of others is a routine feature of face-to-face interaction more generally. Yet there is good reason to suspect that such behavior is contextually variable. A case in point is provided by Anderson's finding that the black street-corner men he studied " 'shoot down' and 'blow away' each other's accounts frequently" (1976: 18). We suspect that one factor that accounts for this difference among the homeless we studied and black street-corner men is that the latter have longer interpersonal histories and greater biographic knowledge about each other, which enable them to judge better the validity of others' claims and the potential danger of calling them into question. Additionally, the men Anderson studied were stratified in a more hierarchical fashion, such that it seemed more acceptable for higher-status men to call their inferiors into question than vice versa. In this regard it is interesting to note that, among the homeless, claim-challenging was most common among the redneck bums, who constituted a fairly well-bounded and hierarchically organized group.

10. For a summary of some of these interpersonal patterns, see Karp and Yoels (1979: 124–29). In general, we suspect that the paradoxical quality of social relationships among the homeless is not peculiar to them but is amplified among them.

11. Liebow (1967) noted a similar disinterest in names among the black street-corner men he studied, observing that they frequently did not know each other's surname. The case of the homeless we studied seems even more extreme, since they often do not even know each other's first name.

12. Homeless who have had repeated encounters with the police benefit particularly from anonymity. It has its drawbacks, however, as it reduces the level of intimacy and the transmission of social information. In our field research, for instance, we often found it difficult to learn about homeless individuals from other street people, because so few knew each other's name.

13. Most discussions of interpersonal relations, whatever the context, invoke one or more of these four dimensions. See, for example, Granovetter (1973).

14. By far the bulk of the literature on social relationships among the homeless has focused on the drinking of alcohol as the primary locus of affiliation and interaction. See Bahr (1967b), Jackson and Conner (1953), Peterson and

Maxwell (1958), Rooney (1961), Rubington (1968), and Wiseman (1970). We observed and will attend to such drinking as a nexus for sociality, but our research also revealed an array of other activities in which social relationships are embedded.

15. This pattern of apprehension decreasing as familiarity increases is common in the initial phases of exposure to various types of deviant behavior as well (Weinberg, 1966; Hong and Duff, 1989). It was also experienced by the buddy-researcher as he proceeded in fieldwork with the homeless.

16. The finding that street relationships are double-edged, providing support on the streets but reducing the chance of getting off the streets, was a relatively consistent observation in research on skid row (see citations in note 14, above) and has also been noted in research on the homeless of the 1980s (see Beauvais et al., 1987; LaGory et al., 1991; Lee, 1987). We will deal with this issue more fully in Chapter 9.

17. The resourcefulness and independence which we observed among traditional tramps have also been well documented in Harper's (1982) tale of his adventures with an avowed tramp. We should point out that our observations of traditional tramps were restricted to their wintertime behaviors, which constitute only one segment of their highly migratory and seasonal activities. Harper's documentary provides a more full-bodied account of the lives of traditional tramps in this regard.

18. This pattern was also noted by Cohen and Sokolovsky (1989) in their study of homeless Bowery men.

19. In many ways the social organization of bottle gangs resembles Yablonsky's (1966) conception of a "near group," in that they are characterized by shifting membership, limited cohesion, impermanence, and limited definitions of membership expectations. However, there are other characteristics associated with Yablonsky's conception, such as minimal normative consensus and emotionally disturbed leadership, that carry stronger pejorative, pathological connotations, and these do not correspond to what we observed in bottle gangs.

20. The pragmatic role of street-based drinking groups in providing homeless alcoholics with consistent access to alcoholic beverages has been noted by many researchers. See, for instance, Jackson and Connor (1953), Peterson and Maxwell (1958), Rooney (1961), and Rubington (1968), among others.

21. This protective function of drinking groups has also been recognized by several other researchers, particularly those who engaged in ethnographic research among skid-row men. See, for instance, Archard (1979), Cohen and Sokolovsky (1989), and Spradley (1970).

22. Many other researchers have also made the observation that the chronically mentally ill compose the most socially isolated segment of the homeless population. See, for instance, Bassuk (1984), Farr et al. (1986), Fischer and Breakey (1986), Lamb and Talbot (1984), Lee (1987), Lipton et al. (1983), Roth and Bean (1986), and Segal et al. (1976).

23. See Rooney (1961, 1976), Rubington (1968), Spradley (1970), and Wiseman (1970).

24. See Beauvais et al. (1987), LaGory et al. (1991), and Lee (1987).

25. Merton originally used the term *retreatist* to describe the homeless, in

his classic essay on anomie and social structure (1968). In that essay he characterized vagrancy as an attempt made by those who lacked the ability to compete in society to escape from it. Merton argued that after repeated failures in the social world, vagrants relinquish both the society's goals and the legitimate means for attaining them, becoming "asocialized" individuals in the process (1968: 208). Merton's analysis provided the theoretic cornerstone for the disaffiliation perspective.

26. Since these findings are derived from survey research, it is interesting to consider why they differ from those of the skid-row-era studies that were also based on survey research. On the one hand, these differences may reflect significant changes in social relations among the homeless of the different historical periods. Perhaps the ecology of skid row, with its SROs, encouraged more solitary survival routines, whereas the context in which the homeless of the 1980s found themselves forced them together for survival. On the other hand, the differences in the findings may result primarily from the recent development of survey instruments that are more sensitive to various types and aspects of social relationships. Cohen and Sokolovsky (1981), for instance, have developed a sophisticated "network analysis profile" in which data are collected on various types and dimensions of social relations. Using this approach to study elderly skid-row men on the Bowery, they found a much higher level of social interaction than did the earlier skid-row studies.

27. See, in particular, Schaefer et al. (1981), LaGory et al. (1991), and Lee (1987).

28. LaGory et al. (1991: 213).

29. The survival value or functionality of weak ties has been observed in other contexts as well. See Baumgartner (1988) and Granovetter (1973).

CHAPTER SEVEN

1. Derber (1979: 42).

2. If expression of concern for and interest in the homeless were associated primarily with cold weather, then media coverage should be greatest during January and February, the coldest months of the year across the country. Instead, public sympathy for the down and out, and perhaps for others as well, is ritualized most conspicuously during the Thanksgiving/Christmas holiday season. As a *Los Angeles Times* editorial noted on Christmas Day, 1988: "The charity of the holiday season is traditional—and welcome. The problem is that so much is seasonal. . . . Come January, when most people go back to their normal routines, the hunger and homelessness recognized in the holiday season will remain. It would be nice if most of the spirit of giving remained too."

3. That sympathy for the homeless would be compressed into a two- to three-month period is hardly surprising theoretically. In his essay on "the visibility of evil," Coser (1969) notes that the degree to which individuals identify sympathetically with victims of catastrophe or injustice varies considerably across time. He argues that "we share at all times the capacity for not seeing what we do not wish to see" (1969: 104), in part because we have only so much emotional energy and yet we live in a world filled with inhumanity and injustice. In

order to protect ourselves both emotionally and morally, we are thus inclined toward denial or what Myrdal (1944) referred to as the "convenience of ignorance." The implication is that there is no necessary or direct correspondence between the magnitude and empirical visibility of injustice or evil in a society and the degree to which it enters the perceptual and emotional field of the more fortunate.

4. For discussion of these and related themes from a sociological standpoint, see Douglas and Johnson (1977) and Fontana (1980).

5. Swidler (1986: 273).

6. For conceptualization and general discussion of luck, see Gunther (1977) and Morrow (1981).

7. This vulnerability thesis is clearly articulated in the parallel works on today's homeless by Rossi (1989a: 143–79) and Wright (1989: 95–114), and it is suggested by a host of other writings focusing on symptoms of mental illness on the streets and particularly on the link between deinstitutionalization and homelessness. We will discuss this thesis more thoroughly in the next chapter.

8. In a review of research on the drinking patterns of homeless men through the 1960s, Bahr suggests that this pattern of spree or periodic drinking was fairly common, occurring among one-third to one-fourth of the drinkers. But, as Bahr cautioned, "[I]t is probable that many of them are merely heavy drinkers whose consumption is periodic because of financial or other factors" (Bahr, 1973: 103).

9. Goffman coined the term to capture the ways that inmates of mental asylums take leave without actually leaving the facility and thereby get "around the organization's assumptions as to what [they] should do and get and hence what [they] should be" (1961a: 189). We think the concept provides analytic leverage when applied to other contexts as well. For a thorough discussion and empirical grounding of the concept in relation to asylums, see Goffman (1961a: 188–320). Material quoted in the text comes from pages 189 and 309.

10. Research on the mental health of the homeless of the 1980s has found that they suffer from considerably higher rates of depression and demoralization than the domiciled, including the domiciled poor (see Rossi, 1989a: 147–52; LaGory et al., 1990). Rossi found, for example, that 47 percent of the sample of homeless he interviewed in Chicago were classified as high on the depression scale he used. As was discussed in note 25 in Chapter 2, such findings do not strike us as surprising. Indeed, not only would we expect to find considerable depression on the streets considering the trials and exigencies of street life, but we suspect such depression might be interpreted as a fairly normal response to a strikingly abnormal situation.

11. For discussion of some mental disorders as "bizarre behaviors," see Eaton (1986: 1–41).

12. Much diagnostic and epidemiological research on mental illness has proceeded as if symptoms of psychosis could be understood out of context. But some students of mental illness have argued instead that symptomatic behaviors are inherently neither normal nor abnormal but have meaning only in relation to the social setting in which they are embedded. See, for example, Coleman

(1967), Eaton and Weil (1953), Edgerton (1969), Goffman (1971), and Laing and Esterson (1970).

13. This dynamic is consistent with Lemert's (1962: 19) observations regarding paranoia. He argues that "while the paranoid person reacts differently to his social environment, it is also true that 'others' react differently to him and . . . that these differential reactions are reciprocals of one another, being interwoven and concatenated at each and all phases of a process of exclusion." Thus, he concludes, "delusions and associated behavior must be understood in a context of exclusion."

14. This is one of the cardinal principles of social interaction. See Stone (1962), Turner (1968), and McCall and Simmons (1978).

15. This conceptualization of social identity is consistent with both Goffman (1963b: 2–3) and McCall and Simmons (1978: 62), as well as with Turner's (1978: 6) "appearance principle," which holds that "people tend to conceive another person [and thus impute social identities] on the basis of the role behavior they observe unless there are cues that alert them to the possibility of a discrepancy between person and role."

16. This conceptualization differs from Goffman's (1963b: 57) and McCall and Simmons's (1978: 62–63) in that they define personal identity in terms of unique, biograpic facts and items that function as pegs upon which social identities can be hung. It is our contention that biographic facts and experiences, like social roles, influence but do not fully determine the construction and assertion of what we call personal identities. In other words, rather than taking for granted the relationship between biography and personal identity, we see it as problematic and variable.

17. These identity statements were not elicited by asking the homeless how they see themselves or other such direct questions. Instead, they arose as the homeless interacted with one another as well as others. The statements were secured primarily by the two relatively unobtrusive forms of listening discussed earlier: eavesdropping and nondirective, conversational listening. All told, we heard 186 statements that we read as bearing directly on the issue of identity. Although these statements came from only 40 percent of our field informants, this subsample was comparable to the larger sample in terms of age, gender, and ethnicity. More important for our purposes, each of the different types of homeless is represented by the identity statements we secured. Consequently, we are reasonably confident that the identity talk we overheard is representative of the homeless living in or passing through Austin.

18. For discussions of such distancing in various contexts, see Goffman (1961b), Levitin (1964), Stebbins (1975), and Sayles (1984).

19. As Anderson (1976: 214) observed, based on his research among domiciled black street-corner men, claims to a particular identity depend in part "on one's ability to manage his image by drawing distinctions between himself and others he does not want to be associated with."

20. See Goffman (1961b) for the initial conceptualization.

21. It was in fact true that some Salvation Army employees loaded bags of groceries into their cars before leaving for the day, but the reason was not, as is

implied in this statement, so that they could take them home for personal use. Rather, they were transporting the groceries to needy families in the community.

22. Wiseman (1970: 187–88, 194–98) similarly noted the "harsh sentiments" of skid-row alcoholics toward their seeming benefactors. Similar patterns of bitching and griping have been observed in relation to more all-encompassing institutions, such as prisons and mental hospitals. In commenting on such verbal insubordination, Goffman (1961a: 319) pushes an interpretation that dovetails with ours: "This recalcitrance is not an incidental mechanism of defense but rather an essential constituent of the self" that allows the individual "to keep some distance, some elbow room, between himself and that with which others assume he should be identified."

23. This conception of embracement is derived from Goffman's (1961b: 106–7) treatment of role embracement, but with two differences. First, we conceive of embracement as a generic process through which attachment to and involvement in a particular entity or activity are expressed, with role embracement constituting only one of many forms of embracement. And, second, we think embracement need not entail disappearance into the activity at hand and corresponding inattention to the flow of other proximate activities. Such engagement should be viewed as a variable feature of embracement, not as a defining characteristic.

24. Anderson (1976) found that the identity work of the black street-corner men he studied was composed mainly of associational distancing and embracement. Evidence of both this and role embracement is also reported by Rooney (1973) in his study of skid-row men in the 1960s. He found that those who were on skid row for longer than a year were much more likely to identify themselves as skid-row members, and that this tendency was even more pronounced among those with friends on skid row. Thus, such embracement appears to be more pronounced the longer the time on the streets and the greater the number of street associates.

25. Given the categorization of this line of talk as "fictive," it is important to make explicit the criteria used to determine whether a particular narration was indeed fictive. We talked with and listened to each of the seventy individuals within our identity subsample, seeing nearly all of them in a range of situations at different times, with an average of 4.5 encounters per individual. We were thus able to monitor many of these individuals across time and space. Any story we identified as fictive contained one or more of three kinds of narrative contradictions: (1) those among multiple stories told by the same individual, as when a street person claims to be thirty-six years old on one occasion and forty-six on another; (2) those between stories and observed behaviors in various situations, as when someone claims to be working regularly but is seen panhandling or intoxicated during the day; and (3) those between current situations and future projections and claims, as when a disheveled, penniless street person claims to have a managerial job awaiting him at a local business. In each of these situations, credulity is strained because of objective discrepancies or because of the vast gap between current and projected realities.

26. Fanciful identities are constructed by other people as well, but it is our

sense that with movement up the class structure they tend to be privatized and temporally or spatially ritualized, rather than publicly articulated, ongoing features of everyday life, as was the case with many of the homeless we studied and the black street-corner men observed by Liebow (1967) and Anderson (1976). Regarding the latter, Liebow (1967: 213) noted that the construction of fictive identities allows them to "be men once again providing they do not look too closely at one another's credentials." Although many of the personal identities they construct, such as "going for brothers," are different in content from those constructed by the homeless, they are functionally similar.

27. That these four factors function as springboards for fanciful identities constructed by homeless men is hardly surprising, considering that success as an adult male in America is defined in large part in terms of job, money, possessions, and women. This thematic connection also suggests that although the life-style of homeless males stands outside the normative order, their dreams and fantasies are nonetheless very much of that order. It could hardly be any other way, of course, since dreams and fantasies are, in large part, culturally embedded.

28. The unsolicited sexual overtures of homeless males understandably make most women uncomfortable. One stereotypic image of the homeless man is that of a potential sex offender, and some of the tactics the men use to gain attention, such as Pat's calling to the young women to undress, overstep public propriety (although the talk and actions certainly are no more lewd than much locker-room humor and singles-bar activities). A large measure of the perceived threat in such interactions may well be a transformation of class offense into sexual terms. In any case, women generally try to avoid encouraging homeless men. Usually the homeless accept this refusal of social involvement, but sometimes, especially when the refusal seems particularly direct, they respond angrily to the loss of face it entails. This can lead to a quick escalation of aggressive interaction, such as that which we witnessed one afternoon in the downtown area when we were hanging out with Ron. He was watching young women walking down the sidewalk after work. As they passed, Ron called out, "Hey, honey, lookin' good!" Most of them responded either by ignoring him or by giving a small grin and accelerating their pace. When one young woman instead scowled and lifted her head in disdain, Ron took off after her, calling out angrily, "Rich bitch! Rich goddamn bitch!" as she hurried up the street.

29. It is important to note that this amplification was elicited by one of us rather than by another homeless individual. As we indicated in the last chapter, we rarely overheard the homeless call into question each other's stories and asserted identities. Whatever the reasons for not challenging publicly another's identity claims, which were discussed in note 9 of the previous chapter, the outcome is a mutually deferential stance that increases the prospect of embellishment and storytelling, thus making the homeless unwitting co-conspirators in the spinning and maintenance of outlandish personal identities.

30. The issue of self-esteem or worth has not been explored in research on today's homeless, but Bahr and Caplow's survey of skid-row men of the 1960s did reveal that they "were much more likely than the non–skid row respondents to admit negative self-conceptions" (1973: 287).

31. See, for example, Goffman's study of asylums (1961a), Liebow's (1967) and Anderson's (1976) ethnographies of black street-corner men, and the observations of Bettelheim (1943), Frankl (1963), and Dimsdale (1980) on the psychological coping strategies of concentration-camp inmates.

32. Maslow (1962).

CHAPTER EIGHT

1. Whenever a social problem becomes a domestic issue, certain positions are customarily taken in public debate. One argument that typically surfaces is that the scope of the problem has been exaggerated and that the problem has something of the character of what Daniel Boorstin (1961) has called "pseudo-events," events or issues that have been deliberately planned in accordance with the interests of some set of actors—the media, a political party or campaign, or a voluntary association or social movement. One line of discussion with respect to the current wave of homelessness, issuing primarily from the commentaries of neo-conservative journalists, is that the magnitude of the problem has been grossly exaggerated and it is thus a pseudo-issue. That argument is clearly off the mark: the issue is not whether there are half a million or three million homeless, but that there are an appreciable number of homeless in a country with a high standard of living and in which hearth and home are almost inalienable rights, and in a world in which throngs of street people are typically associated with Third World cities.

2. For a representative sampling of this literature, see Bratt et al. (1986), Gilderbloom and Appelbaum (1988), Low Income Housing Information Service (1989), Ringheim (1990a), and Zarembka (1990).

3. For discussion of the nature and origins of deinstitutionalization as a social experiment and of some of its presumed consequences, see Bachrach (1976), Dear and Wolch (1987), Gralnick (1985), Grob (1991), Gronfein (1985), and Lerman (1982).

4. These figures are derived from Goldman et al. (1983), table 2 in particular.

5. Bachrach (1976), Dear and Wolch (1987), Grob (1991), Lamb (1984), Okin (1985), and Torrey (1988).

6. Krauthammer (1985: 103).

7. Morganthau et al. (1986: cover).

8. *People* (1986: 29).

9. Quoted in Gamino (1984c: A8).

10. Reported in Gamino (1984f).

11. Gamino (1984a; 1984b; 1984d; 1984e; 1984f).

12. Lipton et al. (1983: 821). See also Arce et al. (1983), Bassuk (1984), and Farr (1982).

13. The study just mentioned, based as it was on an examination of individuals who had already been admitted to New York's Bellevue Hospital for psychiatric problems, thus ensured that a remarkably high incidence of mental illness would be found (Lipton et al., 1983). Another widely cited study was based on interviews with a nonrepresentative sample of seventy-eight homeless in a

single Boston shelter (Bassuk, 1984). For a critical discussion of these and other such studies, see Ropers (1988: 149–53).

14. In *Dangerous Diagnostics* Nelkin and Tancredi emphasize that "the problems of diagnostic uncertainty are greater when a technology developed to identify a pathology in the context of clinical care is transferred to another institutional setting" (1989: 48). This practice is particularly widespread in research on the homeless, and it is pursued with little regard for the potentially contaminating difficulties. For a discussion of some of the problems associated with the application of conventional diagnostic instruments and procedures to the homeless, see notes 25 and 26 in Chapter 2, notes 10 and 12 in Chapter 7, Ropers (1988: 153–68), Snow et al. (1986a: 420–21; 1988), and Toro and Wall (1990).

15. Figures based on those reported in Goldman et al. (1983).

16. Based on the aggregation and analysis of data compiled by the Texas Department of Mental Health and Mental Retardation (MHMR).

17. Farr et al. (1986), LaGory et al. (1989), Lee (1989), Piliavin et al. (1991), Roth et al. (1985), Rossi (1989a), and Wright (1988).

18. One argument made in some quarters in response to findings indicating that deinstitutionalization has been only a minor precipitant of homelessness is that its effects are more indirect than direct. Here a distinction is made between the "ever-institutionalized" and the "never-institutionalized" mentally ill homeless. The argument is that if it were not for the deinstitutionalization experiment, the proportion of never-institutionalized mentally ill on the streets would be much smaller. This proposition is reasonable if we assume that all of the never-institutionalized mentally ill would qualify for institutionalization, that their numbers are as large as was initially assumed, that the chronically mentally ill homeless do not seek mental health assistance, either on an outpatient or an inpatient basis, and that the diagnostic procedures and instruments used in the streets do not err in the direction of misdiagnosis and the identification of false positives. But each of these assumptions is highly suspect. For discussion of some of the problems associated with these assumptions, see Ropers (1988: 149–68) and Snow et al. (1986a, 1988).

19. See Snow et al. (1986a) for a detailed discussion of this and related findings.

20. Reports issued by the U.S. Bureau of the Census since the mid-1980s show a sharp increase in poverty in America (Center on Budget and Policy Priorities, 1985, 1988) and an overall "surge in inequality" (Thurow, 1987). See Wright and Lam (1987) for a discussion of how this "surge" has intensified the demand for low-income housing.

21. Sternlieb and Hughes (1983: 113).

22. Scherer (1984–85: 954).

23. National Coalition for the Homeless (1987: 81).

24. Bahr (1967a), Bahr and Caplow (1973), and Lee (1980).

25. Hamilton, Rabinowitz, and Alschuler, Inc. (1987).

26. Reported in *Newsweek* (1984: 23).

27. Derived from figures presented in Table 6–1 in Hoch and Slayton (1989: 121).

28. Reported in Hopper and Hamberg (1986: 23) and in *Newsweek* (1984: 23).

29. Kasinitz (1984).

30. National Coalition for the Homeless (1989: 5–6).

31. Reported in Lamar (1988) and Schumer (1988).

32. Hartman (1986: 362).

33. For discussion of these processes in relation to the disappearance of low-income housing, see Atlas and Dreier (1980), Brady (1983), Feagin (1986), Marcuse (1985), and Smith and Williams (1986).

34. Hoch and Slayton (1989: 116).

35. Hathcock (1984: 72).

36. Stanley (1985: A1).

37. Szilagyi (1985b: A1).

38. This is not to say that local residents were not displaced. But if they were, most probably doubled up with family or friends, a not uncommon arrangement among low-income citizens in response to the unavailability of low-cost housing.

39. Gilderbloom (1986: 301).

40. Gilderbloom (1986: 301).

41. Ringheim (1990a: 33–34).

42. Gilderbloom (1986: 301).

43. Ringheim (1990b: 11 and Table 6). The eight cities were Baltimore, Boston, Chicago, Detroit, Houston, Minneapolis/St. Paul, Seattle, and Washington, D.C.

44. Center on Budget and Policy Priorities and Low Income Housing Information Service (1989: xii) and Zarembka (1990: 2).

45. Wright (1985: 4).

46. Szilagyi (1985a: A8) and Tyson (1985: H1).

47. Housing and Community Services Department (1985: n.p.).

48. Szilagyi (1985a: A8).

49. Housing Task Force (1984).

50. "The great migration" of over a million black Americans that occurred between 1916 and 1930 is but one example of this process (Marks, 1989).

51. Hodson and Sullivan (1990: 115).

52. Hodson and Sullivan (1990: 116, Table 5.1).

53. Hodson and Sullivan (1990: 116, Table 5.1). It should be kept in mind that the official unemployment rate does not include those unemployed who have become so discouraged that they have quit looking for regular work. As was suggested in Chapters 4 and 5, many of of the homeless fall into that category. If they, along with other discouraged workers, were included in the ranks of the unemployed, the official rate would be much higher.

54. Hodson and Sullivan (1990: 117).

55. This is consistent with Hopper et al.'s contention that homelessness is one of many strategies used by the marginal poor to facilitate their survival, that it is "a routine feature of coping strategies of the marginally situated . . . in urban areas" (1985: 222).

56. That the homeless come from the ranks of the extremely poor is one of the central findings of recent research. See Rossi (1989a), among others.

57. Bluestone and Harrison (1982). For further discussion of the link between deindustrialization and homelessness, see Adams (1986), Hopper et al. (1985), and Ropers (1988: 100–106).

58. For an overview of these parallel processes, see Bluestone and Harrison (1982) and Perrucci et al. (1988).

59. Bluestone and Harrison (1982: 26, 32).

60. Harris (1984).

61. Office of Technology Assessment (1986: 3).

62. Office of Technology Assessment (1986: 11).

63. Office of Technology Assessment (1986: 11).

64. Serrin (1986: 9) and Parker (1986).

65. For evidence of this trend, particularly at the lower reaches of the work force, see Thurow (1987). For discussion of its linkage to homelessness, see Hopper and Hamberg (1986: 18, 25).

66. Such figures were widely discussed by the press and media in conjunction with the debate over minimum wage in the late 1980s, and often in relation to homelessness (*Arizona Daily Star*, 1988: A12; Schumer, 1988; Schmalz, 1988: 414).

67. Bratt (1986), Hartman (1986), Hopper and Hamberg (1986), Lamar (1988), and Schumer (1988).

68. Center on Budget and Policy Priorities (1984: 2; 1985).

69. Hopper and Hamberg (1986: 27) and Hope and Young (1986: 203).

70. *New York Times* (1984: A34).

71. See, for example, Bahr (1970, especially p. 45) and Henslin (1985).

72. A featured essay on homelessness in *Harper's* similarly argued that "many of the homeless are not only hapless victims but voluntary exiles, 'domestic refugees,' people who have turned not against life itself but against us, our life, American life" (Marin, 1987: 41).

73. This finding is consistent with surveys of the homeless that have included voluntaristic choices, such as wanderlust and boredom, in their inquiries about the reasons for homelessness. For example, a survey of 150 homeless in Birmingham, Alabama, found that only 8.0 percent indicated they were on the streets for such reasons (LaGory et al., 1989: 14), and a survey of 979 homeless in Ohio reported a parallel finding of 6.1 percent (Roth, 1989: 154).

74. Victim-blaming is the process by which individuals who suffer a particular fate are blamed for the predicament in which they find themselves. Typically, attention is focused on one or more individual characteristics or attributes as the primary causal agents rather than on the social origins of the problem. See Ryan (1971) for an elaboration of this process.

75. This view is represented in the work of Bahr (1970, 1973), Caplow et al. (1968), Dunham (1953), Levinson (1963), Pittman and Gordon (1958), and Sutherland and Locke (1936), among others. For a brief discussion of its applicability to the homeless of today, see the beginning and end of Chapter 6.

76. These disabilities have been primary focal concerns of virtually every

major community or statewide survey of the homeless conducted in the 1980s and early 1990s. See, for example, Baumann et al. (1985), Breakey et al. (1989), Brown et al. (1983), Farr et al. (1986), Gioglio (1989), Koegel and Burnam (1988), LaGory et al. (1989, 1990), Lee (1989), Piliavin et al. (1989, 1991), Robertson et al. (1985), Rossi (1989a), Roth et al. (1985), and Sosin et al. (1988). Also see Wright's work based on the analysis of data derived from Health Care for the Homeless projects in sixteen major cities (Wright, 1988, 1989; Wright and Weber, 1987). For a review of much of this work, see Fischer and Breakey (1991).

77. Rossi (1989a: 195). This thesis is articulated most clearly by Rossi (1989a: 143–79, 194–95) and Wright (1989: 86–114). Although not all of the researchers cited in the preceding note would explicitly subscribe to this thesis, it is, nonetheless, suggested by the fact that so much of the research has been uncritically fixated on the enumeration of the disabilities of the homeless. This is particularly clear in the case of the voluminous research focusing on mental illness. For overviews of this research, see Arce and Vergare (1984), Fischer and Breakey (1986, 1991), and General Accounting Office (1988). For critical discussion of much of this research and its tendency to "medicalize" the problem of homelessness, see Ropers (1988: 148–68), Snow et al. (1986, 1988), and Toro and Wall (1990).

78. Wright (1989: 90).

79. Rossi (1989a: 179).

80. Rossi (1989a: 195).

81. Wright (1989: 76).

82. Rossi (1989a: 148–79).

83. State figure calculated on the basis of statistics provided by Texas MHMR.

84. The age-standardized arrest rates per 1,000 homeless and non-homeless adult males for property crimes between January, 1983, and March, 1985, were 179.16 and 130.47, respectively. See the discussion of theft in Chapter 5, particularly notes 24 and 25, and Snow et al. (1989) for a discussion of the derivation of these findings.

85. The age-standardized arrest rates per 1,000 homeless and non-homeless adult males for misdemeanors were 647.99 and 133.04, respectively. Misdemeanors accounted for nearly 80 percent of all the offenses for which the homeless were arrested, with substance-related offenses, particularly public intoxication, accounting for 51 percent of all arrests.

86. Some researchers acknowledge this possibility, but typically in passing, as they proceed in their subsequent analyses as though the causal arrow flowed from disabilities to homelessness rather than the other way around. Rossi (1989a: 144) notes, for example, that since "all the data we will consider come from cross-sectional surveys . . . it is always debatable whether a difference between the domiciled and the homeless led to homelessness or whether homelessness created the difference." But this caveat is then ignored in favor of the conclusion that "among the extremely poor, those with disabilities are the most vulnerable to homelessness" (179).

87. Rossi (1989b: 38).

88. Marin (1987: 41–42).

89. Whether Sonny's story is correct is well-nigh impossible to verify, of course. But Sonny never struck us as being mentally ill, much less in need of institutionalization. He was far from a brilliant conversationalist, but he was an amiable person with a good deal of insight into his own situation.

90. Although the family backgrounds of the homeless have not been widely explored, a number of studies similarly report that a significant proportion of homeless have experienced some form of out-of-home care before their eighteenth birthday. For example, a survey of homeless aged eighteen and over in Minneapolis found that 38.6 percent had spent some time in foster care facilities during their youth (Piliavin et al., 1991), and studies in Chicago (Sosin et al., 1988) and New York (Susser et al., 1987) report parallel findings of 14 and 23 percent respectively.

91. Perhaps this is one reason military veterans are so heavily overrepresented among the homeless. Nearly one-half of our tracking sample indicated, when they checked into the Sally for the first time, that they were veterans. This figure is consistent with the Austin street survey conducted in 1984 (Baumann et al., 1985), as well as those reported in other locales, where the range tends to fall between one-third and one-half (Robertson, 1987). Since veterans constitute less than 15 percent of the national population, it is clear that they are highly overrepresented in the ranks of the homeless. Although we do not have data on the proportion of the tracking sample who served during the time of the Vietnam War, studies that do have such data indicate that a large number are included among the homeless veterans (Robertson, 1987). This makes sense, considering that the mean age of the homeless in most communities in the 1980s was about thirty-six. It appears that the ghost of Vietnam has surfaced on the streets of urban America.

92. By *luck,* Jencks (1972: 227) refers to "chance acquaintances who steer you to one line of work rather than another, the range of jobs that happen to be available in a particular community when you are job hunting, the amount of overtime work in your particular plant, whether bad weather destroys your strawberry crop, whether the new superhighway has an exit near your restaurant, and a hundred other unpredictable accidents."

93. This is essentially a paraphrase of Hopper and Hamberg's (1986: 14) summary statement of the structural roots of homelessness.

CHAPTER NINE

1. See Adler and Adler (1983) and Luckenbill (1986).

2. See, for example, Becker's (1963) analysis of the career of marijuana users and Goffman's (1961a) elaboration of the moral career of the mental patient.

3. We are not the first researchers to apply the career concept to the homeless. Over twenty years ago Wallace devoted a chapter in *Skid Row as a Way of Life* (1965) to analyzing the careers of skid-row men. Wallace's analysis is pertinent to this chapter, but he treated homeless careers almost exclusively in terms of socialization processes by which homeless men became "drunks," that is, acculturated alcoholic members of the skid-row community. This focus is too narrow to capture the range of factors that impinge on homeless careers.

Our analysis, although it includes attention to socialization and drinking, is more broadly conceived. Piliavin and his associates (1991) have used the term more recently in their work, but only in a general way in distinguishing between short-term and long-term homelessness. Piliavin's findings in this regard will be noted in the next section of this chapter. Luckenbill and Best (1981) have examined the limitations of the career analogy for studying deviant careers. "Riding escalators between floors may be an effective metaphor for respectable organizational careers," they note, "but it fails to capture the character of deviant careers. A more appropriate image is a walk in the woods. . . . Without a rigid organizational structure, deviant careers can develop in many different ways" (201).

4. Subsequent efforts to locate Willie by tracking him through the Austin police department, city hospital, and Salvation Army yielded no information that went beyond our final contact with him in December of 1984.

5. Another possible way off the streets is through receiving a serendipitous windfall, such as an inheritance or a lottery win. We have occasionally heard of such things in the media (e.g., *Austin American-Statesman*, September 23, 1984), but we witnessed no examples of this in our research.

6. It is possible to distinguish two patterns of episodic homelessness. One pattern, which can be termed end-of-the-month homelessness, entails living in SRO hotels or other cheap housing that is paid for daily or weekly during the first part of the month, followed by homelessness later in the month when money runs out. This pattern seems to be particularly common among older individuals with small but regular first-of-the-month pensions or Social Security checks (see Cohen and Sokolovsky, 1989). A second pattern, which can be termed intermittent homelessness, involves getting off the streets on an irregular basis, usually as a result of serendipitous circumstances, and then returning to the streets when the luck runs out. This second kind of episodic homelessness was the most common pattern among the homeless we encountered. Recent research has fairly consistently found a relatively high level of intermittent episodic homelessness. In Anderson's (1987) study of poverty-level families in the Texas hill country, nearly 81 percent of the homeless families had experienced previous homelessness. In Sosin et al.'s (1988) Chicago survey, approximately half of the homeless respondents had been suffering from episodic homelessness over an average of eight years, with a modal four episodes totaling 3.2 years. Other research that has documented high levels of episodic homelessness includes Farr et al.'s (1986) Los Angeles study; Morse et al.'s (1985) research in St. Louis; Piliavin's Minneapolis study (Piliavin and Sosin, 1987–88); and Rossi's (1989a) Chicago project. Not all research is consistent in this regard, however. For instance, Freeman and Hall (1986) found that once individuals become homeless, they spent an average of 96 percent of the time in that state.

7. See, for example, Brickner et al. (1985), Burt and Cohen (1989a), Cohen and Sokolovsky (1989), Fischer and Breakey (1991), Institute of Medicine (1988), Rossi (1989a), and Wright (1989).

8. Perhaps some of the homeless embellish their educational status on their registration forms at TEC in order to enhance their job prospects. This possibility notwithstanding, it is important to note that many other studies have

yielded rates of high school graduation of over 55 percent (see Baumann et al., 1985; Brown et al., 1983; LaGory et al., 1989; Robertson et al., 1985; and Rossi, 1989a). A few other researchers have found somewhat lower educational attainment (see Lee, 1989; Roth et al., 1985). On balance, though, it appears that the level of educational attainment among the homeless is somewhat higher than might be expected (see Table 1.3).

9. Wiseman (1970: 223).

10. Wiseman (1970: 223).

11. Wiseman (1970: 223).

12. The Salvation Army has upgraded its range of services since the time of our fieldwork, as we discuss in the epilogue, but its primary emphasis insofar as the homeless are concerned continues to be accommodative.

13. For an overview of this tendency see note 27 in Chapter 5.

14. The classic treatment of this problem in relation to treatment programs for skid-row alcoholics is Wiseman's *Stations of the Lost* (1970).

15. Goffman (1961a: 12).

16. It is useful to keep in mind that the homeless often use such phrases as "working the program" differently from the agency staff. For the homeless, to "work the program" usually means to milk it for the individual's own ends; for agency staff, it means commitment to the program and its goals.

17. Rossi (1989a) and Wright (1989).

18. Piven and Cloward (1971).

19. See Brickner et al. (1985), Institute of Medicine (1988), and Redburn and Buss (1986), for example.

20. This observation is also supported by the research of Baumann and his associates in Austin. They found that those who had been homeless for relatively lengthy periods of time exhibited higher levels of psychological functioning and lower levels of perceived deprivation than did those who had been homeless for a short time. See Baumann et al. (1987) and Beauvais et al. (1987).

21. See Pfuhl Jr. (1986) and Schur (1971) for conceptual discussions of role engulfment.

22. Lofland (1969) has suggested that role engulfment and the "denial of role distance" are essentially obverse sides of the same coin.

23. Goffman (1963b: 145).

24. Wallace (1965) and Wiseman (1970).

25. Quoted in Wiseman (1970: 233).

26. See references cited in note 6 in this chapter.

27. Rossi (1989a: 199).

EPILOGUE

1. A chapter of Habitat for Humanity was also established in Austin in late 1985, but it is a small program. During nearly five years of operation, it has renovated only seven homes, four of which were owner-occupied units belonging to low-income elderly individuals or couples. Clearly, it did not constitute a significant resource for the homeless.

2. When we recontacted the Salvation Army in January of 1991, we were

told that they had recently set up a forty-bed transitional unit to help address this need.

3. Several men on the streets used this term, more commonly used for the large cell in which prisoners are held before being brought to court, to refer to the open courtyard beneath the Sally.

4. Foucault (1979: 183–84).

References

Adams, Carolyn Teich. 1986. "Homelessness in the Postindustrial City: Views from London and Philadelphia." *Urban Affairs Quarterly* 21: 527–549.

Adler, Patricia A., and Peter Adler. 1983. "Shifts and Oscillations in Deviant Careers: The Case of Upper Level Drug Dealers and Smugglers." *Social Problems* 31: 195–207.

Agar, Michael H. 1986. *Speaking of Ethnography.* Beverly Hills: Sage.

Allsop, Kenneth. 1967. *Hard Travellin': The Hobo and His History.* New York: New American Library.

Anderson, Elijah. 1976. *A Place on the Corner.* Chicago: University of Chicago Press.

Anderson, Leon. 1987. "Scraping By: A Field Study of Semi-Rural Poverty in the Texas Hill Country." Ph.D. dissertation, University of Texas at Austin.

Anderson, Nels. 1923. *The Hobo: The Sociology of the Homeless Man.* Chicago: University of Chicago Press.

———. 1931. *The Milk and Honey Route: A Handbook for Hobos.* New York: Vanguard.

———. 1940. *Men on the Move.* Chicago: University of Chicago Press.

Appelbaum, Richard P. 1990. "Counting the Homeless." Pp. 1–16 in Jamshid A. Momeni, ed., *Homelessness in the United States: Data and Issues.* Westport, Conn.: Greenwood Press.

Arce, Anthony A., Marilyn Tadlock, Michael L. Vergare, and Stuart H. Shapiro. 1983. "A Psychiatric Profile of Street People Admitted to an Emergency Shelter." *Hospital and Community Psychiatry* 34: 812–817.

Arce, Anthony A., and Michael J. Vergare. 1984. "Identifying and Characterizing the Mentally Ill Among the Homeless." Pp. 75–89 in H. Richard Lamb, ed., *The Homeless Mentally Ill: A Task Force Report of the American Psychiatric Association.* Washington, D.C.: American Psychiatric Association.

Archard, Peter. 1979. *Vagrancy, Alcoholism and Social Control.* London: Macmillan.

Arizona Daily Star. 1988. "Minimum Wage: Republicans Don't Understand the Work Ethic." September 28.

Atlas, John, and Peter Dreier. 1980. "The Housing Crisis and Tenants' Revolt." *Social Policy* 10: 13–24.

Aulette, Judy, and Albert Aulette. 1987. "Police Harassment of the Homeless: The Political Purpose of the Criminalization of Homelessness." *Humanity and Society* 11: 244–256.

Austin American-Statesman. 1981. "Reagan Says Unemployed Not Trying." March 21.

———. 1984. "Heir-raising Arrest Offers Wino New Life." September 23.

———. 1985. "Congress Avenue Bar Victim of Restoration." March 5.

———. 1985. " 'Sally': What Kind of Place Is Austin?" July 28.

———. 1985. "Transients and Jobs" (letter to editor). August 2.

———. 1985. "Center for Homeless Opposed in Galveston." November 30.

———. 1986. "Harvard Blocks Grates to Keep Homeless Away." January 16.

———. 1987. "Neighbors Complain of Shantytown: Men Forced to Leave Area of Wichita Falls." December 13.

Austin–Travis County Health Department. 1984. *Robert Wood Johnson Grant Application: Health Care for the Homeless.* Austin, Texas.

Bachrach, Leona L. 1976. *Deinstitutionalization: An Analytic Review and Sociological Perspective.* Rockville, Md.: National Institutes of Health.

Bahr, Howard M. 1967a. "The Gradual Disappearance of Skid Row." *Social Problems* 15: 41–45.

———. 1967b. "Drinking, Interaction, and Identification: Notes on Socialization into Skid Row." *Journal of Health and Social Behavior* 8: 272–285.

———. 1969. "Lifetime Affiliation Patterns of Early- and Late-Onset Heavy Drinkers on Skid Row." *Quarterly Journal of Studies on Alcohol* 30: 645–656.

———. 1970. "Homelessness, Disaffiliation, and Retreatism." Pp. 39–50 in Howard M. Bahr, ed., *Disaffiliated Man.* Toronto: University of Toronto Press.

———. 1973. *Skid Row: An Introduction to Disaffiliation.* New York: Oxford University Press.

Bahr, Howard M., and Theodore Caplow. 1973. *Old Men Drunk and Sober.* New York: New York University Press.

Baker, Russell W. 1990. "Beggars' Rights in New York." *Christian Science Monitor.* February 13: 7.

Baker, Susan G., and David A. Snow. 1989. "Homelessness in Texas: Estimates of Population Size and Demographic Composition." Pp. 205–217 in Jamshid A. Momeni, ed., *Homelessness in the United States: State Surveys.* Westport, Conn.: Greenwood Press.

Bane, Mary Jo. 1976. *Here to Stay: American Families in the Twentieth Century.* New York: Basic Books.

Banfield, Edward C. 1968. *The Unheavenly City.* Boston: Little, Brown.

Banton, Michael. 1965. *Roles: An Introduction to the Study of Social Relations.* New York: Basic Books.

Barak, Gregg. 1991. *Gimme Shelter: A Social History of Homelessness in America*. New York: Praeger.

Barton, Paul E. 1981. "A Perspective on Work." Pp. 49–61 in John Wilkes, ed., *The Future of Work*. London: Allen and Unwin.

Bassuk, Ellen L. 1984. "The Homelessness Problem." *Scientific American* 251: 40–45.

Baumann, Donald J., Cheryl Beauvais, Charles Grigsby, and F. D. Schultz. 1985. *The Austin Homeless: Final Report Provided to the Hogg Foundation for Mental Health*. Austin: Hogg Foundation for Mental Health.

Baumann, Donald J., Randall Osborne, Mary Osborne, and Doyal Nelms. 1987. "The Subjective Underestimation of Problems by the Homeless: A Puzzle Solved by Theory." Manuscript.

Baumgartner, M. P. 1988. *The Moral Order of a Suburb*. New York: Oxford University Press.

Baxter, Ellen, and Kim Hopper. 1981. *Private Lives/Public Spaces: Homeless Adults on the Streets of New York City*. New York: Community Service Society.

Beauvais, Cheryl, Donald J. Baumann, Charles Grigsby, and F. D. Schultz. 1987. "Social Support and the Streets: Getting By with a Little Help from Friends." Manuscript.

Becker, Howard S. 1960. "Notes on the Concept of Commitment." *American Journal of Sociology* 77: 32–40.

———. 1963. *Outsiders: Studies in the Sociology of Deviance*. New York: Free Press.

———. 1970. "Field Work Evidence." Pp. 39–73 in Howard S. Becker, *Sociological Work: Method and Substance*. Chicago: Aldine.

Beier, A. L. 1985. *Masterless Men: The Vagrancy Problem in England 1560–1640*. New York: Methuen.

Bendiner, Elmer. 1961. *The Bowery Man*. New York: Thomas Nelson and Sons.

Bettelheim, Bruno. 1943. "Individual and Mass Behavior in Extreme Situations." *Journal of Abnormal Social Psychology* 38: 417–452.

Bingham, Richard D., Roy E. Green, and Sammis B. White, eds. 1987. *The Homeless in Contemporary Society*. Newbury Park, Calif.: Sage.

Bittner, Egon. 1967. "The Police on Skid Row: A Study of Police Keeping." *American Sociological Review* 32: 699–715.

Black, Donald. 1976. *The Behavior of Law*. New York: Academic Press.

Bluestone, Barry, and Bennett Harrison. 1982. *The Deindustrialization of America*. New York: Basic Books.

Blumberg, Leonard, Thomas E. Shipley, Jr., and Irving W. Shandler. 1973. *Skid Row and Its Alternatives*. Philadelphia: Temple University Press.

Blumer, Herbert. 1969. *Symbolic Interactionism: Perspective and Method*. Englewood Cliffs, N.J.: Prentice-Hall.

Bogue, Donald J. 1963. *Skid Row in American Cities*. Chicago: Community and Family Study Center, University of Chicago.

Bolin, Robert, and Patricia Trainer. 1978. "Modes of Family Recovery Following Disaster: A Cross-National Study." Pp. 233–247 in E. L. Quarantelli, ed., *Disasters: Theory and Research*. Beverly Hills: Sage.

Boorstin, Daniel J. 1961. *The Image: A Guide to Pseudo Events in America.* New York: Harper and Row.

Brady, James. 1983. "Arson, Urban Economy, and Organized Crime: The Case of Boston." *Social Problems* 31: 1–27.

Bratt, Rachel G. 1986. "Public Housing: The Controversy and Contribution." Pp. 335–361 in Rachel G. Bratt, Chester Hartman, and Ann Meyerson eds., *Critical Perspectives on Housing.* Philadelphia: Temple University Press.

Bratt, Rachel G., Chester Hartman, and Ann Meyerson, eds. 1986. *Critical Perspectives on Housing.* Philadelphia: Temple University Press.

Braudel, Fernand. 1982. *The Wheels of Commerce.* New York: Harper and Row.

Breakey, William R., Pamela J. Fischer, Morton Kramer, Gerald Nestadt, Alan J. Romanoski, Alan Ross, Richard Royall, and Oscar C. Stine. 1989. "Health and Mental Health Problems of Homeless Men and Women of Baltimore." *Journal of the American Medical Association* 262: 1352–1357.

Brickner, Phillip W., Linda K. Scharer, Barbara Conann, Alexander Elvy, and Marianne Savarese, eds. 1985. *Health Care and Homeless People.* New York: Springer.

Brown, Carl, S. McFarlane, Ron Paredes, and Louisa Stark. 1983. *The Homeless of Phoenix: Who Are They? What Should Be Done?* Phoenix: Phoenix South Community Mental Health Center.

Brown, Julie V. 1987. "Peasant Survival Strategies in Late Imperial Russia: The Social Uses of the Mental Hospital." *Social Problems* 34: 311–329.

Bruns, Roger A. 1980. *Knights of the Road: A Hobo History.* New York: Methuen.

Burt, Martha R., and Barbara E. Cohen. 1989a. *America's Homeless: Numbers, Characteristics, and Programs That Serve Them.* Washington, D.C.: Urban Institute Press.

———. 1989b. "Differences among Homeless Single Women, Women with Children, and Single Men." *Social Problems* 36: 508–524.

Calhoun, Thomas C. 1988. "Theoretical Considerations on the Entrance and Stabilization of Male Street Prostitutes." Ph.D. dissertation, University of Kentucky.

Campbell, Donald T., and Donald W. Fiske. 1959. "Convergent and Discriminant Validation by the Multitrait-Multimethod Matrix." *Psychological Bulletin* 56: 81–105.

Camus, Albert. 1946. *The Outsider.* London: Hamilton.

Caplow, Theodore, Howard Bahr, and David Sternberg. 1968. "Homelessness." Pp. 494–499 in D. Stills, ed., *International Encyclopedia of the Social Sciences,* vol. 6. New York: Macmillan.

Caplow, Theodore, Keith A. Lovald, and Samuel Wallace. 1958. *A General Report on the Problem of the Lower Loop Redevelopment Area.* Minneapolis: Minneapolis Housing and Redevelopment Authority.

Caplowitz, David. 1967. *The Poor Pay More.* New York: Free Press.

Castells, Manuel. 1983. *The City and the Grassroots: A Cross-Cultural Theory of Urban Social Movements.* Berkeley: University of California Press.

Caton, Carol L. M., ed. 1990. *Homelessness in America*. New York: Oxford University Press.

Caulk, R. 1983. *The Homeless Poor: Multnomah County*. Portland, Ore.: Social Services Division.

Center on Budget and Policy Priorities. 1984. *End Results: The Impact of Federal Policies Since 1980 on Low Income Americans*. Washington, D.C.: Center on Budget and Policy Priorities.

——. 1985. *Smaller Slices of the Pie: The Growing Economic Vulnerability of Poor and Moderate Income Americans*. Washington, D.C.: Center on Budget and Policy Priorities.

——. 1988. *Poverty Remains High Despite Economic Recovery*. Washington, D.C.: Center on Budget and Policy Priorities.

Center on Budget and Policy Priorities and Low Income Housing Information Service. 1989. *A Place to Call Home: The Crisis in Housing for the Poor*. Washington, D.C.: Center on Budget and Policy Priorities and Low Income Housing Service.

Centre for Contemporary Cultural Studies. 1982. *Making Histories: Studies in History, Writing, and Practice*. London: Hutchinson.

Chambliss, William J. 1964. "A Sociological Analysis of the Law of Vagrancy." *Social Problems* 12: 67–77.

Chandler, Frank W. 1974. *The Literature of Roguery*. Boston: Houghton Mifflin.

City of Austin. 1986. *Final Report: Task Force on the Homeless*. Austin: City of Austin.

Clifford, James, and George E. Marcus. 1986. *Writing Culture: The Poetics and Politics of Ethnography*. Berkeley: University of California Press.

Cohen, Carl I., and Jay Sokolovsky. 1981. "A Reassessment of the Sociability of Long-Term Skid Row Residents: A Social Network Approach." *Social Networks* 3: 93–105.

——. 1989. *Old Men of the Bowery: Strategies for Survival Among the Homeless*. New York: Guilford Press.

Cohen, Lawrence, and Marcus Felson. 1979. "Social Change and Crime Rate Trends: A Routine Activity Approach." *American Sociological Review* 44: 588–608.

Coleman, Jules V. 1967. "Social Factors Influencing the Development and Containment of Psychiatric Symptoms." Pp. 158–168 in Thomas J. Scheff, ed., *Mental Illness and Social Processes*. New York: Harper and Row.

Coles, Robert. 1977. "The Children of Affluence." *Atlantic Monthly*, September.

Coser, Lewis A. 1969. "The Visibility of Evil." *Journal of Social Issues* 25: 101–109.

Costello, Barbara, Joseph Heirling, Frank Hunsaker, and Terry McCulloch. 1990. "Panhandling in Tucson." Paper, Department of Sociology, University of Arizona.

Crouse, Joan M. 1986. *The Homeless Transient in the Great Depression: New York State, 1929–1941*. Albany: SUNY Press.

Dalton, Melville. 1959. *Men Who Manage*. New York: John Wiley.

Danziger, Sheldon, and Daniel H. Weinberg, eds. 1986. *Fighting Poverty: What Works and What Doesn't.* Cambridge, Mass.: Harvard University Press.

Dear, Michael J., and Jennifer R. Wolch. 1987. *Landscapes of Despair: From Deinstitutionalization to Homelessness.* Cambridge, U.K.: Polity Press.

Denzin, Norman K. 1989a. *Interpretive Interactionism.* Newbury Park, Calif.: Sage.

———. 1989b. *The Research Act.* Third edition. Englewood Cliffs, N.J.: Prentice-Hall.

Derber, Charles. 1979. *The Pursuit of Attention: Power and Individualism in Everyday Life.* New York: Oxford University Press.

Dimsdale, Joel E. 1980. "The Coping Behavior of Nazi Concentration Camp Survivors." Pp. 163–74 in Joel E. Dimsdale, ed., *Survivors, Victims and Perpetrators: Essays on the Nazi Holocaust.* Washington: Hemisphere.

Douglas, Jack D. 1976. *Investigative Social Research: Individual and Team Field Research.* Beverly Hills, Calif.: Sage.

Douglas, Jack D., and John M. Johnson, eds. 1977. *Existential Sociology.* New York: Cambridge University Press.

Drabek, Thomas E., and William H. Key. 1983. *Conquering Disaster: Family Recovery and Long-Term Consequences.* New York: Irvington.

Drapkin, Arnold, M.D. 1990. "Medical Problems of the Homeless." Pp. 76–109 in Carol L. M. Caton, ed., *Homelessness in America.* New York: Oxford University Press.

Duncan, James S. 1983. "Men Without Property: The Tramp's Classification and Use of Urban Space." Pp. 86–102 in Robert W. Lake, ed., *Readings in Urban Analysis.* New Brunswick, N.J.: Rutgers University Press.

Dunham, H. W. 1953. *Homeless Men and Their Habitats: A Research Planning Report.* Detroit: Wayne State University Press.

Eaton, Joseph W., and Robert J. Weil. 1953. "The Mental Health of the Hutterites." *Scientific American* 189: 31–37.

Eaton, William W. 1986. *The Sociology of Mental Disorders.* Second edition. New York: Praeger.

Edge, William. 1927. *The Main Stem.* New York: Vanguard.

Edgerton, Robert B. 1969. "On the Recognition of Mental Illness." Pp. 49–72 in Stanley C. Plog and Robert B. Edgerton, eds., *Changing Perspectives on Mental Illness.* New York: Holt, Rinehart and Winston.

Ellwood, David T. 1988. *Poor Support: Poverty in the American Family.* New York: Basic Books.

El Paso Task Force on the Homeless. 1984. *Robert Wood Johnson Grant Application: Health Care for the Homeless.* El Paso, Texas.

Ericksen, Gordon E. 1981. *The Territorial Experience.* Austin: University of Texas Press.

Farr, Roger. 1982. "Skid Row Project." Mimeographed. Los Angeles: Los Angeles County Department of Mental Health, Program Development Bureau.

Farr, Roger, Paul Koegel, and Audrey Burnam. 1986. *A Study of Homelessness and Mental Illness in the Skid Row Area of Los Angeles.* Los Angeles: Los Angeles County Department of Mental Health.

Feagin, Joe R. 1986. "Urban Real Estate Speculation in the United States: Implications for Social Science and Urban Planning." Pp. 99–118 in Rachel G. Bratt, Chester Hartman, and Ann Meyerson, eds., *Critical Perspectives on Housing*. Philadelphia: Temple University Press.

———. 1988. *Free Enterprise City: Houston in Political and Economic Perspective*. New Brunswick, N.J.: Rutgers University Press.

Fine, Gary Alan, and Sherryl Kleinman. 1979. "Rethinking Subculture: An Interactionist Analysis." *American Journal of Sociology* 85: 1–20.

Fischer, Pamela J., and William R. Breakey. 1986. "Homelessness and Mental Health: An Overview." *International Journal of Mental Health* 14: 6–41.

———. 1991. "The Epidemiology of Alcohol, Drug, and Mental Disorders Among Homeless Persons." *American Psychologist* 46: 1115–1128.

Flynt, Josiah. 1899. *Tramping with Tramps*. New York: Century.

Fontana, Andrea. 1980. "Toward a Complex Universe: Existential Sociology." Pp. 155–181 in Jack D. Douglas, Patricia A. Adler, Peter Adler, Andrea Fontana, C. Robert Freeman, and Joseph A. Kotarba, eds., *Introduction to the Sociologies of Everyday Life*. Boston: Allyn and Bacon.

Foote, Caleb. 1956. "Vagrancy Type Law and Its Administration." *University of Pennsylvania Law Review* 104: 615–627.

Foucault, Michel. 1979. *Discipline and Punish*. New York: Vintage.

Frankl, Viktor. 1963. *Man's Search for Meaning*. New York: Washington Square Press.

Freeman, Richard B., and Brian Hall. 1986. "Permanent Homelessness in America." Working paper no. 13. Cambridge, Mass.: National Bureau of Economic Research.

Frost, Robert. 1964. *The Complete Poems of Robert Frost*. New York: Holt, Rinehart and Winston.

Gamino, Denise. 1984a. "Mentally Ill Face Life on Street." *Austin American-Statesman*, December 9.

———. 1984b. "Family Outbreak: Relatives of Mentally Ill Frustrated by Patient Discharges." *Austin American-Statesman*, December 10.

———. 1984c. "Lack of Services in Houston Leaves Mentally Ill Homeless." *Austin American-Statesman*, December 11.

———. 1984d. "Mentally Ill Walled In by Squalor." *Austin American-Statesman*, December 12.

———. 1984e. "Lost Rainbow: Fund Gap Strips Austin Mentally Ill of Dreams." *Austin American-Statesman*, December 13.

———. 1984f. "Discharged Mental Patients Swelling Population of City." *Austin American-Statesman*, June 11.

Gans, Herbert. 1962. *The Urban Villagers: Group and Class in the Life of Italian-Americans*. New York: Free Press.

Geertz, Clifford. 1973. *The Interpretation of Cultures*. New York: Basic Books.

———. 1983. *Local Knowledge: Further Essays in Interpretive Anthropology*. New York: Basic Books.

General Accounting Office. 1985. *Homelessness: A Complex Problem and the Federal Response*. Washington, D.C.: U.S. General Accounting Office.

———. 1988. *Homeless Mentally Ill: Problems and Options in Estimating Trends*. Washington, D.C.: U.S. General Accounting Office.

Gilder, George. 1981. *Wealth and Poverty*. New York: Basic Books.

Gilderbloom, John I. 1986. "Trends in the Affordability of Rental Housing: 1970 to 1983." *Sociology of Social Research* 70: 301–302.

Gilderbloom, John I., and Richard P. Applebaum. 1988. *Rethinking Rental Housing*. Philadelphia: Temple University Press.

Gilmore, Harlan. 1940. *The Beggar*. Chapel Hill: University of North Carolina Press.

Gioglio, Gerald R. 1989. "Homelessness in New Jersey: The Social Service Network and the People Served." Pp. 113–129 in Jamshid A. Momeni, ed., *Homelessness in the United States: State Surveys*. Greenwood, Conn.: Greenwood Press.

Giroux, Henry A. 1983. *Theory and Resistance in Education*. London: Heinemann Educational Books.

Glasser, Irene. 1988. *More than Bread: Ethnography of a Soup Kitchen*. Birmingham, Ala.: University of Alabama Press.

Gmelch, George, and Sharon Bohn Gmelch. 1978. "Begging in Dublin." *Urban Life* 6: 439–454.

Goffman, Erving. 1959. *The Presentation of Self in Everyday Life*. New York: Anchor/Doubleday.

———. 1961a. *Asylums*. Garden City, N.Y.: Anchor.

———. 1961b. "Role Distance." Pp. 85–152 in *Encounters: Two Studies in the Sociology of Interaction*. Indianapolis: Bobbs-Merrill.

———. 1963a. *Behavior in Public Places*. New York: Free Press.

———. 1963b. *Stigma: Notes on the Management of Spoiled Identity*. Englewood Cliffs, N.J.: Prentice-Hall.

———. 1967. "Mental Symptoms and Public Order." Pp. 137–48 in Erving Goffman, *Interaction Ritual: Essays on Face-to-Face Behavior*. Garden City, N.Y.: Anchor Books.

———. 1971. "The Insanity of Place." Pp. 335–390 in Erving Goffman, *Relations in Public*. New York: Harper and Row.

Goldman, Howard H., Neal H. Adams, and Carl A. Taube. 1983. "Deinstitutionalization: The Data Demythologized." *Hospital and Community Psychiatry* 34: 129–134.

Gould, Leroy C., Andrew L. Walker, Lansing E. Crane, and Charles W. Lidz. 1974. *Connections: Notes from the Heroin World*. New Haven, Conn.: Yale University Press.

Gouldner, Alvin W. 1960. "The Norm of Reciprocity: A Preliminary Statement." *American Sociological Review* 25: 161–178.

Gralnick, Alexander. 1985. "Build a Better State Hospital: Deinstitutionalization Has Failed." *Hospital and Community Psychiatry* 36: 738–741.

Granovetter, Mark. 1973. "The Strength of Weak Ties." *American Journal of Sociology* 78: 1360–1380.

Grob, Gerald N. 1991. *From Asylum to Community: Mental Health Policy in Modern America*. Princeton, N.J.: Princeton University Press.

Gronfein, William. 1985. "Psychotropic Drugs and the Origins of Homelessness." *Social Problems* 32: 437–454.

Guest, Edgar A. 1958. "Home." Pp. 391–92 in Kenneth Seeman Giniger, ed., *A Treasury of Golden Memories*. Garden City, N.Y.: Hanover House.

Gunther, Max. 1977. *The Luck Factor*. New York: Macmillan.

Hall, Stuart, and Tony Jefferson, eds. 1976. *Resistance Through Rituals: Youth Subcultures in Post-War Britain*. London: Hutchinson.

Hamilton, Rabinowitz, and Alschuler, Inc. 1987. *The Changing Face of Misery: Los Angeles' Skid Row Area in Transition, Housing and Social Service Needs of Central City East*. Los Angeles: Community Redevelopment Agency.

Harper, Douglas A. 1982. *Good Company*. Chicago: University of Chicago Press.

Harris, Candee S. 1984. "The Magnitude of Job Loss from Plant Closings and the Generation of Replacement Jobs: Some Recent Evidence." *Annals of the American Academy of Political and Social Sciences* 475: 15–27.

Hartman, Chester. 1986. "Housing Policies Under the Reagan Administration." Pp. 362–376 in Rachel G. Bratt, Chester Hartman, and Ann Meyerson, eds., *Critical Perspectives on Homelessness*. Philadelphia: Temple University Press.

Hathcock, Pat. 1984. "With a Bit of Help . . ." *Third Coast*, January: 71–75.

———. 1986. "Inhuman Bondage: The Slave Ranch Trial in Kerrville." *Third Coast*, November: 40–56, 78–84.

Henslin, James M. 1985. "Today's Homeless." Paper presented at the Annual Meeting of the Society for the Study of Social Problems. Washington, D.C.

Herrmann, Gretchen M., and Stephen M. Soiffer. 1984. "For Fun and Profit: An Analysis of the American Garage Sale." *Urban Life* 12: 397–421.

Hirsch, Kathleen. 1989. *Songs from the Alley*. New York: Ticknor and Fields.

Hoch, Charles, and Robert A. Slayton. 1989. *New Homeless and Old: Community and the Skid Row Hotel*. Philadelphia: Temple University Press.

Hodson, Randy, and Teresa A. Sullivan. 1990. *The Social Organization of Work*. Belmont, Calif.: Wadsworth.

Holmes, Urban Tigner. 1966. *Daily Living in the Twelfth Century: Based on the Observations of Alexander Neckam in London and Paris*. Madison: University of Wisconsin Press.

Hombs, Mary Ellen, and Mitch Snyder. 1982. *Homelessness in America: A Forced March to Nowhere*. Washington, D.C.: Community for Creative Nonviolence.

Hong, Lawrence K., and Robert W. Duff. 1989. "Becoming a Taxi Dancer: The Significance of Neutralization in a Semi-Deviant Occupation." Pp. 459–470 in Delos H. Kelly, ed., *Deviant Behavior: A Text Reader in the Sociology of Deviance*. New York: St. Martin's Press.

Hope, Marjorie, and James Young. 1986. *The Faces of Homelessness*. Lexington, Mass.: Lexington Books.

Hopper, Kim, and Jill Hamberg. 1986. "The Making of America's Homeless: From Skid Row to New Poor, 1945–1984." Pp. 12–40 in Rachel G. Bratt, Chester Hartman, and Ann Meyerson, eds., *Critical Perspectives on Housing*. Philadelphia: Temple University Press.

Hopper, Kim, Ezra Susser, and Sarah Conover. 1985. "Economics of Makeshift: Deindustrialization and Homelessness in New York City." *Urban Anthropology* 14: 183–236.

Hostetler, Shari. 1986. "The Demise of St. Martin's." *Seeds*, October: 15–19.

Housing and Community Services Department. 1985. *The State of Housing in Austin*. Austin: Housing and Community Services Department.

Housing Task Force. 1984. "Social Issue Topic for May." Mimeographed. Austin: Housing Task Force.

Housing and Urban Development. 1984. *A Report to the Secretary on the Homeless and Emergency Shelters*. Washington, D.C.: U.S. Department of Housing and Urban Development.

Huggins, Martha K. 1985. *From Slavery to Vagrancy in Brazil*. New Brunswick, N.J.: Rutgers University Press.

Hughes, Everett C. 1945. "Dilemmas and Contradictions in Status." *American Journal of Sociology* 50: 353–359.

———. 1958. *Men and Their Work*. Glencoe, Ill.: Free Press.

Hunter, Albert. 1985. "Private, Parochial and Public Social Orders: The Problem of Crime and Incivility in Urban Communities." Pp. 230–242 in Gerald D. Suttles and Mayer N. Zald, eds., *The Challenge of Social Control: Citizenship and Institution Building in Modern Society—Essays in Honor of Morris Janowitz*. Norwood, N.J.: Ablex Publishing Company.

Illich, Ivan. 1981. *Shadow Work*. Boston: Marian Boyars.

Institute of Medicine. 1988. *Homelessness, Health, and Human Needs*. Washington, D.C.: National Academy Press.

Irwin, John. 1970. *The Felon*. Englewood Cliffs, N.J.: Prentice-Hall.

Jackson, Joan K., and Ralph Connor. 1953. "The Skid Row Alcoholic." *Quarterly Journal of Studies on Alcohol* 14: 468–486.

James, William. 1932. *The Meaning of Truth*. New York: Longmans.

Jencks, Christopher. 1972. *Inequality: A Reassessment of the Effect of Family and Schooling in America*. New York: Basic Books.

Karp, David A., and William C. Yoels. 1979. *Symbols, Selves and Society: Understanding Interaction*. New York: J. B. Lippincott/Harper and Row.

Kasinitz, Philip. 1984. "Gentrification and Homelessness: The Single Room Occupant and the Inner City Revival." *Urban and Social Change Review* 17: 9–14.

Katz, Michael B. 1986. *In the Shadow of the Poorhouse: A Social History of Welfare in America*. New York: Basic Books.

———. 1989. *The Undeserving Poor: From the War on Poverty to the War on Welfare*. New York: Pantheon.

Kennedy, William. 1983. *Ironweed*. New York: Viking Press.

Klapp, Orrin E. 1964. *Symbolic Leaders: Public Dramas and Public Men*. Chicago: Aldine.

Koegel, Paul, and Audrey Burnam. 1988. "Alcoholism Among Homeless Adults in the Inner-city of Los Angeles." *Archives of General Psychiatry* 45: 1011–1018.

Kornhauser, Ruth. 1978. *Social Sources of Delinquency*. Chicago: University of Chicago Press.

Kozol, Jonathan. 1988. *Rachel and Her Children: Homeless Families in America*. New York: Fawcett Columbine.

Krauthammer, Charles. 1985. "When Liberty Really Means Neglect." *Time*, December 2: 103–104.

LaGory, Mark, Ferris J. Ritchey, and Kevin Fitzpatrick. 1991. "Homelessness and Affiliation." *Sociological Quarterly* 32: 201–218.

LaGory, Mark, Ferris J. Ritchey, and Jeffrey Mullis. 1990. "Depression Among the Homeless." *Journal of Health and Social Behavior* 31: 87–101.

LaGory, Mark, Ferris J. Ritchey, Timothy O'Donoghue, and Jeffrey Mullis. 1989. "Homelessness in Alabama: A Variety of People and Experiences." Pp. 1–20 in Jamshid A. Momeni, ed., *Homelessness in the United States: State Surveys*. Westport, Conn.: Greenwood Press.

Laing, R. D., and A. Esterson. 1970. *Sanity, Madness and the Family*. Second edition. Baltimore: Penguin Books.

Lamar, Jacob. 1988. "The Homeless: Brick by Brick." *Time*, October 24: 34–38.

Lamb, H. Richard, ed. 1984. *The Homeless Mentally Ill: A Task Force Report of the American Psychiatric Association*. Washington, D.C.: American Psychiatric Association.

Lamb, H. Richard, and J. A. Talbot. 1984. "The Homeless Mentally Ill: The Perspective of the American Psychiatric Association." *Journal of the American Medical Association* 256: 498–501.

Lasch, Christopher. 1977. *Haven in a Heartless World: The Family Besieged*. New York: Basic Books.

Lee, Barrett A. 1980. "The Disappearance of Skid Row: Some Ecological Evidence." *Urban Affairs Quarterly* 16: 81–107.

———. 1987. "Homelessness and Community." Paper presented at the Annual Meeting of the American Sociological Association.

———. 1989. "Homelessness in Tennessee." Pp. 181–203 in Jamshid A. Momeni, ed., *Homelessness in the United States: State Surveys*. Westport, Conn.: Greenwood Press.

Lee, Barrett A., Sue Hinze Jones, and David W. Lewis. 1990. "Public Beliefs About the Causes of Homelessness." *Social Forces* 69: 253–265.

Lemert, Edwin M. 1962. "Paranoia and the Dynamics of Exclusion." *Sociometry* 25: 2–20.

Lerman, Paul. 1982. *Deinstitutionalization and the Welfare State*. New Brunswick, N.J.: Rutgers University Press.

Levinson, Boris M. 1963. "The Homeless Man: A Psychological Enigma." *Mental Hygiene* 47: 590–601.

Levitin, T. E. 1964. "Role Performances and Role Distance in a Low Status Occupation: The Puller." *Sociological Quarterly* 5: 251–60.

Lewis, Oscar. 1966. "The Culture of Poverty." *Scientific American* 215: 19–25.

Liebow, Elliot. 1967. *Tally's Corner: A Study of Negro Streetcorner Men*. Boston: Little, Brown.

Lincoln, Yvonna S., and Egon C. Guba. 1985. *Naturalistic Inquiry*. Beverly Hills: Sage.

Lipton, Alan A., and Franklin S. Simon. 1985. "Psychiatric Diagnoses in a State Hospital: Manhattan State Revisited." *Hospital and Community Psychiatry* 36: 368–372.

Lipton, Frank R., Albert Sabatini, and Steven E. Katz. 1983. "Down and Out in the City: The Homeless Mentally Ill." *Hospital and Community Psychiatry* 34: 817–821.

Lofland, John. 1969. *Deviance and Identity*. Englewood Cliffs, N.J.: Prentice-Hall.

Lofland, John, and Lyn H. Lofland. 1984. *Analyzing Social Settings*. Belmont, Calif.: Wadsworth.

Lofland, Lyn H. 1973. *A World of Strangers: Order and Action in Urban Public Space*. New York: Basic Books.

Logan, John R., and Harvey L. Molotch. 1987. *Urban Fortunes: The Political Economy of Place*. Berkeley: University of California Press.

London, Jack. 1907. *People of the Abyss*. New York: Macmillan.

Los Angeles Times. 1984a. " 'Troll Busters' in Santa Cruz Prey on the Homeless." October 26.

———. 1984b. "Santa Barbara—A Lid on Hobos' Food?" December 13.

———. 1988. "If Only the Spirit of Giving Could Continue." December 25.

Love, Edmund. 1956. *Subways Are for Sleeping*. New York: Harcourt, Brace, and World.

Low Income Housing Information Service. 1989. *Low Income Housing and Homelessness: Facts and Myths*. Washington, D.C.: Low Income Housing Information Service.

Lozano, Beverly. 1983. "Informal Sector Workers: Walking Out the System's Front Door?" *International Journal of Urban and Regional Research* 7: 340–361.

Luckenbill, David F. 1985. "Entering Male Prostitution." *Urban Life* 14: 131–153. 153.

———. 1986. "Deviant Career Mobility: The Case of Male Prostitutes." *Social Problems* 33: 283–296.

Luckenbill, David F., and Joel Best. 1981. "Careers in Deviance and Respectability: The Analogy's Limitations." *Social Problems* 29: 197–206.

Luther, Martin. 1860. *The Book of Vagabonds and Beggars*, edited by John Camden Hotten. London: John Camden Hotten.

McCall, George J., and J. L. Simmons. 1969. *Issues in Participant Observation: A Text and Reader*. Reading, Mass.: Addison-Wesley.

———. 1978. *Identities and Interactions*. New York: Free Press.

McGrath, Joseph E., Joanne Martin, and Richard Kulka. 1982. *Judgment Calls in Research*. Beverly Hills, Calif.: Sage.

McKinney, John C. 1966. *Constructed Typology and Social Theory*. New York: Appleton-Century-Crofts.

———. 1970. "Sociological Theory and the Process of Typification." Pp. 235–269 in John C. McKinney and Edward A. Tiryakian, eds., *Theoretical Sociology: Perspectives and Developments*. New York: Appleton-Century-Crofts.

McLaren, Peter. 1988. *Life in Schools*. New York: Longman.

MacLeod, Jay. 1987. *Ain't No Makin' It: Leveled Aspirations in a Low-Income Neighborhood*. Boulder, Colo.: Westview Press.

McSheehy, William. 1979. *Skid Row*. Boston: G. K. Hall.

Marcuse, Peter. 1985. "Gentrification, Abandonment, and Displacement: Connections, Causes, and Policy—Response in New York City." *Washington University Journal of Urban and Contemporary Law* 28: 195–240.

Marin, Peter. 1987. "Helping and Hating the Homeless: The Struggle at the Margins of America." *Harper's,* January: 39–49.

———. 1991. "The Prejudice Against Men." *The Nation,* July 8: 46–51.

Marks, Carole. 1989. *Farewell—We're Good and Gone: The Great Black Migration.* Bloomington: Indiana University Press.

Marx, Karl. 1849. "Wage Labor and Capital." Pp. 167–190 in Robert C. Tucker, ed., *The Marx-Engels Reader.* New York: W. W. Norton, 1972.

———. 1932. "Economic and Philosophic Manuscripts of 1844." Pp. 52–106 in Robert C. Tucker, ed., *The Marx-Engels Reader.* New York: W. W. Norton, 1972.

Maslow, Abraham H. 1962. *Toward a Psychology of Being.* New York: Van Nostrand.

Matza, David. 1966a. "The Disreputable Poor." Pp. 289–302 in Reinhardt Bendix and S. M. Lipsett, eds., *Class, Status, and Power: A Reader in Social Stratification.* New York: Free Press.

———. 1966b. "Poverty and Disrepute." Pp. 619–669 in Robert K. Merton and Robert A. Nisbett, eds., *Contemporary Social Problems,* 2nd edition. New York: Harcourt.

Mayhew, Henry. 1985 (1861–62). *London Labour and the London Poor.* New York: Viking Penguin.

Merton, Robert K. 1968. *Social Theory and Social Structure.* New York: Free Press.

———. 1972. "Insiders and Outsiders: A Chapter in the Sociology of Knowledge." *American Journal of Sociology* 78: 9–47.

Miller, Eleanor M. 1986. *Street Women.* Philadelphia: Temple University Press.

Miller, Gale. 1981. *It's a Living: Work in Modern Society.* New York: St. Martin's Press.

Minehan, Thomas. 1934. *Boy and Girl Tramps of America.* New York: Farrar and Rinehart.

Mitford, Jessica. 1974. *Kind and Usual Punishment: The Prison Business.* New York: Vintage.

Momeni, Jamshid A., ed. 1989. *Homelessness in the United States: State Surveys.* Westport, Conn.: Greenwood Press.

———. 1990. *Homelessness in the United States: Data and Issues.* Westport, Conn.: Greenwood Press.

Monkkonen, Eric H., ed. 1984. *Walking to Work: Tramps in America, 1790–1935.* Lincoln, Neb.: University of Nebraska Press.

Morganthau, Tom, Susan Agrest, Nikki Finke Groenberg, Shawn Doherty, and George Raine. 1986. "Abandoned." *Newsweek,* January 6: 14–19.

Morrow, Lance. 1981. "The Importance of Being Lucky." *Time,* April 27: 79–80.

Morse, Gary, Nancy Shields, Christine Hanneke, Robert Calsyn, Gary Burger, and Bruce Nelson. 1985. *Homeless People in St. Louis: A Mental Health Program Evaluation.* Jefferson City, Mo.: Department of Mental Health.

Murray, Charles. 1984. *Losing Ground: American Social Policy, 1950–1980.* New York: Basic Books.

Myrdal, Gunnar. 1944. *An American Dilemma: The Negro Problem and Modern Democracy.* New York: Harper and Row.

National Coalition for the Homeless. 1987. *Pushed Out: America's Homeless.* Washington, D.C.: National Coalition for the Homeless.

———. 1989. *American Nightmare: A Decade of Homelessness in the United States.* Washington, D.C.: National Coalition for the Homeless.

Nelkin, Dorothy, and Laurence Tancredi. 1989. *Dangerous Diagnostics: The Social Power of Biological Information.* New York: Basic Books.

Newsweek. 1984. "Homeless in America." January 2: 20–29.

New York Times. 1984. "Homeless by Choice? Some Choice." February 7.

———. 1985. "Plan to Shelter the Homeless Arouses Concern in Maspeth." June 7.

Office of Technology Assessment. 1986. *Technology and Structural Unemployment: Reemploying Displaced Adults.* Washington, D.C.: Congress of the United States.

Okin, Robert L. 1985. "Expand the Community Care System: Deinstitutionalization Can Work." *Hospital and Community Psychiatry* 36: 742–745.

Oreskes, Michael, and Robin Toner. 1989. "The Homeless and the Heart of Poverty and Policy." *New York Times,* January 29.

Orwell, George. 1933. *Down and Out in Paris and London.* New York: Harcourt Brace Jovanovich.

Parker, Robert E. 1986. "Flesh Peddlers and Warm Bodies: The Temporary Help Industry and Their Workers." Ph.D. dissertation, University of Texas at Austin.

Payne, John Howard. 1958. "Home, Sweet Home." P. 391 in Kenneth Seeman Giniger, ed., *A Treasury of Golden Memories.* Garden City, N.Y.: Hanover House.

People. 1986. "I Never Imagined That I'd Be Homeless." January 27: 27–36.

Perrucci, Carolyn, Robert Perrucci, Dena B. Targ, and Harry R. Targ. 1988. *Plant Closings: International Contexts and Social Costs.* New York: Aldine de Gruyter.

Peterson, William Jack, and Milton A. Maxwell. 1958. "The Skid Road 'Wino.' " *Social Problems* 5: 308–316.

Pfuhl, Erdwin H., Jr. 1986. *The Deviance Process.* Second edition. Belmont, Calif.: Wadsworth.

Piliavin, Irving, and Michael Sosin. 1987–88. "Tracking the Homeless." *Focus* 10: 20–24.

Piliavin, Irving, Michael Sosin, Herb Westerfelt, and Ross L. Matsueda. 1991. "The Duration of Homeless Careers: An Exploratory Study." Manuscript.

Piliavin, Irving, Herb Westerfelt, and Elsa Elliot. 1989. "Estimating Mental Illness Among the Homeless: The Effects of Choice-Based Sampling." *Social Problems* 36: 525–531.

Pittman, David J., and C. Wayne Gordon. 1958. *Revolving Door: A Study of the Chronic Police Case Inebriate.* Glencoe, Ill.: Free Press.

Piven, Frances Fox, and Richard A. Cloward. 1971. *Regulating the Poor: The Functions of Public Welfare*. New York: Vintage.

Plog, Stanley C., and Robert B. Edgerton, eds. 1969. *Changing Perspectives on Mental Illness*. New York: Holt, Rinehart and Winston.

Pollner, Melvin, and Robert M. Emerson. 1983. "The Dynamics of Inclusion and Distance in Fieldwork Relations." Pp. 235–252 in R. M. Emerson, ed., *Contemporary Field Research: A Collection of Readings*. Boston: Little, Brown.

Portes, Alejandro, and John Walton. 1981. *Labor, Class and the International System*. New York: Academic Press.

Redburn, F. Stevens, and Terry F. Buss. 1986. *Responding to America's Homeless: Public Policy Alternatives*. New York: Praeger.

Reiss, Albert J. Jr. 1961. "The Social Integration of Queers and Peers." *Social Problems* 9: 102–119.

Ribton-Turner, C. J. 1887. *A History of Vagrants and Vagrancy and Beggars and Begging*. London: Chapman and Hall.

Ringheim, Karin. 1990a. *At Risk of Homelessness: The Roles of Income and Rent*. New York: Praeger.

———. 1990b. "The Structural Determinants of Homelessness: A Study of 8 Cities." Paper presented at the Annual Meeting of the American Sociological Association, Washington, D.C.

Ritzer, George, and David Walczak. 1986. *Working: Conflict and Change*. Englewood Cliffs, N.J.: Prentice-Hall.

Robertson, Marjorie J. 1987. "Homeless Veterans: An Emerging Problem?" Pp. 64–81 in Richard D. Bingham, Roy E. Green, and Sammis B. White, eds., *The Homeless in Contemporary Society*. Newbury Park, Calif.: Sage.

Robertson, Marjorie J., Richard Ropers, and Richard Boyer. 1985. *The Homeless of Los Angeles County: An Empirical Evaluation*. Document no. 4. Los Angeles: Basic Shelter Research Project, School of Public Health, University of California, Los Angeles.

Rooney, James F. 1961. "Group Processes Among Skid Row Winos: A Reevaluation of the Undersocialization Hypothesis." *Quarterly Journal of Studies on Alcohol* 22: 444–460.

———. 1973. "Friendship and Reference Group Orientation Among Skid Row Men." Ph.D. dissertation, University of Pennsylvania.

———. 1976. "Friendship and Disaffiliation Among the Skid Row Population." *Journal of Gerontology* 31: 82–88.

———. 1980. "Organizational Success Through Program Failure: Skid Row Rescue Missions." *Social Forces* 58: 904–924.

Ropers, Richard H. 1988. *The Invisible Homeless: A New Urban Ecology*. New York: Human Sciences Press.

Rosaldo, Renato. 1989. *Culture and Truth: The Remaking of Social Analysis*. Boston: Beacon Press.

Rose, Lionel. 1988. *Rogues and Vagabonds: Vagrant Underworld in Britain, 1815–1985*. New York: Routledge.

Rossi, Peter. 1989a. *Down and Out in America: The Origins of Homelessness*. Chicago: University of Chicago Press.

———. 1989b. *Without Shelter: Homelessness in the 1980s*. New York: Priority Press.

Rossi, Peter, James D. Wright, Gene A. Fischer, and Georgianna Willis. 1987. "The Urban Homeless: Estimating Composition and Size." *Science* 235: 1336–1341.

Roth, Dee. 1989. "Homelessness in Ohio: A Statewide Epidemiological Survey." Pp. 145–163 in Jamshid A. Momeni, ed., *Homelessness in the United States: State Surveys*. Westport, Conn.: Greenwood Press.

Roth, Dee, and Gerald J. Bean. 1986. "New Perspectives on Homelessness: Findings from a Statewide Epidemiological Study." *Hospital and Community Psychiatry* 37: 712–719.

Roth, Dee, Gerald J. Bean, Nancy Lust, and Traian Saveanu. 1985. *Homelessness in Ohio: A Study of People in Need*. Columbus, Ohio: Ohio Department of Mental Health.

Rothman, David J. 1971. *The Discovery of the Asylum: Social Order and Disorder in the New Republic*. Boston: Little, Brown.

Roy, Donald. 1957. "Quota Restriction and Goldbricking in a Machine Shop." *American Journal of Sociology* 57: 427–442.

Rubington, Earl. 1968. "The Bottle Gang." *Quarterly Journal of Studies on Alcohol* 29: 943–955.

———. 1971. "The Changing Skid Row Scene." *Quarterly Journal of Studies on Alcohol* 32: 123–135.

Rubington, Earl, and Martin S. Weinberg. 1981. *Deviance: The Interactionist Perspective*. New York: Macmillan.

Ryan, William. 1971. *Blaming the Victim*. New York: Vintage.

Salgado, Gamini, ed. 1972. *Cony-Catchers and Bawdy Baskets: An Anthology of Elizabethan Low Life*. Baltimore: Penguin Books.

San Antonio Urban Council. 1984. *Robert Wood Johnson Grant Application: Health Care for the Homeless*. San Antonio: San Antonio Urban Council.

Sarbin, Theodore R. 1969. "The Scientific Status of the Mental Illness Metaphor." Pp. 9–31 in Stanley C. Plog and Robert B. Edgerton, eds., *Changing Perspectives in Mental Illness*. New York: Holt, Rinehart and Winston.

Sayles, Marnie L. 1984. "Role Distancing: Differentiating the Role of the Elderly from the Person." *Qualitative Sociology* 7: 236–252.

Schaefer, Catherine, James Coyne, and Richard S. Lazarus. 1981. "The Health-Related Functions of Social Support." *Journal of Behavioral Medicine* 4: 212–241.

Scheff, Thomas J. 1966. *Being Mentally Ill: A Sociological Theory*. Chicago: Aldine.

Scherer, Andrew. 1984–85. "Is There Life after Abandonment? The Key Role of New York City's In Rem Housing in Establishing an Entitlement to Decent, Affordable Housing." *New York University Review of Law and Social Change* 13: 953–974.

Schmalz, Jeffrey. 1988. "Belying Popular Stereotypes, Many of Homeless Have Jobs." *New York Times,* December 19.

Schumer, Charles E. 1988. "Homelessness: A Side Effect of Reaganomics." *Arizona Daily Star,* March 13.

Schur, Edwin M. 1971. *Labeling Deviant Behaviors: Sociological Implications.* New York: Harper and Row.

Sedgwick, Peter. 1982. *Psycho Politics.* New York: Harper and Row.

Segal, Steven P., Jim Baumohl, and Elsie Johnson. 1976. "Falling Through the Cracks: Mental Disorder and Social Margin in a Young Vagrant Population." *Social Problems* 24: 397–400.

Serrin, William. 1986. "Part-time Work, New Labor Trend." *New York Times,* July 9.

Siegal, Harvey A. 1978. *Outposts of the Forgotten: Socially Terminal People in Slum Hotels and Single Room Occupancy Tenements.* New Brunswick, N.J.: Transaction Books.

Sjoberg, Gideon. 1960. *The Preindustrial City.* Glencoe, Ill.: Free Press.

Sjoberg, Gideon, Richard A. Brymer, and Buford Farris. 1966. "Bureaucracy and the Lower Class." *Sociology* and *Social Research* 50: 325–337.

Sjoberg, Gideon, and Roger Nett. 1968. *A Methodology for Social Research.* New York: Harper and Row.

Smith, Charles W. 1989. *Auctions: The Social Construction of Value.* New York: Free Press.

Smith, Neil. 1983. "Toward a Theory of Gentrification: A Back to the City Movement by Capital, Not People." Pp. 278–298 in Robert W. Lake, ed., *Readings in Urban Analysis.* New Brunswick, N.J.: Rutgers University Press.

Smith, Neil, and Peter Williams. 1986. *Gentrification of the City.* London: Allen and Unwin.

Snow, David A. 1989. *The Homeless Street People of Austin: A Team Field Study in the Mid-1980s.* Final Report for the Hogg Foundation for Mental Health. Austin, Texas.

Snow, David A., Susan G. Baker, and Leon Anderson. 1988. "On the Precariousness of Measuring Insanity in Insane Contexts." *Social Problems* 35: 192–196.

———. 1989. "Criminality Among Homeless Men: An Empirical Assessment." *Social Problems* 36: 532–549.

Snow, David A., Susan G. Baker, Leon Anderson, and Michael Martin. 1986a. "The Myth of Pervasive Mental Illness Among the Homeless." *Social Problems* 33: 407–23.

Snow, David A., Robert D. Benford, and Leon Anderson. 1986b. "Fieldwork Roles and Informational Yield: A Comparison of Alternative Settings and Roles." *Urban Life* 15: 377–408.

Snow, David A., Louis Zurcher, and Gideon Sjoberg. 1982. "Interviewing by Comment: An Adjunct to the Direct Question." *Qualitative Sociology* 5: 285–311.

Social Policy Advisory Committee Task Force on Transients. 1983. "Recommendations" (memo). Austin, Texas.

Sosin, Michael, Paul Colson, and Susan Grossman. 1988. *Homelessness in Chicago: Poverty and Pathology, Social Institutions and Social Change.* Chicago: University of Chicago, School of Social Service Administration.

Southern Regional Council. 1988. *Hard Labor: A Report on Day Labor Pools in Temporary Employment.* Atlanta, Ga.: Southern Regional Council.

Spradley, James. 1970. *You Owe Yourself a Drunk: An Ethnography of Urban Nomads.* Boston: Little, Brown.
————. 1980. *Participant Observation.* New York: Holt, Rinehart and Winston.
Stake, Robert E. 1978. "The Case-Study Method in Social Inquiry." *Educational Researcher* 7: 5–8.
Stanley, Dick. 1985. "Life in Public Housing Project Has Peaceful Side Despite Woes." *Austin American-Statesman,* January 26.
Stebbins, Robert A. 1975. "Role Distance, Role Distance Behavior and Jazz Musicians." Pp. 133–141 in D. Brissett and C. Edgely, eds., *Life as Theater: A Dramaturgical Sourcebook.* Chicago: Aldine.
Stein, Bruno. 1971. *On Relief: The Economics of Poverty and Public Welfare.* New York: Basic Books.
Sternlieb, George, and James W. Hughes. 1983. "Housing the Poor in a Postshelter Society." *Annals of the American Academy of Political and Social Sciences* 465: 109–122.
Stinchcombe, Arthur L. 1964. *Rebellion in a High School.* Chicago: Quadrangle Books.
Stone, Gregory P. 1962. "Appearance and the Self." Pp. 86–118 in Arnold M. Rose, ed., *Human Behavior and Social Processes.* Boston: Houghton Mifflin.
Susser, Ezra, Elmer Struening, and Sarah Conover. 1987. "Childhood Experiences of Homeless Men." *American Journal of Psychiatry* 144: 1599–1601.
Sutherland, Edwin, and Harvey Locke. 1936. *Twenty Thousand Homeless Men.* Chicago: J. B. Lippincott.
Suttles, Gerald D. 1968. *The Social Order of the Slum.* Chicago: University of Chicago Press.
Swidler, Ann. 1986. "Culture in Action: Symbols and Strategies." *American Sociological Review* 51: 273–286.
Szasz, Thomas S. 1961. *The Myth of Mental Illness.* New York: Dell.
Szilagyi, Peter. 1985a. "Affordable Homes Prove Elusive." *Austin American-Statesman,* April 14.
————. 1985b. "Forecasts for Housing Inflation Predict Varied Futures." *Austin American-Statesman,* April 16.
Tannahill, Reay. 1980. *Sex in History.* New York: Stein and Day.
Texas Health and Human Services Coordinating Council. 1985. *Final Report on the Homeless in Texas.* Austin: Texas Health and Human Services Coordinating Council.
Thurow, Lester. 1987. "A Surge in Inequality." *Scientific American* 256: 30–37.
Time. 1985a. "Coming In from the Cold." February 4: 20–21.
————. 1985b. "Harassing the Homeless." March 11: 68.
————. 1988a. "Can You Spare a Dime—for Bail." January 11: 33.
————. 1988b. "Begging: To Give or Not to Give." September 5: 68–74.
————. 1990a. "Buddy, Can You Spare a Dime?" February 12: 55.
Titmuss, Richard M. 1971. *The Gift Relationship: From Human Blood to Social Policy.* New York: Vintage.

Toro, Paul A., and David D. Wall. 1990. "Research on Homeless Persons: Clarifying Some Methodological Issues." Manuscript.

Torrey, E. Fuller. 1988. *Nowhere To Go: The Tragic Odyssey of the Homeless Mentally Ill.* New York: Harper and Row.

Turner, Ralph H. 1968. "The Self-Conception in Social Interaction." Pp. 93–106 in C. Gordon and K. J. Gergen, eds., *The Self in Social Interaction.* New York: John Wiley and Sons.

———. 1978. "The Role and the Person." *American Journal of Sociology* 84: 1–23.

Turner, Victor. 1969. *The Ritual Process: Structure and Anti-structure.* Chicago: Aldine.

———. 1974. *Dramas, Fields, and Metaphors: Symbolic Action in Human Society.* Ithaca, N.Y.: Cornell University Press.

Tyson, Kim. 1984. "Lender Reports Lack of Affordable Housing Lots." *Austin American-Statesman,* August 1.

U.S. Bureau of the Census. 1981. *1980 Census of the Population: General and Social and Economic Characteristics.* Volume 1: *U.S. Summary.* Washington, D.C.: Government Printing Office.

U.S. Bureau of the Census. 1981. *1980 Census of the Population: Texas.* Vol. 1. Washington, D.C.: Government Printing Office.

U.S. Conference of Mayors. 1985. *Health Care for the Homeless: A 40-City Review.* Washington, D.C.: United States Conference of Mayors.

U.S. House Committee on Government Operations. 1985. *The Federal Response to the Homeless Crisis.* Hearings before a Subcommittee of the Committee on Government Operations. House of Representatives, 98th Congress, 2d Session. Washington, D.C.: U.S. Government Printing Office.

U.S. Department of Labor, Employment and Training Administration. 1977. *Dictionary of Occupational Titles.* 4th ed. Washington, D.C.: U.S. Government Printing Office.

Uzzell, J. Douglas. 1980. "Mixed Strategies and the Informal Sector: Three Faces of Reserved Labor." *Human Organization* 39: 40–49.

Valentine, Charles. 1968. *Culture and Poverty: Critique and Counterproposal.* Chicago: University of Chicago Press.

Vander Kooi, Ronald C. 1973. "The Mainstem: Skid Row Revisited." *Society* 10: 64–71.

Van Maanen, John. 1988. *Tales of the Field: On Writing Ethnography.* Chicago: University of Chicago Press.

Wallace, Samuel. 1965. *Skid Row as a Way of Life.* Totowa, N.J.: Bedminister Press.

Waxman, Chaim I. 1983. *The Stigma of Poverty: A Critique of Poverty Theories and Policies.* New York: Pergamon.

Webb, Eugene J., Donald T. Campbell, Richard D. Schwartz, Lee Sechrest, and Janet Belew. 1981. *Nonreactive Measures in the Social Sciences.* Second edition. Boston: Houghton Mifflin.

Weinberg, Martin S. 1966. "Becoming a Nudist." *Psychiatry: Journal for the Study of Interpersonal Process* 29: 15–24.

Werner, Oscar, and G. Mark Schoepfle. 1987. *Systematic Fieldwork: Eth-*

nographic Analysis and Data Management, vol. 2. Newbury Park, Calif.: Sage.

Whyte, William F. 1943. *Street Corner Society: The Social Structure of an Italian Slum.* Chicago: University of Chicago Press.

Wiegand, R. Bruce. 1990. "Sweat and Blood: Sources of Income on a Southern Skid Row." Pp. 111–122 in Jamshid A. Momeni, ed., *Homelessness in the United States: Data and Issues.* Westport, Conn.: Greenwood Press.

Willis, Paul. 1977. *Learning to Labour.* New York: Columbia University Press.

Wilson, Colin. 1965. *The Outsider.* Boston: Houghton Mifflin.

Wilson, James Q. 1975. *Thinking About Crime.* New York: Basic Books.

Wilson, William Julius. 1987. *The Truly Disadvantaged: The Inner City, the Underclass, and Public Policy.* Chicago: University of Chicago Press.

Wiseman, Jacqueline. 1970. *Stations of the Lost: The Treatment of Skid Row Alcoholics.* Chicago: University of Chicago Press.

Worden, Steven K. 1987. "Bums, Barrios and Baptists: An Interactionist Inquiry into the Pieties of Place." Ph.D. dissertation, University of Texas at Austin.

Wright, Arthur L. 1985. *The Texas Housing Affordability Index.* College Station, Tx.: Texas Real Estate Research Center.

Wright, James D. 1988. "The Mentally Ill Homeless: What Is Myth and What Is Fact?" *Social Problems* 35: 182–191.

———. 1989. *Address Unknown: The Homeless in America.* New York: Aldine de Gruyter.

Wright, James D., and Julie Lam. 1987. "Homeless and the Low Income Housing Supply." *Social Policy* 17: 48–53.

Wright, James D., and Eleanor Weber. 1987. *Homelessness and Health.* New York: McGraw-Hill.

Yablonsky, Lewis. 1966. *The Violent Gang.* Baltimore: Penguin Books.

Yin, Robert K. 1984. *Case Study Research: Design and Methods.* Beverly Hills: Sage.

Zarembka, Arlene. 1990. *The Urban Housing Crisis: Social, Economic, and Legal Issues and Proposals.* New York: Greenwood Press.

Index

Accommodative response, 196, 290, 301, 305; and Angels House, 78, 84–86, 283; and Caritas, 78, 83–84, 86; organizational, 77–79; and Salvation Army, 78–82, 86, 134, 283, 290, 307

Adaptive response: and alcohol use, 203, 208–11, 258; and criminal activity, 167, 258, 278; extrication from street life compromised by, 195, 290–91, 294–95, 299–300, 302; and mental illness, 203, 208, 211–13, 257–58; and social relationships, 195, 197, 291; subcultures as, 39, 40, 70, 76, 208, 339n2

Address Unknown (Wright), 234

Age composition, 17, 31–33, 49, 144, 321n67; of hippie tramps, 49, 61, 326n22; of institutionally adapted straddlers, 49, 55; of mentally ill persons, 49, 68; of recently dislocated persons, 49; of redneck bums, 49, 192; of regular straddlers, 49; in skid-row districts, 16, 320n56; of traditional bums, 49, 63; of traditional tramps, 49, 59

Agricultural laborers: in colonial period, 12; effect of mechanization on, 14; and industrial expansion, 13

AIDS epidemic, 341n14

Aid to Families with Dependent Children (AFDC), 138, 139, 251

Alcoholics Anonymous, 136, 301, 306; compulsory participation in, 137, 288; resistance to, 93, 288–89; and successful rehabilitation, 222, 276, 301, 311

Alcohol use, 18, 42, 291, 348n8; as adaptive response, 203, 208–11, 258; as cause of homelessness, 253, 255, 256, 257, 269, 271, 278, 318n12; correlated with time on the streets, 209, 278; and hippie tramps, 45, 61, 189, 209; and institutionally adapted straddlers, 45, 56, 258; as locus of affiliation, 189, 190, 345–46n14, 346nn19–21; and mentally ill persons, 45; and recently dislocated persons, 45, 209; and redneck bums, 45, 65–66, 192, 209; and regular straddlers, 45, 54; and rehabilitation programs, 78, 87, 92–94, 136, 283, 286–89; and resource sharing, 173, 189, 190; in skid-row districts, 16, 42, 146, 321n61, 325nn8–9, 357n3; and traditional bums, 45, 62–65, 93, 189, 190; and traditional tramps, 45, 59, 93. *See also* Bottle gangs; Detox facilities; Drug use

Alienation, 132–34, 169, 302

Anderson, Elijah, 173, 345n9, 349n19, 350n24

Anderson, Nels, 14, 15, 42, 111, 331n22

Angels House, 23, 78, 84–86, 200, 254, 283, 304, 330nn13–14

Appelbaum, Richard P., 317n1

Arrests, 308, 310, 356nn84–85; and

Compositor: Maple-Vail Book Mfg. Group
Text: 10/13 Sabon
Display: Sabon
Printer: Maple-Vail Book Mfg. Group
Binder: Maple-Vail Book Mfg. Group

DEMCO